QUEER PHILOLOGIES

MATERIAL TEXTS

Series Editors

Roger Chartier   Leah Price

Joseph Farrell   Peter Stallybrass

Anthony Grafton   Michael F. Suarez, S.J.

QUEER PHILOLOGIES

Sex, Language, and Affect
in Shakespeare's Time

JEFFREY MASTEN

PENN

University of Pennsylvania Press

Philadelphia

Published by
University of Pennsylvania Press
Philadelphia, Pennsylvania 19104-4112
www.upenn.edu/pennpress

Printed in the United States of America on acid-free paper
1 3 5 7 9 10 8 6 4 2

Library of Congress Cataloging-in-Publication Data

Names: Masten, Jeffrey, author.
Title: Queer philologies : sex, language, and affect in Shakespeare's
time / Jeffrey Masten.
Other titles: Material texts.
Description: Philadelphia : University of Pennsylvania Press, [2016] |
2016 | Series: Material texts | Includes bibliographical references and
index.
Identifiers: LCCN 2015038860 | ISBN 9780812247862 (alk. paper)
Subjects: LCSH: English literature—Early modern, 1500–1700—
History and criticism. | Language and sex—England—History—16th
century. | Language and sex—England—History—17th century. |
Homosexuality and literature—England—History—16th century. |
Homosexuality and literature—England—History—17th century. |
English language—Early modern, 1500–1700. | Sex in literature.
Classification: LCC PR428.H66 M37 2016 | DDC 820.9/003—dc23
LC record available at http://lccn.loc.gov/2015038860

For

Jay Grossman

Phylologie. *Loue of much babling.*
　　　　　—Henry Cockeram, *The English Dictionarie: Or,*
　　　　　　　An Interpreter of hard English Words (1623)

Der Zweck der Philologie ist die Historie.
[The purpose of philology is history.]
　　　　　—Friedrich Schlegel, "Zur Philologie" (1797)

Since the term has so many and such divergent meanings,
it is best to abandon it.
　　　　　—René Wellek and Austin Warren, *Theory*
　　　　　　　of Literature (1949)

It is thought that philology is finished—and I believe it
hasn't yet begun.
　　　　　—Friedrich Nietzsche, "We Philologists" (1875)

[T]o remain enchanted by the phantom of a political
engagement outside and above an engagement with
issues of rhetoric, figuration, and fantasy is to ignore
the historical conceptualization of homosexuality
in a distinctive relation to language.
　　　　　—Lee Edelman, *Homographesis* (1994)

CONTENTS (A)

CONTENTS (Q)

NOTE ON CITATIONS AND QUOTATIONS

For reasons that are discussed in the Introduction and Chapter 1, quotations from early modern printed and manuscript sources retain their original spellings (including early modern usage of i/j, u/v, and vv, though both long and short "s" are rendered in modern type).

Except where noted, I have translated a text's blackletter, italic, or other early modern typeface (when used as the default typeface of the text or section of the text) into modern roman type, using italics to indicate the text's emphases. In quotations, second capitals following a larger printed intial capital have also been eliminated silently. In early modern book titles, including in the notes and bibliography, words composed entirely of capitals have generally been rendered as words with initial capitals, and title fonts are made uniformly italic; early modern spelling of titles has been maintained, with some resulting oddities (for example, "Scriptvres," "Qvip"). On meanings conveyed by early modern capitals, see the Introduction and Chapter 4. Given this book's emphasis on type and letters, I regret the loss of contextual meaning sometimes incurred by these changes but encourage readers to consult the earlier editions.

Except where noted, all citations of the *Oxford English Dictionary* refer to the online edition of the *OED* and reflect the *OED*'s revisions as of its June 2015 update.

References to *Mr. VVilliam Shakespeares Comedies, Histories, & Tragedies* (1623) cite through-line numbers (TLN) in *The Norton Facsimile: The First Folio of Shakespeare*, prepared by Charlton Hinman, unless otherwise noted.

On Q: An Introduction to Queer Philology

Capitals are increased by parsimony, and diminished by
prodigality and misconduct.
> —Adam Smith, *An Inquiry into the Nature
> and Causes of the Wealth of Nations*[1]

Quin. . . . and so euery one according to his cue.
> —*A Midsommer Nights Dreame*[2]

Q, Without A

Introducing "queer philology," I should start at the very beginning: with the
letter Q. Q is a letter with quite a history, something of a tale to tell, and we
might as well begin with Samuel Johnson's erroneous tale, writing in his *Dictionary* of 1755: "Q, Is a consonant borrowed from the Latin or French . . . the name
of this letter is *cue*, from *queue*, French, tail; its form being that of an O with a
tail."[3] This statement is, the *Oxford English Dictionary* (*OED*) carefully informs us,
wrong: "[An entirely erroneous guess.]"[4] This is to say, Q is known, by the time of
the nineteenth-century philology that made possible the *OED*, to have been derived and named "really" from a letter (*koppa*) in certain early Phoenician and
Greek alphabets.[5] But let us, for the moment, and in the spirit of what I hope to
introduce as a queer philology, follow Johnson's cue, or his erroneous guess, back
to the period with which this book is most closely concerned, the early modern,
and see where this erroneous Q may lead, or (in Latin) intro/duce, us.[6]

Q, writes the sixteenth-century French printer and humanist language reformer
Geofroy Tory, in the second book of his magisterial treatise on majuscles, *Champ
Fleury [the Art and Science of the Due and True Proportion of Classical Letters]* (1529),[7]

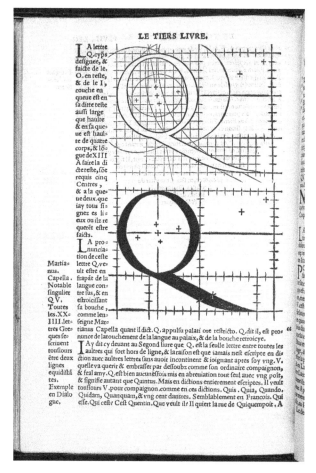

FIGURE 1. The letter Q in *Champ Fleury*, f. LIII'.
© The British Library Board. Shelfmark 60.e.14.

est la seulle entre toutes les autres lettres qui sort hors de ligne par dessoubz, & . . . iay trouue q' [que] le. Q. sort hors de ligne pource quil ne se
laisse escripre en diction entiere, sans son compaignon & bon frere. V. &
pour monstrer qui le desire tousiours apres soy, Il le va embrasser de sa
queue p [par] dessoubz cõe ie figureray cy apres en son renc. (f. XII')

[is the only one among all the other letters that goes outside the line un-
derneath, and . . . I have found that the Q goes outside the line because it/
he does not let himself be written in a complete word, without his companion and good brother V, and in order to show who always desires him
after himself, he will embrace him/seeks to embrace him with his tail [*sa
queue*] from below, as I will hereafter illustrate in its/his place.][8] (Figure 1)

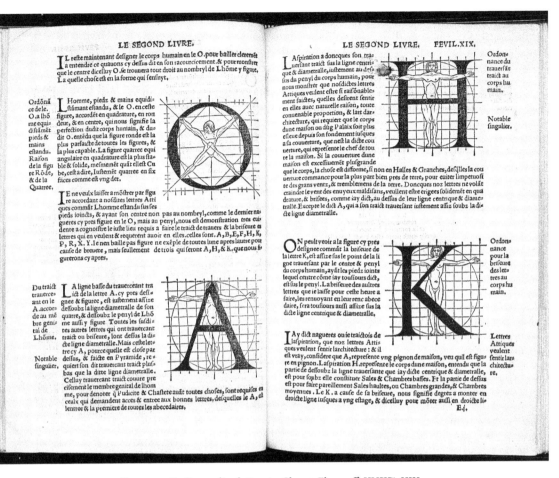

FIGURE 2. Bodies and/as letters in *Champ Fleury*, ff. XVIII^v–XIX.
© The British Library Board. Shelfmark 60.e.14.

As Tom Conley has observed in his important reading of *Champ Fleury*, Tory's plotting of majuscules within the square is part of a larger ensuing humanist project seeking the standardization of the letter. Tory's work "reflect[s] a growing uniformity of patterns of script,"[9] and, as Conley shows in his analysis of the book as a cartographic text, Tory's book works not only to map the letters of the alphabet, but also to align, within these plottings, the body of the letter and the body of the body, in what are taken to be their correct proportions (Figure 2). This is to say, this book not only hails, or *introduces,* its reader into a kind of literacy (the proper proportion of letters) but also introduces his/her body into this map; the reader imagines his/her body as or in a letter. The letter becomes standardized, and the body (here, a male body) either becomes or is already understood as the form of that standardization.

It is worth pointing out, however, that Q is one point at which Tory's humanist project of standardization falters—that Q persists in *Champ Fleury* as the exceptional letter, the only one among all the other letters, as we have already seen, who goes outside the line (Figure 3; "LETTRES FLEVRIES"). Q is anomalous, too, in never being written by himself in a word; Q is thus an exception to the paradigm shift out of which Tory qua printer writes: if the innovation of movable type capitalizes on the mobility of letters (their willingness to be separated and deployed, printed and redistributed in multiple combinations), Q is, except within abbreviations, never permitted to appear singly, without his companion, V.[10] Q is, in this sense, *the letter which is not one*: never alone, never functioning only *as* a letter, always conjoined, always desiring companionship. Johnson's history of Q leads to one even more erroneous, or errant, than the *OED* has imagined: we are beginning to approach the queerness of Q.

For it is not only the case that the letter Q is, in *Champ Fleury*, exceptional, but that Q's exceptionality is a tale tied to his tail, his errant queue. Further, the discourse that articulates Q's difference, Q's anomaly, or his going outside the line from below, is not only discourse that recent scholarship can help us recognize as anal (Q's name as well as his queue/tail homonymically suggest a *cul*, an "arse, bumme, tayle, nockandroe, fundament" as Cotgrave's 1611 French-English dictionary would translate[11]), but also discourse widely associated with male-male relations during this period. Recent histories of sexuality have demonstrated that in early modern culture there was not (as there is said to be in modernity) a single "homosexuality," but rather multiple *homoeroticisms*—homoerotic discourses, practices, or structures[12] that are neither self-identical (sodomy is not friendship is not pederasty) nor the same as the modern notion of "homosexuality" qua identity.[13] If it is then, perhaps, somewhat surprising to see, in his mapping of the letter Q, Tory deploying simultaneously *two* of these discourses (the language of sodomy, usually condemned, and the language of homoerotic male-male friendship, usually promoted[14]), this may again signal the extent of Q's queerness: it (or shall I say "he"?) is exceptional both as the letter with a constant friend and companion *and* as the letter that couples with another, with his tail from below.[15]

When Tory returns to the letter Q in *Champ Fleury*'s third book, which is devoted to the description and plotting of each of the twenty-three letters in alphabetic order, we learn that Q seems always tending toward jointure; indeed, Q is initially formed by a copula—made, Tory says, of the O "en teste" (*tête*, literally the *cap*/ital) and the I lying or couched "en queue" ("faicte de le. O. en teste, & de le I, couche en queue" [f. LIIIᵛ]; see Figure 1). Further, Tory's discourse in this extended description of Q retains both his sodomitical and his friend/ly commitments: if V is Q's ordinary companion and faithful friend ("son ordinaire compaignon, & feal amy"), Q here again seeks out and embraces V upward,[16] from

FIGURE 3. "LETTRES FLEVRIES" in *Champ Fleury*, f. LXXVIII^v.
© The British Library Board. Shelfmark 60.e.14.

below ("querir & embrasse par dessoubz" [f. LIII^v]). We can also notice Tory's discourse for the immediacy and position of Q and V's relation: they are linked "incontinent & ioignant" (f. LIII^v).[17] This phrasing not only suggests *immediate* linkage ("as soone as may be," says Cotgrave of "incontinent" as an adverb), but may also bring with it the resonance of Q as incontinent or unchaste, with a physical proximity that is also a joining, a coupling, a touch. (As an adjective, Cotgrave translates *ioignant* as both "Neere vnto, hard by, . . . almost touching" *and* as "Ioyning, coupling" [sig. Aaa.iiii].)

The corporeal ligature of the faithful friends is embodied even more sodomitically when Tory maps the two letters in relation to each other, in an illustration that, we can notice, disrupts the otherwise serial, alphabetic order of Tory's third book, by anomalously figuring two letters together (Figure 4):

> Pour monstrer ce que iay dit, que Q. tire & embrasse de sa queue le V. Iē [J'en] ay faict cy pres vng deseing au quel peut veoir que le bout de la ditte queue saccorde a la pointe du bout dembas de le V. (f. LIIII)

> [To show what I've said, that Q pulls/leads and embraces the V with his tail, I've made nearby a design in which one can see that the end/tip of the said tail accords/agrees with the point of the bottom end/tip of the V.]

The tail accords (itself) with, agrees with, the bottom of its faithful friend and ordinary companion, but again, supplementing the sodomitic, a term like *s'accorde* in this context may bring with it a range of friendly and even marital resonances: "Accorder vne fille," translates Cotgrave: "To handfast, affiance, betroath himselfe vnto a maiden" (sig. B.iiii^v). The agreement of the tail and the bottom may also alert us here to the confused sodometrics[18] (or positionings) of this configuration, the strangeness (even as it appears to be already sodomitic) of a coupling of *tails*. Embodying in the letter a trope that is, as several critics have shown, the rhetorical figure of sodomy during the period,[19] Q's tail is literally *preposterous*, a confusion of before and behind, for it leads while it also follows; simultaneously, this *tail*, as in English of the period, begins to function not (or not *only*) as tail but as yard, as penis.[20] Embracing this tail, not unlike other yards, may eventuate in a loss of virtue; quoting Priscian, who speaks of the "vertu" (the virtue or power/value) of letters, Tory accords with, or follows the lead of, the ancient author:

> Priscian autheur iadis tresillustre, en son premier Liure ou il parle de la vertu des lr̄es [lettres], dict bien q' Q. veult tousiours apres luy V. pour monstrer que le dit V. pert sa vertu & son / son estant escript deuāt vne vocale en vne mesme syllabe. (f. XII^v)[21]

[Priscian, the very illustrious author of old, in his first book, where he speaks of the virtue/power of the letters, indeed says that Q always wants V after himself to show that the said V loses his virtue/power and his sound when written before a vowel within the same syllable.]

Following Q, the V loses his *vertu*—his power, which is also his *"valour, prowess, manhood,"* as Cotgrave translates. Normally himself *une vocale* (a vowel), V loses as well his voice or sound ("son / son," as Tory is careful to write, aware of the homograph that joins voice and self-possession), his vocality. A subordinate sexual positioning, as elsewhere in this culture, eventuates in a loss of power understood as manhood understood as voice. This is to say, there are powerful implications to where and how one is led, or intro/duced.

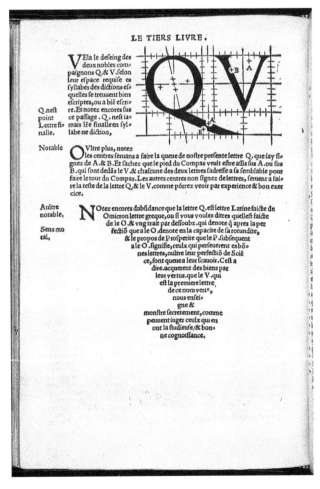

FIGURE 4. Les "deux nobles compaignons Q. & V." in *Champ Fleury*, f. LIIIIʳ.
© The British Library Board. Shelfmark 60.e.14.

In moving toward an introduction to philology, the love of the *logos*, I have instead introduced you to the love of the letter, love among the letters. But, lest you think I am overemphasizing the sexiness or *corporeality* of letters—lest, that is, you think I am leading you erroneously to read a metaphorical discourse of the letter as having to do with actual bodies—it is important to recall the insistence of the bodily in Tory's orthography. *Champ Fleury* is subtitled "the Art and Science of the due and true Proportion of classical Letters, . . . proportioned according to the Human Body and Face." As Conley has shown in detail, Tory maps the human body, and what he calls the "body" of the letters, onto a ten-by-ten grid; the graphing of letters produces an elaborate conjunction of rhetorical terms, the disciplines of classical education, and the body. In the graphing of the letter O and a recognizably Vitruvian man (f. XVIIIᵛ), for example (Figure 5), the diagonals cross, forming a *chi*, at the center of the letter and the man, and it then comes as no surprise, in Tory's explanation of a figure he calls "LHOMME LETRE" (Figure 6), that the letter X should correspond with "Dialectica" and the navel (ff. XXIIᵛ–XXIII). This "lettered," "learned," or "literal man" brings the twenty-three letters of the "Roman" alphabet[22] into relation with, presents them as a parallel realization *of*, the "most noble members and places of the human body" ("le nōbre des. XXIII. lettres Attiques accorde, comme iay dit, aux membres & lieux pl[us] nobles du corps humain"), and with the nine muses, seven liberal arts, four cardinal

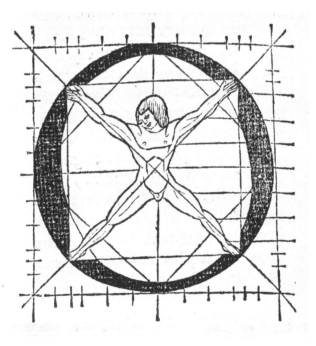

FIGURE 5. Man/chiasmus/letter in *Champ Fleury*, f. XVIIIᵛ.
© The British Library Board. Shelfmark 60.e.14.

virtues, and three graces,[23] reproducing some familiar early modern hierarchies of the body: upper and lower, right and left (*dextre* et *senestre*), and so forth (ff. XXII^v–XXIII).[24] The letter A, for example, accords with *Iusticia* and the right hand. The placement of Q makes corporeal and witty sense within these correspondent systems: as Conley notices, Q here makes use of "a common pun and rebus on *cul*" (81). Q marks "the place for discharging the belly" ("Le lieu pour decharger le ventre") with a pun also on wind (*vent*) and is wittily therefore associated with Euterpe, the muse of music (f. XXII^v).[25]

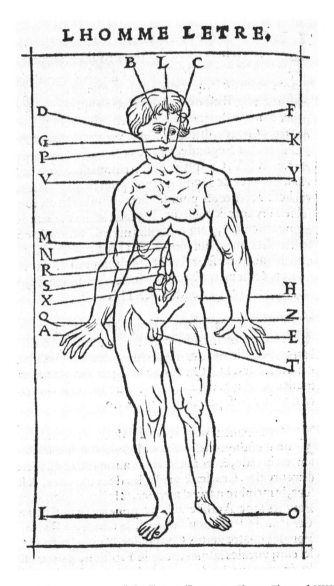

FIGURE 6. "LHOMME LETRE," the "lettered" man, in *Champ Fleury*, f. XXII^v.
© The British Library Board. Shelfmark 60.e.14.

But we should also notice Q's persistent anomaly, his queerness, within these schema: like the penis, Q figures one of two body parts of the literal man that here lacks a name: "the place for . . . ," rather than the straightforward nouns naming the other parts; a function, rather than an identity; a "does" as much as an "is." He is furthermore the only letter attached to the unseen backside of the lettered man, the only letter whose location cannot be seen on the map of the body. Tory writes:

> Les lettres ainsi logees que voyes cy dessus, ne sōt pas logees en leur ordre Abecedaire quon tient communement, mais tout a mon essient les ay mises & appliquees selon ma petite Philosophie. (f. XXIII)

> [The letters thus lodged as seen above are not placed in their alphabetical order, to which one commonly adheres, but altogether intentionally/consciously I have placed and associated them/set them out according to my little philosophy.]

But even out of the common order, outside the logic of the alphabet, "as seen above," Q cannot be seen above, is not visibly *logé* in this logic.

Lest you think I can lead you to such conclusions only by engaging in the *jouissance* of a French text, let me assure you that Q resists assimilation to the rule as well in English, the language at the center of this study.[26] Q, explains Richard Huloet in his 1552 *ABCEDARIVM ANGLICOLATINVM*, "[i]s a mute, whych also taken as *Litera super uacue*, dothe desyre no letter to hym but V."[27] *Supervacue* is a term rarely found in English contexts, but Wyclif translates it as both "over-void" and "over-vain." (The threat of such a letter may not be obvious to us, but, especially to a group of spelling reformers who, as we will see in Chapter 1, want to rationalize English into a one-letter/one-sound system, the threat of the mute and supervacuous letter is significant.) John Higgins, revising Huloet twenty years later, again refers to Q as a "mute" and "vnneadfull."[28] In John Baret's *Alvearie Or Triple Dictionary* (1574), this discourse is expanded:

> **Q** Hath long bene superfluously vsed in writing english woordes, whereas the Grekes neuer knew it, neither could the English saxons euer abide the abuse thereof, but alwaies vsed *K* when such occasion serued. As for *Q* in latin woordes, I meddle nothing with it here, leauing that language to be refourmed by better learned men. Yet *Quintilian lib. 12. cap. 10.* saith it is but a needelesse and voide letter: and *Priscian* also affirmeth that both *K*, *Q*, and *C*, haue all one power. . . . Yf then *K* by it selfe will serue, what neede we pester our crosrew with such superfluous letters?[29]

The discourse surrounding Q here continues to be of superfluity,[30] but we should also note that added to this supervoid is the notion that the use of Q was an "abuse" for the Anglo-Saxons. The letter further seems to call forth the need for the reform of another language of illustrious precedent, Latin, in a passage stuffed with quotations from Latin authors, who are here adduced to testify in the service of their own deconstruction; Baret virtually makes Quintillian drop his own name into the void that Q spells out here. Once again, Q creates a disturbance in alphabetic order, "pestering" the cross-row (that is, the arrangement of letters in the alphabet used to teach children their letters). Pestering was worse, less trivial, in early modern England than it has come to be: "to pester" was to "overcrowd" and to "annoy," but also to "intricate, intangle, trouble, incomber" (Cotgrave, sig. Gg.i[v]).[31] As a term, *cross-row* mingles *ortho*graphic and sacred orders (it was also known as the *Christ-cross-row*, because in hornbooks the row of letters usually began with a cross before the A [Figure 7]),[32] and this may signal the extent to which the threat of Q in Baret is

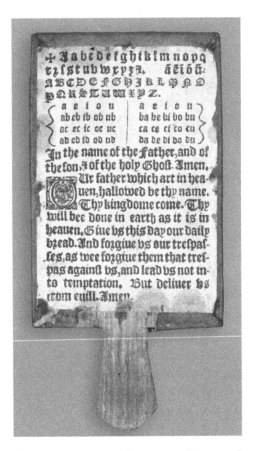

FIGURE 7. The cross-row on an early seventeenth-century hornbook.
By permission of the Folger Shakespeare Library.

significant. *Abuse* in this culture carried with it religious and sodomitic associations we have since lost: among those who "shall not inherite the kingdome of God" in the Authorized Version of the Bible (1611) are "fornicatours, nor idolaters, nor adulterers, nor effeminate, nor abusers of themselues with mankinde,"[33] and Tyndale (1530) associates the "abuse [of] men's wives" with "sodomitry."[34]

If Q has lost his gender in Baret, he has given it over to K in Ben Jonson's *English Grammar*, where Q is described as

> a Letter we might very well spare in our *Alphabet*, if we would but use the serviceable *k*. as he should be, and restore him to the right of reputation he had with our Fore-fathers. For, the *English-Saxons* knew not this halting Q. with her waiting-woman *u*. after her, but exprest

quaile.		*kuaile.*
quest.		*kuest.*
	by	
quick		*kuick.*
quil.		*kuil.*

> Til *custome* under the excuse of expressing enfranchis'd words with us, intreated her into our Language, in

quality,	*quantity*
quarel	*quintessence, &c.*

> And hath now given her [the] best of *ks*. possession.[35]

If Jonson is unusual in giving a letter a feminine gender, it is perhaps not surprising that the playwright of *Epicoene, or the Silent Woman* would make the letter that can be spared a female.[36] Q has eroded the reputation of the patriarchally derived K of the Anglo-Saxons; Q's femininity is furthermore "halting" (i.e., limping, or imperfect). (Again, the translators of the Authorized Version, describing their work, help to contextualize: "if [in prior translations] any thing be halting, or superfluous, or not so agreeable to the originall, the same may bee corrected, and the trueth set in place."[37]) The only letter with an attendant, Jonson's Q is a foreign interloper and usurper of the prerogatives of natural male English letters—an accident of custom, the "enfranchisement" (i.e., naturalization) of alien words. Not only female, she becomes an alien or slave-born letter, in the other related sense of *enfranchise*: having political privileges she did or should not have.[38] *Qu*: two women together, taking liberties. We may even hear, in this Jacobean text of Jonson's, the play of the majuscules Q and K as queen and king: a plea, not so long after Elizabeth and in the time of Anna, against queens, for an Englished Salic law, or against foreign queens. To think like Christopher Marlowe for a moment: is the *emigré(e)* Q a Gaveston (desiring no other to him but V?) or an Isabella?

Indeed, to find a defense of errant, alien Q, one must go to the borders of English, to the text of a Scottish orthography reformer, Alexander Hume, writing his treatise *Of the Orthographie and Congruitie of the Britan Tongue* (c. 1617). Like Baret, Hume is concerned with "use" and "abuse," and he titles his fifth chapter "Of Our Abusing Sum Consonants."[39] Abuse, for Hume, in a way that should remind us of Tory, is associated with the arrangement of the body and the formation of letters; in his chapter titled "Of the Rules to Symbolize," Hume insists upon the clarity and differentiation of parts of the body as registered in writing: "it is clere that soundes pronounced with this organ can not be written with symboles of that; as, for exemple, a labiel symbol can not serve a dental nor a guttural sound; nor a guttural symbol a dental nor a labiel sound" (18). This is the trouble with the *under-use* of Q in English, which produces in Hume's text an unusual narrative break from his sequence of numbered orthographical rules:

8. [In "Of the Rules to Symbolize"] To clere this point, and alsoe to reform an errour bred in the south and now usurped be our ignorant printeres, I wil tel quhat befel my self quhen I was in the south with a special gud frende of myne. Ther rease, upon sum accident, quhither quho, quhen, quhat, etc., sould be symbolized with q or w, a hoat disputation betuene him and me. After manie conflictes (for we often encountered), we met be chance, in the citie of Baeth, with a Doctour of divinitie of both our acquentance. He invited us to denner. At table my antagonist, to bring the question on foot amangs his awn condisciples, began that I was becum an heretik, and the doctour spering [i.e., asking][40] how, ansuered that I denyed quho to be spelled with a w, but with qu. Be quhat reason? quod the Doctour. Here, I beginning to lay my grundes of labial, dental, and guttural soundes and symboles, he snapped me on this hand and he on that, that the doctour had mikle a doe to win me room for a syllogisme.[41] Then (said I) a labial letter can not symboliz a guttural syllab. But w is a labial letter, quho a guttural sound. And therfoer w can not symboliz quho, nor noe syllab of that nature. Here the doctour staying them again (for al barked at ones), the proposition, said he, I understand; the assumption is Scottish, and the conclusion false. Quherat al laughed, as if I had bene dryven from al replye, and I fretted to see a frivolouse jest goe for a solid ansuer. (18)[42]

[To [make] clear this point, and also to reform an error bred in the south and now usurped by our ignorant printers, I will tell what befell myself when I was in the south with a special good friend of mine. There rose, upon some accident, whether *who*, *when*, *what*, etc., should be symbolized with *q* or *w*—a hot disputation between him and me. After many conflicts (for we often encountered), we met by chance in the city of Bath, with a Doctor of Divinity of both our acquaintance. He invited us to dinner. At table, my antagonist, to bring the question on foot amongst his own con-disciples, began that I was become an heretic, and, the Doctor [asking] "How?" [my friend] answered that I denied *who* to be spelled with a *w*, but [rather] with *qu*. "By what reason?" quoth the Doctor. Here, I, beginning to lay my grounds of labial, dental, and guttural sounds and symbols, he snapped me on this hand and he on that, that the Doctor had [much] ado to win [myself] room for a syllogism.[43] "Then," said I, "a labial letter cannot symbolize a guttural syllable. But *w* is a labial letter; *who*, a guttural sound. And therefore *w* cannot symbolize *who*, nor no syllable of that nature." Here the Doctor, staying them again (for all barked at once): "The proposition," said he, "I understand; the assumption is Scottish, and the conclusion false." Whereat all laughed, as if I had been driven from all reply, and I fretted to see a frivolous jest go for a solid answer.]

This passage—an extraordinary tale of national shaming around the use of the letter Q—brings together a number of the discourses we have been examining. If the allegation of heresy against the Q-user begins as an exaggerating jest, we can nevertheless notice that Hume's argument in this episode is with a Doctor of Divinity; the question of Q's supervacuity is again brought into the realm of the theological—the Christ-cross-row again troubled. If the level of affect Hume accords this incident seems to us extravagant, we can further notice that significant homosocial bonds and relations are at stake: Hume is encountering again a "special gud frende of myne" who, in the course of the tale, becomes his "antagonist"; the doctor is of their mutual "acquentance"; the friend crosses over to the side of other "condisciples." Also at issue is the proper disposition of the body, its members, and their inseparable link to the alphabet; the corporeal "grundes" of speech and writing are being undermined, to Hume's obvious discomfort: even as the question is brought "on foot" and he is being disciplined on the one hand and on the other, throat and labia are being confused. The episode also adjudicates national boundaries; according to the doctor, Q is the province of heresy, of Scottish assumptions that lead to false conclusions. To Hume, to the contrary, the under-use of Q, the "errour bred in the south," requires reformation; it involves an error or errancy of the body, the wandering away of the "special gud frende," a perverse turn away from bodily and national grounds.[44]

Practicing Philology

But I seem to be leading you away from, rather than introducing you to, as promised, a kind of philology, so it is perhaps time to lay down some groundwork, some fundamentals—to make room for some syllogisms, some rules of philology. "If the fundacion be not sure," writes Hume in his dedication to King James VI and I, "the maer gorgiouse the edifice[,] the grosser the falt."[45] Let us start again, then, from the beginning:

A. This book argues that the study of sex and gender in historically distant cultures is necessarily a *philological* investigation—in this case, a detailed study of the terms and related rhetorics that early modern English culture used to inscribe bodies, pleasures, affects, sexual acts, and, to the extent we can speak of these, identities.

B. As this catalog will suggest, the project builds on the work of theorists and historians who have, following Foucault, investigated the historical and cultural specificity of words like *homosexual, sodomy,* and *tribade.*[46]

C. Thus interested in practicing the detailed analysis of linguistic evidence employed by an older philological study, the book proposes a renewed historical philology that investigates the etymology, circulation, transformation, and constitutive power of some "key words" within early modern lexicons and discourses of sex and gender.[47]

D. In the first sense that we will give to the term *queer philology,* this is to practice a philology *of the queer*—that is, of sexual practices, the positioning of bodies and body parts, and "identities" that seem nonnormative, whether in their own time or, especially, from this historical distance.[48]

E. The book is organized around a series of terms that function as a variorum for analyzing sex/gender and their manifold associations in early modern English culture—terms chosen to illustrate both the continuities of early modern language with our own, and its alterities.

F. This lexicon—including, for example, *conversation* and *intercourse, fundament* and *foundation, sweet* and *amorous, tup* and *top*—is proposed not as a comprehensive account of early modern sex/gender vocabularies, but rather as a set of sites for thinking both about structures of sex and gender (what does it mean, for example, that *conversation* and *intercourse* have exchanged meanings since the seventeenth century?) *and* about early modern structures of language (what does it mean that *fundament, fundacion,* and *foundation* are sometimes used interchangeably?).

G. Beginning from the analysis of a specific term, each chapter moves toward a broader analysis of the circulation of sex/gender discourses and their relation to other formative but often undernoticed languages of this culture, as located in a variety of other texts.

H. It is thus the project of this book both to spell out the historical particularities of early modern orthography, structures of rhetoric, and vocabulary *and* to read anew the textual record left by this culture—a record, as Q emblematizes and Chapter 4's discussion of boys in/as letters demonstrates, that sometimes straddles a boundary we would erect between the literal (letteral), textual, and visual.

I. There can be no nuanced cultural history of early modern sex and gender without spelling out its terms—for what alternatives of historical access do we have? Comprehension of sex will require philology. (As we will see in Chapter 3, even a term as apparently clinical and transparent as *sexual intercourse* requires philological attention.) As Stephen G. Nichols writes, in an introduction to "New Philology" in medieval studies, "philology is the matrix out of which all else springs."[49] (We will return to Nichols's matrix and this claim.)

K. We are practicing philology, so this may require attending, with all the objectivity we can muster, to philology's concerns, in the language of its discipline: to its *matrices* (whether of tongues or of pieces of type, type-faces); to the *etymologies* (which is, to translate, the true origins, the *genealogies*) of words; to *families* of related languages; to the pursuit of linguistic *roots*; to *stemmata* (that is, the *family* stems or trees or *pedigrees*) of manuscripts and printed texts, their *lines* of *descent, contamination,* and *corruption*; to the fidelity or *faithfulness* of translations; to the *mongrelization* of literary genres; to *spurious* (which is, to translate, "illegitimate, false . . . bastard, adulterous") words.

L. We may notice that the orderings of philology will lead us to edit, to eliminate, to *castigate* as the early modern humanists would say (which is to say, we may find ourselves led toward making chaste or pure) the guesses we can identify as "entirely erroneous."[50] The word *guess* is, of course, of obscure descent, but seems to come from *get*, "to get, obtain, to beget."[51] What then is Samuel Johnson's Q, from the French *queue* for tail, but a bastard child?

Queer Philology

By escalating the critical rhetoric here—imitating the assured pronouncements of some earlier practitioners of philology and reaching the impasse of L. above, putting pressure on a number of philology's terms, a process that will continue throughout this book—I hope I have begun obliquely to draw attention to some of the assumptions and problems of traditional philology as it emerges out of classical textual recovery, editing, correction, errata sheets, and "castigation" in the Renaissance; as it reaches an extensive flowering in the late eighteenth- and nineteenth-century comparative linguistic philology of William Jones, Friedrich Schlegel, Franz Bopp, Jacob Grimm, and many others; as it comes to dominate scholarship in European and eventually American universities and produces a *New English Dictionary* that will become the *OED*; and as it continues as a deep, if contested, disciplinary structure inflecting later literary, editorial, historical, linguistic, philosophical, and cultural scholarship. Erich Auerbach's mid-twentieth-century association of a culture of "civilization" and its emergent "need to constitute authentic texts" suggests the persistence of philology in the rhetoric of editorial work on early modern texts at least into the late twentieth century, a connection that motivates the final section of this book.[52]

This story of philology as an emergent and then hegemonic discipline has been told by others—perhaps, as Seth Lerer and Gregory Nagy suggest, from its very beginnings.[53] At the outset of the twentieth century, Ferdinand de Saussure's notes for the *Course in General Linguistics* famously begin with a critical, pocket history of philology and comparative philology as prelude ("erroneous and insufficient") to the emergence of a "true science of linguistics,"[54] and in recent decades scholars, including Hans Aarsleff, Anthony Grafton, Geoffrey Galt Harpham, Stephanie Jed, and Lerer, have elaborated aspects of this story, often including critical discussion of philology's ideological assumptions and blind spots.[55] It is not the goal of this book to tell that story comprehensively again; that is a task perhaps best left to the classicist, Germanist, or Victorianist I am not, though, as Aarsleff's history shows, the English influence on and development of this story have been undernoted, given later hegemonies within the discipline. Neither is it the goal of this book to draw a bright, definitional line around "philology": as these histories have suggested and as other critics have observed, to hazard a definition of this discipline—this historically variant, enlarging/narrowing set of practices—can seem like folly. Writing in the mid-twentieth century, René Wellek and Austin Warren opine that "[s]ince the term has so many and such divergent meanings, it is best to abandon it."[56] Indeed, as Aarsleff recounts in demonstrating the early emergence out of debates in philosophies of language and as Roberta Frank succinctly summarizes, philology (gendered female in Frank's account) seems perpetually defined in opposition: "Philology resists regularization or definition. Her identity is relational, dependent on a constantly shifting opposite principle, variously called philosophy, linguistics, psychology, theory, dialectics, antiquarianism, truth, social utility, or didacticism."[57] Aarsleff proposes to use "the term 'study of language' rather than 'philology,'" arguing that "the history we seek will gain neither continuity nor coherence if we in advance decide to limit it to such work as may deserve the name of philology in the narrower sense, a decision that has by and large been left to German scholars."[58]

Thus, instead, while relying on a general (and capacious, not-strictly-bounded) understanding of philology as an uneven and historically shifting set of transnational practices that has variously incorporated comparative linguistic study, the histories of languages, etymology (on a spectrum we might describe as ranging from "impressionistic" to "scientific"), textual editing, translation, modernization, and correction (and incorporating within such editorial practice the study of original documents in manuscript and print),[59] *Queer Philologies* seeks as part of its project to draw critical attention, as in my alphabetic progression above, to the ways in which philology's manifold methods and rhetorics of investigation are often themselves thoroughly implicated in the languages of sex, gender, and the body that I am studying.

You may have noticed that the increasing adamancy of my alphabetized pronouncements above begins to border on what Carla Freccero brilliantly terms "phallolog[y]."[60] Philology's investments in phallology—more precisely, its self-construction *through* normative languages of sex, gender, reproduction, and the body—are evident at least since the Renaissance, as Jed persuasively showed in her analysis of languages of castigation and chastity at the heart of humanist textual practice. To take a familiar English example that may resonate anew here, the actors acting as text-gathering editors of the Shakespeare first folio collection (1623) argue that they seek to provide the playwright's textual "Orphanes" the surrogate parentage of "Guardians" (i.e., *patr*ons) and that they present the previously "maimed, and deformed" bodily members of his textual corpus as "cur'd, and perfect of their limbes."[61] While not systematically developed, such corporeal and familial rhetoric resonates with later examples drawn from the late eighteenth- and nineteenth-century emergence and apogee of philology's disciplinary practice: Johann Gottfried von Herder's influential *Treatise upon the Origin of Language* (1771; English trans., 1827) employs "often-repeated organic metaphors" and sees language as a "natural being" governed by "natural laws";[62] James Ingram's *Inaugural Lecture on the Utility of Anglo-Saxon Literature* (1807) argues "we must study, if I may use the expression, the *comparative anatomy* of human language; we must *dissect*";[63] Bopp, writing in the 1820 English version of the treatise that essentially founds comparative philology, is one of many to use eventually standard rhetoric of a "family of languages," "kindred dialects," and "sister languages."[64] As Lerer notes in emphasizing the aspirations of philology by analogy to science, Schlegel, too, sees a relation between the comparative grammar of languages and comparative anatomy, and, later, the American philologist William Dwight Whitney uses the suggestive title *The Life and Growth of Language*

(1875).[65] Lerer in particular has noted the way in which Bopp's terms "all come together to inflect the rhetoric of comparative philology with the idioms of biology" (Raymond Williams also remarked the methodologically parallel, contemporary development of evolutionary biology and comparative philology[66]), and Lerer remarks that "[c]omparative philology, in these terms, reads like an investigation into family relationships"—though he does not analyze the heteronormative and reproductive implications of this dominant rhetoric.[67] Indeed, this rhetoric sometimes inflects Lerer's own discussion, as when he writes that Sir William Jones "*sired* the modern discipline of comparative philology."[68] (A queer philology is here bound to ask: sired with or "on" *whom*?) Saussure, for all his revolutionary critique of traditional philology, remains deeply embedded in the familial paradigm of languages: "Scientific observation of linguistic similarities proves that two or more idioms may be akin, i.e. that they have a common origin. A group of related languages makes up a family."[69]

So ingrained has this mode of description become in our default modes of thinking about language that it seems almost impossible to think outside of them. Jed's exposition of two sets of terms, implicated both in the texts on the rape of Lucretia she analyzes *and* in subsequent editorial and interpretive accounts of those texts, "words related to touching or the absence of touching—*tangible, contaminate, contact, integrity, intact,* etc." and "words related to cutting—*chastity, castigate, caste,* and Latin *carere* ('to be cut off from, to lack')," brings brilliantly to the surface the implication of humanist editorial practice in rhetorics of sexual/power-ful contact and contamination. (These terms find remoter echoes in my treatment of textual "corruption" in mid-twentieth-century New Bibliography's study of compositors in Chapter 1.) Yet Jed also describes these sets of terms as two joined but "conflicting lexical *families* of terms." The analysis of bodily and lineal integrity central (one could say "integral") to her analysis of humanism's "chaste thinking" is surely also embedded in theories of "Indo-European" language "families" and the tracing of their etymological "roots."[70]

These examples—many more from the vast annals of philology could be supplied—begin to suggest the ways in which philology's rhetoric and practice are susceptible to queer analysis and critique, requiring a revision of the assurance (above) of what philology can enact with regard to the history of sexuality. This is to say, revising dictum I. above, that,

I.[v]   Even as "comprehension of sex will require philology," at the same time, this book does not (cannot) seek simply to illuminate, in positivist mode, terms of sex, gender, and the body via a philological method that would seem to make them yield up their truth as discourses.[71] Rather, we will also see that there is rarely philology without sex—rarely, that is, an analysis of language and textual transmission, contamination, and correction that does not draw upon or intersect with terms from the lexicons of sex, gender, reproduction, the body, and the family.

What does it mean, for example, to think of some words (and works) as "spurious"? And therefore of proper words as having a readily identifiable parent, a traceable lineage? Why are words, languages, and sometimes literary genres (as we will see in Chapter 7) understood as necessarily heterosexual, or at least reproductive—familial in their circulation, transmission, dispersal, and alteration?[72] To return to an example cited above, when Nichols argues that "philology is the matrix out of which all else springs,"[73] we should notice that philology is both being described as an order or system that preexists the objects of its study *and* being figured in specifically sex/gendered terms: the mother (*matrix*, or "womb," *mater*) of its inventions.

To practice a queer philology is, in part, to attempt to denaturalize these powerful rhetorics. Though not explicitly focused on philology's queering and queerable potential, Jonathan Culler remarks that "the notion of philology as a basis which is somehow prior to literary and cultural interpretation is an idea that one should seriously question, and an idea, moreover, that philology itself, in principle as well as in practice, provides us with the tools for questioning."[74] A number of critics have joined Culler in remarking philology's capacity for self-critique; Frank notes that philology "is perhaps best recognized by her skeptical stance and disruptiveness, her unwillingness to commit herself quickly, not by her shape, which is always changing" and Lerer sees self-critique at work in Auerbach's *Mimesis*: "The paradox of philological inquiry, then, lies in its claim to rescue a *patrimoine spirituel* while at the same time exposing the underminings of that patrimony."[75] But the language of patrimony, the "ravages of time" (related etymologically to ravishment and rape) from which Auerbach says it must be saved,[76] as well as (female) philology's changing shape, can again remind us of the need for a specifically *queer* philology attuned to sex/gender nonnormativity. This is not to exclude other forms of critique and engagement; Harpham has explored the reliance of comparative Indo-European philology on concepts of Aryan race/ nation and, as Lerer pointedly notes and Aarsleff also documents, "[t]he history of orientalism in the nineteenth century *is* the history of linguistics."[77] In a Shakespearean editorial context, Chapter 8 attempts to engage philology at the intersection of gender, sexuality, and race.

Why take Q as an emblem of such a queer philology? Part of an answer, as I've begun to suggest, is implicit in Johnson's etymology of Q and the *OED*'s treatment of it. For it is one of the contentions of this project that

M.   An analysis of historically prior languages, rhetorics, genres, words, spellings, and even letters will lead us in the direction of "queer" philologies that have been de-emphasized or submerged in more traditional accounts of language.

Johnson's conclusion, and indeed his method (a method the *OED* editors call "guessing"), must be carefully policed by the *OED*'s bracketing: it must be made to seem a queer philology.[78] But as we have seen—however "erroneous" it now seems as a "guess," however "false" Johnson's etymology from the perspective of a book and now website originally known as the *New English Dictionary on Historical Principles; Founded Mainly on the Materials Collected by the Philological Society*—Q's tail *did* make sense in early modern culture, in a way that has some significance both for our understanding of early modern language and for our understanding of early modern sex/gender discourses and practices. Q and, by extension, these "queer" or anomalous philologies have significant explanatory power for a cultural study of early modern England.

The story of Q is a queer philology, but Q itself can be an emblem for queer study in another sense: as the exceptional letter or term that stands outside the (contingent) orderings of an emergent early modern philology of letters.[79] If we can shorthand those orderings as *ortho/graphy* ("right-writing," spelling order allied to rectitude, an emergent early modern idea, as we will see in Chapter 1), then to study Q, to practice a queer philology, is, by contrast, to investigate moments of early modern *skaiography*—crooked writing, to use the antonym of *orthography* proposed by Hume, our shamed Scottish user of Q.[80] *Skaiography* comes from *skaio-*, "left, left-handed, awkward, crooked,"[81] related to the Latin *scaeuitas*, "[i]nstinctive choosing of the wrong; perversity."[82] We could turn back to the preposterous trajectory of Q's tail in Tory, the perverse tail that leads rather than follows; skaiography is writing leftward, backward, against the grain.[83]

Like several of the examples of queer philology that structure this book, like skaiography, Q is the letter that does not maintain good order and moves beyond the square; the letter that functions (unletterlike) only inseparably with another letter; the letter whose correspondence with the body is marked as unseen, whose location on the backside is said to exist outside of legibility (a place not *of* the body, but for "discharging" the body, a place said to be, in the normative order of things, a void); the letter that disrupts the common order by leading in another letter prematurely, out of his place. In these ways, Q seems to work within and against orthography and philology as they begin to emerge in their early modern forms.

As the letter that can be spared, Q further stands for both the alterity and the historical contingency of the early modern alphabet, the cross-row. Q demonstrates that the alphabet, as a rudimentary technology for the study of language (a philology), is a product of its culture: a structure (like philology as a discipline) that is at once contested, re/formed, persistent, changing, ideologically marked.[84] If the alphabet were always and already the same, we would have no trouble singing Thomas Morley's early modern cross-row song (Figure 8), with its twenty-four letters, its "double w," and its now-cryptic conclusion "tittle tittle. est Amen."[85] Further, if Jonson, Baret, and others had had their way, the alphabet might have lost Q (just as it has gained U and J). Thus, Q may also be the emblem of the persistence of disseminated linguistic practice over the prescriptions of theory, the persistence of the "custom" that "enfranchises" alien words over linguistic discipline. (As we will see in Chapter 1, it is relevant to remember that when spelling standardization eventually does take place in English, it does so *not* along the lines prescribed by sixteenth- and early seventeenth-century spelling reformers.) Q thus exposes the attempted *performativity* of the cross-row, its striving after order; this is the cross-row: *Amen*, so be it. Q pesters the *notion* of the cross-row.[86] A queer philology thus might dwell on the contingencies and perturbations of the alphabet and other philologies, the moments of cited supervacuity—it might forego the possibility of singing, as if it were a possible conclusion to reach: "now I *know* my ABC's."[87] Or, remembering the historical specificity of alphabets, one might sing "*now* I know my ABC's—only for now, only for *this* 'now.'" Q signals letters' alterity and continuity.

Taking Q as an emblem of queer philology, I want to broaden this project of reading through and against the discipline of traditional philology to apply to the other activities of a queer philology in this book beyond the (in)dividual letter. In the chapters that follow I will attend to other "sodometries" within our critical

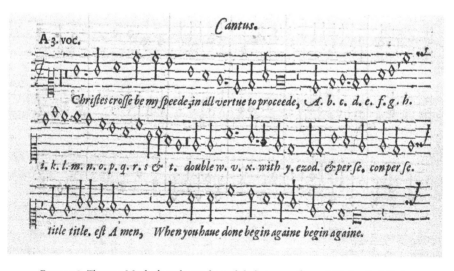

FIGURE 8. Thomas Morley's early modern alphabet song, from *A Plaine And Easie Introdvction To Practicall Mvsicke*. By permission of the Folger Shakespeare Library.

reading practices; as Jonathan Goldberg has pointed out, *sodometry* is an early modern term for both sexual positionings and the argument that seems to be false. I will thus be attending to what we call "false" etymologies,[88] as we have seen—but also to:

N. Ostensible textual cruxes thought to be nonsensical and thus in need of modern emendation (especially in Chapters 1, 8, and 9);

O. Early modern spellings that have been modernized (translated?) by later readers and editors (especially in Chapters 6, 8, and 9); and

P. The overlapping, or co-extant, senses that the indispensable philology of the *OED* would nevertheless separate into discrete meanings and separate words (especially in Chapters 3 and 5–9).[89]

In this second sense of queer philology, then, I mean to rely upon (as I hope that I have been illustrating) the utility of the discipline of philology, but also to insist that this discipline be read and practiced in a way that will highlight its own normativizing categories and elisions: "discipline" in another sense. This rereading of philology's disciplin(ing) will extend as well to the textual and editorial practices that have played a significant role in philology's development and practice (from at least the Renaissance to the present, as Grafton emphasizes[90])—including textual bibliography, its terms, and techniques (Chapters 1, 4, 8–9); paleography (Chapter 3); and glossarial commentary (Chapters 2, 4, 5, 9, and especially 8).

We have already noted, in Q, that concerns about perversities of sexual practice often arise simultaneously with concerns about such perversities of representation (superfluity, exceptionality). Lee Edelman has theorized this conjunction in modernity, describing "the critical . . . significance that our culture has come to place on the identification of 'the homosexual,' . . . the historical relationship that has produced gay sexuality in a discourse that associates it with figures of nomination or inscription."[91] Noting the traditional designation of sodomy as "the horrible crime/sin not to be named among Christians,"[92] Edelman emphasizes that "homosexual practices have been placed in [a] powerful, and [a] powerfully proscriptive, . . . relation to language" (5). To translate Edelman back into Huloet's terms: Q "[i]s a mute, whych also taken as *Litera super uacue*, dothe desyre no letter to hym but V." (Homoerotic desire and representational difficulty coexist.) If my translation is in some particulars unfaithful (as we say) to Edelman, and if we must be wary, when speaking of early modernity, of some modern terms Edelman uses even under erasure (e.g., *homosexual* and *identity*), I think that we can nevertheless see the queer philology I am trying to introduce through Q as usefully related or conjoined to the critical practice Edelman calls *homographesis*: "Like writing . . . , homographesis would name a double operation: one serving the ideological purposes of a conservative social order intent on codifying identities in its labor of disciplinary inscription, and the other resistant to that categorization, intent on *de*-scribing the identities that order has so oppressively *in*-scribed" (10, emphasis in the original). Q is both writing (inscribing) and unwriting (de-scribing). Translating into the terms we have been reading, and into a historically prior period,[93] we can observe this double operation: on the one hand, the labor of philology's disciplinary inscription (call it Tory's ten-by-ten grid, accompanied by the liberal arts and muses; or orthography; or alphabetical order; or the cross-row; or, in a different historical register, the *OED*) *and, simultaneously* (as our double operation, on the same hand), the *de*-scription (the written unwriting) spelled out by Q (call this going outside the line; or writing on the unseen backside; or skaiography; or pestering the cross-row; or, in the critical practice this book seeks to enact, philology made queer).[94]

The Body and the Letter

Like bodies, the bodies of letters have positions and, in early modern English, desires. Largely this is no longer the case: your word-processing software, unless it is queerer than mine, won't let you extend the kern (or tail) of the Q under the bottom point of the V. In the late seventeenth century when Joseph Moxon was writing his manual on printing, this was still possible: "every next *Letter* is turned with its *Nick* downwards, that the *Kern* of each *Letter* may lie over the *Beard* of its next."[95] For us, as for Moxon, Q no longer is seen to desire, or attributed the perverse monogamy he has in Huloet, to "desyre no letter to hym but V."[96] What do these positionings of letters, this desire of a letter to have another *to* him, tell us about the positions of the bodies of persons and their desires? In an undated, probably late sixteenth-century English alphabet of calligraphic "grotesques" (Figure 9), the body of the Q includes and extends into other bodies, across and within species—including two men who face each other within the letter, with another facing forward (or is it backward?). With their unusual facial features, the possibly racialized marking of the figure on the right, and the exaggerated foreheads that may suggest—if not actually depict—turbans, these figures may (or may not) evoke period portraits of Ottoman Turks. Or their scrolling elaboration, seeming to grow out of and reference the knot work and cross-hatching of the letter's decorative "cadels" may, through writing, lead at last to an "encounter with the idea of Turks," as Bronwen Wilson has suggested to me in correspondence. Western European associations of Turks with discourses of sexuality and sodomy are, of course, not unrelated to the directional questions the tale of Q has raised for us in the introduction. Two further examples of bodies and letters follow.

The first turns us back to French for a moment, or at least to a French moment in an English play. In what has become Act 3, Scene 6, of Shakespeare's *Henry V*,

FIGURE 9. Men in Q, in an English calligraphic letterbook (sixteenth century?). Photo courtesy of The Newberry Library (Wing MS folio ZW 141.59, vol. 2).

the French herald Mountioy (Montjoy) enters to Henry and his army and, speaking for the French king, says, "Now wee speake vpon our Q. and our voyce is imperiall" (Figure 10).[97] What does it mean for the French king to speak upon his Q? Of course we know what this means in the English context. The "Q." upon which Mountioy speaks is his "cue": "The concluding word or words of a speech in a play, serving as a signal or direction to another actor to enter, or begin his speech" (*OED*). Along with *kew, ku, quew, q, quue, que*, and *kue* (the *Henry V* quarto text's spelling[98]), capital *Q* is a circulating early modern spelling of *cue*.

But why? Is this Q from *queue* (French, for tail) as the *OED* suggests, noting at the same time the apparent lack of evidence? Might we follow seventeenth-century hard-word lists in seeing Q instead as an abbreviation? In the 1625 edition of his *Guide into the Tongues*, John Minsheu writes, "Qu, *a terme vsed among* Stage-plaiers, à Lat. *Qualis*, . . . at what manner of word the *Actors* are to beginne to speake one after another hath done his speech."[99] Or compare Charles Butler, in his *English Grammar* (1633): "**q** a note of entrance for Actors, (because it is the first letter of *quando*, when) shewing when to enter and speak."[100] Does the king,

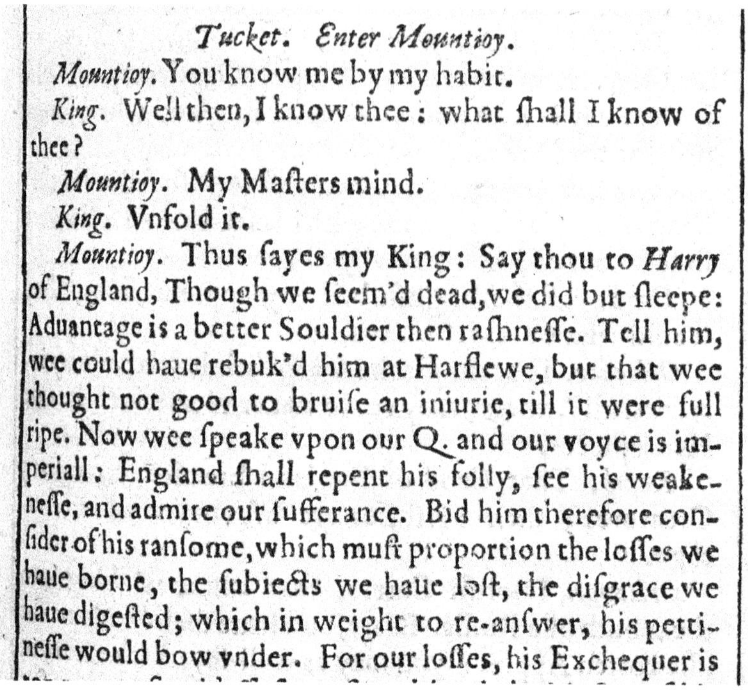

> *Tucket.* Enter *Mountioy.*
> *Mountioy.* You know me by my habit.
> *King.* Well then, I know thee : what ſhall I know of thee?
> *Mountioy.* My Maſters mind.
> *King.* Vnfold it.
> *Mountioy.* Thus ſayes my King: Say thou to *Harry* of England, Though we ſeem'd dead, we did but ſleepe: Aduantage is a better Souldier then raſhneſſe. Tell him, wee could haue rebuk'd him at Harflewe, but that wee thought not good to bruiſe an iniurie, till it were full ripe. Now wee ſpeake vpon our Q. and our voyce is imperiall: England ſhall repent his folly, ſee his weakeneſſe, and admire our ſufferance. Bid him therefore conſider of his ranſome, which muſt proportion the loſſes we haue borne, the ſubieɛts we haue loſt, the diſgrace we haue digeſted; which in weight to re-anſwer, his pettineſſe would bow vnder. For our loſſes, his Exchequer is

FIGURE 10. "Now wee speake vpon our Q," in William Shakespeare, *The Life of Henry the Fift*, in *Mr. VVilliam Shakespeares Comedies, Histories, & Tragedies*, p. 81 of the Histories. By permission of the Folger Shakespeare Library.

then, speak upon some*thing* (his *qualis*, on some manner, or quality of word, of his own)? Or does he speak at some *time* (his *quando*, following upon some prior Q)? Who or what can Q a king?

No matter whom you follow here (Minsheu or Butler), Q, in acting, is about positioning: *upon* a quality; *after* what's prior. Henry addresses Mountioy[101] upon both these grounds: "I know thy *qualitie*," he says, then (instructing him to break sequence): "Turne thee *back*, / And tell thy King, I doe not seeke him now."[102] Which way does the herald's Q lead: back or forth? Does it matter that, in the *franglais* of English heraldry, *queue* is also a term for tail?[103]

The French king's Q is somewhat past ("Though we seem'd dead, we did but sleepe"), and there is an abundance of anticipated or missed Qs in Shakespeare. "Mistris *Page*, remember you your *Qu*."[104] Beatrice says, "Speake Count, tis your Qu."[105] Bottom is above all the subject of the missed Q: "you speake all your part at once, cues and all," says Quince. "*Piramus* enter, your cue is past."[106] "When my cue comes, call me, and I will answer. My next is, most faire *Piramus*."[107] "*Deceiuing me*, / Is *Thisbies* cue; she is to enter."[108] (Bottom's dream, itself a kind of sodometry, is dreamt in the space of the missing Q.) The centrality of women's "cues" (and boys acting women's cues)—especially in proximity to the frequent *Count/cunt* homograph, as in one of these examples—may mean that additional kinds of bodies and body parts are at stake in these lines. The Schoolmaster in *The Two Noble Kinsmen* tells his morris dancers, who are lacking a woman to complete their dance, to "marke [their] Cue."[109] Minsheu defines "a Cu &c." as "*a womans &c. a Quaint, as* Chaucer *termes it.*"[110] (Does Mountioy's Q coincide with the "Count"/cunt/gown on which Princess Katherine's body-centered language lesson ends two scenes earlier?[111]) In print at least, Shakespeare's "cues" seem to move without friction among spellings—some "Qu," some "cue," and "Q." What did an early modern audience hear when it heard actors marking cues, missing cues, speaking upon their Qs? Is a Q a character, a word, an ideogram or -graph, a "hieroglyph," an emblem, a body, or a body part?[112]

My second example of the relation of letters to bodies is a pedagogical one, and it is also about bodily positioning, the relation of heads and tails and horns and Qs. "Mounsieur, are you not lettred?" says the Braggart to the Pedant in the 1623 folio text of Shakespeare's *Loues Labour's lost* (5.1); "Yes, yes," says the Braggart's Boy, "he teaches boyes the Horne-booke: What is A b speld backward with the horn on his head?"[113] The conjunction of bodies (horns and heads), books, and backward letters seems a mere joke, but this confluence, as we have come to expect, is more than simply occasional. To gloss it, to expand on what Patricia Parker has noted as the conjunction of "paederastic . . . 'tutoring'" and "the inversion of alphabetical sequence,"[114] we can turn to an obscure 1622 publication, *Hornbyes Hornbook*, a nineteen-page poem in celebration of the hornbook, the near homograph of its author, William Hornbye.[115] Hornbye's verse is not exactly memorable, but other aspects of this publication are, in bringing together for us the conjunction of letters, bodies, and the alterity of the early modern pedagogical scene—of teaching boys the hornbook and thus inculcating the alphabet.

Hornbye's book is in large part taken up with a celebration of the hornbook (the sheet of paper containing the cross-row and the Lord's Prayer, usually tacked on a piece of wood and covered with transparent horn; Figure 7). Anticipating an aspect of the eighteenth- and nineteenth-century philological debates, Hornbye argues that the hornbook is the key to all culture: "The *Horn-booke* of all books I doe commend, / For the worlds knowledge, it doth cõprehẽd" (sig. B1), the poem begins, and all "vertues first doe flow / From the *Originall,* the *Christ-crosse-row*" (sig. B2). The poem goes on like this for a dozen or so pages, describing the usefulness of the hornbook for all the lettered professions, criticizing schoolmasters who "basely doth abuse it, / Because they want discretion how to vse it" (sig. B7). If the antecedent of "it" here is not entirely clear, we can note (with Elizabeth Pittenger's, Alan Stewart's, and Wendy Wall's important contextualizations)[116] that the passage seems strongly to allude to the ubiquitous allegations of schoolmasters' violence in beating. As if signaled by this connection, Hornbye suddenly breaks off his encomium to the hornbook in order "[t]o tell a tale, the like was neuer told," and the poem begins its only subsection, with a solid line across the text and a centered title: "A Tale." As Hornbye notes, this is a tale of tails (like Q, a homograph), for it concerns his own traumatic beating at the hands of a schoolmaster:

> Now I begin to tell a tale of sorrow
> Euen of my taile: I went to *Peterborrow*
> To reape more learning, then before I had;
> But yet I prou'd more backward, and more bad,
> By reason that my Masters strict correction,
> Turn'd quite from him my loue, and my affection,
> That unto learning then I had no mind,
> To which before I greatly was inclind. (sig. B7ᵛ)

We can note in passing some ideas we have already engaged, here describing the positioning of the student: he is backward (which is the direction of the tail?); his affection is turned; he had an inclination toward learning. The poem then proceeds to narrate, in astonishingly anal detail, an episode that begins with the boys locking the schoolmaster out of the schoolhouse ("We shut him forth of dores incontinent"). All but six of the sixty boys defect (they "[w]ent to their Master, and themselues submitted; / Because (indeed) their bumbs began to itch, / They all went crouching for to saue their britch, / Thus they esteemed more their nether part, / Thē foule disgrace . . . ," and they thus "saue their tayles"). At the end of the revolt, Hornbye and his schoolmates are beaten: they are taken to the bake-house and treated (literally) as meat:

> When I came there, my heart began to faile,
> To see such cost prouided for my taile:
> For he prouision priuily had got,
> Which made my brich to sting, it was so hot;
> There was prepared Rods a large elne long,
> Of tuffe-red-willowes binded very strong;
> Pepper and salt he did together blend,
> Full halfe a pecke he on our tayles did spend:
> Twixt euery fower yerkes, we a handfull had
> On our bare-bumbs, which almost made vs mad. (sig. C1)

When Hornbye has finished narrating this "tayle of lamentation, / Euen of our tayles great grief" (sig. C1ᵛ), he returns immediately to his discussion of the hornbook, but, surprisingly, to a discussion of how the hornbook also contains the knowledge necessary for a good marriage ("a Coniunction Copplatiue most chaste" [sig. C2]), with strong advice for men against sex outside marriage:

> But they which other womens kindnes proue,
> There is a breach of Wedlocks honest loue.
> These doe euen *Hell* for a iust stripe earne,
> And so (indeed) the *Horn-booke* backwards learne. (sig. C2ᵛ)

Much more could be said about *Hornbyes Hornbook* and its peculiar conjunctions, but I want to notice here the correlation of discourses of alphabetic backwardness (for the married man as well as for the backward student boy) with sodomitical scenes (whether this is extramarital sex for men, or the hint of bare-bumb pederasty for the boy, linked in curious sequitur).

But we can also notice, in a way that anticipates our discussion of early modern boy-desire in Chapters 4–5, that the alternative to the harsh schoolmaster and his attention to the "hinder parts" of his boys while teaching them the hornbook is not, shall we say, a hands-off pedagogical approach. The boy William Hornbye's backwardness is the result of a lack of affection for his schoolmaster, and the solution to the problem of learning is not a total dissociation, but rather a conjunction illustrated in Hornbye's dedicating his book to three young gentlemen, possibly his students, in an affectionate language that may seem oddly positioned to modern eyes.[117] This Mr. W. H., for so he signs himself,[118] both writes of his "love" and affection for these three young men (dwelling upon their "chaste eyes" and "youthful yeares" [sig. A3ᵛ]) and positions them in affectionate relation to each other:

> Conioyning you together, as tis right,
> Because a Simpathie in loue you vse:
> As you are Fellowes both at Schoole and play,
> (I hope) I blameless ioyne you partners may. (sig. A5ᵛ)

These are the other copulative conjunctions of the schoolmaster. "[Y]ong children," writes Roger Ascham, in his Præface to *The Scholemaster* (1570), "[are] soner allured by loue, than driuen by beating, to atteyne good learning."[119] The options are alluring, or driving: *seduction* and an *introduction* into philology are etymologically related. A problem in early modern pedagogy, in teaching boys the hornbook, is how to position bodies while they are learning their letters. Is the proper position beating (which, as Stewart has suggested, we may have evi-

HORNBYES
HORNBOOK.

Iudge not too rashly, till through all you looke ;
If nothing then doth pleafe you, burne the Booke.

By *William Hornbye*, Gent.

London,
Printed by *Aug. Math.* for *Thomas Bayly*, and are to be
fold at his fhop in the middle Row neere Staple Inn. 1622.

FIGURE 11. The title page of *Hornbyes Hornbook*. © The British Library Board.
Shelfmark C.30.b.20.

dence to see as widespread institutional violence and possibly rape, one possible relation to the boy's queue or tail)?[120] Or is the proper position the positioning of affection, of allure—a less violent, if no less powerfully marked, kind of conjunction or joining? Do these texts spell out embracing with the tail, or the joining of friends? The question of the introduction to letters is *orthopaedic*, in the etymological sense of that later term.

One position is taken on the title page of *Hornbyes Hornbook* (Figure 11). The master's book is on the table, along with the reminder, even in this apparently affectionate scene, of the disciplinary rod. The schoolmaster holds an apple, thus offering an unexpectedly Edenic, potently rewritten scene of original knowledge acquisition. Teaching a boy the hornbook, which the boy holds in his hand, the schoolmaster positions himself behind and around the boy. Thus aligned in queue, we might say, the boy points out a letter, perhaps marks his Q. Before but following his master, he is introduced into a queer philology.

Hornbyes Hornbook is perhaps a particularly lowbrow version of early modern humanist philology. But with its conflations of tail/tale/alphabet and its title-page resignification of the Eden story—a resignification from hetero-reproductive to same-sexual (pedagogical reproduction), while also deleting women's (condemned, enabling) place in that story—it joins with Tory to show that philology, in its early modern emergences, is already queer. As Tory's text, its significance at the advent of humanism, and its transmission into print similarly show, it is not that queer and feminist work come in, after the fact, *après la lettre*, to superimpose such queerness, even as it may require queer and feminist analysis to identify it as such. At a formative early modern moment in the history of Western knowledge production and technologies of language, the emergence of the standardization of the letter, humanism is fully entangled with (one might say "en-tailed to") the body, its genders, its associations, its sodomitical and affective encounters—entailed as well to what is disavowed in the standardizations of the body/letter. Through the letter as body, the body as letter, queer philology exposes (and is) humanism's fraught relationship to embodiment. Or (and) to reverse this: modern Western embodiment reflects humanism's fraught account of the letter.[121]

FIGURE 12. A boy reading in Q, from Theodōros Gazēs, *Introdvctionis grammaticae.*
Photo courtesy of The Newberry Library.

This Book

Only "perhaps" does the boy in *Hornbyes Hornbook* (Figure 11) mark his Q; closer scrutiny now permitted by digital photography shows that, with only three letters to choose from on his abbreviated hornbook, the boy seems to mark his B. But allow the possibility of two different letters as points of departure to signify the two differing, overlapping, but simultaneous modes of organization in the book that follows.

On the one hand, the book is divided into five sections. This Introduction and Chapter 1 outline the more fluid linguistic situation that obtains in early modern English prior to orthographic standardization, setting the central linguistic context for the analyses that follow; at the same time, these chapters emphasize the implication of philological modes of analysis in discourses of sex/gender, both in the early modern period and in book-historical, philological, and editorial approaches today. Given textual editing's long association with philology and the fact that it is now often credited (or maligned) as a last bastion of philological work, the implications of modern editorial practices and choices recur as a focus throughout the book (see Chapters 1, 4, and 5); the last section of the book ("Editing Philologies") advocates explicitly for a more active engagement of editorial practice with philologies of sex, sexuality, and gender. In between, three sections treat three Lexicons, concentrating on discourses that have become integral to historical analyses of especially male same-sex relations in early modern England, a structure that also serves to emphasize this book's affiliation with and revision of Williams's *Key Words* and William Empson's *Structure of Complex Words*, as well as its resonance with the "critical semantics" approach recently articulated in Roland Greene's *Five Words*. Lexicon 1 elaborates languages of male same-sex friendship. Lexicon 2 focuses on early modern pederasty, or what I call "boy-desire," in order to emphasize that this discourse concerns both early modern culture's attraction *toward* young men as well as its conception of *their own* desires, if any, toward others. Lexicon 3 attempts to take the critical discussion of early modern "sodomy" and its linguistic surround in new directions, by considering both the question of the "foundational" body part most closely associated with this "confused category" in the period, and the proliferation of sodomitical discourse as seemingly far afield as the definition of Renaissance dramatic genres. Sodomy also animates the primary editorial examples in the final section, where the analysis takes up its connections to early modern conceptions of race and female riot, respectively, in a set of textual cruxes and glosses in *Othello* (as contrasted with the editorial treatment of friendship in *The Merchant of Venice*) and in the text and canonicity of the disputed Shakespearean play *Sir Thomas More*. This set of five sections is the book's more conventional mode of organization.

On the other hand, one might choose to start with Q (as perhaps you already have) and move through or about this book as one might a dictionary or glossary, encountering chapters organized around a set of key, or at least *remarkable*, words for thinking about sex/gender in early modern England. This glossary, I probably hardly need write at this point, does not proceed from A to Z: beginning with Q, it proceeds (in a way that cannot only be described as "proceeding") through *spell, orthography, skaiography, his, hir, sweet, persuasion, conversation, intercourse, boy, amorous, fundament, foundation, mongrel, tup, top, bumbast*. (See the alternative table of contents.) As I have suggested, these "glossary entries"—discursive essays on a glossarial theme—are by no means an attempt to provide a comprehensive account of early modern "sexual" language (nor could they be). As chapters that begin to outline how one might begin to do that, this book has as one of its objectives to encourage, via the exploration of method, the expansion of such glossaries and the knowledges they may generate by other scholars—including, as especially the final section emphasizes, by editors who prepare the early modern texts that others rely on and by those of us (all of us, I argue) who must in effect become editors in order to read early modern sex and gender.

It may be argued that the words I have chosen to concentrate on are not uniformly important or central to early modern culture, but, as the preceding pages have made clear, this book aspires both to a topical contribution to the history of sexuality in early modern Europe—I hope to have convinced you that something so apparently ancillary and unremarkable as the letter Q can and did make a difference—*and* to a methodological intervention. In that methodological regard, the book seeks to demonstrate—through a number of kinds of examples, sites, discourses, genres, words, and writers—the utility of patiently unraveling the connections of even the most initially unlikely words for understanding this culture, which is to say, for understanding how to continue to read this culture. In the final section of Chapter 4, which focuses on the visual representation of boys in historiated alphabetic initials—the body of a boy, like the body of a Q, in a letter—these examples extend to (or continue to trouble our line between) the textual and visual.

As the appearance of "Shakespeare" in my subtitle will suggest, texts associated with the most canonical of English writers are frequently the site of investigation in this book not because I seek to preserve the exceptional status often assigned to Shakespeare, but because his texts are widely referenced sites of cultural knowledge and consequence for many readers and also are a preeminent site for *methodological* articulation, expansion, and revolution for early modern

philological, textual, bibliographical, editorial, and sex/gender work—from the
now-aging New Bibliography through the newer New Textualism, for feminism,
sexuality studies, and the new (anti)historicism in queer studies, and beyond.
Along the way, a chapter that begins with *Twelfth Night* illustrates how the career
of "the" cross-dressed boy character/heroine/actor changes in the seventeenth
century if, turning away from Shakespeare, we instead examine the long career of
the boy-woman at the center of Beaumont and Fletcher's popular *Philaster* and
read "the boy" onstage in relation to "boy alphabets" in early modern printed
books. Christopher Marlowe's texts, too, are particularly prominent here, not for
some peculiar status I would afford Marlowe (somehow alongside Shakespeare,
but above texts written by any other number of other writers one might name),
but rather for the *methodological* traction they provide both for analyzing early
modern discourses of sex/gender and for thinking about early modern sexual
"identity." How can a queer reading practice, a queer philology, add to our comprehension of a writer once presumed to be "gay" (in a more or less modern
sense), but recently the subject of a critical "straightening out" project (Chapters
3 and 5)? To what extent do Marlowe's contemporaries' revisions and continuations of his texts exemplify queer affiliation or even (proto-) "gay shame"—in a
way that extends the ambit of queerness *beyond* writerly identities, as the discussion of the unlikely figure of George Chapman in Chapter 5 suggests? Even as I
believe the approach I take here is attentive to particular local exigencies, I hope
that readers may see, through a queer-philological approach, a mode other than
author(ship)-based approaches for considering texts generated by these writers
and, by extension (extensions that may, of course, require their own local adjustments, their own queer philologies), those of others.

Because the book is methodological in its aspirations, the chapters, in ways
that exceed my reference to them above, engage with some of the flashpoints and
nodes of controversy in early modern literary and cultural criticism, including
the following: authorship and attribution (Chapter 3); the ideological investments
and effects (intentional or not) of New Bibliography (as in Chapter 1's discussion
of compositor analysis and Cold War homophobia), which is the basis for the
editing of most modern editions of Shakespeare and the other early modern texts
we read, study, and teach; the stakes (for gender and sexuality) of the editorial
distinction between "good" and "bad" quartos (the discussion of *Philaster* in Chapter 4); the "sexuality" of particular characters and writers (Hamlet in Chapter 2;
Marlowe in Chapters 3 and 5); the meaning(s) of early modern pederasty in relation to classical and modern "homosexuality" (Chapters 4 and 5); the definition
of literary genres (if not exactly a flashpoint, certainly an underquestioned foundation on which many of us teach, write, and organize curricula and hiring within
Renaissance studies and literature departments; Chapter 7); the relation of edito-

rial practice to interpretation and the (artificial?) division between textual emendation and glossing (Chapters 8–9); and the intersectionality of sexuality, gender,
and race (Chapters 8–9 again). Although the book's analysis of sexuality largely
focuses on men, there are a number of places throughout, and especially in particular readings in Chapters 1, 4, 6, 8, and 9, that take up the sometimes contested
relation of feminist and queer readings (which are sometimes also readings of
women) in early modern texts and criticism. This list represents, you will have
noticed, a third hand with which to open or read this book.

At the same time, I hope that *Queer Philologies* will present a methodological
intervention of relevance to scholars and theorists of sexuality and gender interested in other periods and locales of history, language, literature, and culture,
including of our own moment, and in queer historiography generally. The book's
emphases on the alterities of early modern "sexuality," sexual practices, body
parts, "identities," eroticism, affect, and so on, should help further to defamiliar-
ize what we now think we know about sexuality and sexualities in the present,
"render[ing] less destructively presumable 'homosexuality as we know it today,' "
as Eve Kosofsky Sedgwick formatively argued—heterosexuality, too, we can
add.[122] (Critics and theorists especially interested in the present may find Chapter
3's trajectory from *conversation* to *intercourse* and on toward *fuck buddy* one generative place to begin.) At the same time, this book's emphasis on the *textures* of
alterity will help demonstrate, I believe, that what has been called the "tyranny of
historicism" in early modern sexuality studies misapprehends the nature of at
least some sexual history projects, like this one, that travel under historicism's
large and varied label.[123] Readers of the alterity/continuity debate in queer historiography will already have recognized that this is not an "unhistoricist" book, to
use the revisionary term introduced by Goldberg and Madhavi Menon and elaborated by Menon; nor does it see all historicisms—whether old, "New," newer, or
other—as necessarily undermined by a "compulsory heterotemporality" in which
historical difference becomes elided with or collapsed into other irredeemably
"hetero" normativities.[124] Throughout this book, my questions will often be: why
and how is historical alterity also potentially queer—though not necessarily always so? What queerness can be mobilized and deployed by and through—not
despite—recognizing and analyzing alterity?[125] As Goldberg's formative anthology of essays demonstrated (but did not exhaust) two decades ago, there is more
than one way to queer a Renaissance.[126]

Emphasizing the *textures* of alterity means, on the one hand, that this book
embraces the simultaneous, overlapping, and sometimes mutually excluding
models that Sedgwick theorized and that historian-theorists of premodern sexuality who disagree on other aspects of queer historiography have nevertheless
embraced: Smith's multiple "myths"; Halperin's multiple "discourses, practices,

categories, patterns, or models"; Traub's "cycles of salience" as well as her co-extant and eventually mutually inflecting tribades and femmes as they intersect as well with "domestic heterosexuality" and with something both like and unlike modern lesbianism; Goldberg and Menon's "multiplicity of the past" leading "to the possibilities of different futures"; DiGangi's plural "sexual types."[127] Even in Foucault's "utterly confused category" of sodomy, the very etymology of the adjective (in both the original French and the English translation's Anglo-Norman cognate) may transport into an apparently singular "category" a resonant plurality of things con/founded, poured or mixed together: "cette catégorie si *confuse*."[128] On another hand (a hand confounded with the first), *textures* may indicate both the uneven surface(s) we are analyzing—a past that cannot itself be understood to be fully "self-identical" or singular, as Goldberg and Menon emphasize[129]—and the tactile interpretive interaction of the visiting philologist. My queer philologies will emphasize that this past is (these pasts *are*) discursively woven *text*ures discernibly different in weave from the similarly non-self-identical textures of the present—to which this plural past is connected by some *but not all* of its threads, only some of which are currently perceptible or (to continue the language of seeing or making by hand) *man*ifest. (There will be numerous examples of troubled continuity throughout this book, but *Q, conversation,* and *friend*—each an early modern term that is still, now, in some version of overlapping same-different use—may serve to illustrate.) This is a problem of historical-textual method that Goldberg suggestively addressed earlier: "The logic of textuality that is the logic of historicity means also that the *virtually unbounded* possibilities of difference are *relatively bound* within any textual/historic instance."[130]

Researched, written, and revised over the course of much of the continuism versus alteritism debates in queer historiography (debates that, as Traub's recent, thoroughgoing critique and its varied responses suggest, seem likely to continue), *Queer Philologies* does not, then, see a need to read "unhistorically," as Menon advocates, or for a new "unhistoricism." As my resistance to the *OED*'s only apparently precise datings of initial and changing meanings will suggest throughout this book, for example, my historicism is not interchangeable with a historicism defined by dates of literary composition, publication, or the ostensible first "invention" of particular semantic meanings—though I will sometimes refer to them.[131] Rather, this book seeks to practice a more labile, deconstructive history of sexuality and sexual meaning—a history that is (unabashedly but, I hope, critically) a new and renewing "historicism" in its attempt to focus on the methods of its own historiography (a *queer* philology), and a historicism attentive to alterity *and* continuity, while also alert to the multiple and sometimes contradictory possibilities circulating in the synchronic moment, as traced through that moment's language. Etymology, as I have just hinted via Foucault's *confuse* and as I argue in the analysis of the words *sweet* and *persuasion* in Chapter 2, can be precisely such a tool, analyzing as it does the persistence(s) of the past into the multiplicity of possible meanings in the present or in the less remote past. Etymologies—shorn, I advocate in Chapter 2, of any guarantee of definitive, determinative, singular origin—can function, in this sense, as Elizabeth Freeman's "[q]ueer temporalities": "points of resistance to this temporal order [of "history 'proper'"] that, in turn, propose other possibilities for living in relation to indeterminately past, present, and future others: that is, of living *historically*."[132] To redeploy another of Freeman's resonant terms, etymologies can point out to us the "temporal drag" that language is: the present written and spoken in—bound and enabled by—the textured, sometimes out/landish garb or costume of its pasts.[133]

Such an attempt at a textured, plural, cultural history through language will call forth both deliberation and playfulness, qualities I have attempted to enact in the sometimes atypical formats of this Introduction and the following chapters, which seek to resist the expectation and plod of standard academic forms. I hope at least some of those assays provide pleasure and introduce/seduce readers into philology as a lovable method that may move beyond the adjective "narrow" routinely assigned it. ("[A] corresponding 'wide philologist,'" Frank remarks, "does not exist."[134]) My attempts in this regard are not separable from the concerns of history and alterity discussed above; as Roland Barthes (*licence*d philologist) writes, remarking on the productivity of the "historical meaning of a word" even as he explicitly points beyond "the narrow acceptation of philology," "sometimes, on the contrary, *history serves to revivify a word* and then we must rediscover this historical meaning as an enjoyable, not authoritarian element, witness of a truth, but free, plural, consumed in the very pleasure of a *fiction* (that of our reading)."[135] In part it is through the revivifying pleasures of reading and writing that *Queer Philologies* will attempt to re-mark historicism's alleged "tyranny" with plurality. At least one philologist trained at the height of Germanic philology's traditional methods also emphasized a method that would move deliberately, enticingly, open-endedly. Reflecting on his chosen specialty, Nietzsche's words, at the end of the 1886 preface to *Daybreak*, resonate uncannily with our own hurried time, with its emphasis on tweetable arguments and definitive, scientized proofs and outcomes. "It is not for nothing that I have been a philologist," he writes:

> [P]hilology is that venerable art which demands of its votaries one thing above all: to go aside, to take time, to become still, to become slow. . . . But for precisely this reason it is more necessary than ever today, by precisely this means does it entice and enchant us the most, in the midst of an age of "work," that is to say, of hurry, of indecent and perspiring haste, which

wants to "get everything done" at once, including every old or new book:—this art does not so easily get anything done, it teaches to read well, that is to say, to read slowly, deeply, looking cautiously before and aft, with reservations, with doors left open, with delicate eyes and fingers.[136]

If there is a queerness, a slight gender nonnormativity, to be heard in a male scholar's embrace of a method that requires "delicate" fingers and eyes (*zarten Fingern und Augen*), temporal *drag* in both senses, I also hope that this book beginning with Q will allow scholars, students, and readers of the past and present alike to go aside, to experience the reservations and pluralities that are a part of its evidence, the doors left open, the entirely erroneous guess that leads to knowledge before and aft, the tail or queue that introduces us beyond the square.[137]

FIGURE 13. Q in an Italian calligraphic alphabet book.
Photo courtesy of The Newberry Library, Wing MS ZW 5351.99.

Spelling Shakespeare: Early Modern "Orthography" and the Secret Lives of Shakespeare's Compositors

[I]t is even more important that we should discover, if we can, through the identification of compositors on the basis of their spellings, *what kind of minds* may have affected the readings of substantive editions of Shakespeare's plays, since *this question* is fundamental to the editing of any text.

—Alice Walker, *Textual Problems of the First Folio*[1]

A password is more than just a flaky kind of fingerprint. We still want passwords to be romantic, not just utilitarian. We reveal ourselves in our passwords. . . . Choosing **xerxes** or **donjuan** is a grown-up equivalent of wearing Power Ranger underwear.

—James Gleick, in the *New York Times Magazine*[2]

Putting aside my title for a moment, I will begin instead with a more modern secret life. When a twentieth-century American student—let's call him Student A—was in about the sixth grade, a teacher corrected his repeated spelling of the word *occasion* in a composition. Student A was in the habit of spelling this word *o-c-c-a-i-s-i-o-n*, because he knew that a correct spelling of this word would need to register (as his spelling did) a long "a" vowel in the second syllable. O-c-c-a-i-s-i-o-n. Student A no longer recalls the composition or most of the sixth grade, but the moment of correction—or, more accurately, the memory of his confident, repeated, peculiar spelling—sometimes recurs, when he writes or types the word. How all *occasions* do inform against him, now.

As I hope to show in more detail, such a narrative would be largely impossible to have lived or told in the early modern period—say, around 1600—because, as is widely known, there was no one standard of correct English spelling with which to discipline the young student, although, as we will see, within certain contexts there was beginning to be the idea of a standard. Second, the anecdote might be taken to suggest that there are, in a way to which I will return, naturally occurring spelling preferences—as suggested by Student A's apparent individualized preference, when questioned in his untutored state, for the spelling *occaision* over *occasion*, and the fact that he continues sometimes to hesitate over the "i" of the keyboard when typing this word, even after years of advanced literary training. But the anecdote also obviously suggests that Student A wasn't untutored and was attempting to conform to a notion of standardized, phonetic spelling.

The problematic of compositor study—the study of the workmen who set by hand the type of early printed books, and the intense analysis of their spellings as a central feature of mid-twentieth-century Shakespearean editorial practice—resides in this anecdote in another way. For if we were to apply Student A's story to the seventeenth century without attention to some important epistemic differences, we would reproduce, I think, the way in which twentieth-century textual bibliography has applied, without enough examination, its own assumptions about spelling, regularity, and, as we'll see, individuality, to conditions of language and subjectivity before the modern era. The words of Charlton Hinman are exemplary in this regard; writing in a 1940–41 essay that precedes and provides a rationale for his immense labor collating and dividing up the compositorial shares of the first folio collection of Shakespeare's plays, Hinman says that "*it is to be expected* that any compositor of the sixteenth or seventeenth century would develop certain individual spelling habits, and that these habits may serve to distinguish his work from that of other compositors."[3] Hinman here tells us what he expects, or rather what "is to be expected" of early modern spellers, but there is no evidence supplied for these twentieth-century expectations.

In the course of this chapter, I hope to demonstrate, first, that compositor study—this highly specialized subfield of editorial philology—has instrumentally affected the early modern texts we read and study, especially those texts associated with Shakespeare; second, that the paradigm within which compositor spelling analysis operates is demonstrably related to other deforming narratives about the production of early modern texts and about the early modern "linguistic field"[4] more generally; third, that these narratives came to life within a particular mid-twentieth-century epistemology that has had, in other spheres, demonstrably toxic effects on actual persons living and dead; and, finally, that there are other ways in which we might think, historically and theoretically, about the people who spelled and pressed the texts we read and study—ways that might be more useful for the study of the history of the book, the history of the language, the history of the subject, and the history of sexuality.

Spell-check

If there were no spelling bees in early modern England, this is not because that culture had not perfected other modes through which the spectacle of a particular subject's submission to (or divergence from) a larger cultural value could be exhibited, but because spelling was only in the process of becoming such a value and, relatedly, only in the process of becoming an action, a transitive activity—and not yet predicated on the absorption and reproduction of particular "correct" spellings. In fact, one of the earliest meanings of the word *spell* (as a verb) in English was "[t]o read (a book, etc.) letter by letter; to peruse, or make out, slowly or with difficulty" (ca. 1300–1848).[5] To spell in English, from about 1300 well into the nineteenth century, meant to *read* something, to consume a supplied text—to puzzle out a particular exemplar. A set of what the *Oxford English Dictionary* (*OED*) calls "figurative" meanings continued to spin out from this spelling-as-reading meaning in the sixteenth and seventeenth centuries: "To discover or find out, to guess or suspect, by close study or observation" (ca. 1587–1879); "To make out, understand, decipher, or comprehend, by study" (ca. 1635–1886); "To consider, contemplate, scan intently" (ca. 1633–1859).[6] "[T]he vast discourses of wisest and most learned men," writes Kenelm Digby in 1644, "are beyond the spellinges of infantes: and yet those discourses spring from the same roote, as the others spellinges doe, and are but a raysing of them to a greater height."[7] Digby's context (an extended metaphor within a scientific discussion) suggests that *spellinge* for him signifies reading or comprehension—the belabored understanding of children. The acting company's famous preface to the first folio collection of Shakespeare's plays can be re-read, re-spelled, in this context: "*To the great Variety of Readers*," it begins, "From the most able, to him that can but spell."[8] What knowledge of spelling is required to spell Shakespeare?

The date of the folio's formulation of spelling/reading is 1623, and, as we have seen, Digby's 1644 text also invokes spelling-as-reading (he also uses the phrase "spellingly reade"), suggesting that this meaning continues to circulate even after the tentative beginnings of what we think of as spelling. According to the *OED* at least, the recognizably modern meaning of spelling—"To name or set down in order the letters of (a word or syllable)"—appears first around 1595 (Shakespeare is cited among its earliest users, in 1598), though I am not at all sure that the early examples of this usage I know of are (upon rereading) about the production of "correct spellings" in our terms. Spelling in the fully modern sense does not clearly emerge in the *OED*'s examples until much later in the next century, around 1693.[9]

If spelling in early modern English is about reading (that is, the ability to make sense of particular graphic shapes and forms on the page),[10] we should also note that these shapes might be different, within a certain range, while at the same time not necessarily registering as "different words" in our understanding. As Margreta de Grazia has argued in an important essay on English prior to lexical standardization, in a culture in which there was constant, multiple graphic and phonic overlap among (what we would refer to as) discrete words, there was more polysemic possibility/activity built into this system—if early modern English can even be called a "system."[11] Bourdieu's "linguistic field" is a better term, taken alongside Juliet Fleming's reminder that English was "not unruled, but ruled differently—perhaps in accordance with a rhetorical rather than grammatical, lexical, and orthographic order."[12]

The variability of pronunciations, the intersection of dialects, the ongoing shift from an inflected to a largely uninflected grammatical practice (and the corresponding migration of words among "parts of speech"),[13] the nonexistence of dictionaries regulating the usage/spelling of everyday words, etymological thinking that linked rather than dissevered similar words[14]—all of these factors made for a more fluid and unfixed linguistic field. What we call "single words" were spelled in multiple ways, often by the same person. In *Sir Thomas More*, the play manuscript often adduced to illustrate Shakespeare's spelling (and the subject of Chapter 9), Hand D (the handwriting sometimes associated with Shakespeare) spells nearly a fifth of the words he writes more than once in more than one way.[15] An extraordinary, compact example is a line spoken by the crowd ("all") addressing Sheriff Thomas More and spelled out by Hand D as "Shreiue moor moor more Shreue moore."[16] The line's six word forms contain what we would consider two words: one spelled two ways and another spelled three ways. The word *sheriff*, as Philip Gaskell writes of one Hand D passage, "appears five times in . . . five lines in five different spellings."[17]

Furthermore, as this example (from Shakespeare's "own" spelling, if such it is)[18] can help to suggest, the *OED*'s focus on discrete words, sorted into particular (so-called) parts of speech, attached to particular (also discrete) meanings associated with a variety of (past) forms obscures, and imposes a modern order on, the fluidity of early modern practice(s), in which *ay* sounded like both *I* and *eye/eie* and could be spelled *I*, *aye*, and *ay*. Or, to take some other examples we will examine in more detail elsewhere in this book, the pairs of words *conversation* and *conversion*, *discreet* and *discrete*, even *foundation* and *fundament*, were interchangeable. In this context, *spelling* was conceptualized as the process of *processing* these forms, not *producing* them. Production is called not *spelling*, but *writing*.

Those familiar with the decades around 1600 might say that I am simplifying the issue: that there were in fact those in English culture who saw this linguistic situation as an issue, a problem, and attempted to fix it. In the 1560s to 1580s, with Thomas Smith's *De recta & emendata Lingvæ Anglicæ Scriptione*, John Hart's *An orthographie*, and William Bullokar's *Bullokars Booke at large, for the Amendment of Orthographie*, there were recurrent attempts to standardize English spelling—that is, to focus on the production of uniform spellings.[19] Such attempts continued in the early seventeenth century. As Jonathan Goldberg has importantly observed in his discussion of some of the texts of this movement, sixteenth-century spelling reform is not devoid of ideological aspirations and effects,[20] and the etymological resonance of Smith's, Hart's, and Bullokar's titles can begin to emphasize for us the cultural values with which uniform spelling is associated for its reformers. Spelling reform is concerned with *orthography* (literally, right-writing); *orthos* is straight, upright, standing, the opposite of crooked.[21] Alexander Hume's unpublished treatise *Of the Orthographie and Congruitie of the Britan Tongue* (c. 1617)—the Q-defending text we encountered in the Introduction—makes the connection explicitly: "the printeres and wryteres of this age, caring for noe more arte then may win the pennie, wil not paen them selfes to knau whither it be orthographie or skaiographie that doeth the turne."[22] Hume both dedicates his text to the king and coins a perverse opposite to rectitude in delineating his system of right-writing; *skaiographie*, as noted above, comes from *skaios*, "left, left-handed, awkward, crooked,"[23] related to the Latin *scaeuitas*, "[i]nstinctive choosing of the wrong; perversity."[24]

Whether orthography or skaiography doeth the turn, orthography seems always, nevertheless, to have the potential to turn against, to turn *back* on its advocates, who frequently don't fare well in the popular culture that registers their efforts. In *Loues Labour's lost* (1594–97?), to take a familiar example, the spelling reformer (in this case, the advocate of more Latinate spellings in English) is often referred to in the folio's stage directions and speech headings as simply "the Pedant," rather than as Holofernes, and is associated with both sodomy and cuckoldry.[25] Bullokar's name is misunderstood as "ballocks" (testicles) and "bullocks" (castrated bulls) in the Middleton, Rowley et al. play *The Old Law* (1618–19?).[26] Or consider Benedick's description of the lovesick Claudio in *Much Adoe about Nothing*: "he was wont to speake plaine, & to the purpose (like an honest man & a souldier) and now is he turn'd ortho-graphy, his words are a very fantasticall banquet, iust so many strange dishes: may I be so conuerted, & see with these eyes?"[27] Right-writing is made to take a turn here; the right (ortho-graphy) becomes strange and fantastical, the sign of a perverse conversion to what we would call "heterosexuality."[28] As Elizabeth Pittenger and Juliet Fleming have shown, language learning during this period often registers complicated structures and anxieties of sex/gender.[29]

Spelling reform is thus contested.[30] Furthermore, it cannot be understood as a smooth history of gradual adherence to a modern, rational standard, for, again as Goldberg notes, the reformers aren't successful, and when English spelling eventually becomes (more) standardized, it does not become so along the lines advocated by those who have "turn'd orthography."[31]

For the purposes of this chapter, this is the crucial point about spelling as articulated in the late sixteenth and early seventeenth centuries: the spelling reform of these earliest English philologists—Hart, Bullokar, Hume, and others—does not have as a shared value the erasure of variable spellings of English words; the existence of multiple possibilities for the spelling of any given word does not register as a concern in these reform texts (or *antireform* texts).[32] Mulcaster, for example, writes against the reform of what he calls "our customarie writing"[33] without registering the spelling variances that are for us an apparent feature of period writing. Instead, spelling reform (as Goldberg's analysis demonstrates and deconstructs in detail) seeks to produce an ostensibly mimetic relation between the sounds of words and their orthography—a system in which each letter or combination of letters will be matched with a single spoken sound.[34] The development of this aspiringly mimetic system might in fact seem to eventuate in the reduction of variability, but the difference in emphasis is a central one for understanding the early modern English linguistic field. What is at stake in the early modern debate is not the reduction of variability but the cohesion of sound and graphic depiction; "in true Ortography," Bullokar writes (with a redoubled excess), "*both* the eye, the voyce, and the eare consent most perfectly, without any let, doubt, or maze."[35] The consent is among bodily members, not among spellings.

Further, the relation of spelling to allegedly "individual" members of the body politic (and here I am building on Peter Stallybrass's important critique of the notion of the *individual*, as opposed to the *subject*, in this period[36]) is not what we have come to expect. When Thomas Whythorne goes to write what is now often said to be one of the first "autobiographies" in English, he writes his extraordinarily self-scrutinizing narrative not in conventional (i.e., *variable*) spelling or in an idiosyncratic system of his own devising but in a version of Hart's orthography; the individual life spells itself out by aspiring not to individuation but to standardization, uniformity. Yet even here, as the modern editor of Whythorne's manuscript notes, the autobiographical subject practices no fully auto-orthographical consistency: "'use' may be spelt 'yowze' or 'iuwz' or in ten variant ways" (lvii), and "on the same page he will write 'laf' and 'lawf' for 'laugh'" (lxvi).[37]

Thus far I have said little about a subject that will occupy the ensuing sections of this chapter—the relation of spelling to an emergent print culture, the links between philology and bibliography—and I want to note the fact that a number of orthographers (and anti-orthographers) register the possible importance of print in their projects. Bullokar, for example, laments that "for lacke of true ortography our writing in Inglish hath altered in euery age, yea since printing began," but he argues that "printing be the best helpe to stay the same, in one order."[38] As we have seen, Hume's citation of English "skaiographie" indicts both writers *and* printers. But, contra Bullokar and the more recent print historian Elizabeth Eisenstein, we should note that the spelling of early modern English compositors may actually have *resisted* the progressive stabilization of spelling that print is said to have enacted.[39] As D. G. Scragg notes, "[J]ustification [during this period] was achieved by varying the spelling of words in a line, and words which had a variable length extending from *pity* to *pyttye* became very valuable to printers."[40] Examining the 1611 King James Bible, A. W. Pollard writes, "In my innocence I was prepared to find [the spelling] both scholarly and consistent." But he finds that the "only consistency is that the form is always preferred *which suits the spacing*."[41] From our perspective this undernoticed point can hardly be *over*emphasized, because it is utterly foreign to modern practice: where our newspapers and word-processing programs use spacing to justify a line of printed or displayed text, early modern printers used *both* spaces *and* variable spellings to fill out their lines.[42] Whatever its eventual effect in solidifying a common spelling practice, early print may have seized on the variance of spellings that *already* existed in early modern English and may have encouraged, promoted, expanded, circulated, and/or inculcated that variance by continuing to reproduce variant spellings that might then have been seen as even more widely available—even more available to compositors themselves, who might reproduce them in contexts that required no justification.

The relatively unstructured linguistic field I have been describing had begun to change significantly by 1643, when Richard Hodges published his book *A Special Help To Orthographie: Or, The True-writing of English. Consisting of such Words as are alike in sound, and unlike both in their signification and Writing: As also, of such Words which are so neer alike in sound, that they are sometimes taken one for another*.[43] This is the advent of spelling *standardization*, and something different from spelling *reform*, for Hodges assumes that there are now already-correct spellings (not mimetically related to sound) that need to be inculcated. For Hodges, unlike for many of his fellow literate English subjects of the preceding century, *assent* cannot be *ascent* or "*A sent* or savour."[44] At the same time, this book registers the possibility that, as late as 1643, there are (else what market for this book?) those who could still (as we would say) "confuse" these (as we would say) "discrete" "words."

Spelling and the Individual Talent

Barnardo. Who's there?
Fran. Nay answer me: Stand & vnfold
your selfe.

—*Hamlet*[45]

The fundamental assumption of twentieth-century analysis of early modern English compositors is that, even if the language as a whole did not operate according to principles of standardized spelling, each individual writer, and therefore typesetter, operated according to a personal, largely self-standardized, glossary. The central study in this field, Charlton Hinman's division of compositor labor in the Shakespeare folio, is based largely on his analysis of variations in the words *do*, *go*, and *here*; "quire tt [*Othello*]," he says, "was set by a man with a marked preference for *do*, *go* and *heere*. And such a man was Compositor B, as he is now generally called."[46] In contrast, some pages in gathering o, which includes parts of *2* and *3 Henry VI*, "were quite as certainly set by someone else—by a man who, unlike B, strongly preferred *doe*, *goe*, and *here* to *do*, *go* and *heere*. . . . This man was Compositor A; and . . . he was almost as constant to his habit of spelling these words in the manner indicated as B was to his habit of spelling the same words in a different way" (1:184–85). Hinman eventually analyzes some other spellings that are not as seemingly common and arbitrary as these, but I want to notice here, first, the way in which letters on the page are made to produce a compositor with strong preferences and constant habits, and, second, the way in which that subject is made to seem immediately to have an identity in real life, a name—even though that name is almost comically an obvious bibliographical construction: "Such a man was Compositor B. . . . This man was Compositor A."[47]

I am not sure that it is possible to prove to current satisfaction that compositors *did not* have self-standardized spelling glossaries that they habitually employed and that can therefore be used to identify them. Perhaps the only way to demonstrate this empirically would be to compare known printers' records connecting particular compositors to particular pages, with the actual printed pages, and then to show how the spellings on those pages do, or do not, disclose compositors with individualized, consistent practices. We do not have such records for the Shakespeare folio or for most early seventeenth-century printed books, but in his brilliant critique of the use of spacing to distinguish compositors, D. F.

McKenzie has shown that, in cases where we *do* have such records, the compositors fail to line up in the way the individuating methodology of compositor study predicts.[48]

The first section of this chapter has, I hope, begun to suggest the problematic of the assumption of individualized spelling practices, at a cultural level—the way in which it would require an individual speller resistant to the unstandardized linguistic context surrounding him. Hinman, in the 1940–41 essay I quoted earlier, writes that "[t]he standardization of spelling was of course in progress, particularly in printing houses; yet there was still, even among printers, such a variety of acceptable alternative spellings that *it would be remarkable indeed* if individual compositors did not form individual habits" ("Principles," 79). As before, Hinman notes what he would find remarkable, if lacking, but without substantiation. Indeed, Hinman's own logic is itself remarkable: there was no larger cultural system of standardization, *so that* there must have been, compensatorily, standardization at the level of the individual. The sheer lack of a standardized linguistic field seems to *necessitate* standardization at the more local level; no individual, Hinman suggests, could countenance the variety of available spellings.

If the available evidence allows me only to cast doubt on the notion of individuated orthography, I think I *can* show that the study of compositors as individuals—as we have already begun to see—partakes of peculiarly modern notions of agency and subjectivity, and that our study of this method has something to say about our approach to Shakespeare. Hinman writes that "[t]he habits of Compositor D with respect to other words than 'do,' 'go,' and 'here'—both his preferences and his *tolerances*—are yet to be thoroughly studied. So too are such non-spelling peculiarities as may be discovered in his work" (*PPFFS*, 1:199). As Hinman saw it, the work of compositor analysis is to convert characters into characters—spellings into an individual constituted as a range of (ortho)graphic behaviors, habits, preferences, and even tolerances (by which term Hinman means that a compositor "tolerates" some spellings he prefers not to use himself, if they are present in the copy from which he is setting type). But the rhetoric, as we have seen it thus far, is not particularly careful to distinguish apparently unconscious habits from tolerances and strong preferences; if the compositor is a creature of his habits, he is also a "man" who prefers and tolerates. Hinman's comment at the end of this passage—on Compositor D's "non-spelling peculiarities"—figures the trajectory of compositor analysis itself, for the larger point, as Walker puts it, is to know "*what kind of minds* may have affected" Shakespeare's text—to discover the peculiarities that go beyond the bounds of mere spelling.

Indeed, though most of the compositor analyses published since the 1940s have been taken up with identifying compositors in various texts, the larger editorial *use* of this analysis is said to reside in a next step that ties it deeply to the text-establishing and -authenticating function of editorial philology. Compositor analysis seeks to know what kinds of errors particular compositors were ostensibly prone to making and thereby to determine when a supposed error in Shakespeare's text is likely made by a compositor (and therefore to be corrected through emendation)—and when an error was introduced by Shakespeare.[49] The result has been a kind of composite compositor sketch, the delineation of characters that proliferate out from the surface of these texts: Compositor A, we learn, "was by habit conservative."[50] Or "[t]he important thing to remember, in connection with A's habits, is that he was systematic" (Walker, "Compositor Determination," 15n8). So secure is A's personality that his behavior can be predicted even in hypothetical situations: "He could normally maintain a system, and I have no doubt that if A had decided to turn every tenth 'e' he could have held his head to the business" (15n8). Gary Taylor has attempted to reverse this characterization: "A's reputation as a uniquely reliable and trustworthy compositor, whose work editors should be loath to emend, is almost wholly unfounded."[51] In contrast, the "notorious"[52] Compositor B's "more erratic ways" ("Compositor Determination" 15n8) are

> marked by a combination of misdirected ingenuity, deliberate tampering, and plain carelessness that makes him an interesting example of how far a compositor could go in the intentional and unintentional alteration of copy while setting it into type—although it should be understood that B appears to have gone a good deal further than most.[53]

Hinman's index entries for the compositors themselves read like character composites:

> Compositor E, . . . spelling peculiarities of . . . ; his spelling 'mixed', much influenced by copy, his true preferences therefore hidden . . . ; no strong preferences evident at first . . . ; non-spelling peculiarities . . . ; set [type] only in absence of one or both 'regulars' and used their cases . . . ; why he began with quire dd, not cc . . . ; . . . was very inaccurate, was expected to make errors, and much of his work proofed . . . ; set only for the six Tragedies which F reprints from quartos. . . . ; his essential function . . . ; his dual role . . . ; set most of *Titus* and *Romeo*, all of pre-cancellation *Troilus*, had a share in *Ham.*, *Lear*, *Oth.* . . . . ; was slower than B. . . . ; final disappearance. . . . ; although heretofore confused with B, his work now relatively easy to identify. . . . ; his share in F summarized. . . . (*PPFFS*, 2:536)

I will return to E's characteristics, but notice here that a chronological log of E's activities in the progress of folio printing oscillates with, and becomes, a rehearsal of personality traits, with a fully bounded subjectivity—a subjectivity so complex that even some of E's "true preferences" (preferences culled from the printed page) remain somehow hidden from view. The spelling evidence may be composed of temporary aberrations, but the compositor is now a species.[54]

The kind of individuation of printing-house labor delineated here is both essential to the method of compositor analysis and, apparently, that which can thwart its success, as Fredson Bowers (Hinman's teacher and the dean of postwar American textual studies) suggests, writing in 1959 that

> the uniqueness of each compositor, and of his mental and physical habits and reactions, lends to the detailed study of his work an unpredictable basis in which the human equation is often of the first importance. . . . [E]ach compositor is a law to himself, subject to all the irrationality associated with human operations under individual responsibility.[55]

Individuation, as Bowers makes clear, is at the center of this method, doubly so, for even as the passage seems edgily to approach an admission of the method's impossibility, it suggests that the ideal compositor for analysis is one who is outrageously, clinically idiosyncratic (and therefore identifiable), but at the same time absolutely consistent in his idiosyncrasy.

This methodological paradox brings us back to Hinman's Compositor E, who is, as we have seen, hardly the ideal compositor; indeed, he further suggests some of the internal inconsistencies of the methodology. For Compositor E is an impressionable individual of astonishing malleability. Hinman notes that the habits and preferences of E actually *change* over the course of the pages of the folio he works on: he begins as "a novice who had not at first had any really strong spelling preferences"; early on in the job he "follows copy" closely but quickly develops "strong spelling preferences" of his own—what Hinman calls "a *do-go* habit" (*PPFFS*, 1:213n2). This habit also characterizes Compositor B, and Hinman in fact finds E working closely with B. Commenting on Hinman's work, T. H. Howard-Hill emphasizes "the closeness of E's working relationship with compositor B . . . [;] throughout the Tragedies, we can observe E's gradual acquisition of typographical expertise. . . . He was, as the Nurse in *Romeo* puts it, 'a man of wax.'"[56] Another bibliographer notices Compositor E's "strong imitative tendency, which has so effectively concealed his presence and caused such confusion."[57]

Once we start to notice variability, imitative tendencies, and the acquisition of others' habits—where before there had only been solid identity and consistency—these more flexible characteristics begin to appear everywhere: Hinman admits that "both [compositors] A and B now and again used non-characteristic spellings, and sometimes without ascertainable reason" (*PPFFS*, 1:185). As we have

, B's work is sometimes difficult to distinguish from that of Compositor E 2, 1:226); and what characterizes E, as he is initially delineated by Hinman, is his lack of character, or lack of his own characters: he has "B-like spelling prefer-ences but also a strong tendency to follow copy" (1:212). If this evidence under-mines the separability of B and E, and the separation of E's work from that of the other compositors who composed Shakespeare,[58] the very flexibility and mallea-bility of E's spellings make it possible, by Hinman's own logic, to find the impres-sionable E almost *anywhere* (1:213n2).[59]

Habits and Intolerances

Spelling-habit is the way in which any person spelt;
it is usage, mostly unconscious, sometimes grotesquely
self-conscious. Spelling-pattern, however, is the investigator's concept of individual tendency.
                —T. H. Hill, "Spelling and the Bibliographer"[60]

Both A and B made mistakes, but B made more than A
and was especially given to particular kinds of aberration.
Unlike A, Compositor B took frequent and various
liberties with his copy.
                                —Charlton Hinman (*PPFFS*, 1:10)

[F]or every obvious homosexual, there are probably nine
nearly impossible to detect.
                                —*Life* magazine (1964)[61]

The analysis of compositors' spelling begins in a 1920 letter to the *Times Literary Supplement* about spellings in *Macbeth*, appears as an occasionally useful inferen-tial method in R. B. McKerrow's widely taught *Introduction to Bibliography for Literary Students* (1927), and is first employed in earnest as a textual method in Edwin Willoughby's 1932 book on the first folio.[62] Hinman publishes on spelling identification in 1940–41, but it is only after the hiatus of the Second World War that compositor study becomes central to the conduct of Shakespearean bibliog-raphy. Take down from the shelf the row of early issues of *Studies in Bibliography*, the annual volume of papers that Bowers began to edit in 1948, and you find at least one article each year on compositor identification in the period directly after the war. Then there is an explosion of interest in the mid-1950s: five articles in 1955, four in 1956, three in 1957, three more in 1958.

But *hiatus*, to backtrack for a moment, is not the best word for what happened to American bibliographic study during the Second World War, for, as I want to suggest, compositor analysis was not so much suspended as *produced* by the war, in some important ways. Before the United States entered the war, Bowers "had been given secret instruction as a cryptanalyst in a naval communications group being formed at the university [of Virginia]"; during the war he moved to Washington "to supervise an intelligence unit working on deciphering enemy codes."[63] Among a number of prominent literary/bibliographic scholars, the unit included Charlton Hinman (33).[64] Hinman in fact got the idea for the collating machine he later invented to compare Shakespeare folio pages from "the method followed in the intelligence unit for comparing successive photographs of enemy fortifications, to see whether changes had been made" (34).

Were compositors to become the code-producing enemies of postwar bibliographic scholarship? The connections between postwar bibliography and cryptanalytic work didn't escape another bibliographer, G. Thomas Tanselle, reviewing Bowers's life and work: "the goal of both activities," he writes, "is to find meaningful patterns in what at first seems to be chaotic data" (34).[65] But surely there are other questions to ask: what are the differences between intentionally produced codes disclosing the locations of Japanese warships, and the codes, or inscriptions, of seventeenth-century spellings? What if chaotic data, as I've suggested, are instead data that lie outside our standards for the behavior of the chaotic and the ordered? These are not the only questions to be asked of the methods of compositor analysis, and I want briefly to think more broadly about the discourses that surrounded, informed, and structured compositor study in the late 1940s and early 1950s.

If the enemies of the United States and its bibliographers from 1941 to 1945 were fascists abroad, some of the most extravagant battles of the postwar Cold War, as a number of political and social historians have argued, were fought against (real and ostensible) homosexuals and communists within. The historian David Johnson has carefully demonstrated that, although it has been overshadowed in the subsequent historiography by the Red Scare, "the Lavender Scare—a fear that homosexuals posed a threat to national security and needed to be systematically removed from the federal government—permeated 1950s political culture."[66] If the publication of the Kinsey report on *Sexual Behavior in the Human Male* in 1948 taught and then sought to reassure Americans that homosexuals were potentially everywhere, the 1950 Senate inquiry into the *Employment of Homosexuals and Other Sex Perverts in Government*[67] also marshaled Kinsey's evidence to argue that homosexuals were everywhere *in the government* and necessary to detect.[68] And like the pre–First World War chief of Austrian intelligence (a homosexual) that the Senate committee produced as its lone example—a man who gave secrets to (not incidentally in 1950) the Russians and even altered the texts of Austrian intelligence reports—these infiltrating homosexuals were ostensibly blackmailable and unstable. As the report gratuitously (which is to say, from its perspective, approvingly) added, the Austrian homosexual, upon discovery of his "traitorous acts," committed suicide (*Employment of Homosexuals*, 5).[69]

Detection, as the historian John D'Emilio summarizes the Senate report "was not an easy task . . . , because too many [homosexuals] lacked the 'outward characteristics or physical traits that are positive as identifying marks of sex perversion.'"[70] (One senator asked a witness: "There is no quick test like an X-ray that discloses these things?" [qtd. in Johnson, *Lavender Scare*, 114].) Detection was nevertheless deemed important because "[t]hese perverts will frequently attempt to entice normal individuals to engage in perverted practices. This is particularly true in the case of young and impressionable people who might come under the influence of a pervert" (*Employment of Homosexuals*, 4).

Beginning in the early 1950s, then, and extending into the 1960s, as Lee Edelman has brilliantly analyzed and Johnson decisively documented,[71] the United States experienced an explosion of discourse related to the visible signs and detection of homosexuality.[72] Throughout this period the discourses of detection remain similarly constituted: surveillance is concerned with detecting homosexuality through its visible signs on the body, with the "habits," "practices," "tendencies," and "aberrations" of the homosexual, and his/her "perversion" of government agencies (particularly the State Department), the larger body politic, and the fighting corps during and after the Second World War, as Allan Bérubé has documented. Johnson notes that a "1952 procedures manual for [State Department] security officers contained a nine-page section devoted entirely to homosexuality, the only type of security offense singled out for such coverage"; officers were to "report 'any unusual traits of speech, appearance, or personality'" (73). During the postwar period, in the armed forces, the federal government, and civilian life, more and more citizens were subject to these forms of detection and screening, which ranged from individual interrogations of federal employees and federal job applicants, to the homosexual gag-reflex test developed by the Army, to Rorschach testing, to the other psychiatric tests for detection advocated by the Senate committee.[73] As D'Emilio has shown, the attempt to detect homosexuals (and, relatedly, communists) "extended far beyond a search for those in the military and the federal bureaucracy" (46) to states, municipalities, private industries, and universities.[74]

You will have detected already the tendency of my argument, so let me provide a caveat before I proceed. I do not mean to suggest that Hinman and other Shakespearean bibliographers believe(d) that sexual preferences or behaviors can be ascertained on the basis of spelling habits, or that Hinman and others intentionally applied this rhetoric, in their work, with the virulence intended by the Senate committee, subsequent federal investigators, or Hinman's and Bowers's colleagues in the armed forces. On the other hand, I *do* mean to suggest that the language of mid-twentieth-century compositorial study, in its search for essences/ identities that can be read out from spelling habits, behaviors, tendencies, and practices, bears resemblance to, and is startlingly contemporaneous with, other mid-twentieth-century attempts to monitor and detect identities—*sexual* identities—on the basis of visible physical signs and behaviors.

That this rhetoric would have been available to Hinman and Bowers and the other scholars, mostly Americans, who worked on compositor study—through their experience in the wartime navy and also simply by reading the newspaper and watching television in the early 1950s—I have already tried to suggest. Hinman, who was in Washington at the Folger Shakespeare Library working on folios at his collating machine (at least in 1952–53), lived in the midst of it. President Eisenhower strengthened President Truman's "loyalty" program in April 1953 and, for the first time, explicitly prohibited the hiring and retention of federal employees engaged in "sexual perversion" (D'Emilio, 44); the new policies were elaborated by the attorney general in President Eisenhower's first televised appearance from the White House and discussed by the president himself in a subsequent news conference and the 1954 State of the Union address (Johnson, 123, 134). In addition to the widespread "vice" squad campaigns during this period in Washington, D.C., the results of which were used extensively against federal employees and applicants suspected of being gay, the State Department (the origin of the "security" scandal and investigations) reported that in the first nine months of 1953 "192 persons had been removed [from their jobs] for 'Security (Exclusive of Homosexuality),' while 114 had been removed for 'Security (Homosexuals)'" (Johnson, 130). Earlier in the Scare, at the time of the Senate report in 1950, which was covered in the *Washington Post* (117), fifteen gay employees of the Library of Congress (across the street from the Folger) were under investigation for sex perversion—nine had resigned, one was dismissed, and five cases were "pending" (*Employment of Homosexuals*, Appendix III, 25). In mid-1954, after his son was arrested in Lafayette Park, across from the White House, and later tried, under Republican senatorial pressure, on a "morals" charge, Senator Lester C. Hunt withdrew from his reelection campaign and killed himself with a shotgun in his Senate office (Johnson, 140–41). The next year, a two-part *Reader's Digest* article, reprinted in *U.S. News and World Report* and entitled "How About Those Security Risks?," cited a convicted spy's "instability" and "aberrant habits" (qtd. in Johnson, 140). By 1958, an independent study "estimated that *one of every five em-*

ployed adults in America had been given some form of loyalty or security screening" (137, my emphasis); such screenings often involved questions about homosexual behavior, "tendencies," and associations.[75] Consultants at the Department of Health, Education, and Welfare who worked on the Salk vaccine, for example, were "asked to sign a loyalty oath, and warned against 'drunkenness, sexual perversion and associating with spies,'" as reported in the press (137). As Johnson's book eloquently demonstrates, during the Lavender Scare, there is no separating the overlapping rhetorics of sexuality and related "security risk" discourses in this period—in Washington, in the press, and in the broader public understanding.

Nor would a certain rhetoric of homosexuality have been foreign to the University of Virginia in the 1950s, where Bowers was editing the volumes of *Studies in Bibliography* and their articles on compositor identification and also working on an edition of a new cache of Whitman manuscripts—manuscripts of the poems that had become the "Calamus" section of *Leaves of Grass*. Bowers, for his part, displays a certain avoidance of the word "homosexual" throughout his first published essay on the manuscripts (in the 1954 volume of *Studies*),[76] almost as if he had searched and replaced the term *homosexual* with *calamus*, which appears lowercased throughout the essay and without quotation marks:

> another spurt of poetic activity produced additional poems, many of these of a calamus nature (258)

> one of these [poems] is perhaps the most specifically calamus poem he wrote (259)

> even this frankly calamus poem (259)

Is it the unusual use of the noun *calamus* as an adjective or the "spurt" of Whitmanian activity that leads me to hear the faint echo of another (nonce)word here—"additional poems . . . of a *calumnous* nature"—as if, in these frankly calamus poems, Whitman is seen as casting an aspersion on his own reputation?

When Bowers does finally use the much more frankly calamus term, the syntactic discomfort is striking: "In th[e]se manuscripts . . . , there is a small amount of homosexual references but no serious emphasis on it" (258). The troubled agreement of this sentence—what is the "it" that lacks serious emphasis, but the apparently unmentionable entity *homosexuality*?—can suggest for us a larger problematic we have witnessed in the rhetoric of compositor study. For, like Hinman's index entry for Compositor E, Bowers's sentence seems lodged between a series of acts or behaviors in the text ("homosexual references") and an undefined entity or identity ("it") that, however unemphasized in the texts under analysis, seems to govern the rhetoric of his reading.[77] The trajectory of Bowers's discussion of Whitman's "homosexual references," however confused, resembles that of the compositor's aberrations and perversions said to lie upon the surface of Shakespeare's text.

For I do think, to return to Shakespeare, that nothing less than the security of the state of Shakespeare's text, or corpus, is at stake in the rhetorics of compositor analysis. Hinman stresses again and again that Shakespeare's text is only as reliable as the trustworthiness of the compositors who set it in type. In the same volume of *Studies* that included Bowers on Whitman, Walker writes, "[W]e are faced with the possibility that there may be at least two hundred errors in the Folio *Lear* and *Othello* for which compositor B was solely responsible. Must we assume that these two texts are pitted with holes and corrupted by interpolations and perversions of the wording?"[78] For Hinman, at least, the security of the Shakespearean text and national security during the Cold War years might have been even more firmly linked. Hinman had been a fellow at the Folger, beginning work on Shakespeare compositors, in 1941–42 (Tanselle, 33); after Pearl Harbor and for the duration of the war, the Library (which sits two blocks from the U.S. Capitol) had moved 30,000 of its most valuable books to a secret location on the more remote Amherst College campus.[79] In the midst of collating the folios, Hinman himself writes in 1953 that the Shakespeare folios had been moved again, and the Cold War resonates in his language: "As a precaution against possible disaster, only about half of the irreplaceable Folger copies are being kept in the Library in Washington; but the other copies will be brought back for collation as soon as work has been completed on the copies now available."[80]

But let another bibliographer—for reasons that will become clear, I will refer to him as Bibliographer B—speak about the more textual disasters threatening Shakespeare:

> [T]ype-setters played a role the importance of which can hardly be over-emphasized. . . . Thus in a given text we may find what a printing house employee *thought* Shakespeare wrote, or what he thought Shakespeare *might* have written, or—more disastrous still—what a printing house employee thought Shakespeare *should* have written, rather than what he actually wrote.[81]

Like Hinman, Bibliographer B was a dissertation student of Bowers's, and he came back to the University of Virginia after a few years elsewhere to be Bowers's colleague. He published in *Studies* on compositor analysis in a number of Shake-speare plays, and, early one morning in March of 1955—and now I am quoting from the local newspapers—Bibliographer B, "who was 37 and unmarried, shot himself in the right side of the head with a .22 calibre pistol."[82]

I do not know much else about Bibliographer B, but it is difficult not to read the signs, bodily and other, proffered by the newspaper accounts of his death as anything but, say, "a small amount of homosexual references but no serious emphasis on it." There is the gratuitous linking of his age, his (un)marital status, and the shot, which in the logic of the sentence seems almost consequential. There is the statement that Bibliographer B "was known to be suffering from 'extreme worry and strain' . . . according to reliable sources."

What were B's habits and preferences, I find myself wondering. There is not much to go on. He habitually appears on time for his nine o'clock class, or else an alarmed colleague would not have come looking for him. His grooming habits are likewise impeccable: "At the time he was found [Bibliographer B] was cleanly shaven and dressed." (The suggestion that one might have expected to find him in another state seems only a further sign, an offering up of the worried and strained body to further view.) Regrettably, a set of "[p]apers related to the death of" Bibliographer B and two sealed envelopes with committee reports on his "case" have since been destroyed by the University of Virginia library.[83]

I find myself examining the habits of his prose, in the lecture on compositor study I have already quoted. Does it matter, I wonder, that he explicitly avoids discussing compositor *identification* in this talk on compositor study? "I shall not discuss the methods by which compositors can be identified, but assuming that identification is possible, I should like to examine some of the implications."[84] Does it signify that, speaking as he is to the assembled members of the 1954 English Institute, on a panel with Bowers and Walker, with Hinman in the chair[85]— speaking, a few months before his death, of the potential disasters to be uncovered by compositor study—he avoids the rhetoric of detection, perversion, aberration, and irrationality, though he is attuned to "habits"?

I do not think that it matters whether Bibliographer B was gay or not—although of course he lived in a context where it mattered immensely. Either way, there seem to be no more signs, but, when I go back to Hinman and find him looking at the infiltrated, compromised fortifications of the folios through his collating machine, counting aberrant spellings not of *xerxes* or *donjuan*, but of *traitor*, *young*, and *grief*—the spellings that, along with *do*, *go*, and *here*, he tracks to detect compositors throughout his book—it is hard not to see, through that apparatus, an identity for Bibliographer B.[86]

Pressing Subjects

[I]t is of greatest concernment . . . to have a vigilant eye
how Bookes demeane themselves as well as men; and
thereafter to confine, imprison, and do sharpest justice on
them as malefactors: For Books are not absolutely dead
things, but doe contain a potencie of life in them to be as
active as that soule was whose progeny they are; nay they
do preserve as in a violl the purest efficacie and extraction
of that living intellect that bred them.

—John Milton, *Areopagitica*[87]

Joseph Moxon's *Mechanick Exercises: Or, the Doctrine of handy-works. Applied to the Art of Printing* (1683) is the repository of much of what we think we know about seventeenth-century English printing, outside of other printed books themselves. As the first extant guide to English printing-house practice, Moxon's text is the basis for some of Hinman's assumptions about the conduct of printing, press speed, and the importance of nonstop work and efficient production—assumptions that themselves led to the narratives we have seen regarding the alternation of different compositors. Moxon is also in part the basis for McKenzie's important critique of Hinman's postindustrial assumptions about efficiency and standardized production. Much of the discussion of Moxon centers on how reliable he is as a factual guide to English printing-house practice[88] and to what degree a late seventeenth-century account is a reliable guide to early seventeenth-century practice.

But the *Mechanick Exercises* for printing—part of a series of exercises that includes smithing, joining, and carpentry—is more instrumental in its intentions and effects than this discussion usually allows. Moxon's publications function as do-it-yourself guides to these various "arts"—in this case as a kind of self-interpellating manual for the production of printers. To set up a press, you learn these terms for the parts of the press; you set up the parts in this fashion; you move the parts in this way to produce print. This process in itself is highly self-reflective and reflexive; as de Grazia has shown, the parts of the press in Moxon's description are anthropomorphic and reproductive: tongues, heads, bodies, cheeks, matrices, screws, and so on.[89] Moxon's title, *Mechanick Exercises*, is in this context ambiguous, for *mechanick* during this period can mean "manual" *or* "mechanical";[90] likewise, *exercises* might signify exercises, in the pedagogical sense, for the reader to go through, to rehearse; practices; "habitual occupation or employment"; or even a "disciplinary suffering, 'trial'" (*OED*). Are *Mechanick Exercises* the exercises of the press or of the person training him/herself to operate the press? Who or which is (the) mechanick? Who or what is being trained, disciplined in this applied art?

One might proceed, then, to produce a larger reading of the descriptive and performative qualities of Moxon's *Exercises* as a cultural document.[91] I will restrict myself here to suggesting how we might use Moxon to move toward a more historically attuned notion of the compositor—as a "pressing subject," one pressed, pressing, and impressed, rather than as the erratic, obstructionist individual of New Bibliographic accounts.

Moxon writes of the compositor's duties as a kind of negotiation, with the compositor not as an intruding perverter in the ideally unmediated transmission of the text, but as a kind of useful double agent negotiating among others: "A good *Compositor* . . . reads his *Copy* with consideration; . . . and consequently considers how to order his Work the better . . . As how to make his *Indenting*, *Pointing*, *Breaking*, *Italicking*, *&c.* the better sympathize with the *Authors* Genius, and also with the capacity of the Reader."[92] The good compositor orients himself in two directions, toward the author and toward the reader, and lest we too quickly assume, as in modernity, that only authors have genius, we should note that "*a good natural Genius*" is one of the attributes Moxon desires, too, in his compositor (2:197).

But if the compositor is a negotiating agent, there are also ways in which the printing house and the press train, discipline, and *produce* the compositor, as in Moxon's description of the disciplining of a printing-house employee who fails to pay fines levied for in-house infractions:

> The Workmen take him by force, and lay him on his Belly athwart the *Correcting*-stone, and held him there while another of the Work-men, with a Paper-board, gave him 10 *l. and a Purse*, viz. Eleven blows on his Buttocks; which he laid on according to his own mercy. For Tradition tells us, that about 50 years ago one was *Solaced* [the term used for this punishment] with so much violence, that he presently Pissed Blood, and shortly after dyed of it. (2:357–58)

Lain athwart the "Correcting-stone" like a page to be proofread, or a forme filled with type, disciplined, too, with the implied textuality of a "Paper-board"—the composer of text has become text, produced by, subject to, the press. It may be in this context that the impressionable Compositor E becomes, for us, if not for the New Bibliographers, the most appropriate model of the early modern compositor: impressionable, a man of wax, he has imitative tendencies; he follows copy closely; and copy follows him.

You will perhaps not be surprised that *beating* itself is a term in printing—it refers to the inking of the press. The press-man, in Moxon's words,

> keeps a constant and methodical posture and gesture in every action of *Pulling* and *Beating*, which in a train of Work becomes habitual to him, and eases his Body, by not running into unnecessary divertions of Postures or Gestures in his Labour. . . . And a *Pull* of the same strength upon the same *Form*, with the same *Beating*, and with the same *Blankets*, &c. will give the same Colour and Impression. (2:334)

These are the mechanick exercises of the press-man. But is there any way to emerge—theoretically—from this constant shuttle of pressing subject and machine, mechanick and mechanical? I have spoken of interpellation, but the better term here—for Moxon's reader, the compositor, and the press-man alike—is Bourdieu's concept of the *habitus*. Bourdieu defines the habitus as "systems of durable, transposable dispositions, structured structures predisposed as structuring structures, that is, as principles which generate and organize practices and representations that can be objectively adapted to their outcomes without predisposing a conscious aiming at ends."[93] Thinking more particularly about the compositor and his spellings, we might speak not of spelling habits but of spelling habitus:

> Because the *habitus* is an infinite capacity for generating products— thoughts, perceptions, expressions and actions—whose limits are set by the historically and socially situated conditions of its production, the conditioned and conditional freedom it provides is as remote from creation of unpredictable novelty as it is from simple mechanical reproduction of the original conditioning. (55)

Neither unpredictable novelty nor simple mechanical reproduction, the compositor's spelling, in these terms, becomes not a conduit of identity, but, again quoting Bourdieu, "a product of history, produc[ing] individual and collective practices—more history—in accordance with the schemes generated by history" (54). More particularly, we might define the spelling habitus as the collision of a number of dispositions (seen historically): public tastes and traditional practices; the availability of different traditions of spelling in different classes, regions, dialects within and on the borders of English; current (synchronic) spelling practices as they intersect with and diverge from (diachronic) etymology, seen as a digest or palimpsest of historical practices; the attempts at orthographical reform; and the exigencies of printing, spacing, and justification—the press training the compositor to spell, limiting the spellings possible.[94] A queer philology of early modern English spelling, in other words, will want to be alert not only to the historically distinct or continuous forms and meanings of particular "words," but also, given spelling's connections with "right-writing" and eventually with conceptions of aberrance, to the ways in which "identity" and these multifactorially produced habits of the spelling habitus are potentially dissociated or incommensurate.

This is how Moxon describes the secret/inner life of the compositor, the pressing subject:

> first [he] reads so much of his *Copy* as he thinks he can retain in his memory till he have *Composed* it. . . . And having read, he falls a Spelling in his mind; yet so, that his Thoughts run no faster than his Fingers: For as he spells A, he takes up A out of the A *Box*, as he names n in his thoughts, he takes up n out of the n *Box*, as he names d in his thoughts he takes up d out of the d *Box*; which three *Letters* set together make a Word, viz. And; so that after the d he sets a *Space*: Then he goes on to the next word, and so *Composes* on. (2:212–13)[95]

If Moxon in 1683 is some distance from the unfixed linguistic field of the earlier seventeenth century—he says the compositor should know "*the present traditional* Spelling *of all English Words*" (2:197)—if, that is, spelling has become a process of "naming [letters] in his thoughts," of producing spellings, we should nevertheless notice that Moxon is at the same time not merely describing but also working to *produce* such a system, to compose compositors for/in whom the production of spellings on this model will occur. Once you have gone through your mechanick exercises, is the "A *Box*" in the upper case, or in your mind?

Spelling, in 1683, may still be reading, and writing, from reading; the compositor "falls a Spelling in his mind": he writes, reading his mind, reading what is written in his mind, in the space(s) provided.

Recomposing

We have seen how compositor study requires some queer-philological analysis of some of its highly consequential, historically situated terms—*corruption, aberration, perversion,* and so forth. I want, in concluding, to spell out some of what I think are the larger ramifications of a critique of compositor analysis for a queer-philological approach to Shakespeare and early modern texts more generally.

Even with the elevated prominence recently of studies in the history of the book, compositor studies can continue to seem an arcane subfield to those outside its discipline, and it is important to note that it is part of a larger movement in twentieth-century treatments of Shakespearean and other early modern texts that relies on a precise individuation of agents at every stage of textual production, in ways that are often strikingly anachronistic. In this way, compositor analysis closely parallels the work of Cyrus Hoy and those following his influential work, who have sought to discern and separate out of collaboratively written texts the individuated "shares" of particular playwrights—to separate, say, Shakespeare and Fletcher's words in *The Two Noble Kinsmen*—on the basis of "linguistic habits" or "preferences," the ostensible difference in usage of words like *'em* and *them*, *ye* and *you*.[96] (Like Hinman's work, Hoy's was also done under Bowers's supervision at the University of Virginia; Hoy's attention to "habits" and "preferences" is also a legacy of the 1950s, published between 1956 and 1962.) The most extreme version of this is the bibliographic treatment of a play like *Pericles*, where various, related New Bibliographic methods have located two (or more) playwrights, two memorial reporters of the text, and *three* compositors (named x, y, and z, two of whom are said, in one still influential account, to be "immoral").[97] All of this individuated activity is isolated in order to explain the ostensible "badness" of a text that, as Barbara A. Mowat has shown, was in the early seventeenth century acted on tour from the text of the *same* printed book now so widely maligned in twentieth-century bibliography and criticism.[98]

By contrast, a historicized—even queered—sense of identity in relation to the spelling and printing habitus might help us to rethink the complex problem of agency in and around Shakespeare's texts. As I hope I have also suggested, a queer philology of the less remote past—a discursive analysis of the overlaps among Cold War rhetorics of secrecy, corruption, detection, and homosexuality—may help us to think more seriously about what is at stake in essentialized notions of identity in the twentieth and twenty-first centuries. These important meta-methodological concerns aside, however, what can such a queer-philological account of compositors and their spellings do for and with Shakespeare's text? How will a queer analytic help us see how compositor study might affect, reform, or deform the folio text?

Let us look briefly at page 206 of the Comedies section of the first folio. There, in the final moments of *As You Like It*, with a number of weddings seemingly both imminent and impossible, and with Rosalind (disguised as the young man Ganymede) having promised to return, sort out the marriage plots, and "make all this matter euen" (TLN 2594),[99] this text appears in the folio, the only early printed text of the play:

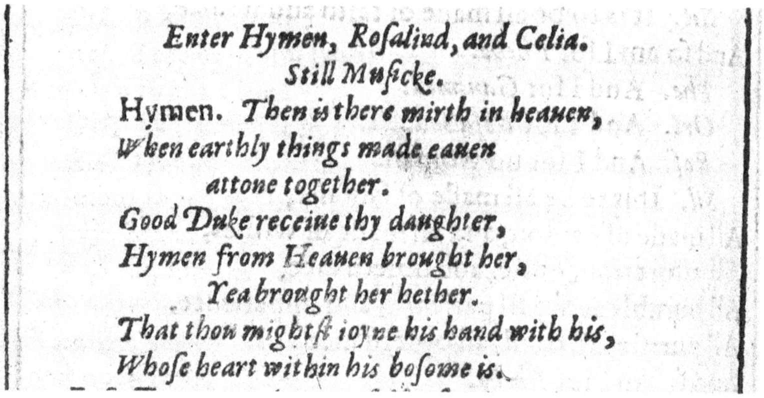
Enter Hymen, Roſalind, and Celia.
Still Muſicke.
Hymen. *Then is there mirth in heauen,*
When earthly things made eauen
attone together.
Good Duke receiue thy daughter,
Hymen from Heauen brought her,
Yea brought her hether.
That thou mightſt ioyne his hand with his,
Whoſe heart within his boſome is.

FIGURE 14. "[H]is hand with his" at the conclusion of *As You Like It*, in *Mr. VVilliam Shakespeares Comedies, Histories, & Tragedies*, p. 206 of the Comedies. By permission of the Folger Shakespeare Library.

Who marries Orlando at the end of this play—Ganymede, Rosalind, or both?[100] The folio text is almost universally emended to eliminate that question or simplify its answer;[101] the New Variorum Shakespeare notes in its survey of previous editions that "editors are almost unanimous in finding *his hand* an error for *her hand* . . . —COLLIER (ed. 1842) notes that *his* is an easy misreading of *hir*—but are deeply divided over whose bosom is the repository of whose heart."[102]

The Variorum note proceeds to quote a number of the "deeply divided" editors, but notice that they are deeply divided on this second issue only once one has decided that the first (two male hands joined in the last scene of a Shakespearean comedy) is simply "an error" or "an easy misreading." In the context of another emendation of *his* to *hir*/*her*, Gary Taylor expands on Collier's theory: "In an Elizabethan secretary hand, terminal *s* was often almost impossible to distinguish from *r*, and in contemporary orthography *her* could be spelled with a medial *i*; in such circumstances, a 'hir' and a 'his' are materially identical, and can only be differentiated by cultural context."[103]

Whatever the force with which this comedy moves toward a marital ending (and that force is significant), cultural context does not easily settle the question in this instance. Critics who see the folio's reading as a *mis*reading will remark that Rosalind and Celia have returned to the stage dressed "as themselves,"[104] and Rosalind has been referred to as "her" in the lines that directly precede "his hand with his." However, those critics are likely reading out of an editorial tradition that has routinely inserted a stage direction indicating for Rosalind a return to women's dress, and, if Rosalind in this speech is referenced as both female and male, it is neither the first nor the last time in the play that this occurs, as the play's epilogue demonstrates. In any event, we would not want to exclude too quickly the possibility of two male hands joined in the last scene of a play that repeatedly directs attention to the boy actor playing the part of Rosalind, has emphasized the choice of the homoerotically charged name "Ganymede," has that character invoke Jove/Jupiter several times in the course of the play, and has earlier, in Act 4, Scene 1, staged a version of this same marriage, bringing together these same hands: "Come sister," Rosalind-as-Ganymede says, "you shall be the Priest, and marrie vs: *giue me your hand Orlando*" (TLN 2033–34, my emphasis).[105] As Alan Bray's work has demonstrated, the image of two joined hands (a handfast) is central to the iconography of same-sex friendship in this period, appearing on friends' joint graves and monuments.[106] That what Taylor calls an "exceptionally easy misreading, well attested elsewhere" seems to occur in other plays, then, does not guarantee the correctness of this correction in the context of *As You Like It*.[107]

Whose "error" or "misreading" is this—whose *his*? Hinman asserts, on the basis of particular spellings and types in the text, that page 206 of the Comedies was set by Compositor B from typecase y (2:448), and this is where we may see the larger ideological investments of emending (on the basis of compositor error) this potentially locally queer moment in this more broadly queer text. To put the case bluntly: if Compositor B, notorious and erratic, known for his textual perversions, can be said to have erred or misread a pronoun in his manuscript, the text can be adjusted accordingly, and Shakespeare's hand—which is to say, in this case, a pair of "heterosexual" hands—can be restored. The compositor's skaiography (*his*) can be replaced by Shakespeare's presumed orthography (*hir*), and interpretation may proceed.

Paying attention to compositors has the distinct payoff of bringing other agencies into the text, but, even in the terms of conventional compositor study, as we have seen, these are complex agencies. Does Compositor B "prefer" *his* here? Or does he merely "tolerate" it? Is Compositor B's setting of this word a moment of (ostensibly uncharacteristic?) adherence to the text, an accidental misreading, or a deliberate revision? (Recall that he has been credited with "a combination of misdirected ingenuity, deliberate tampering, and plain carelessness" and has "gone a good deal further than most."[108])

There are other potential agencies that lie between Shakespeare and the text of *As You Like It* as it reached its eventual readers: a scribe or playhouse bookkeeper, since the play is sometimes hypothesized to have been set in print "either from a promptbook or, less probably, from a literary transcript of either the promptbook or Shakespeare's foul papers";[109] potentially a later revising playwright (who could be Shakespeare or someone else);[110] several songwriters; the actors (potentially including Shakespeare, acting in another role); the publishers of the folio volume; and the proofreaders who either failed to correct this "error" or didn't see it as such.[111] I don't mean to shield Shakespeare's own complex and opaque agency here from analysis by suggesting some other possible textual agents: I think it is more than possible that "his with his" was initially written into the play by Shakespeare. But I also think that, lacking a manuscript in Shakespeare's hand, this is an unanswerable question, and even were we to possess such a manuscript, we would not know whether Shakespeare made an error or performed an easy misreading of his own intention, in writing "his hand with his."

As I hope I have suggested, typecasting compositors is unlikely to solve this dilemma—if we understand the situation of a mediated text produced by multiple and potentially self-contradictory agencies to *be* a dilemma. As mentioned above, Compositor E's "imitative," "man of wax" "tendencies" throw into question his separability from other workers. Hinman finds E only in the Tragedies, but, while disputing some of Hinman's findings, Andrew Cairncross has, by Hinman's methods, found "unequivocal" evidence of E's "presence" in the Comedies and on the page in question.[112]

By questioning some of the assumptions of and offering a critique of compositor analysis, I do not seek to foreclose discussion of the labor of those engaged in producing books in early modern England. Indeed, I hope to suggest that compositor studies' tendency to rely on a historically inappropriate notion of impeded, solitary authorial agency has largely occluded what Moxon observes—as late as the end of the seventeenth century—about the proper function of compositors in (re)writing, (re)ordering, (re)emphasizing texts initiated by other hands. Why not produce a history of composition that is attuned to the labors of compositors in this way?—not as obstructing the ideally unmediated transmission of the authorial text, but as co-laborers in the working(s), mediations, transformations of textual production and reproduction. Mediation, after all, is what we have—all that we have. Even a manuscript—if *Sir Thomas More* is any indication—will stymie an attempt to locate Shakespeare's "own" spellings.

"[T]hat some demonstrable features of Shakespeare's holographs may eventually be recovered from the prints is not entirely a dream," Bowers writes, examining Compositor E in the folio *Othello*,[113] and Walker articulates the extraordinary fantasy, even if under negation, of stripping away compositors' spellings and translating the folio texts of Shakespeare back into Shakespeare's own spellings ("Compositor Determination," 8).[114] These authorial fantasies remain prominent with more recent literary and cultural critics as well; Richard Helgerson's book on the rise of an English national culture in the late sixteenth century, for example, modernizes spellings "[e]xcept when quoting from Spenser's verse, where archaism has authorial warrant."[115] But which archaisms, a queer philology will ask, even in Spenser, carry the warrant of authority, and which are the collective habits, or habitus, of the sixteenth century? What interpretive arrest is produced by this warrant? And when we re-compose Shakespeare's spellings, will we have Shakespeare's spellings, or the spellings that spelled Shakespeare?

Hinman, for his part, tries to close this potentially disastrous loop, appealing to apparent coincidence to produce a more reassuringly familial fantasy. Reading a list of employees of the print shop where the folios were produced, he notices that "one John Shakespeare, son of a Warwickshire butcher, was bound apprentice to William Jaggard . . . and took up his freedom . . . in May, 1617" (*PPFFS*, 2:513). "It is pleasant to wonder," he writes, near the end of his monumental study, "if the man who set more than half of the Folio into type (and who also took many liberties with its text)—to wonder if Compositor B was by any chance this same John Shakespeare" (2:513). The name seems to bring the anonymous perverter of the text back within the bounds of the playwright's family and, through the patronymic, to guarantee continuity (this Shakespeare gains his freedom a year after another Shakespeare's death) and a certain implicit level of textual fidelity.

But there is another fantasy, a different secret life, that a queer philology might see or "out" here, and—while I stress in all its doubtfulness that is *only* an alternative fantasy—it is structurally similar to the hand of Orlando joined with Ganymede's onstage in an early seventeenth-century performance of *As You Like It*, as well as the joined hands of the sharer or hired man who played Orlando's role and the boy apprentice with a marked imitative tendency who played Rosalind/Ganymede.[116] It is "pleasant to wonder" whether we may see this same John Shakespeare (but let's call him Compositor B) and Compositor E at work together on page 206: the hands of the adult worker and the apprentice who imitates him, producing meanings, spellings, of uncertain origin. Whose hand is "his"?

Having engaged in the Introduction and this chapter some detailed aspects of the linguistic "surround" in early modern England prior to lexical standardization, as well as some early modern and modern philological practices aspiring to address it and their interimplication in languages of sex, gender, and sexuality, *Queer Philologies* now moves to explore three distinct "lexicons" of sex/gender in early modern discourse. Throughout these analyses of terms and rhetorics, we will repeatedly encounter the challenge of reading early modern texts without also addressing the editorial-philological work explored here that has prepared and framed them for modern audiences; discussion of modern editorial methods approaching early modern texts will be woven throughout. The chapters, however, are centered on three of the primary ways in which same-sex "sexuality," affect, desire, and bodily practices—principally though not entirely directed toward men—circulate in early modern discourse. In the book's final section, we will return to explore directly the additional ways in which revised forms of editorial approach—supported by the queer philology practiced in these lexicons—might challenge and reimagine current editorial work.

LEXICON 1

FRIENDSHIP

CHAPTER 2

"Sweet Persuasion," the Taste of Letters, and Male Friendship

Epithets

Beginning to address my topic, allow me, patient readers, scholars, and friends, to begin with some possible addresses and some scenes in the history and theory of the address. First, a familiar modern scene:

> ideology . . . "recruits" subjects among the individuals (it recruits them all), or "transforms" the individuals into subjects (it transforms them all) by that very precise operation which I have called *interpellation* or hailing, and which can be imagined along the lines of the most commonplace everyday police (or other) hailing: "Hey, you there!"
>
> Assuming that the theoretical scene I have imagined takes place in the street, the hailed individual will turn around. By this mere one-hundred-and-eighty-degree physical conversion, he becomes a *subject*. Why? Because he has recognized that the hail was "really" addressed to him, and that "it was *really him* who was hailed" (and not someone else).[1]

Second, here is Erasmus, in *On the Writing of Letters*, considering salutations and the writing of "[t]he usual epithets of kindred and relatives":

> "Best of fathers," "most gracious mother," "dearest brother," "esteemed uncle," "dearest sister," "*sweet* wife," "darling grandson," "dear son-in-law, relative, comrade, fellow-soldier." Of the rest, who are distinguished by no clear indication, we shall call wealthy and influential men "estimable," "eminent," "in the first rank," "illustrious," "respected," "most respected"; those endowed with virtue or outstanding in learning "esteemed," "honourable," "commendable," "accomplished," "excellent," "surpassing," "wise,"

"estimable," "respectable," "clear-sighted," "prudent"; married women "noble," "distinguished," "best," "blameless," "virtuous," "modest"; girls "pretty," "beautiful," "lovable," "well-mannered," "chaste," "charming," "*sweet*"; young men "talented," "virtuous," "restrained," "promising," "of outstanding character," "of noble character"; soldiers "valiant," "well-tried"; workmen "hard-working," "clever," "skilled," "expert," "painstaking." From the examples I have given each will discover the rest for himself. But here is caution needed . . . against transferring what suits one group to another, such as calling a girl "venerable," an old man "charming," a king "modest," and a matron "invincible."[2]

Third, an editorial gloss from Clifford Leech's second-generation Arden edition of *The Two Gentlemen of Verona*, discussing line 149 of Act 2, Scene 4: "The use of 'sweet,' absolutely, as a form of address between man and man on equal terms, is rare in Shakespeare."[3]

Fourth, selected salutations drawn from the letters of James I, writing to the Duke of Buckingham, and to Buckingham and Charles together:

My only sweet and dear child, | Sweet boys, | My sweet boys and dear venturous knights, worthy to be put in a new romance, | My sweet boys, | My sweet Steenie gossip, | My sweet Steenie, | My sweet Steenie and gossip, | Sweet heart, | My sweet dear child, scholar, and friend.[4]

Fifth, Jacques Derrida, beginning *Politics of Friendship*, and quoting Montaigne referencing Aristotle:

"O my friends, there is no friend."

I am addressing you, am I not?
How many of us are there?[5]

Sweetness and Affect

"Good night, sweet prince," a man addresses his dying friend at the end of a familiar play, "And flights of angels sing thee to thy rest."[6] If this line has much of the timeless, monumental, and therefore unheard quality that much of the surrounding play has attained in the time since its initial performances in urban

England in the first years of the seventeenth century, there is nevertheless here a slight catch—an unusual aftertaste—in its smooth delivery into timelessness. Perhaps a modern audience finds this justified by the trauma that has preceded it; perhaps we hear it, if we hear it, as "merely" metaphorical, nothing at stake— surely no director would cut the line—and yet it is the syrupy adjective that I linger over as Horatio addresses Hamlet, one last time. After all the butch heroics of the preceding scenes, the stoicism, the shouting and jumping in of graves, the tabulation of competitive Ophelia-loving, the fencing—after he has, after all, killed several people with his own hand and earlier dispatched a couple longtime friends to their early deaths, all of this known to Horatio—it is nevertheless "Good night, *sweet* prince."

This is not a line that has attracted much attention. Of the flights of angels, whole chapters if not books have been written,[7] but, within the ample glossing of the *Hamlet* text, "Good night, sweet prince" rarely scores a mention. There is no comment on the line in the Variorum edition; the phrase passes unnoted in the *Norton Shakespeare*, the *Riverside Shakespeare*, the third-generation *Arden Shakespeare* edition, and other prominent modern teaching and scholarly editions. The Variorum edition's index (a place "sweet" *is* finally mentioned) works to make this word, uttered between men, common, conventional, anesthetized: "Sweet lord," reads the index listing, citing not Horatio but the fawning courtier Osric, and distancing itself further with a bracketed explanation, "[a common mode of address]."[8] Harold Jenkins's second-generation Arden edition provides the "sweet" in "sweet prince" with a note, "Frequent as an epithet of affection," a gloss it gives in expanded form at Horatio's first hailing of Hamlet as his "sweet lord" in Act 3, Scene 2: "A frequent epithet in complimentary or affectionate address."[9] Working in several directions, the term *epithet* marks *sweet*'s commonness as a term of male intimacy but simultaneously layers it with discomfort: on the one hand, "epithets," in the Erasmian sense, both describe and function beyond or in excess of the thing "itself"; on the other hand, in the modern era, they are often understood to be contemptuous, to be expunged in polite company. The Arden's terms, in other words, may distance *sweet* as a common but naughty word; the epithet here (merely conventional, or ignorable) is reduced into insignificance.

I probably would not have noticed Hamlet's dying sweetness if it had not been for a production I saw of Shakespeare's *The Two Gentlemen of Verona* several years ago.[10] Having previously written about the friendship of the play's title protagonists, Valentine and Proteus, and specifically about the first scene of the play, in which they reluctantly take leave of each other as Valentine departs for the court,[11] I noted a missing "sweet" in the early lines of the performance I witnessed. "Wilt thou be gone?" says Proteus to his friend, in line eleven,

> Sweet *Valentine* adew,
> Thinke on thy *Protheus,* when thou (hap'ly) seest
> Some rare note-worthy obiect in thy trauaile.[12]

In this performance, Valentine was no longer "sweet," at least at this formative initial moment of the play's unfolding; the performance retained some of the later instances of *sweet* between men, but only after dropping this initial one. It may be that the missing *sweet* was accidental and occurred only in the single performance I witnessed; what matters to me is not who "wrote" or intended this elision (whether actor or director), but instead, my perception, sitting with a modern audience at a contemporary performance, that the *elision* could seem to pass as utterly natural in a play reset in the early twentieth century—that the address of sweetness between male friends would seem, as in the *Hamlet* instance, to fit so uncomfortably with a standard modern conception of male-male relations.[13] Given that the early modern rhetoric of sweetness is used across a number of kinds of relationships (e.g., hierarchical and non-, same-sex and cross-sex, etc.), what became clear to me in the course of this performance was that a modern audience could invest the rhetoric of sweetness, when spoken between men and women, with intense affect (as in Proteus's later line about a letter from Julia, "Sweet Loue, sweet lines, sweet life!" [TLN 40]), while simultaneously *not* registering—by erasing into the realm of the dead-metaphorical, the "conventional mode of address"—a rhetoric of sweetness between men. Understand "Good night, sweet prince," then, as a line that also carries a historiographical imperative: as modern readers, editors, performers, and audiences, we have largely put the notion of affectionately meaningful male-male sweetness to bed.

The queerness of this early modern rhetoric comes in two modes. First, as I have noted, it is spoken across *kinds* of relationships in early modern England, including those we would now separate into homosexual and heterosexual.[14] In this sense, it represents yet more evidence for the mobile quality of desire, erotics, and affect, as distinct from identities in the modern sense, in this culture. Second, it is *historically* "queer"—used between men in a way that now seems to offend against normative codes of gender (sweetness now seems effeminizing).

Without effacing the queerness of *sweet* in the first sense (its mobility across kinds of relationships), I want in this chapter to reinvigorate this language as it is used between men, to bring it back to legibility. Or rather: to bring it back upon the palate (though we will return to the synaesthesia of this rhetoric, its ability to migrate not only across kinds of relationships but also among the senses). I hope not to do so, however, in the usually prophylactic terms of its conventionality as a mode of address. And so a brief further tasting is in order.

"But let me hear the letter of your friend," Portia says to Bassanio, in *The Merchant of Venice*, and Bassanio reads:

> *Sweet* Bassanio, *my ships haue all miscaried, my Creditors growe cruell, my estate is very low, my bond to the Iewe is forfaite, and since in paying it, it is impossible I should liue, all debts are cleerd betweene you and I if I might but see you at my death: notwithstanding, vse your pleasure, if your loue do not perswade you to come, let not my letter.*[15]

Lest one think that the homo-intimacy around sweet Bassanio dissipates in the cross-sex marriages of the play's comic ending, note that Bassanio himself deploys the identical rhetoric in the play's concluding lines, addressing his wife in the person of her earlier male disguise as a doctor of laws: "(Sweet Doctor) you shall be my bedfellow" (sig. K1ᵛ). No less a masculine icon than Henry V, addressing in anguished terms the betrayal of Lord Scroope, whom this play notes in advance as "the man that was his bedfellow," speaks in similar terms:

> Thou that didst beare the key of all my counsailes,
> That knew'st the very bottome of my soule,
> . . . .
> Oh, how hast thou with iealousie infected
> The sweetnesse of affiance?[16]

There may be more to this persistent rhetoric than typically meets the tongue. Usually viewed, however nervously, as nonerotic male friendships, these instances can be set alongside others more clearly erotically charged: in the opening lines of Christopher Marlowe's *Edward II*, for example, to which we will return, Gaveston says of Edward's letter calling him back to England: "Sweete prince I come, these these thy amorous lines, / Might haue enforst me to haue swum from France." "Thy woorth sweet friend is far aboue my guifts," says Edward a few moments later, in the first of his several uses of the word; "Therefore to equall it receiue my hart."[17]

This rhetoric is by no means restricted to Shakespeare, Marlowe, or drama; it extends across a wide range of friendship texts during this period, including a formative source, the friendship of Musidorus and "Sweet Pyrocles" in the *Arcadia*, and particularly including letters, onstage and off.[18] As a number of cultural historians, including Alan Bray, Mario DiGangi, Laurie Shannon, Bruce Smith, Alan Stewart, and myself, have argued, the rhetoric of these relationships is centrally concerned with describing ideally persons of absolute identicality, indistinshability, and interchangeability—qualities that Shannon has summarized as likeness, parity, equality, and consent."[19] Without particular emphasis (it is not theorized, as in Montaigne's friendship essay or even made explicit, as in *Two Gentlemen*), Hamlet's first meeting with Horatio seems to aspire to this interchangeability and absolute likeness of friends:

Hor.   Hail to your lordship!
Ham.   I am glad to see you well.
       Horatio—or I do forget myself.
Hor.   The same, my lord, and your poor servant ever.
Ham.   Sir, my good friend—*I'll change that name with you.*
               (1.2.159–62, my emphasis)[20]

Though Horatio continues to reinscribe their class difference, Hamlet seeks to "change names" at the moment of their first mutual hailing in this text, and the passage echoes Montaigne's announcement of the same structure: "If a man vrge me to tell wherefore I loued him, I feele it can not be expressed, but by answering; Because it was he, because it was my selfe."[21] Or, as Valentine says of Proteus, "I knew him as my selfe: for from our Infancie / We haue conuerst, and spent our howres together" (TLN 712–13). Such relationships were both celebrated by and constitutive of the broader social fabric, in ways that were, as Bray demonstrated in his posthumous volume *The Friend*, not necessarily at odds with or separable from the system of cross-sex patriarchal marriage. Together with *conversing*, a term that links speaking together, dwelling with, and conversion, sweetness is a part of the syntax of affective male relations.[22]

Queer Sweets

"What ho, Horatio!" shouts Hamlet. "Here, *sweet lord*, at your service," is the immediate response. "Horatio, thou art e'en as just a man / As e'er my conversation cop'd withal," comes the reply to that (3.2.52–55).[23] The historical queerness of this rhetoric, the way sweetness and the undisputed masculinity of male friendship in the period seem to us strangely to jostle, is partly a function of what we might think of as the emergent effeminacy of sugar—the way that, as Kim F. Hall has analyzed, sugar, following the advent of its colonial importation and over the course of its increasing use in early modern English households and cuisine, developed increasingly feminized associations.[24] (What, after all, are little girls made of?)

Even within a discourse of affect, however, it is not the case that sugar *was* one thing (masculine) and became another (feminine). In the evidence examined above from around 1600, sweetness is portable across our standard categories—as a language of affection between men, between men and women, and between women. This is true even within most of the texts I've mentioned thus far; indeed, the line I quoted from the end of *The Merchant of Venice* (Bassanio speaking to his wife as if she were still dressed as a doctor) encodes this when followed to its conclusion: "(Sweet Doctor) you shall be my bedfellow, / vvhen *I* am absent then lie with my wife" (sig. K1ᵛ). Anyone, it seems, can be sweet to anyone, perhaps in this instance even including *herself*, and including as well male-male relationships conceptualized as more explicitly hierarchical and thus unlike the male friendships I've already cited: Achilles and Patroclus repeatedly address each other as "sweet" in *Troilus and Cressida*, and, in perhaps the most explicitly pederastic literary text of the period, Richard Barnfield's 1595 sonnets address "Sweete Ganymede," a "sweete youth" and "sweet boy" with "hony-combs" "dropping" "from his lips."[25] Shakespeare engages this rhetoric in a similar context, especially but not only in the early sonnets of his sequence (those apparently to a young man), for example, sonnet 6, which encodes in its own complicated syntax the portability of the rhetoric of sweetness:

> let not winters wragged hand deface,
> In thee thy summer ere thou be distil'd:
> Make sweet some viall; treasure thou some place,
> With beautits treasure ere it be selfe kil'd.[26]

One of the sonnet's imperatives here is, of course, the exhortation to the young man to reproduce, to "make some vial sweet" (impregnate some womb). But, as I have argued elsewhere, there are multiple other possibilities for this line (possibilities that the indispensable Booth edition calls "logically incidental" but that I would view as logically "co-incidental"): "sweeten someone (something?) vile," and (as a direct address, because *sweet* was often used in this way, Leech's defensive gloss on *The Two Gentlemen of Verona* notwithstanding) "make, Sweet, some vial," as well as "construct some vial that is sweet."[27] Each of these potential meanings plays around the rhetoric of vile sodomy, through the staged lack of bodily referent: *some* vial, *any* vial. Indeed, the sonnet's original spelling, *viall*, signifying both the noun *vessel* and the adjective *disgusting*, blends in its multiplicity the "vile vial," the "improper vessel" (the anus) here sweetened.[28] As a reading of John Harington's water-closet treatise and Gail Kern Paster's work on it suggest, sweet smells, evacuation, anality, and desire are often inextricably bound in this culture, in ways that await further exploration.[29]

You may think this baseness far afield from the sweetness of the Prince and his friendship with Horatio, and yet I follow the scent, as Hamlet says to Horatio:

Dost thou think Alexander looked o' this fashion i'th'earth?

Hor. E'en so.

Ham. And smelt so? Pah!   [*Puts down the skull.*]

Hor. E'en so, my lord.

Ham. To what base uses we may return, Horatio! Why may not
imagination trace the noble dust of Alexander till [he] find it
stopping a bung-hole? (5.1.191–98)

What "bung-hole," you ask? "A beer-barrel," Hamlet elaborates (5.1.205); "the opening of a cask," notes the *Norton Shakespeare*, but Marlowe provides another gloss in a catalog of classical male-male relations: "The mightiest kings haue had their minions, / Great *Alexander* loude *Ephestion* [Hephaestion]."[30] Tracing the dust of Alexander, Hamlet (or the playwright, or both) may become a queer philologist here for a moment, imag/ining (picturing) in this word *bung-hole* a history of Alexander's male relations and a body part potentially involved. Though modern editions do not see such a picture here, as contemporaneous a source as Randle Cotgrave's 1611 French-English translation dictionary equates "the bung-hole, fundament, nock-androe" in glossing French *trou*.[31] The play provides no suggestion of how Hamlet smelled to Horatio, but Thomas North's Plutarch records of Alexander that "his skin had a maruelous good sauor, & . . . his breath was very swete, insomuch that his body had so swete a smell of it selfe, that all the apparell [he] wore next vnto his body, tooke thereof a passing delightfull sauor, as if it had bene perfumed."[32]

Etymology and Memory

Can a smell, or a taste, be remembered, evoked, brought back to life from memory? Scientific opinion is divided on this question.[33] Can the history of a taste's or a smell's accumulated meanings or associations be reconstituted in the present? An aspect of my argument in this chapter and in the larger book is that, in our study of the erotic and affective past, we have not sufficiently attended to *etymology*—the history of words (the history *in* words). I do not mean that we need to occupy ourselves with the pursuit of "word origins" or of etymology for its own sake, but rather to be more carefully attuned to the ways that etymologies, shorn of their associations with "origin," persist in a word and its surrounding discourse, as a diachronic record of practice in the midst of language as a synchronic system.[34]

What, then, lingers in *sweet*—a very old English word, traceable back through Old English and associated Teutonic uses, to a hypothesized Indo-European root? It is closely related to the Greek verbs for "to rejoice" and "to please," and, according to the *Oxford English Dictionary* (*OED*), to Latin *suavis* (sweet) and *suadere* (to advise) "properly, to make something pleasant to." *Sweet* is thus related etymologically to *persuade* and its shortened early modern synonym, *suade*. Both *sweet* and *suade* are related to *suave*, which in early modern English signified "[p]leasing or agreeable to the senses *or the mind*; sweet."[35]

The *OED* places these associations in the dim, even *hypothetical*, linguistic past, but the linking of persuasion and sweetness is ubiquitous in English around 1600, even though or perhaps because *persuade* is a comparatively late arrival in English, "not in general use until [the] 16th c." In *The English Secretorie*, one of Angel Day's Erasmian categories of letters is "swasorie" (suasory).[36] Thomas Campion, Thomas Middleton, Thomas Dekker, Shakespeare, Ben Jonson, Cyril Tourneur, and Philip Massinger, to name a few, all use the phrase "sweet persuasion(s)," or the words in similar close proximity to each other, in the early seventeenth century. An astonishing example of this recurrent phrase (etymologically "redundant," as we have seen) appears in a commendatory poem to William Cartwright's *Comedies, Tragi-comedies, With other Poems* of 1651, describing the writer's effect:

> A pleasing horror strook through every limb,
> And every Ear was close chain'd up to Him:
> Such Masculine vigour ravish'd our assent;
> What He Perswaded, was Commandement:
> A sweeter plenty Rhetorick ne'r knew
> In *Ch[r]ysostome's* Pulpit, nor in *Tully's* Pew.[37]

Notice that the redoubled instrumentality of the phrase "sweet persuasion" is strongly present in the instances of male friendship I have already quoted, several of these involving letters, a connection that perhaps should not surprise us, given Erasmus's emphasis on the persuasive as a major type of letter: "Cease to perswade, my louing *Protheus*," says "sweet *Valentine*" (*Two Gentlemen*, TLN 4, 14). "Sweet Bassanio," says Antonio's letter, "if your loue do not perswade you to come, let not my letter." Like Cartwright's commanding vigor, Edward II's epistolary persuasion is yet more ravishing: "Sweete prince I come," says Gaveston, "these these thy amorous lines, / Might haue *enforst* me to haue swum from France" (my emphasis).

Etymology, then, in its lingering tastes of the past in the present, forces us to develop ever-expanding lexicons of erotic and affective terms and their relations. Not only a backward-looking *history*, etymology as a practice looks forward to remind us that words that seem identical and familiar to modern eyes and tongues we might better see as false cognates ("false friends," as we used to say in French class)—words that only *pass* as "the same" as ours, words that, when pressed, release whole new contexts, while also holding within themselves the genealogical seeds of their eventual direction. *Friend* and *sweet* are both examples. Seeing (or rather, smelling, tasting, even feeling, as in Cartwright's "pleasing horror" in "every limb") the embodied, instrumental dynamics of the *persuasion* embedded in *sweet* is central to an understanding of early modern male relations and the letters that write them. There is no reading the queer address without philology.

Sweet Thing

Allow me to sketch one of several directions in which an understanding of early modern male-male sweetness might proceed. What does it mean to think of a friend as "sweet" in early modern culture? Sugar and spices, Sidney W. Mintz argues, were not initially considered food in early modern culture,[38] and Patricia Fumerton follows Mintz to argue, in her analysis of the early modern practices of the banquet and the "void" course, that sugar was, instead, a medicine: "Ingested with full consciousness of their rareness, the sugar and spice of void confectionary . . . became a sort of ornamental talisman worn within the body. They were jewel-laxatives serving to 'open obstructions,' 'purge superfluous humors,' purify or 'cleanse the body,' aid digestion . . . , refresh or comfort 'the spirits and vital parts,' and cherish 'the whole Body exceedingly.'"[39] Is *this* the sweet prince Horatio is tasting? "No medicine in the world can do thee good," Laertes says to Hamlet in the play's final moments (5.2.320), but Horatio survives. Is the sweet friend of early modernity not only "swasorie" (persuasive) but also curative?

By virtue of this rhetorical and etymological surround, sweetness may ask us to collate two observations about early modern bodies: first, the commonplace, copied out of Aristotle and endlessly recirculated, that friends are "one soul in two bodies"; second, the idea of the fungible, humoral body, a conduit for liquids, humors, passions, and so forth.[40] As a recurrent term in friendship's vocabulary, *sweet* indicates the fungibility of male friends—not merely the exchangeability and indistinguishability of identities or selves, but also the way in which what we have regarded as an identity trope is imagined in this culture as literally embodied. Responding to Horatio's hailing, "sweet lord," and hailing Horatio as "e'en as just a man / As e'er my conversation cop'd withal," Hamlet had earlier juxtaposed to this friendship "the candied tongue" of the flatterer that "lick[s] absurd pomp," but concludes:

> Give me that man
> That is not passion's slave, and I will wear him
> In my heart's core, ay, in my heart of heart,
> As I do thee. (3.2.60, 71–74)

How many souls, how many bodies here? Bray describes a 1619 chapel monument to Thomas Legge built by his friend John Gostlin; it shows two hands holding aloft a flaming heart and the inscription reads, in translation, "Love [Amor] joined them living. So may the earth join them in their burial. *O Legge, Gostlin's heart you have still with you.*"[41] Alongside this rhetoric and iconography, consider Cotgrave, translating the French verb *persuader*: "To persuade; aduise, exhort, moue, induce, vnto; to make beleeue, breed beliefe, put *into the head*, make *sinke into* the thought, or mind."[42]

Margreta de Grazia and Juliet Fleming have each asked whether words may function as things in early modernity,[43] and, by sketching all too briefly this array of associations, I seek to ask whether in this context words, and specifically the discourse of sweetness, are conceptualized as part of the material that constitutes and flows across and through the fungible bodies of early modern male friends. Lynne Magnusson's comments on the materiality of Erasmus's epistolary rhetoric are striking in this sense, whatever he might have said about using *sweet* as an epithet for boys as well as girls: "For Erasmus, the dialogic forms of address developed in the epistolary scripts for various occasions are not just forms in words: they are forms of life, the material substance of relationships."[44]

From this perspective, there is an astonishing passage in Florio's translation of Montaigne's friendship essay that I continue to return to, having elsewhere read it as an attempt to imagine mutual and unhierarchized same-sex intercourse,[45] for it seems to acknowledge the idea of friendship as material ingestion and incorporation—the taste or smell of the friend as refined, medicinal, "ornamental talisman," in Fumerton's phrase:

> [Friendship] is I wot not what kinde of quintessence of all this commixture, which having seized all my will, induced the same to plunge and loose it selfe in his, which likewise having seized all his will, brought it to loose and plunge it selfe in mine, with a mutuall greedinesse, and with a semblable concurrance.[46]

At least as ideally imagined in these texts, the sweetness of the friend, I would argue, is immersed, embedded, plunged, set loose within; it circulates; it inhabits. Hamlet reminds Horatio near the moment of his death of the earlier heart exchange: "If thou didst ever *hold me in* thy heart, / Absent thee from felicity a while . . ." (5.2.351–52, my emphasis). Further, Horatio invokes *as his own* Hamlet's "mouth" twice in the final speeches of the play: "Of that I shall have also cause to speak, / And from his mouth whose voice will draw on more" (5.2.396–97).[47] The rest is not silence, but Horatio.[48] A similar sense of incorporating the friend's sweetness is suggested in

Three Proper, and Wittie, Familiar Letters, where, in a passage that Jonathan Goldberg illuminates, Immerito (Edmund Spenser) wishes from G.H. (Gabriel Harvey), "'a Reciprocall farewell from your owne sweete mouth'" and G.H. reciprocally desires that "'I may personally performe your request, and bestowe the sweetest Farewell, upon your sweetmouthed Mastershippe.'"[49]

Such reciprocal, material sweetness between men is not addressed just onstage or in letters; in one of the first references to Shakespeare as a writer, Francis Meres indicates his fungibility, in a passage stuffed with epithets: "the sweete wittie soule of *Ouid* liues in mellifluous & hony-tongued *Shakespeare*." "[W]itness," Meres adds, "his sugred Sonnets among his priuate friends."[50] Sweetness is here again a trope for circulation or fungibility, not just among bodies but (again) across senses: "Mellifluous," glosses Thomas Blount in his 1656 *Glossographia*, "sweet as honey, that out of which honey flows: Also elequent of speech"; "Eloquent," Cotgrave translates, "well-spoken, of a sweet deliuerie."[51] Like Alexander, the persuasive smell, or sound, of Shakespeare persists. In his poem prefacing the Shakespeare first folio, what is Jonson tasting when he addresses the "*Sweet Swan of* Auon"? What is Milton tasting, smelling, hearing, incorporating, curing, when he addresses "Sweetest Shakespear fancies childe"?[52] What are little boys (and English authors) made of?

Postscript (Self-Addressed)

As my discussion has already suggested, addressing the mode of address in letters between men and (as Magnusson shows) some of the other verbal forms that take them up, like stage plays, may bring to our attention something crucial about the relationship between friendship and letters. Friendship, as is well known, is both the condition of possibility for letter writing in early modern culture—whatever the variety of their address in practice, letters were at least conceptualized, most influentially by Erasmus, as "a conversation [mutual exchange of speech] between absent friends"[53]—and a potentially deconstructive reduplication. Why should one soul in two bodies seek to address itself? What is the effect of conceptualizing a genre as self-addressed? Hey, me there! (Hey, us here?)

This is a question that the letter that opens *Edward II* plays with, in performance if not in the printed text. Onstage there is the following scene: an unnamed man, a mystery, appears with a letter, which he reads:

My father is deceast, come *Gaueston*,
And share the kingdom with thy deerest friend
Ah words that make me surfet with delight:

What greater blisse can hap to *Gaueston,*
Then liue and be the fauorit of a king? (sig. A2)

This relationship is immediately visible as another of what Stewart has called "reading friendship[s],"[54] but, without the stage direction in the printed text ("*Enter* Gauestone *reading on a letter that was brought him from the king*") or the speech heading that appears in modern editions, it is possible for at least two lines of the performance, and perhaps five, to experience this letter as read by either its addresser or its addressee. And then the man addresses a reply and becomes not-Edward:

Sweete prince I come, these these thy amorous lines,
Might haue enforst me to haue swum from France,
And like *Leander* gaspt vpon the sande,
So thou wouldst smile and take me in thy armes.

The play's play with this problem is famously emphasized later in the scene, when Edward first hails his friend:

What *Gaueston*, welcome: kis not my hand,
Embrace me *Gaueston* as I do thee:
Why shouldst thou kneele,
Knowest thou not who I am?
Thy friend, thy selfe, another *Gaueston*[.] (sig. A4ᵛ)

In its opening sleight-of-hand/letter/person, the play brings together the fungibility (here heavily stigmatized by the nobles of the play) of friends who address each other in the rhetoric of sweetness/persuasion.

I would also want to emphasize the way that friendship as incorporation and simultaneity may give us some analytic purchase on Erasmus's predication of letters on absence. As Goldberg argues, "The 'original' that the letter replaces (bodily presence of the face-to-face and the oral; mental intuition and intention) is also structured as the letter is, since such proximities are always already distanced by the letter (in its linguistic definition). Letters, which cover distance, also function in the gap that divides any moment, and their space and modes of presence are how presence is constituted."[55] Put another way, we might see the (only ostensibly) absent address of sweetness as a performative address that, in its absence, creates the conditions of presence, in a world in which the constant reinscriptions of friendly relations between men are a powerful social structure. What taste, what smell or other remnant of affect, is a letter addressed to "Sweet Bassanio" said to carry and restore?[56] To imagine such a possibility is therefore explicitly not to treat sweetness (or the rhetorics of affection more generally) as mere rhetorical flourish; the epithet—the supplement here—is both additive and constitutive, and friendly presence itself is thereby seen not as a presence to be lost, but as a production of exchange. Or, translating "production" into early modern English (and attempting to actualize all possible puns and etymologies), we might say that, in a world that apparently did not take (what I will call) male-order sweets as lightly as we do, the epithet is a confection. A "medicinal preparation compounded of various drugs," the epithet-as-confection "sweeten[s]"; it is a "prepared dish or delicacy," "a preserve, sweetmeat, comfit."[57] Like friendship and friendship's letters, it is compounded, confected, comfit—etymologically "made or done *with*."

Extended "Conversation": Living with Christopher Marlowe; a Brief History of "Intercourse"

I myselfe readinge mine owne woorkes, am sometime in that case, that I thincke *Cato* telleth the tale, and not myselfe.

I woulde that for a while you shoulde not thincke vpon me, but suppose that *Lælius* hymselfe speaketh.

—Cicero to his friend Atticus, as translated by Thomas Newton, in the Preface to *The Booke of Freendshippe*[1]

[T]hey vsed not onely one boord, but one bedde, one booke (if so be it they thought not one to many) . . . all things went in cõmon betweene them, which all men accompted cõmendable.

—John Lyly, *Euphues*[2]

Conversation

In the sixteenth and seventeenth centuries, the word *conversation*, along with the related terms *converse* and *conversant*, had a much more complex aura of meanings than it has for us today. By far the oldest meaning of *conversation*, from the fourteenth century onward, concerns living in a place or dwelling among a group of people, as in the question the *Oxford English Dictionary* (*OED*) locates in 1483, "where conuersest thou"?,[3] or the 1611 Authorized Version's use, "For our conuersation is in heauen,"[4] a usage for which the 1881 Revised Standard Version tellingly substitutes "citizenship."[5] A related obsolete meaning of *conversation* is "[t]he action of consorting or having dealings with others; . . . commerce, intercourse, society, intimacy." As Valentine says of his friend Protheus in Shake-speare's *Two Gentlemen of Verona*, "from our Infancie / We haue conuerst, and spent our howres together."[6] Some other related meanings circulating in the sev-enteenth century are one's "conversation" or "Circle of acquaintance, company, society" and "behaviour, mode or course of life." Indeed, according to some hard-word lists and translation dictionaries that the *OED* does not cite, these are the most prominent seventeenth-century meanings of the term: John Bullokar's *An English Expositor* (1616) glosses "*Conuersant* [as] Vsing much in ones company;"[7] John Minsheu's *Ductor in Linguas, The Guide into the tongues* (1617) defines *con-verse* as "*accompanie, or associate much or often*";[8] and John Florio translates the Italian "Conuersatione" as "*conuersation, societie.*"[9]

Add to this the closely related sense that is now largely the *only* meaning for *conversation*, beginning around 1586: "Interchange of thoughts and words; famil-iar discourse or talk"—what Cyril Tourneur called in 1609 "[c]onversation (the commerce of minds)."[10] One specialized meaning that persisted at least until the end of the sixteenth century we might understand to be related, through the per-suasive quality of familiar discourse: conversation as conversion, what Coverdale, translating the Acts of the Apostles in 1535, called "the conuersacion of the Heythen."[11] (Here the Latin etymology, through French, of the related terms seems especially resonant: "to turn oneself about, to move to and fro, pass one's life, dwell, abide."[12])

I have largely kept out of (the) conversation thus far an important resonance of this word, the meaning the *OED* dates from the early sixteenth century as "[s]exual intercourse or intimacy."[13] According to the *OED*, at least, this early modern mean-ing remains in circulation until just after the emergence of the term *sexual inter-course*, which seems in some sense to take its place around 1800, as Juliet Fleming has noted.[14] (We will return to this intersection, along with the later legal term *criminal conversation*, toward the end of this chapter.) There are some key differ-ences between early modern *conversation* and modern *sexual intercourse* to which we will return, but here I cite briefly some appearances of conversation-as-intercourse: Shakespeare's Richard III's condemnation of Lord Hasting's "Conuer-sation with Shores Wife"; a clearly sexual 1649 discussion of "a conjugall conversa-tion"; or, most succinctly, a 1646 Thomas Browne usage of cross-race, cross-sex exchange that makes related or synonymous the terms "converse or copulation."[15]

Sexual conversation, in this sense, seems often to be figured as illicit or explic-itly condemned, at least when it refers to what we would now call heterosexual relations. In *Richard III*, Hastings's severed head is displayed onstage as recom-pense for his "conversation with Shore's wife." Arcite and Palamon, conversing together in prison in Fletcher and Shakespeare's *The Two Noble Kinsmen*, usefully illustrate this meaning: "We are young," Arcite says,

> and yet desire the waies of honour,
> That liberty and common Conversation
> The poyson of pure spirits; might like women
> Wooe us to wander from.[16]

The passage suggests that one kind of conversation—between kinsmen—must ostensibly be protected from other kinds of conversation: "common" conversation (conversation among/across social classes) and cross-gender conversation (associated with "liberty," promiscuity, and wandering). Cross-sex *conversation*, in this and many other instances, seems always potentially to register a transgression; the *OED*'s citation of a 1656 sermon demonstrates this in its very insistence on the condoned nature of the intercourse: "They may *lawfully* converse together as man and wife."[17] As this evidence begins to suggest, the problem for early modern culture may be the uneasiness (in both senses) of imagining the possibility of an equitable conversation between the heterosexes—as well as the problem, as perceived from the hegemonic masculinist perspective, of men's potential effeminization through heterosexual practices. In 1615, George Sandys writes of men who are "[e]nfeebled with the continual conuerse of women,"[18] and John Florio, translating Montaigne's friendship essay in 1603, neatly outlines the misogynist assumption, employing two closely related terms: "the ordinary sufficiencie of women, cannot answer [the] *conference* and *communication* [of male friendship] . . . , nor seeme their mindes strong enough to endure the pulling of a knot so hard, so fast, and durable."[19] "Cannot answer": cannot aspire to, but also, in the context of the exchange of words and ideas, cannot reply, cannot converse.[20]

In contrast to this pejorative portrayal of the impossibilities and dangers of cross-sex conference and communication, *conversation*, in the discourse of male-male friendship explored through the discourse of persuasive "sweet"-ness in Chapter 2, inscribes a model of the exchange of ideas, discourse, talk, even identities based in a notion of equitableness.[21] (Whether it brings with it, from "heterosexual" contexts into this privileged same-sex space, some of the derogated sense of what we would call "sexual" [genital] conversation remains to be seen, but certainly a heavy charge of affect and intimacy accompanies it.) Thus, as we saw in Chapter 2, male friendship in Montaigne's essay is figured as a "semblable concurrence," and I emphasize here that all of these terms associated with the exchange of discourse and ideas are also insistently *spatial*. Etymologically, a *concurrence* is a running together; to *converse* is to dwell or live together; *conversion*, as Bullokar defines it, is a "*turning* from euill to good";[22] to *converse* is also to turn about, to reverse course and discourse.[23] Speaking of space, these terms situate a study of conversation—and also, I argue, of textual exchange and replication—at a complicated nexus of interrelated discourses. *Conversation* can be dwelling in a place or among a group of people; interchange of thoughts and words; commerce, society, intimacy; sexual intercourse or intimacy; or conversion.

Shuffling

> When J was first suspected for that Libell that concern'd
> the state, amongst those waste and idle papers (which J
> carde not for) & which unaskt J did deliuer vp, were
> founde some fragmentes of a disputation toching that
> opinion affirmed by Marlowe to be his, and shufled with
> some of myne (vnknown to me) by some occasion of our
> wrytinge in one chamber twoe yeares synce.
> —Thomas Kyd[24]

These words, taken from one of the few texts we can closely associate with the playwright Thomas Kyd, are from his letter—somewhat frantic in tone, befitting someone who has recently been tortured by order of the Privy Council—to Sir John Puckering, the Lord Keeper and a member of that council. Kyd's words in this letter are usually read as evidence that he and Christopher Marlowe lived together during the time that both were writing plays for the Lord Strange's Men, among other companies; as Jonathan Goldberg carefully (if somewhat chastely) phrases it in "Sodomy and Society: The Case of Christopher Marlowe," Kyd was Marlowe's "fellow playwright and sometime roommate."[25] For the purposes of the present discussion, I do not want to lose sight of the probability that Kyd and Marlowe lived together, but I do want to note that the evidence that suggests this emphasizes Marlowe and Kyd's *intellectual* conversation as a part of their domestic and/or sexual converse: their pages get "shufled," Kyd says, on "some occasion of our wrytinge in one chamber." Kyd is at some pains, probably literal pains, to separate himself and his papers from Marlowe, but, far from discounting this evidence as the tattletaling of a terrorized early modern subject (though it is certainly also that), I want to point out that implicit in Kyd's letter, the story that he circulates because it is believable to Elizabeth I's secret service, is the story that the papers of playwrights get "shufled" together. This is also the implicit assumption of, for example, the title page to *The Spanish Tragedy*, the only play attributed to Kyd in the period;[26] early seventeenth-century editions describe the play as "[n]ewly corrected, amended, and enlarged with new Additions of the Painters part, and others, as it hath of late been diuers times acted."[27] These may or may not be the famous "additions" to this play, also known as *Jeronimo*, for which Philip Henslowe recorded payment to Ben Jonson in 1601–2—

vnto bengemy Johnsone
Lent ^ at the a poyntment of E Alleyn
& w^m birde the 22 of June 1602
in earneste of a Boocke called Richard   x^ll
crockbacke & for new adicyons for
Jeronymo the some of . . . .[28]

But for the purposes of the present analysis (an analysis of the shuffling of play-wrights' papers) it makes little difference. In fact, the undecidability of the question (whose adicyons?) further illustrates the point.[29] As the manuscript of the play *Sir Thomas More* strongly suggests—a play, as Scott McMillin has argued, written for the Lord Strange's Men at about the time Marlowe and Kyd were writing in one chamber, a play concerned, as we will see in Chapter 9, with incidents of anti-alien riots and libels of the same kind that eventuated in Kyd's arrest—early modern playwrights were far less interested in keeping their hands, pages, and conversation separate than are the twentieth-century critics who have studied them.[30]

Thinking about Marlowe and Kyd writing together in one chamber, we could indeed start with the hands of the documents in question, since, unlike the man-uscripts of most plays from this period, these manuscripts exist, and include one signed letter from Kyd to Puckering,[31] one apparently unsigned letter from Kyd to Puckering,[32] and some pages of what Kyd calls "some fragmentes of a disputation toching that opinion affirmed by Marlowe to be his."[33] The letters are written in a legal style of secretary hand; the "fragmentes of a disputation"—an extract from a sixteenth-century printed theological tract on the Arian heresy—are in an en-tirely different hand, an italic hand, an observation that might at first seem to support Kyd's implication that they are Marlowe's. But looking more closely, we can also notice, as has Marlowe's biographer, C. F. Tucker Brooke,[34] that the hand of the disputation, the italic hand, is also a style of hand that Kyd has and uses, in the signed letter, for emphasis (e.g., in the words *Atheisme* and *Atheist* [Figures 15–16]) and, as we shall see, for Latin quotations and commonplaces, like his quo-tation on male friendship, from "Tullie" (Cicero) (Figure 17).

FIGURES 15 and 16. Excerpts from a letter of Thomas Kyd concerning Christopher Marlowe, Harley MS 6849, f. 218. © The British Library Board.

Keeping in mind that one signature is all that may remain of Christopher Marlowe's handwriting,[35] and keeping in mind that Thomas Kyd, if he is the Thomas Kyd we think he is, was the son of a scrivener, is thought briefly to have followed his father into that trade,[36] and could (as we see in his letter) write with at least two hands, we have a number of questions to ask. Whose hand is whose? Are the fragments, already a quotation from an earlier tract, also written out *by* Kyd *for* Marlowe?[37] How do we read the ambiguity (ambidexterity?) of Kyd's syntax, "some fragmentes of a disputation toching that opinion affirmed by Marlowe to be his and shufled with some of myne"? Are the papers, or the opinion in them, or *both* "affirmed by Marlowe to be his"? How closely does Marlowe's opinion touch the disputation? How closely do Marlowe's opinions touch Kyd's? What has been shuffled? What is the extent of the shuffling?

I do not favor bringing out the paleographical evidence as if it could answer these questions or as if these are the pertinent questions to ask in the first place.[38] We should notice that these questions, which seem to be called up by the evidence itself, and which seem also to be very much like default modern questions about the authorship of Renaissance plays (who wrote which pages?), are questions structurally akin to those formulated by the intervention of early modern power into this shared chamber. In the words of the Privy Council order that eventuated in (though it did not call specifically for) the arrest of Thomas Kyd, the civil authorities were ordered

> to make search and apprehend every person . . . to be suspected [in this matter], and for that purpose to enter into all houses and places where any such may be remaining. And, upon their apprehension, to make like search in any the chambers, studies, chests, or other like places for all manner of writings or papers that may give you light for the discovery of the libellers. And after you shall have examined the persons, if you shall find them duly to be suspected, and they shall refuse to confess the truth, you shall by authority hereof put them to the torture in Bridewell.[39]

Separating the authorship of the Kyd/Marlowe papers, though it is apparently Kyd's idea at this juncture, is a strategy produced in reaction to the state and the state's regulation of an apparently extra-theatrical matter. It does not seem to have occurred to Kyd to mark with such precision the authorship of anything else he wrote. The same holds for Marlowe.

I want to consider Marlowe and Kyd's relation (and thus potentially consider early modern male-male relations more generally)[40] in terms that are both less anachronistic in resisting "solving" questions of individual authorship and less on the side of a certain mode of state power, by looking instead at the language of conversation—of society, acquaintance, intimacy—that pervades these documents. Perusing the terms, manuscripts, and intertexts that constitute that intimacy will require queer philology.

To be sure, Kyd's discussion of friendship with Marlowe (freshly and usefully dead at the moment of Kyd's writing) is entirely in the negative. Though he discloses that they have in some sense shared one chamber and an unnamed patron for whose company they both wrote plays, he also refers to Marlowe distantly as "this Marlowe" ("My first acquaintance with this Marlowe, rose vpon his bearing name to serve my Lord although his Lordship never knewe his service, but in writing for his plaiers"). And Kyd's repudiation of Marlowe, when it comes, could hardly be more emphatic:

> That J shold Loue or be familer frend, with one so irreligious, were verie rare when *Tullie* saith *Digni sunt amicitia quibus in ipsis inest causa cur diligantur* which neither was in him, for person, quallities, or honestie, besides he was intemperate & of a cruel hart, the verie contraries to which, my greatest enemies will saie by me.[41]

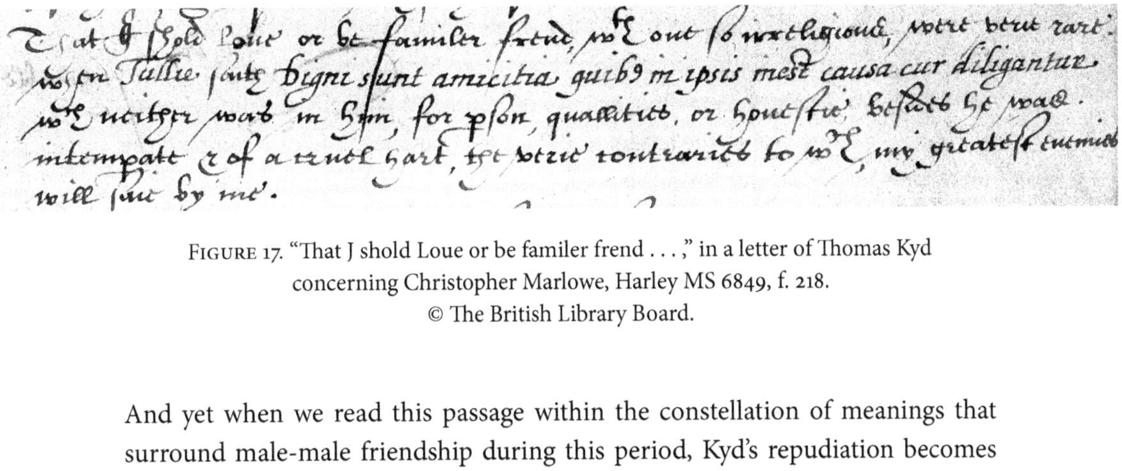
That J shold Loue or be familer frend, wth one so irreligious, were verie rare.
when Tullie saith Digni sunt amicitia quib9 in ipsis inest causa cur diligantur.
wch neither was in him, for pson, quallities, or honestie, besides he was.
intemperate & of a cruel hart, the verie contraries to wch, my greatest enemies
will saie by me.

FIGURE 17. "That J shold Loue or be familer frend . . . ," in a letter of Thomas Kyd concerning Christopher Marlowe, Harley MS 6849, f. 218. © The British Library Board.

And yet when we read this passage within the constellation of meanings that surround male-male friendship during this period, Kyd's repudiation becomes much more complicated. Inscribed in italic hand (see Figure 17), the Latin quotation, from Cicero's "De Amicitia," or dialogue on friendship, is straightforward enough: "they bee worthye of Frendshippe, in whom there is good cause why they should be loued," reads the 1577 Thomas Newton translation.[42] The quotation thus implies that Kyd and Marlowe were never friends, because Marlowe was not worthy. But the quotation derives from a section of the dialogue on the ending of intimate male-male friendships that *have* existed: "There is also somtimes (as it were) a certain calamity or mishap," Cicero writes (and Newton translates), "in the departure from frendes."[43] Read in relation to Cicero's dialogue, the letter denying friendship seems suddenly suffused with, haunted by, a dead friendship.

"That J shold loue or be familer frend, with one so irreligious, were verie rare," Kyd writes, and Cicero's text uses the same word, *rare* (*rara*), in an exclamation that directly follows the line Kyd quotes, to describe the "rare class" (*rarum genus*) of friends worthy to be loved, and then again to amplify on this rarity: "It is a rare thing [*Rarum genus!*] (for surely al excellent things are rare [*rara*]) & theris nothĩg harder, then to finde a thing which in euery respect in his kinde is throughlye perfect."[44] "All excellent thinges are rare," declares the marginal gloss on this sentence in the 1577 translation, and in this context, Kyd's rare love or familiar friendship with Marlowe begins to look not only rare (unusual), but also rare (valuable, excellent).

Read through the classical text it prominently cites, Kyd's letter is haunted by Marlowe in another sense as well, for Cicero's dialogue, often called "Laelius on Friendship," stages a conversation in which several interlocutors question Laelius on his feelings of grief upon the death of his close friend Scipio. Kyd, writing a few days after Marlowe's death, repudiating his acquaintance with "this Marlowe," quotes a classical dialogue on friendship in which the central figure speaks of his grief for the death of a close friend.[45] (It is perhaps not inappropriate, in contextualizing the playwright Kyd's quotation of Laelius at a central moment in his letter about another playwright, to note that, in the words of the Loeb edition's introduction, "Laelius was such a master of elegant diction that the plays of his poet-friend Terence, which were so much admired for the purity of their Latinity, were by many attributed in whole or in part to him."[46]) Given Kyd's allusive writing practice elsewhere in the letters to Puckering, a queer philology can read the recourse to classical quotation, in Latin, as itself a marker for, inscription of, a kind of male relations in this context: Marlowe, Kyd writes, "wold report St John to be our saviour Christes *Alexis* J cover it with reverence and trembling that is that Christ did loue him with an extraordinary loue."[47] To cover it with reverence and trembling is to allude to Virgil's homoerotic second eclogue, to cite Corydon's desire for Alexis; extraordinary love (*rarum genus*?) is made to speak Latin, and Kyd's denial of love and friendship with Marlowe, written in Latin and another hand, begins to speak another language, the language of male-male conversation.

What—we might pause for a moment to ask—is covered by reference to Tullie? "The Romaine *Tullie* loued *Octauis*," says Marlowe's character, Mortimer Senior, in his catalog of the "mightiest kings" and "their minions," "[a]nd not kings onelie, but the wisest men."[48] Editors have been quick to straighten out the relation of the "real" Cicero and Octavius, but what matters here is what these Latin names may have covered, or referenced, for Marlowe, Kyd, and others in their culture.

Walter J. Ong has argued that the learning of Latin itself functioned as a male puberty rite in English culture, separating the men from the boys and the women,[49] and it is worth recalling that the reading of Latin, and particularly of the Romaine Tullie, was an everyday part of male education during the period.

While at Cambridge, for example, Marlowe and his fellow students would have attended "a rhetorick lecture, of some p[ar]t of Tully, for the space of an houre," every afternoon at three o'clock.[50] (Kyd's education at the Merchant Taylors' School would have been similar in style and curriculum.[51]) Cicero is built into the structure of, and central to the rhetoric of, the everydayness of male-male relations in this era. These are some of the cultural associations of Kyd's recourse to Cicero; even as the letters to Puckering deny close acquaintance or conversation with Marlowe, they inscribe it, in terms that also closely recall what both Goldberg and Bruce R. Smith have identified as the early modern homoerotic classical pastoral and Stephen Guy-Bray has called pastoral's "homoerotic space."[52] "*Eglogue*," says the definition in a dictionary of 1613, "a talking together." This, the *OED* insists, is an "erroneous" definition of *eclogue*,[53] but we are reading here in conversation's intersecting spaces: "Come *live with me* and be my love," Marlowe writes elsewhere, precipitating a number of reply poems from other men, shuffled (as Arthur Marotti and Wendy Wall have noted) in numerous commonplace books and manuscripts: "Come live with me . . . / And we will *all the pleasures* prove."[54]

The covering and uncovering of male relations in the Kyd/Marlowe case seems to play the line Alan Bray has identified between condemned sodomy and condoned male friendship during this period, and the larger discursive problem in these letters (and here I would include the more famous testimony of Richard Baines in the same case, which Goldberg has analyzed in detail) is one of distinguishing, if and where appropriate, the languages of male relations.[55] Baines, too, says Marlowe associated Christ and St. John the Evangelist, though unlike Kyd he does not "cover it with reverence and trembling," writing instead that Christ "vsed him as the sinners of Sodoma."[56] For Baines the problem is to remain outside Marlowe's discourse of male relations, even as he announces its proselytizing dangerousness: he testifies that "this Marlow [marlow in MS] doth not only hould [these opinions] himself, but *almost into every Company he Cometh* he perswades men to Atheism . . . as J Richard Baines will Justify & approue both by mine oth and the testimony of many honest men, and *almost al men with whome he hath Conversed* any time will testify the same."[57] Marlowe's conversation, in this context, is *conversion*, the "conuersacion [to] the Heythen"—and again can be read over into other modes of persuasive conversation: "If these delights *thy mind may move*; / Then *live with mee*, and be *my love*."[58] Such conversation/conversion must be marked as both irresistible (and thus threatening to the state) *and* as not fully successful (thus allowing Baines to testify as one not "perswade[d] . . . to Atheism"). Kyd's attempts, too, to separate himself from Marlowe's papers, person, and circle of conversation face the same problem: to disclose an intimate knowledge of Marlowe and at the same time to disavow acquaintance, society, intimacy, conversion: "[For] more assurance that J was not of that vile opinion [of atheism],

Lett it but please your Lordship to enquire of such as he *conversd* withall; that is (as J am geven to vnderstand) with *Harriot, Warner, Royden* and some stationers in Paules churchyard, whom J in no sort can accuse nor will excuse by reson of his companie; of whose *consent* if J had been, no question but J also shold haue been of their *consort*."[59]

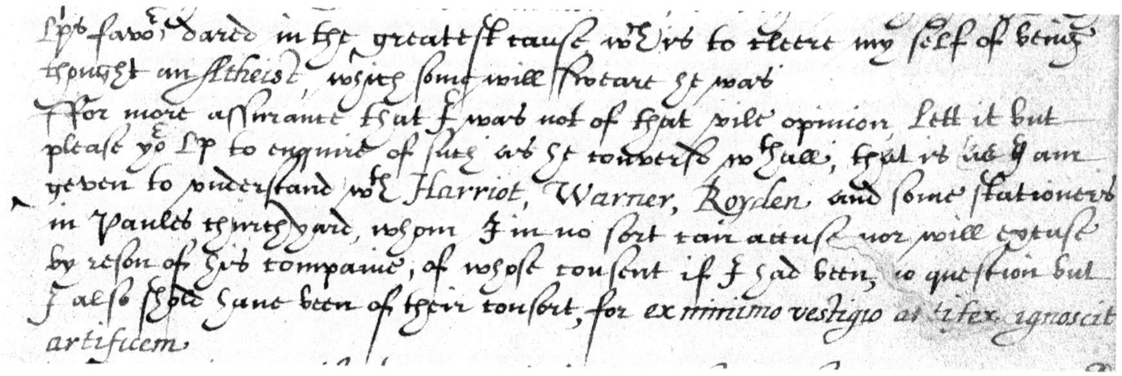
Lps fauors haue in this greatest cause wch is to cleere my self of being
thought an Atheist, which some will sweare he was
For more assurance that I was not of that vile opinion Lett it but
please yor Lp to enquire of such as he conversd w^thall, that is (as I am
geven to vnderstand) wth Harriot, Warner, Royden, and some stationers
in Paules churchyard, whom I in no sort can accuse nor will excuse
by reson of his companie, of whose consent if I had been, no question but
I also shold haue been of their consort, for ex minimo vestigio artifex agnoscit
artificem.

FIGURE 18. "[S]uch as he conversd withall . . . ," in a letter of Thomas Kyd concerning Christopher Marlowe, Harley MS 6849, f. 218. © The British Library Board.

Consent goes with consort and with conversing. To agree is to be in the same place. This link is perhaps dangerous ground for Kyd, who has already admitted consorting with Marlowe. The closeness of a later conduct book's phrase to describe male "acquaintance" (there it is called "consenting Consort")[60] can serve as a reminder of the continuing strength of that linkage within the discourse of male friendship in the seventeenth century—even if, in Kyd, it appears under negation ("as J am geven to vnderstand . . . if J had been").[61] Again, it is important to emphasize that there is no such thing as a simple factual reading of these documents; Baines's and Kyd's attempts to separate themselves from networks of conversation, conversion, and acquaintance, like Kyd's attempt to straighten up his shuffled papers, are a reaction to state intervention, in the context of a political situation that, for reasons we do not fully understand, was considered by the authorities to have been extremely volatile.[62]

Dwelling

In belaboring Kyd's (and Baines's) remarks about Marlowe, I seek to extend our notion of early modern *converse* or *conversation*, to use a philological problem—the problem of translating out of (or back into) early modern English some of the range of meanings we no longer associate with these terms—in order to open out a discussion of some wider questions of material practice: of what we would call writing practices and domestic practices, affect, and their interrelation. These documents employ this discourse here only under negation—only in the disclosures they make that seem to oppose their expressed intent of distance from, rather than proximity to, Marlowe. But, again, following the cue of *converse* to think spatially, we might place Marlowe and Kyd, writing in one chamber of undisclosed location, next to another circle of acquaintance that conversed, or dwelt among, some other houses and playhouses, on the Bankside in Southwark.

"Item," writes Thomas Pope, a resident of St. Saviour's parish in Southwark, an actor in the Lord Chamberlain's Men, and a shareholder in the Globe and the Curtain, "I geue and bequeth to robart gough [his apprentice, later himself an actor with the King's Men] and Iohn edmans [another apprentice of Pope's and an actor in Queen Anne's company] all my wering aparrell and all my armes to be equally deuided betwene them."[63] About two years later, in his 1605 will, Augustine Phillips—an actor in the Lord Chamberlain's and then the King's Men and, like Pope, a shareholder in the Globe—gives "vnto Samuell Gilborne my Late Aprentice the some of ffortye shillinges and my mouse Colloured veluit hose and a white Taffety dublet A blacke Taffety sute my purple Cloke sword and dagger And my base viall. [. . . and] to Iames Sandes my Aprentice the some of ffortye shillinges and a Citterne a Bandore and a Lute."[64] Phillips leaves each forty shillings plus the other property (valuable clothes, the musical instruments); that is ten shillings more than he gives to his fellows in the company (William Shakespeare, Henry Condell, Lawrence Fletcher, Robert Armin, among others).

In a liveried culture, a culture of sumptuary laws that reflect but also constitute identities,[65] what gets transferred, transmitted, in these exchanges of the living and the dead? We might think of these bequests as transmitting identity, or identification,[66] in a way not unrelated to fellow-ship and to master-apprentice relations. "Watch what I do, which is also what I wear. I will train you to become me." Does James Sandys inherit the cittern, the bandore (another stringed instrument), and the lute, because he should learn to play or because his master Phillips has already taught him? Does Gilborn inherit the fancy clothes because he has learned to act or *so that* he will? Phillips is witnessed, as he bequeaths these items, by Robert Goffe, his son-in-law, a King's Man, and apparently the same "robart gough" named the recipient of half of all Pope's wearing apparel and arms.

In the church of the parish where Pope lives and dies, and in which later the writers Massinger and Fletcher are buried in the same grave, in the same parish where Beaumont and Fletcher share a house and clothes and cloak, another actor, William Hovell, leases (he says in his will) "Tenementes in Vnicorne Ally vppon the Bankside in the saide parishe of St Saviour" from "one master Phillipe Henslow Esquire," noted in a will in which he (among other things) "bequeath[s] vnto [his] apprentice Michael Bowyer [an actor with Queen Henrietta's Men] xl s/ And to [his] apprentice William Wilson [connected with Palsgrave's Men] xx s."[67] He also gives to two other actors "my fyfte parte of my stocke of apparell and other thinges which I haue in the companie wherein they playe . . . to be equallie shared or de-vided betwene them Two."[68] As Fletcher and Massinger apparently did, Hovell asks that his "bodie [be] buryed in the Chancell or in one of the vpper Iles" of this church on the Bankside.[69]

I dwell on the details of these wills and anecdotes, because I think that it is through an attentiveness to these particularities of material culture—the details of locations, the literal dwelling in and among, the mobility and transfer of important property (in these cases, clothes)—that we can begin to see another subject of *conversation*: a complicated culture of male relations, sometimes domestic rela-tions, in this case around the theater. (That this culture did not escape the notice of others, who gave it a different valence, may be glimpsed in the writings of the Pu-ritan artisan Nehemiah Wallington, who wrote in 1633/34 that he had heard of "a group of married men in Southwark who had 'lived in the sin of buggery and were sworn brothers to it' some seven years."[70]) While we may need to distinguish adult-apprentice relations from those of conversing friends (and friendship's emphasis, at least in theory, on a lack of hierarchy), we would also want to notice the overlap-pings of these discourses and structures of male-male relation and affect, and the way in which there may have been diachronic continuities for (some) participants: Goffe apprentice becomes Goffe sharer and Goffe son-in-law, made conversant by marriage. (Chapters 4 and 5 also speak to this trajectory.)

Through an analysis of these relations, we may begin to see the "subjects" of conversation in yet another sense: the specific and peculiar modes of identity and identification produced out of the practices of this culture. *Conversation*: "behav-ior, mode, or course of life." Modes of life transmitted, handed down to and across or between "fellows," "sharers," apprentices. (Is apprenticeship a kind of peda-gogy, or conversion?) As in Chapter 1, this is to engage Bourdieu's conception of the *habitus* and to extend it to a full etymological capaciousness: a habitus of practices or habits, but also the habitus of habits or clothes, and the habitus of habitation—of living or dwelling among.[71] To extend *conversation* to this—to think out from this term spatially about the peculiar locations of early modern London, to think, too, about the shuffling of clothes that are also costumes, of musical instruments that are also properties, of papers that are fragments and also scripts—is to say that we cannot begin fully to understand the early modern theater and those working in it until we see it as enmeshed in, located within, dwelling upon, *conversant* with (in the earlier senses) other specific material practices and discourses.

Further Conversation

> Not so common as commendable it is, to see young
> gentlemen choose thē such friends with whom they may
> seeme beeing absent to be present, being a sunder to be
> conuersant, beeing dead to be aliue.
>
> —Lyly, *Euphues*[72]

In thinking about Kyd's and Marlowe's circle of extended conversation, I am suggesting a Marlowe somewhat different from the one we have become used to: Stephen Greenblatt's Marlowe-as-Other (and an Other simultaneously in the service of hegemonic Elizabethan culture), or Emily Bartels's Marlowe as a part of the spectacle of strangeness he stages, an alienated Other.[73] "This Marlowe"— Marlowe held at a distance; the Marlowe whose genealogy extends to Harry Levin's "overreacher";[74] the Marlowe of the repeated charges of disorderly conduct; a Marlowe who is also discussed in relation to his Other, solitary characters—should not, I am arguing, occlude for us the trace, in these documents, of another Marlowe: a Marlowe conversing with his culture, with other playwrights; a Marlowe who sometimes speaks *with*, rather than alone in alienation *from*.[75] A Marlowe replied to, brought into conversation in *As You Like It*, where, as a "Dead Shepheard," he is invoked, quoted, and agreed with:

> Dead Shepheard, now I find thy saw of might,
> Who euer lov'd, that lou'd not at first sight?[76]

"*Eglogue*," "a talking together." Phoebe's and Shakespeare's conversation with Marlowe here is also the space of the homoerotic pastoral, as the exit of a character named Ganymede directly before these lines makes emphatic.

I do not seek to propose merely an opposite to the oppositional Marlowe we have been living with for some time now—as if these other historicizings of him were wrong—but rather a complicated, mixed Marlowe. As we will examine in Chapter 5, he is an Other (without doubt), but also a Marlowe in conversation: accused of sodomy, but also valued for passionate shepherding. ("This Marlowe" allows a revisionary reading of, among other texts, *Edward II*; for, to place Edward oppositionally—as if a homoerotically inclined English king is at odds with his culture in the same way that, say, a Maltese Jew, a Scythian barbarian, or a German scholar-magician-heretic is—is to ignore the simultaneous presence of validated, condoned, homoaffection in this culture: its centrality to domestic arrangements, educational structures, the rhetoric of male friendship.[77]) Prompted by Kyd, this is to ask, which Marlowe have we fashioned for ourselves, which have we desired, and at what moments in the history of criticism?

Reading Kyd's conversation, his living and shuffling with Christopher Marlowe, will also help us to think about the figure of Kyd and give us a frame for reading the other bits of evidence that survive about this person—his conversation in some extended senses. The evidence is admittedly scarce and fragmentary, but it speaks in the discourses we have been analyzing, and it speaks more resonantly than in a critical discourse that seeks first and foremost to deliberate the facticity of the events of Kyd's life and to settle the authorship of texts that have been attributed to him. These bits might include the following:

☞ Investigating Kyd's conversation—whom he "lived among"—we find that his circle of relations, to the extent that we can reconstruct it, seems to have been largely extrafamilial; after his death, his mother and father declined to participate in the administration of his estate (for reasons not available to us), a fact that also suggests he did not have a spouse or heirs.[78]

☞ The few texts we can associate with Kyd are collaborations (if we count *The Spanish Tragedy* as such, as it was certainly seen in the period) and translations (most relevantly, his translation of Garnier's tragedy *Cornelia*, published in 1594). At his most heteroglossic, as in the "play of Hieronimo in sundry languages . . . set down in English" in *The Spanish Tragedy*, Kyd is both collaborator and translator. We can add to this Hieronimo's Latin speech at the end of Act 2, which the Revels edition of the play quotes F. S. Boas describing as a "pastiche, in Kyd's singular fashion, of tags from classical poetry, and lines of his own composition," adding that "[t]here are reminiscences of Lucretius, Virgil, and Ovid."[79] But what do "singular" and "fashion" mean in Kyd's shuffling context? *Digni sunt quibus inest causa . . .*

☞ Another example of Kyd as translator that converses in the discourses we have been analyzing is a volume published in 1588, identified by the initials T. K. With his waste and idle papers, his pages and fragments shuffled unbeknownst to him, Kyd would have the Privy Council think that he was no great housekeeper, but there is evidence to suggest that he is the T. K. who translated Tasso's *Padre di Famiglia*, a book T. K. calls, in English, *The housholders philosophie. Wherein is perfectly described, the true oeconomia of housekeeping.* Conversation: interchange of words or ideas; dwelling in a place. . . .

☞ *The Spanish Tragedy* had an afterlife not only in its manifold and continual revision, revival, and republication, but also in *The Spanish Comedy.* Also apparently known as *Don Horatio* and *The Comedy of Jeronimo*, this play was a sequel or prequel to the now more-famous *Tragedy*,[80] and Henslowe's records show that it was performed frequently in 1591–92, often in repertory with the *Tragedy* (*Jeronimo*), for example, on March 13–14, 1591; March 30–31, 1591; April 22 and 24, 1592; and May 21–22, 1592.[81] Another related title, *The First Part of Jeron-*

imo, published in 1605, may or may not be the same play as the *Comedy,* or it may be a revision of it; in either case, it registers the continued survival and popularity of "Kyd's" Jeronimo play(s)—whether or not Kyd participated in its composition at some point.[82]

We should include here the continued circulation of *The Spanish Tragedy,* later subtitled *Hieronimo is mad againe,* in other plays through allusion, quotation, emulation, and parody. Hieronimo's Act 3 lament for his dead son, for example—

> Oh eies, no eies, but fountains fraught with teares,
> Oh life, no life, but liuely fourme of death:
> Oh world, no world but masse of publique wrongs[83]

—is replayed at the end of the Middleton, Rowley et al. collaboration *The Old Law* (1618–19). (We will return to this passage in Chapter 7 for an analysis of tragicomedy.) The play's Clown learns that, as a result of a law's repeal, he will lose a two-to-one bet (what he calls his "venter"/venture) because he will not be able to have his old wife put to death and marry a new, younger wife on the same day:

> Oh Musick, no musick, but prove most dolefull Trumpets,
> Oh Bride no Bride, but thou maist prove a Strumpet,
> Oh venter, no venter, I have for one now none,
> Oh wife, thy life is sav'd when I hope t'had been gone.[84]

Other playwrights continue to live with Kyd, well after his death in 1594; Hieronimo is mad, again and again. *The Old Law*'s absorption of *The Spanish Tragedy* may remind us once more of some of the problematic questions an individuated model of writing (as opposed to a model of conversation) asks but is hard-pressed to answer: Who shuffled these particular papers? Who wrote the Clown's speech? Middleton? Rowley? Massinger (to whom the play is also attributed)? Kyd? (If Kyd, then Marlowe?) A murderous/witty Clown, perhaps written in part by a playwright who also played clowns (Rowley), speaking in the voice of a mourning father who is both player and playwright, written by the two-handed son of a scrivener? What manner of linguistic analysis will sort this conversation out? (And, of course, with what assumptions, and toward what end?)[85]

☞ There are two other theatrical figures, living in a house in another theater district, the Blackfriars, in 1610, changing and sharing costumes and roles: Captain, Doctor, Jeremy the Butler, Priest of Faery, and their more familiar names, Face and Subtle, the alchemist of the play's title. "Thou must borrow," they tell one of their gulls, a "*Spanish* suite. Hast thou no credit with the Players? / . . . *Hieronimo's* old Cloke, Ruffe, and Hat will serue."[86] These are Jonson's papers, shuffling

Kyd's, bringing in a cloak Jonson is thought himself to have worn, acting Hieron-imo, in the play to which he wrote additions, before adding reference to the additions into his "own" script. The costume and Kyd's fragments are shuffled even within Jonson's well-ordered papers: Doll Common speaks the first line of *The Spanish Tragedy* amid other dialogue in the sundry languages of *The Alchemist*; the Spanish cloak is worn by Surly, speaking Spanish then English, then taken by Face from Drugger, to be worn ultimately by Lovewit, master and keeper of this house near a theater, in a theater.[87]

   ☞ Unlike two other playwrights—Massinger and Fletcher—recorded in a poem by Aston Cockayne as lying in a single grave, Kyd seems to have had a solitary burial.[88] But he is figuratively interred, together with Marlowe, in another poem that takes up the question of the burial of playwrights, together or apart— Ben Jonson's poem on the dead Shakespeare in the 1623 first folio. "My *Shakespeare*, rise;" Jonson writes,

> I will not <u>lodge thee</u> by
> *Chaucer*, or *Spenser*, or bid *Beaumont* lye
> A little further, to make thee <u>a roome</u>:
>   Thou art a Moniment, without a tombe,
> . . . .
> That I not <u>mixe thee</u> so, my braine excuses;
>   I meane with great, but disproportion'd *Muses*:
> For, if I thought my iudgement were of yeeres,
>   I should <u>commit</u> thee surely with thy peeres,
> And tell, how farre thou didstst our *Lily* out-shine,
>   Or sporting *Kid*, or *Marlowes* mighty line.[89]

"Sporting *Kid*": in the appearance of "sports" (erotic slang during the period, perhaps not unrelated to the term's more theatrical meanings) and the pun on kid/ goat (a figure of playfulness, wantonness, even lechery)[90] there is a hint here of another Kyd whom we have *not* seen in his terrorized letters to the Privy Council. What has this Kyd written? "Sporting Kid" seems no allusion to *The Spanish Tragedy* or *Cornelia*, though perhaps to *The Spanish Comedy*; Jonson's gloss must also be set alongside Dekker's "industrious *Kyd*"[91]—an evocation suggesting that Kyd's shape may change more than we have yet reckoned, for "industrious" does not seem fully appropriate to Kyd's currently slender canon.[92]

Unlike Cockayne's burial poem, Jonson's is a poem *against* mixing, *against* conversation—a poem that performs the separation of Shakespeare from his acting company and fellow playwrights, urging him toward a singular apotheosis. But even Jonson (greatly invested in this process of singularization, whether in the Shakespeare folio or his own) does not keep Kyd and Marlowe separate. His *"sporting* Kid" is lodged with Marlowe; they are written together, if not writing together, conversing in one line.

Marjorie Garber has analyzed the inwardness of Marlowe's lines—a thematics and formal poetics of enclosure in Marlowe's plays she finds epitomized, for example, in familiar lines from *The Jew of Malta*:

> And as their wealth *inc*reaseth, so *inc*lose
> *Infin*ite riches *in* a little room.[93]

If we follow this reading in seeing spatial homologies in the little room, the line, and Marlowe "working within the confines of the tiny Elizabethan stage,"[94] we can, by beginning to read Kyd writing with Marlowe, see that the confines of the chamber, the early modern stage, and Jonson's line may enclose or disclose *several* writers, speaking together. In a word, *conversation*. The little room, the early English playhouse, and the "oeconomia of housekeeping" in these related houses may enclose and include practices and affects we are only beginning to reckon, discourses we are only beginning to translate, terms whose extensive and culturally particular meanings we are only beginning to extend.

Coda: A Brief History of *Intercourse*

In a brilliantly speculative essay based on demographic research, Henry Abelove has noted the extraordinary rise in "sexual intercourse so-called" in the late eighteenth century, arguing not only for recognition of a rise in this behavior ("penis in vagina, vagina around penis, with seminal emission uninterrupted") but also for its cultural revaluation or redefinition as "productive" in the context of the economic discourses of the Industrial Revolution in Britain. Abelove's corollary hypothesis is that, with the invention of "sexual intercourse so-called" as productive, other sexual behaviors "are reorganized and reconstructed in the late eighteenth century as foreplay . . . , as what precedes that sexual behavior which alone is privileged, intercourse so-called."[95] Working in a more philological and linguistic register, and from the perspective of the sixteenth century, Juliet Fleming remarks, " 'Conversation' and 'intercourse' have . . . a complex and mutually involved history; . . . in the sixteenth and seventeenth centuries, 'conversation' was carrying a sexual freight that it later handed over to the word 'intercourse.' "[96] We have been examining *conversation*, but these distinct observations prompt an obvious question: did sexual intercourse exist in the sixteenth and seventeenth centuries?

The answer must be "almost certainly," if we take Abelove's as our working definition.[97] And yet, as Fleming's and Abelove's arguments begin to suggest, a queer philology that is attuned to the difficulties of translating just such "sexual" behaviors and terms across time yields a more complex answer that will sound like "almost certainly not"—at least not in the modern sense.

The story of how *intercourse* takes on at least some of the meanings earlier carried by *conversation* is no doubt a complex one, one that I hope queer historians and philologists who study the later seventeenth and eighteenth centuries will take on in more detail. But what at least speculating briefly about this problem may bring into view for us is the way in which, as historians of sexuality, even our most apparently clinical ways of describing "sexual" practices—what, after all, could be clearer or more neutral than the term *sexual intercourse*?—must remain subject to queer-philological scrutiny and revision.

During the seventeenth century, as the *OED* outlines, the primary meanings of *intercourse* were (1) commerce, traffic, and communication between countries; (2) "social communication between individuals"; and (3) the "continuous interchange or exchange of" something, like letters, or Adam and Eve's "sweet intercourse of looks and smiles" in *Paradise Lost*.[98] In this period, in other words, *intercourse* carries some of the meanings we now attribute to *conversation*—apparently without the potentially sexual or erotic meanings associated with that term and discussed above. (Milton's usage here may be proleptic of a transition, for reasons I will suggest below.) The first uses of *intercourse* in a "sexual" sense, in fact, do not seem to occur until the mid- to late eighteenth century—indeed, in the very era of the transition Abelove analyzes. Many of these eighteenth-century uses appear in natural-science contexts, as in the first *OED* citation for "sexual intercourse," from 1753, also the first I have been able to locate, which notes the "sexual intercourse" of worms and snails in comparison to humans.[99] These earliest uses of the term often differ from our now-default syntax for the term by employing a definite or indefinite article—for example, noting the lack of "*any* sexual intercourse"[100] or, more frequently, discussing "*the* sexual intercourse": "The sexual intercourse [of the toad] takes place in March or April, and is mostly carried on in the water."[101] These uses eventually extend into human contexts and into the controversy and debate over "sexual" behavior, morality, population growth, and economy in texts by William Godwin and Thomas Robert Malthus; Godwin mentions "the sexual intercourse" in the second edition of *Enquiry concerning political justice* (1796),[102] and Malthus, in the second, enlarged edition of *An Essay on the Principle of Population* (1803) that reacts to Godwin, uses "intercourse" twenty-eight times—twenty-six instances are in contexts we would consider "sexual" (including "the sexual intercourse").[103]

Malthus is only one user of words in this culture, of course, but his text is worth taking seriously both because of its controversy and influence and also because it may illustrate, as it assists in the influential transmission of this term from a natural-science context to an emergent social-science and moral-philosophical context, that *sexual intercourse*—the term we now see as least value-laden for describing certain types of human "sexual" interaction—seems first to appear in English with a heavily pejorative penumbra: "an illicit intercourse between the sexes" (12n, 137, 300); "promiscuous intercourse," a favored phrase (11, 51, 52, 56, 58, 59, 101, 110, 111, 178n, 370, 496, 504, 520, 559); "a vicious intercourse with the sex," meaning women (155, 599); and "the premature intercourse of the sexes" (103).[104] Malthus continues to use *intercourse* in its earlier non-"sexual" senses as well (17, 60). Why?

The answers, I think, lie in the term *sexual*, in at least three ways. First, that the adjective *sexual* is even necessary for Godwin, Malthus, and these other early users is important, marking the semantic effort required to pull *intercourse* away from its other dominant, historically precedent meanings: this is not *commercial* intercourse, or sociable conversation or interaction, or, to cite another of the *OED*'s meanings, "[c]ommunion between man and that which is spiritual or unseen."[105] This is *sexual* intercourse.

But, second, the word *sexual*, transparent as it may now seem to us, itself requires our serious historicizing, philological attention—and thus my persistent quotation marks around it above—for it begins its life in English as a description of things "[c]haracteristic of or peculiar to the female sex; feminine," a meaning that the dictionary traces forward into the mid-nineteenth century.[106] Further, at the time of these uses and indeed from about 1651 until sometime in the twentieth century,[107] *sexual* referred to "the attribute of being either male or female" —that is, what we now call "gender" or "sexual difference."[108] In 1803, *sexual intercourse* meant intercourse between persons or animals of different genders: genderal intercourse; cross-sexual intercourse; or (though the term had not yet been invented) *heterosexual* intercourse.[109] (To put this another way: rather than referring to the *quality or domain of the action*, as it now does for us, the term referred to the *identity of the participants*.)

This is, third, a meaning that is underscored by the use of the (mostly) definite article in early usage: "the sexual intercourse." That is to say, not the *other* kinds of intercourse, those not involving gender difference. "The sexual intercourse" is "sexual," at the moment of its arrival, not because it is "sexy" or related to some (as-yet-to-be-coined) notion of un-gender-differentiated "sexuality" in the modern sense, but because it involves the (potentially) reproductive cross-sexual act.

As the *OED*'s citations and other uses of *intercourse* prior to 1800 suggest, the introduction of *sexual* at a particular moment in the history of *intercourse* may then signify the introduction of *difference* into a term that seemed often to lack, in its apparent reflexivity, an explicit hierarchy or differentiation in its earlier uses. In

Robert Cawdrey's *Table Alphabeticall* (1604), for example, *intercourse* is defined as "mutuall accesse, or passage one to another" and as "[p]assing or sending one to another," in Bullokar's *English Expositor* (1616).[110] As Minsheu's 1617 etymological dictionary put it, it is "an entercourse of marchandise from place to place."[111] In John Florio's 1598 translation dictionary, *A Worlde of Wordes*, the Italian *intercorrente* was glossed as "running or going between."[112] *Intercourse*, in these earlier English uses, is focused on a mutuality, reciprocality, and two-way transit that is, at least ideologically, largely imagined as possible only within certain male-male contexts.

But just as, later, around 1800, *sexual* introduces hierarchy and difference into a term previously distinguished by its horizontality, we could also speculate about the meanings and effects of the etymological force of *intercourse* still resonant at that date. *Inter+course* as "running between" is now a dead metaphor, a meaning now almost entirely lost to us. But is it possible that this sense of *inter/course* produces an equalizing function into "the" sexual act between genders—as a cultural fantasy, if not, of course, in actual fact? Could we productively see this new, more mutual sense of "the sexual intercourse" as accompanying an (ever-emerging, still not fully emerged) idea of "companionate" marriage or "domestic heterosexuality" in English culture,[113] as well as a more "mutual" biological account of reproduction (supplanting an earlier model of active male spirit or "idea"),[114] and even Abelove's sense that "sexual intercourse so-called" rises as a late eighteenth-century practice tied squarely to (mutual?) production? I am not, of course, arguing that hierarchies in cross-sexual relations ("the" act, or the domestic or other social relations and structures organized in relation to it) simply drop away with the adoption of *intercourse* as a potentially less hierarchical term in sexual theory and practice. Nevertheless, *sexual inter/course* as a term may at least imagine or inscribe the possibility of intercourse—mutual exchange—between the sexes, in a way not contemplated by some earlier terms.

Conversation, to return to our earlier term, persists in English in a "sexual" sense in the restricted legal context of "criminal conversation," a tort abolished in England in 1857 but still on the books in a number of U.S. jurisdictions in the twenty-first century. This usage, which demonstrates among other things that *conversation* and *intercourse* have not simply exchanged places since the sixteenth century, may indeed stem from the earlier meaning that encoded a perceived transgression against the nonhierarchical senses of (male) *conversation, converse*, and *conversing* we analyzed in the earlier sections of this chapter. In this sense, the conversation between two noble kinsmen quoted earlier is worth recalling:

> We are young and yet desire the waies of honour,
> That liberty and common Conversation

The poyson of pure spirits; might like women
Wooe us to wander from.[115]

Associating "liberty" (in the sense of both freedom from their imprisoned state and a broader sense of "license") and "conversation" with "women" as poisonous and at odds with "honour," the passage may encode the threat that women are thought to pose to this earlier, class-aligned, and noble (noncommon) sense of men conversing (living, speaking, exchanging) together. (This understanding of gendered hierarchy is performed visually in the ensuing scene, as the kinsmen look down from their prison-tower space "above" on the early modern stage, to see Emilia, the woman whose arrival interrupts their conversation in several senses, on the stage/garden "below.") Can conversation, in this earlier universe of discourse, happen across lines of gender difference or is it effectively "criminal conversation," unsanctioned intercourse?

The idea that (what counts to premodern persons as) premodern sex is generally understood as hierarchical has become a commonplace in the history of sexuality, and the complex and intersecting histories of *conversation* and *intercourse* as we have explored them in this chapter suggest the difficulty, in that context, of confidently tracing what we would see as the erotic or "sexual" (genital-reproductive) in relation to discourses of male-male *converse*, *conversation*, and *conversing*. (That is, can something in sixteenth- and seventeenth-century England be seen as "sex" in our sense if it does not include hierarchy? Does male-male conversation in this period pass over into "sodomy" once inter/course among men becomes legibly hierarchical?) I stress that this speculative coda is only the beginning of such thinking and will involve research that may eventually be enhanced by larger, more accurately searchable swaths of text. At the time of this writing, for example, the Google Books Ngram viewer, initially much vaunted as producing illuminating graphs of historical word usage across the available Google "corpus" of scanned texts, cannot adequately distinguish "suck" from "fuck" (or "such," or even, as some readers of Shakespeare will be interested to know, "Puck"), distinctions that would be useful for a serious queer philology of "sexual" terms.[116]

Nevertheless, it is worth thinking, with the tools we do have, about the more hierarchical, less equitable terms for "sexual" practice that precede "sexual intercourse, so-called." Perhaps in part because they were not difficult or Latinate terms in need of elucidation as hard-word lists became dictionaries in the sixteenth and seventeenth centuries, such terms are not particularly common in these texts, but the following series of entries from Florio's Italian-English *A Worlde of Wordes* is instructive:

Fottarie, *iapings, sardings, swiuings, fuckings.*
[…]
Fottere, fotto, fottei, fottuto, *to iape, to sard, to fucke, to swiue, to occupy.*
[…]
Fottitrice, *a woman fucker, swiuer, sarder, or iaper.*
Fottitore, *a iaper, a sarder, a swiuer, a fucker, an occupier.*
Fottitura, *a iaping, a swiuing, a fucking, a sarding, an occupying.*
[…]
Fottuto, *iaped, occupied, sarded, swiued, fuckt.*[117]

The hierarchical, transitive quality of the verb *fuck* is obviously enough still with us (erased though it is by the *OED*'s glossing of it as to "have sexual intercourse with [a person]"),[118] and it is echoed in the usage of the now-obsolete (but etymologically hazy) terms *jape*, *sard*, and *swive*. The sexual *occupy* movement, well attested in Shakespeare and elsewhere around 1600, likewise carries with it a "sexual" hierarchy that the *OED* finds stretching into the early nineteenth century.[119] But, as I hope I have been suggesting, a queer philology will ultimately seek to read more closely, and more politically, less obvious sixteenth- and seventeenth-century terms for what we now call more equitably "intercourse," a running between.

I have largely left pleasure out of a consideration of "the sexual intercourse" in this discussion and had thought that I would conclude with a word about it, by noting the term *enjoying*—a term that turns up with some frequency in early modern heteroerotic contexts. Indeed, just after the "common conversation" passage from *The Two Noble Kinsmen* quoted above, *to enjoy* pops up as a verb, in the argument between Palamon and Arcite over Emilia.

Pal. You love her, then?
Arc. Who would not?
Pal. And desire her?
Arc. Before my liberty.
Pal. I saw her first.
Arc. That's nothing.
Pal. But it shall be.
Arc. I saw her too.
Pal. Yes, but you must not love her.
Arc. I will not, as you doe; to worship her;
As she is heavenly, and a blessed Goddes;
(I love her as a woman, to enjoy her)
So both may love.[120]

However, to discuss *enjoy*, I quickly found, is also to note that—whatever our pleasant associations with that term now, its seeming closeness with *joy* and *jouissance*—enjoying is, at least sometimes in early modern discourse, associated with possession (occupation, we might say). As Minsheu's *Ductor in Linguas* puts it, to "*haue the possession of*, [from the French] Iouir, *quod deduci videtur a Lat*: gaudere. . . . *Vi. to* Possesse."[121] A reader who does turn to *possesse* finds a discussion of two kinds of property rights in common law.[122] If our vocabularies of (sexual) pleasure have not been entirely stripped of these explicit resonances of property and possession, we can nevertheless notice that, for *enjoy*, Minsheu gives no other definition but this. If the evidence of these word-books is to be believed, then, the culturally sanctioned male-male forms of *conversation* and *intercourse*—as mutual commerce, what Montaigne calls "equitable jouissance"— may thus be at odds with sex understood (fundamentally) as *enjoying*.[123] Imagine for a moment the impossibility of translating into early modern English the late twentieth-century American, originally gay-male relation signified by the term *fuck buddy*, with its impossibly modern mélange of sex, masculinity, nonintimate intimacy, friendship, and familiar, hierarchy-erasing tone (modern *enjoying* without early modern *enjoying*).[124]

There are potentially surprising corollaries to this for early modern England. First, certain kinds of erotic *conversation* between early modern men, at least men of close rank/race/national identification, might appear to be more equitable and thus more in line with certain of our own political values in a strangely complicated way, than relations between early modern women and men. (This is to say, there are contexts in which *shuffling* and *enjoying* are opposites.) Second, pleasure(s) might need to be mapped on to, read out of, these relations in a way more complicated than we have imagined thus far or I have studied here. (Early modern women's *enjoying* must be high on that list.) But I leave that potentially queer philology to others and another time. I have been dominating this conversation—or, in early modern English, "I have enjoyed our intercourse."

LEXICON 2

BOY-DESIRE

CHAPTER 4

Reading "Boys": Performance and Print

For when yeares thrée times fiue and one he fully lyued
    had,
So that he séemde to stande béetwene the state of man and
    Lad,
The hearts of dyuers trim yong men his beautie gan to
    moue
And many a Ladie fresh and faire was taken in his loue.
    —Ovid, *Metamorphoses*, in Arthur Golding's translation[1]

Neither a borrower nor a lender boy,
                —*Hamlet*, the "good" quarto (1604)[2]

Boys Onstage

[W] hy did the English stage take boys for women?" Stephen Orgel has influentially asked.[3] But why did the English stage take boys for boys? Better yet, what did the English stage take boys for, as "boys"?[4] To begin to think about these questions, allow me to catalog some of the terms used to address and describe the young woman Viola when she becomes Cesario in *Twelfth Night*. Of course, to refer to this figure onstage as Viola is already to get ahead of ourselves, since, as is well known, Viola is not named in the play's dialogue as "Viola" until 235 lines into the play's Act 5; in her first scene, she is simply "lady" and "madam."[5] Like Violenta, the ghost-name of which she is apparently the subject in an entrance direction in the folio text, one might say that the name "Viola" is an effect of script and print—of stage directions and speech prefixes and only eventually of dialogue.[6] In performance, in her female gender, she has no name until the end of the play. Whatever we may make of this apparent lacuna, the terms of address and description become only more variable after her first appearance.

Concealing herself, this lady becomes "an eunuch" (1.2), a "gentleman" (1.5), and self-addresses "As I am a man" and "As I am a woman" (2.2). The dialogue first refers to this figure as "Cesario" in Act 1, Scene 4. He speaks of himself as part of the group "We men" in Act 2, Scene 4—a label Orsino corrects or amends by addressing him as "boy" almost immediately thereafter. He speaks as a "friend" to the adult Feste in Act 3, Scene 1 (thus presuming a kind of equity), swears by his "youth," and is "almost sick" for a beard in the same scene.

Orsino calls him "good youth" (1.4.15), "good Cesario" (2.4.2), and "Dear lad"—[not yet] "a man" in Act 1, Scene 4 (29–31). He often addresses him directly as "boy": "Come hither, boy" (2.4.14); "Hath it not, boy?" (24, also 31); "died thy sister of her love, my boy?" (2.4.119); and then, threatening to kill him in Act 5, "Come, boy, with me, my thoughts are ripe in mischief" (5.1.125).[7] Once Olivia has disclosed her marriage with (it seems) this boy, Orsino hails him as "your minion" (5.1.121); he is also "the lamb that I do love" (5.1.127). The diminutives continue with "sirrah" and "thou dissembling cub" shortly thereafter (5.1.141, 5.1.160).[8] Moments later, Orsino refers to him as "My gentleman, Cesario" (5.1.177), and the play famously concludes with Orsino insisting on the future use of this name "while [he is] a man" (5.1.375–76).

Olivia, for her part, calls him several times "this youth" (1.5.286, 295) and directly addresses him as "youth" and "good youth" (3.1.98, 129), but also as "[t]he County's man" (1.5.290)—though in Act 3, Scene 1, she implies that he is not yet "reap[ed]" as "a proper man" (3.1.131). Mistaking Sebastian, she addresses him as "dear Cesario" and "gentle friend" (3.4.48–49). Later it is "Cesario, husband" (5.1.139, 140)—though just a few lines later "this youth" (5.1.151, referring to Cesario, but mistaking for Sebastian). In the end, still called "Cesario" while he is a man by Orsino, she is to Olivia a "sister" (5.1.317).[9]

Who is Cesario, what is he, that all our swains and more commend him, and in such disparate terms? Man, boy, eunuch, youth; there is still more: Maria sees "a young gentleman" (1.5.94), "a fair young man" (1.5.97), but also "the youth of the Count's" (2.3.123–24). Sir Toby sees a "gentleman" (1.5.113–15), but also "the Count's youth" (3.2.31), "the youth" (3.2.55–56; 3.4.183, 186), and yet "the gentleman" (3.4.186, 294) and "the young gentleman" (3.4.179). Sir Toby refers obliquely to Cesario's "manhood" (3.4.174) and in jest to "such a virago" (3.4.265), but also to a "very dishonest, paltry boy" (3.4.376). Fabian sees "the youth" (3.2.60), as does Sir Andrew (3.1.84), who also sees "the Count's servingman" (3.2.5), and later (mistaking Sebastian) the "Count's gentleman, one Cesario" (5.1.175).[10]

Describing him initially as "yon young fellow" (1.5.133), Malvolio provides the most extensive gloss. Olivia asks, "What kind o' man is he?" and Malvolio replies, "Why, of mankind" (1.5.144–45)—like a man, of man's kind or likeness.

OLIVIA   What manner of man?
MALVOLIO Of very ill manner: he'll speak with you, will you or no.

(1.5.146–47)

However frustrating to Olivia, Malvolio's semiotic riffs on her terms only further complicate any attempt firmly to distinguish or categorize Cesario. He is "of mankind," which is to say like any man, but also of a man's mere kind or likeness, perhaps a little less than kin. He is also a man who is of an ill manner: ill-mannered, certainly, but also perhaps only able to man, to be or play man, in an ill fashion. The question "What manner of man?" may come to signify, after Malvolio's reply, how does one man (how does one manner, or play) a man? Undeterred, Olivia continues to refine her question: "Of what personage and years is he?" Malvolio answers:

> Not yet old enough for a man, nor young enough for a boy: as a squash is before 'tis a peascod, or a codling when 'tis almost an apple. 'Tis with him in standing water between boy and man. He is very well-favoured, and he speaks very shrewishly. One would think his mother's milk were scarce out of him. (1.5.150–55)

Malvolio's analysis draws attention to the proliferation of the list I have so far recited—that is, to the procession of conflicting, overlapping terms the play uses to refer to this figure in its male gender—but it also establishes a set of metaphoric associations for the boy or man or young fellow upon his second entrance in boy's, or man's, or young fellow's clothes. On the one hand, the lines establish a developmental model of boyhood: not *yet* a man, though no longer a boy; a squash *before* it is a peascod; a codling *before* an apple; in "standing water"—at the turning of the tide, say the glosses in almost all the editions—between boy and man. The tide will turn: boys will be men.

Yet, on the other hand—a hand that potentially works against this developmental sense—Malvolio's lines, when lifted out of editorial attempts to pin them down and instead opened out philologically into the context of the other early modern discourses they engage, set off a chain of associations that here only *intensify* the problematic of the figure he describes. *The Oxford English Dictionary* (*OED*), for example, has no evidence, outside Shakespeare's own usage, for the typical gloss of "squash" as "undeveloped pea-pod (*peas-cod*)"[11]—and thus for boy as not-yet-developed man (or, more accurately, shell or husk of a man). The dictionary has no etymological explanation for why this sense developed, as it argues, "[r]elated to, or directly from," the verb *to squash*, and this development apparently dies out with William Shakespeare in any event—if indeed it ever lived: one of the other Shakespearean uses of the term cited by the *OED*, in *A Midsummer Night's Dream*, sees the relation of squash to peascod as gendered, not developmental: "I pray you commend mee to mistresse *Squash*, your mother," Bottom says, "and to master *Peascod* your father."[12] Thus Malvolio's comment may gesture toward the gender instabilities I take to be axiomatic in the play's denotations of Cesario, a transitivity already well described in the play's criticism.[13]

Stripped of an editorial desire to delimit and stabilize their meaning, the passage's other terms similarly ramify outward: *codling* seems to take off from *peascod* and signifies not only an unripe apple, but also (as one might expect) a small fish, and, also, since *cod* means "bag" and thus "scrotum," "a small bag, or testicles." Denoting Cesario seems to require mixing apples and apricocks.[14]

A final example: as W. Roy Mackenzie pointed out in a 1926 note unregistered in recent editions of the play,[15] there is no period evidence for reading Malvolio's line, "in standing water between boy and man," to mean "at the turn of the tide"[16]—the identical gloss in all the major recent editions. The line is much more likely to have meant a stagnant or standing pool or pond, a swamp between the states of land and water. In the uses of the phrase that Shakespeare, his fellow actors, and his audiences were most likely to know, God, in Psalm 107, "reduceth a wyldernes into a standing water: and a drye ground into water springes" and, in Psalm 114, is said to have "turned the harde rocke into a standing water: and the flint stone into a springing well of waters"—translations that persist from the Bishops' Bible through the Authorized Version.[17] "Standing waters," writes Robert Burton in *The Anatomy of Melancholy*, are "thick and ill-coloured, such as come forth of pools, and moats, where hemp hath been steeped, or slimy fishes live, are most unwholesome, putrified, and full of mites, creepers, slimy, muddy, unclean, corrupt, impure, by reason of the sun's heat, and *still-standing*."[18] "The fattest standing water is always the best," writes William Harrison in *The Description of England*, "whereon the sun lieth longest, and the fattest fish is bred."[19] Clearly this phrase is part of Malvolio's vocabulary of derision, but it also suggests a Cesario between water and land, liquid and solid. In a pool not subject to tides or flow, he is *categorically*, not *temporally*, between boy and man. As the fish in these contextualizing quotations may also suggest, "standing water" may emerge into the text here not as yet another metaphor for developmental boyhood-as-incipient manhood, but as a metonymic connection to the codling—the little fish, the little testicle—above. If so, then we may also hear in this passage a further phallic insult in the oxymoronic sense of "standing water." Can standing water "stand," get it up?

I have gone fairly deep (as it were) into the text's historical and philological resonances here in part to remind us that Cesario—this boy played by a woman played by a boy—is indicated in the play through a range of categories, from "boy" to "man" (including "youth"), categories whose relation to each other is neither mutually exclusive, nor always logically developmental (boy *to* man), nor entirely systematic. The inability to categorize Cesario—or, more precisely, the ability of this figure to call forth repeated and divergent categorizations—exceeds, I argue, the often critically discussed gender transitivity of the figure (a "fellow" who "speaks shrewishly"; a "lad" whose "small pipe / Is as the maiden's organ" and "semblative a woman's part"), since this bundle of categories is, as the play emphasizes, entirely and repeatedly also misrecognized, or simply *recognized*, as "Sebastian."[20] Insofar as these multiple categorizations, recognitions, and hailings figure the responses of a variety of represented persons to this performing figure, they may also figure what an early modern audience saw, in all its multiplicity, when it saw boy actors playing women, sometimes playing boys and men.

My attention to such questions of categorization in part stems from a desire to historicize the languages of masculinity in early modern England, a critical project that has been ongoing in the field for some time. But I am also suggesting that we need to pursue this project not only between genders, but even more carefully *within* them. As Ilana Krausman Ben-Amos's book *Adolescence and Youth in Early Modern England* argues,

> the boundaries between childhood and youth on the one hand and between youth and adulthood on the other could become extremely imprecise. Even in scientific theories which aimed at explaining the passage from childhood to old age, and which abounded in numeric divisions and categories, there was no universally accepted division between childhood, adolescence, youth, and so on. . . . [A] person might be considered mentally and emotionally mature for specific rights and obligations at different times during his teens, as well as legally mature at 21; but in terms of social experience, the requirements of some professions, or responsibility for a family, he could be considered, at 18, 20, or even 25, as still quite young.[21]

As Ben-Amos's book suggests, our modern Anglo-American default sense of something called adolescence is strongly inflected by our own institutionalized and routinized educational system, a set of transitions the early modern system cuts across both in terms of age and in the variabilities of social class, geography, and other factors. In a culture where life expectancy was, comparatively speaking, quite low and the mean age of marriage for men (one indicator of full entrance into adulthood) "fluctuated between 27.6 and 29.3,"[22] nonadulthood could in fact occupy the majority of a life. Further, as Bruce Smith has shown, the range of reference for the term *boy* was itself hugely elastic from our point of view, including, in one sodomy trial, a "boy" described as "aged 29 years or thereabouts."[23]

A current Google search for the phrase "boys will be boys" requires .24 seconds and produces 892,000 results, suggesting that, in Anglo-American modernity at least, we think of this category as self-evident.[24] My point is not only to ask that, in thinking about early modern figures like Cesario and Sebastian and the boys who played them in plays like *Twelfth Night*, we develop more subtle and historically appropriate ideas of masculinity, its ages and modes. I am also urging that we think about the relation of this definitional and categorical fluidity to the perceived erotic desirability of boys, youths, and men in early modern culture.[25] As Stephen Orgel summarizes, "[B]oys were, like women—but unlike men—acknowledged objects of sexual attraction for men. . . . [T]he homosexual, and particularly the pederastic component of the Elizabethan erotic imagination is both explicit and for the most part surprisingly unproblematic."[26] Pressing Orgel's point further, a consensus of critics has begun to recognize the category of the boy or youth or young man as a "universal object of desire" during this period—a figure of erotic and affective attraction and availability for early modern men and women alike.[27] Golding's Ovid's Narcissus is in this sense exemplary: at the age of sixteen, "The hearts of dyuers trim yong men his beautie gan to moue / And many a Ladie fresh and faire was taken in his loue." Standing water has its attractions for everyone, including, of course, Narcissus himself.

What can a renewed queer-philological attention to the categories "boy," "youth," "man," and so forth tell us about the range of eroticisms in early modern English culture? In his essay "How to Do the History of Male Homosexuality," David M. Halperin has brilliantly delineated a set of prehomosexual discourses or structures that circulate from classical antiquity through the early modern period and into the present, representing structures or configurations of homoeroticism that eventually contribute to, but are not the same as, the category of modern "homosexuality."[28] Several of these structures, including pederasty, are constituted through hierarchies of age, status, or gender affinity. Building on Halperin's formulation, I want, in emphasizing the categorical unfixity of "the boy," first, to highlight the complexity of a structure like pederasty as its attractions are enacted in plays like *Twelfth Night* (the way in which the "ped" in "pederasty" is a moving target, and thus the way in which the term, at least if understood in its ostensible modern self-evidentness, is not precisely what we are seeing here). Second, I seek also to indicate the ways in which pederasty overlaps with, slides into, sometimes becomes or comes from, other kinds of love, attraction, affection in this period. This is to say, even as the lexicons of this book (and the columns of the categorizing chart that Halperin provides at the end of his essay) seem to erect boundaries between same-sex male discourses, we will see below, particularly in the section entitled "The Boy/friend," additional ways in which these discourses can overlap with and draw on discourses (like friendship, above, and sodomy, below) that seem typically to carry different valences of sexual hierarchy/equality.[29] To further explore these issues, and to consider how they might differently figure in performance and in print, I turn now to the roughly contemporaneous *Philaster, or Love Lies A-Bleeding*, another King's Men's play that raises philological and editorial issues centered on a boy.

Love of Boys

"The love of boys unto their lords is strange," Philaster says, near the beginning of Act 2 of the play that bears his name (2.1.57).[30] Speaking of Bellario, the boy "[s]ent by the gods" whom he found in the woods while hunting, Philaster enlarges on this strange boy-man love: "I have read wonders of it, yet this boy / For my sake— if a man may judge by looks / And speech—would outdo story" (1.2.112, 2.1.58– 60). Philaster's speech both registers this structure as normative (a love whose name he's seen spoken before) and as (in Bellario's case) willfully exceeding the wonder-full, outgoing the standard accounts. "Strange," but not unprecedented— and perhaps also strange because Philaster is accustomed in the classical sources to seeing the affection flow in the other direction.[31]

The boy Bellario is, in fact, the object of concerted erotic interest in *Philaster*, and not only *from* Philaster. Or more precisely (and this bears comparison with *Twelfth Night*), the boy functions as a figure for the possibility of eroticism, a figure always on the verge of eroticization. There is, first, the long pastoral monologue that interrupts the action, in which Philaster introduces Bellario—in Philaster's superlative terms, "[t]he trustiest, lovingest, and the gentlest boy / That ever master kept" (1.2.138–39). In fact, the boy's value in the play seems to be that he can, at whatever point, be invested with meaning. Dion is only one of many characters to dwell upon the word *boy* in the play, and, as he says after Philaster has given Bellario to his beloved, the princess Arethusa, Bellario is "that boy, that princess's boy, that brave, chaste, virtuous lady's boy, and a fair boy, a well-spoken boy!" (2.4.186–88). The courtesan Megra, however, invests the boy with less chaste erotic meaning. "The princess has a Hylas, an Adonis" (2.4.17), she says, thus citing the boy's classical availability as the subject of erotic interest for both Hercules and Venus, men and women. Bellario himself cites another classical scene of erotic investment (the story of Ganymede, a figure hovering over the whole play) and thematizes his own tractability, when he notes to Philaster early on:

> Sir, you did take me up
> When I was nothing, and only yet am something
> By being yours. You trusted me unknown.
>
> (2.1.5–7)

Defined, constituted by, his relation to the master who has taken him up,[32] Bellario emphasizes a few lines later his availability for pedagogic instruction and transformation:

> Sir, if I have made
> A fault of ignorance, instruct my youth:
> I shall be willing, if not apt, to learn.
> Age and experience will adorn my mind
> With larger knowledge, and if I have done
> A wilful fault, think me not past all hope
> For once. What master holds so strict a hand
> Over his boy that he will part with him
> Without one warning? Let me be corrected.
>   (2.1.29–37)

As the work of Elizabeth Pittenger, Alan Stewart, and Wendy Wall on the prevalence of pedagogic beating in early modern schools has shown, this imagined scene of correction is itself not necessarily separate from or devoid of eroticism in this period.[33] Taking up Bellario's willful multivalence, I argue that the play records and extends the erotic slippage available in the figure of the boy, the page, the servant, as the pedagogical scene and classical resonances that get attached to him begin to suggest: a Ganymede "taken up," "a Hylas," "an Adonis."[34] This is so much the case that, when Megra finally articulates a specific erotic allegation against Bellario, the charge is immediately assimilable by other characters in the play: "I know the boy / She keeps, a handsome boy, about eighteen; / Know what she does with him, where and when" (2.4.154–56).

As I have already noted, the term *boy* has a capaciousness of reference in this period that may in fact bear some discursive responsibility for Bellario as a site of definitional struggle—denoting age (a *young* boy), but also often denoting servitude and/or social inferiority. Some of this breadth of reference may replay a more specific cultural ambiguity: to take one possible site of boy (in)definition, the ecclesiastical canons of 1604 ambiguated the age of marital consent, continuing to allow marriage at fourteen for boys, while adding the requirement of parental or guardian consent until age twenty-one.[35]

Bellario's eroticization is the product not only of his age—though his age comes to function as a marker of his erotic availability—but also of his clothes. "'Tis a sweet boy," says Dion. "How brave she keeps him!" (2.4.26). "Where's the boy?" Arethusa asks her waiting-woman.

GENTLEWOMAN   Within, madam.

ARETHUSA   Gave you him gold to buy him clothes?

GENTLEWOMAN	I did.
ARETHUSA	And has he done't?
GENTLEWOMAN	Yes, madam.
ARESTHUSA	'Tis a pretty, sad-talking boy, is it not?

(2.3.1–7)

Bellario becomes here a liveried servant of the princess—a point made emphatically at the beginning of the scene—and this "brave" livery itself becomes a further mark of his eroticization, in a way that the text suggests as potentially excessive: "She has made thee brave!" accuses Philaster, who has himself earlier made Bellario something out of nothing (3.1.158). "My lord," Bellario replies, "she has attired me past my wish, / Past my desert" (3.1.159–60). The liveried status of Bellario—his mark, badge, habit of service—becomes even more controversial, as the King's interrogation of Arethusa on the charge of boy-love hints:

KING
   Tell me, have you not a boy?
ARETHUSA   Yes, sir.
KING
   What kind of boy?
ARETHUSA   A page, a waiting boy.
KING
   A handsome boy?
ARETHUSA   I think he be not ugly;
. . . .
KING
   He speaks and sings and plays?
ARETHUSA   Yes, sir.
KING
   About eighteen?
ARETHUSA   I never asked his age.
KING
   Is he full of service?
ARETHUSA   By your pardon,
   Why do you ask?
. . . .
KING
   Put him away, I say. He's done you
   That good service shames me to speak of.

(3.2.10–20)

In this play, the erotic risk posed by Bellario's clothing here is a result of a gendered structure: to be the kept boy of Philaster—to be the "trustiest, lovingest, and the gentlest boy / That ever master kept"—is to be endowed with affect apparently without risk, as Philaster's long introductory aria on Bellario suggests. But to be the kept-boy/man (the eighteen-year-old liveried servant) of the princess is to open the possibility of multiple kinds of "service," and a service, as Philaster jealously fantasizes, in which the servant may become a kind of master to the princess who is said to "yield thee [Bellario] all delights / Naked, as to her lord." "I took her oath / Thou shouldst enjoy her," Philaster lies (3.1.198–200).

Fantasized here, and alluded to in *Twelfth Night* in Orsino's sending his page to Olivia, this kind of erotic danger is enacted in the Act 4 hunting sequence of *Philaster*, a phantasmatically isolated forest space first set up in Arethusa's speech in the last lines of Act 3. The forest and this speech explicitly ally the hunt with sexual desire and wounding with penetration, as R. A. Foakes notes,[36] even as the speech encodes the prospective polymorphous perversity of the multiple erotic woundings that will follow. "I am in tune to hunt," Arethusa says:

> Diana, if thou canst rage with a maid
> As with a man, let me discover thee
> Bathing, and turn me to a fearful hind,
> That I may die pursued by cruel hounds
> And have my story written in my wounds.
>
>   (3.2.168–73)

The hunt imagined here by Arethusa is multivalent and multidirectional. Like Orsino in the first scene of *Twelfth Night*, Arethusa writes herself as Actaeon and thus, if only in the conditional ("*if* thou canst rage with a maid"), within a scene of self-endangering female-female voyeurism and desire. This is a scene in which, moreover, she imagines viewing the bathing Diana—to whom Arethusa's classical namesake was originally bound in service, before she (Arethusa) was herself hunted by Alpheus and turned into a fountain. The passage is explicit in linking desire with what we might call unsafe hunting practices, and it suggests that the resulting wounds themselves will become the text of the tragedy the play at this point threatens to unfold.

Let me quickly recount the woundings of Act 4 of *Philaster*. Philaster wounds Arethusa. A "Country Fellow," whom the wounded Arethusa accuses of "intrud[ing] [him]self / Upon our private sports, our recreations" (4.5.91–92), then wounds Philaster. Philaster, fleeing, finds Bellario asleep, and, in an attempt to thrust guilt for Arethusa's wounding upon him, wounds *him* by replicating his own wounds: "Sword, print my wounds / Upon this sleeping boy" (4.6.23–24). To use the words of the play's subtitle, all "loves" lie "a-Bleeding" in Act 4.

The end of *Philaster*, of course, binds up these wounds, and in doing so it reintegrates Bellario, the figure of the boy, into the combined household of the betrothed Philaster and Arethusa.[37] The text is careful to make prophylactic at least some of the eroticism around which it had earlier elaborated tensions, by disclosing that Bellario is "really" Euphrasia, a maiden apparently chastely devoted to Philaster.[38] If the play has, in other words, significantly expanded the erotic availability and meaning of "the boy" over the course of the play, it seems here largely to shut down that experimentation by the last-minute disclosure—news to everyone but herself, including the audience—that the boy Bellario is in fact the woman Euphrasia.[39]

The Habit of a Boy

That is at least one of the stories one might derive from *Philaster*, though we should notice that the play also simultaneously leaves open some of the possibilities it had earlier exhibited. The disclosure of the truth of Euphrasia's gender is, for example, greeted with significant ambiguity:

DION

    It is a woman; let her speak the rest.

PHILASTER

    How? That again.

DION   *It* is a woman.

. . . .

PHILASTER

    It is a woman, sir! Hark, gentlemen,

    It is a woman! . . .

    . . . *It* is a woman!

. . . .

                        But Bellario—

For I must call thee still so—tell me why

Thou didst conceal thy sex.

                (5.5.126–46, my emphasis)

Philaster's request in turn produces another narrative that is *simultaneously* a genealogy of Bellario's/Euphrasia's true gender *and* a second version of Philaster's earlier speech explaining the love of boys unto their lords. Yet Euphrasia's now "female" version of her story is nevertheless still structured by the rhetoric of "taking up," associated with the shepherd Ganymede:

> I saw *a god,*
> I thought—but it was you—enter our gates.
> My blood *flew out and back again* . . .
> . . . .
>   Then was I called away in haste
> To entertain you. Never was a man
> *Heaved from a sheepcote to a sceptre, raised*
> *So high* in thoughts as I. . . .
>   (5.5.156–63, my emphasis)

Euphrasia's story, ostensibly the backstory of her true gender, simultaneously re-stages the shepherd Ganymede's flight, legible, as Leonard Barkan has pointed out, as his ravishment and/or his education: the story of awakened desire here is also the story of rising thoughts.[40] Having dressed herself "[i]in habit of a boy," Euphrasia continues, she sat "by the fount / Where first you *took me up*" (5.5.173, 182–83). Discovered to be a woman, Euphrasia's rhetoric and narrative continue to mark her as a boy.

Is this why Philaster must "call [Bellario] still so"? Is it the persistence of the boy clothing that she still wears—the force of "habit"?[41] Or what Orgel describes as her "deci[sion] to remain permanently in drag"?[42] Even to ignore these ambiguities, to ignore the persistence of Bellario's boyhood and concentrate on Euphrasia, is not to arrive at an ending without eroticism. In the shared household, the threesome with which it concludes, the play supplies an ongoing man-boy relationship (Philaster still calls this girl "Bellario"; she still tells that story), as well as what we might see—following Valerie Traub's foundational work—as a relationship of "chaste femme" love between Arethusa, and her former boy, now a girl, Euphrasia.[43] But that relationship is itself a mirror image of Arethusa's speech before the hunt, as we have already noticed: the servant girl viewing her naked, bathing mistress, who is imagined, at least, as capable of raging with maid as well as man. "O, never," says Arethusa, earlier in the play, "never such a boy again / As my Bellario!" As if noting that this excess might eventually be read as a different story, Philaster responds, "all this passion for a boy?" (3.2.74–75, 81).

Printing Bellario

Thus far, in considering the figure of the boy in *Philaster*, I have worked in a relatively familiar interpretive vein: noting the play's emphasis on the boy, Bellario; noting the text's seeming offering of nonheteronormative erotic possibilities; noting the foreclosure of those possibilities by the exposure of the boy's "real" gender as a woman; then noting the way in which that foreclosure is itself not closed, and in a number of directions—the residual of a man-boy attraction at the end of the play; the possibility of female-female eroticism broached by Arethusa that may persist in the play's dénouement; the unresolved erotic triangle in the household the play sets up at its end. (In this sense, my general approach is like any number of readings of *As You Like It* that emphasize the space of erotic play in the Rosalind-as-Ganymede scenes, the seeming foreclosure of these possibilities in heterosexual marriage at play's end, the persistence of Rosalind's boy gender and what, homoerotically, it may represent, even—as Orgel and I have each argued— in the wedding scene of the play and in the erotic multivalence that many critics have located in the play's epilogue.[44]) In doing so, I have relied implicitly on a model of what may have been visible and audible in a *performance* of *Philaster*, even saving my reminder that Bellario is "really" a woman, within the representation, until late in my discussion.

I have chosen the example of *Philaster*, however, because it differs from the usual suspects in discussions of cross-dressing boys both in performance and, significantly, in print. First, unlike the usual Shakespearean examples, *Philaster* presents and eroticizes a boy who is, throughout, a boy, until the last lines of the play. There is no initial scene establishing the boy actor as a woman who then dresses up; thus, in its eroticization and argument over the erotic meaning and function of the boy, this play lacks the potential prophylaxis, the protection in advance, with which plays like *As You Like It* and *Twelfth Night* present their audience (however briefly, in the latter case)—an audience that knows, yes, that this is a boy actor (and thus a Ganymede or Cesario) and simultaneously that, within the representation, he is "really" a woman. *Philaster* provides such an out only in retrospect, and it presses this possibility to the very limit of theatrical titillation in performance by emphasizing, describing, and finally threatening to reveal the body of the boy actor and boy Bellario before apparently resolving the problem. That is, the disjunction between the boy gender that Bellario has embodied throughout the play and his "real" female gender emerges only in the last scene of the play as the King, first, conjures up the image of an offstage torture and further wounding of Bellario ("Bear away that boy / To torture" [5.5.64–65]). (Just as wounding has already been set by the play within a context of Ovidian sexuality, torture has been glossed elsewhere in the play as "ravish[ment]" [4.6.82–85].[45]) A few moments later, the King then proceeds to order the performance of this torture onstage and commands, "Sirs, strip that boy," an imperative that proposes to reveal an erotic possibility the play has held out from the beginning (5.5.81). In its threat to strip both the livery of Bellario and the costume of the boy actor, the play emphasizes its absolute equation, to this point, of the player-apprentice and the liveried servant.[46] Unlike the Shakespearean examples often adduced, then, a performance of *Philaster* might be said to reiterate the boyness of the boy actor (whatever that may be) from beginning to end.

But what about *Philaster* in print? First, there is a lot of it, and an initial review of the terrain is required: it is an extraordinarily popular play. Between its first appearance in 1620 (Q1) and the end of the seventeenth century, there are ten quartos and an appearance in the second Beaumont and Fletcher folio (1679). Since Leo Kirschbaum's 1938 "Census of Bad Quartos," the 1620 first quarto has usually been considered one. "Comparison of Q1 and Q2 reveals in the former," Kirschbaum writes, "all the phenomena of bad quartos: . . . 'mishearings' . . . , addition, omission, substitution, restatement, transposition, mislining, corrupt blank verse, and the giving of speeches to the wrong characters."[47] Q2 (published in 1622) has been taken as the good and authoritative text, and, in the usual construal of things, according to Robert K. Turner, the editor who has studied the texts most minutely, "[a] comparison of [the later] editions reveals little more than the progressive degeneration of the text that is inevitable in a long series of reprints."[48] These views are shared by Dora Jean Ashe in her Regents edition of 1971 and Andrew Gurr in his Revels edition of 1969 (recently republished); Gurr calls the first quarto "botched" and "inferior," "with nonce-constructions and variants that are evident misreadings of the Q2 text's readings on an average of one line in four."[49] Suzanne Gossett's edition, the most recent, concurs that Q1 is "a very bad text."[50]

It is not my purpose here to save a "bad" quarto (as much fun as that can be); it is true that Q1 is a tough read and certainly less tidy than a modern reader might prefer, though I would also note that Q2 has its own extensive share of what is taken to be mislineation, a number of speeches attributed to what seem like the wrong characters, and so forth. Instead, I want to suggest that one person's textual corruption and "progressive degeneration" may be another person's history of sexuality. It might be argued that this has been the case since 1622, when, in the striking and familiar address to the reader of the second quarto, Thomas Walkley, the publisher of the first two quartos, wrote that "*Philaster,* and *Arethusa* his loue, haue laine so long a bleeding, by reason of some dangerous and gaping wounds, which they receiued in the first Impression."[51] Very early in its printing history, in other words, Walkley, deploying the language of wounding, inserts the text into a discourse of eroticism employed by the play itself; if editorial work on this play, including editorial work over the course of its printing in the seventeenth century, has seen itself as following the less wounded text, it may well also have been led, through Walkley's antiwounding rhetoric (which is to say, in this context, anti-Ovidian-erotic rhetoric), to look away from other eroticisms.

I propose, then, provisionally to rename Q1 from "the Bad Quarto" to "the Boy Quarto."[52] Following Kirschbaum, this may entail a subsequent "Census of

Boy Quartos," but I leave that for another time. For, though this text features, as Kirschbaum notes, "addition, omission, substitution, restatement, transposition, . . . and the giving of speeches to [different, if not exactly] the wrong[,] characters," what may be most striking about *Philaster* Q1 is the way in which some of these additions and restatements (which are, of course, actually differences and *pre*statements) figure the character I have been calling Bellario, but who is most often figured in Q1, the Boy Quarto, simply as "Boy."[53] The first description of him, in all the texts, as I have already mentioned, occurs in Philaster's speech beginning "I haue a boy, sent by the gods" (Q1, sig. C2ᵛ), and the presentation of this figure throughout the Q1 text emphasizes this generic quality. This is the case in the dialogue that Q1 predominantly shares with Q2, from which I quoted above, but it is even more emphatically the case in Q1's textual apparatus. With this figure's first entrance in Act 2, Scene 1, Q2 has "Enter *Philaster* and *Bellario*":

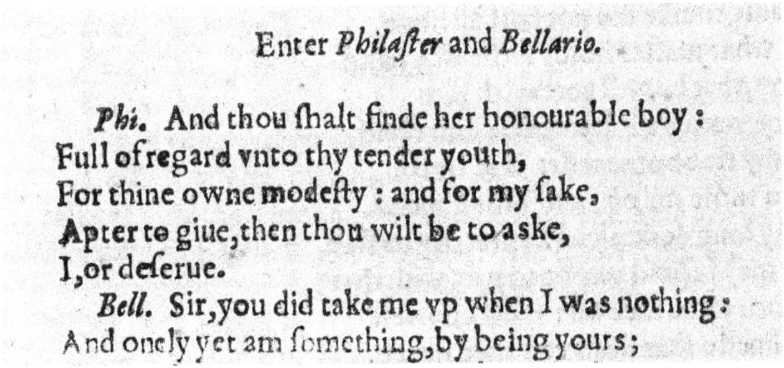

Enter *Philaster* and *Bellario*.

Phi. And thou shalt finde her honourable boy :
Full of regard vnto thy tender youth,
For thine owne modesty : and for my sake,
Apter to giue, then thou wilt be to aske,
I, or deserue.
Bell. Sir, you did take me vp when I was nothing :
And onely yet am something, by being yours;

FIGURE 19. "Enter *Philaster* and *Bellario*," in *Philaster* (Q2), sig. D1, p. 17.
By permission of the Folger Shakespeare Library.

Q1, however, instead emphasizes the boy:

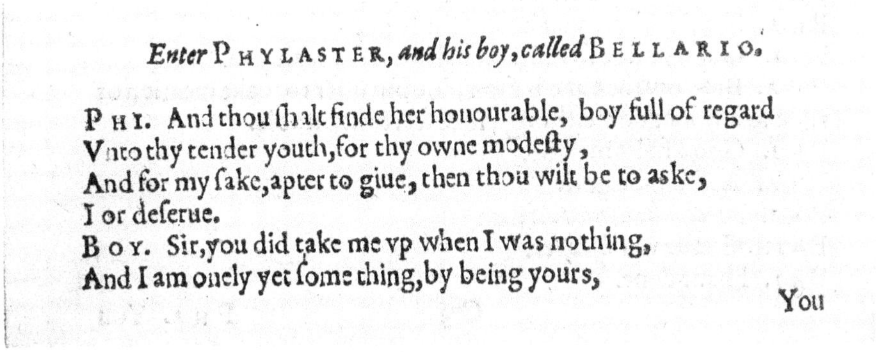

Enter P H Y L A S T E R, *and his boy, called* B E L L A R I O.

P H I. And thou shalt finde her honourable, boy full of regard
Vnto thy tender youth, for thy owne modesty,
And for my sake, apter to giue, then thou wilt be to aske,
I or deserue.
B o Y. Sir, you did take me vp when I was nothing,
And I am onely yet some thing, by being yours,
                                                    You

FIGURE 20. "*[H]is boy, called* BELLARIO," in *Phylaster* (Q1), sig. C3ᵛ, p. 14.
Reproduced by permission of The Huntington Library, San Marino, California.

As these photoquotations suggest, whereas Q2 thereafter begins its practice of using the speech prefixes "*Bell.*" and sometimes "*Bel.*" throughout, the boy called Bellario in Q1 speaks through the speech prefix "Boy," in small caps, until a moment in the last scene (to which I will return). Hailed and described in the dialogue as "boy" throughout, he is likewise "boy," generic boy, throughout Q1's stage directions, appearing there by name only in his first and last entrance indications. Thus, at the level of its dialogue and its apparatus, the text is a litany of summonses to a generic boy: "*Exit boy*," at the end of this scene, is followed immediately by "The loue of boyes vnto their Lords is strange" (Q1, sig. C4ᵛ, p. 16). "*Enter boy*" (38); "*Exit*Boy" ([*sic*] 39). "*Enter* Boy" (42); "*Exit* Boy." ([4]3). "*She sits downe, Enter* Boy" (45); "*Exit* Boy" ([46]). "*Enter the* Boy" (49); "*Boy falls downe*" (50). "*Enter* Phi. *Princesse,* Boy, *with a garland of flowers on's head*" (55).

Enter PHYLASTER, *Princeſſe,* BOY, *in priſon.*
PRIN. Nay, faith *Phylaſter,* grieue not, we are well.
BOY. Nay, good my Lord forbeare, we are wondrous well.
PHI. Oh *Arethuſa* and *Bellario,*

                                       H 3   Leaue

FIGURE 21. The "Boy" quarto, *Phylaster* (Q1), sig. H3, p. 53. Reproduced by permission of The Huntington Library, San Marino, California.

From a modern vantage point (particularly a modern editorial and readerly viewpoint that has tended to favor proper names over generic tags), the love of this text unto this *term* seems strange, but I hope I have begun to suggest the way in which the Boy Quarto seems, in print, to maintain and even to amplify some aspects of the play that, as I have argued above, would have been central to a performance of this play.[54] The one departure from this rule is the list of "The Actors Names" that prefaces the Q1 text; there, this character is figured as

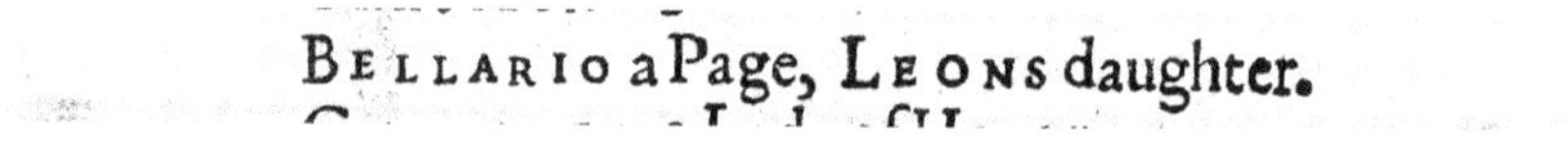

BELLARIO a Page, LEONS daughter.

FIGURE 22. Excerpt from "The Actors Names" in *Phylaster* (Q1), title-page verso. Reproduced by permission of The Huntington Library, San Marino, California.

This entry may well depict the emerging difference between *Philaster* in performance and *Philaster* in print (or, rather, *Philaster* and what it further performs in print). For, unlike what may have been the performance experience for either of these earliest texts in the theater, this moment in the printed text attempts to insert into the otherwise resolutely Boy Quarto a prehistory for the character Bellario's "true" gender that the quarto does not otherwise share. (To put this another way: "The Actors Names" here acts the function of Rosalind before the forest, or the unnamed lady Viola emerging from the shipwreck—the establishment of a gender that is then thrown off or covered over for the bulk of the play.)

In the dialogue text of the Boy Quarto, Bellario as daughter emerges in the last three pages of the play, but her gender (disclosed by her kneeling to Leon and the stage direction *"discouers her haire"*) is accompanied *not* by her emergence from the speech prefix "BOY" into a named female identity (indeed, she has no female name in this text), but by her taking on, for the first time in this text, the speech prefix "BEL." for Bellario:

> That boy there ----
> BEL. If to me ye fpeake Lady,
> I muft tell you, you haue loft your felfe
> In your too much forwardneffe, and hath forgot
> Both modefty and truth, with what impudence
> You haue throwne moft damnable afpertions
> On that noble Princeffe and my felfe : witneffe the world ;
> Behold me fir.   *Kneeles to* LEON, *and difcouers her haire.*
> LEON. I fhould know this face ; my daughter.
> BEL. The fame fir.
> PRIN. How, our fometime Page, *Bellario*, turn'd woman ?

FIGURE 23. From "BOY" to Bellario, in *Phylaster* (Q1), sig. I4ᵛ, p. 64. Reproduced by permission of The Huntington Library, San Marino, California.

For a reader of this quarto, this text maintains or performs a persistent ambiguity around this figure: *he* is a daughter in a list at the outset; *she* goes by her male name when she "turn[s] woman." "How, our sometime Page, *Bellario*, turn'd woman?" asks the Princesse. "I doe beleeue thee," the Princesse says a moment later, and then (simultaneously disbelieving) "*Bellario* I shall call thee still" (64–65). (Here again the play both makes impossible and practices a same-sex female eroticism, to use Traub's terms, because its impossibility both absolves the Princesse from the accusation of having slept with a boy and remains present in her affection for her page turned woman.[55])

The second quarto—call it the Bellario Quarto—maintains a similar ambiguity, though differently articulated: there is no list of the actors' names, but Bellario remains Bellario consistently throughout, in stage directions and speech prefixes, before and after his/her gender transformation. For a reader of the Bellario Quarto, the dissonance or ambiguity emerges most visibly at the moment Bellario speaks his/her (other name) (see Figure 24): the speech prefix announces "Bellario," and Bellario announces "Euphrasia." "What's thy name?": "*Bel. Euphrasia.*"

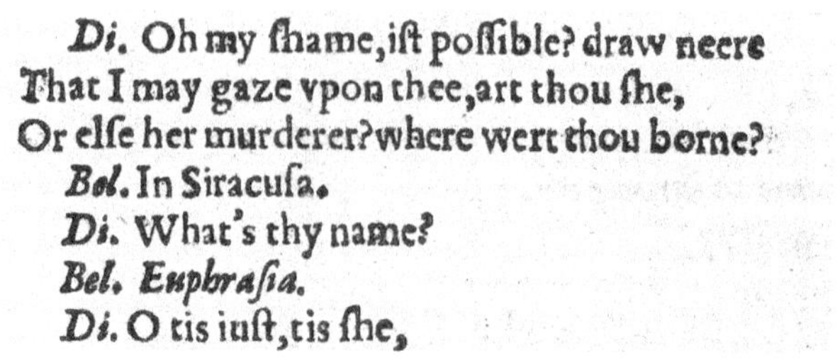

> *Di.* Oh my fhame,ift poffible? draw neere
> That I may gaze vpon thee,art thou fhe,
> Or elfe her murderer?where wert thou borne?
> *Bel.* In Siracufa.
> *Di.* What's thy name?
> *Bel. Euphrafia.*
> *Di.* O tis iuft,tis fhe,

FIGURE 24. "What's thy name?" in *Philaster* (Q2), sig. L2, p. 75. By permission
of the Folger Shakespeare Library.

It is perhaps useful for me to pause here in this history that attempts to avert corruption and degeneration to comment on my reconfiguring of the first two texts of *Philaster*. I bother to think about this at all because I think that, even with several good twentieth- and twenty-first-century editions of the play based on the Good (Bellario) Quarto available, there is a way in which these editions fail to register aspects of the ostensibly "bad" text (the boy text)—aspects that nevertheless disclose something crucial about *Philaster* as it is registered even in the "good" text and in early seventeenth-century performance practice. (This is only more the case when one observes the fact that the middle sections of these texts are, in the dialogue they inscribe, more or less identical, with only parts of the first and last acts showing marked divergence.[56]) I emphasize that I do not rename these texts as the paired "Boy Quarto" and "Woman Quarto," for *neither* text fully begins with or finally restores a female Euphrasia even in the ambiguated ways in which Rosalind and Viola end their plays. Neither do these texts map easily onto something that might look like pederasty versus heteronormativity, since the Boy Quarto is, if anything, more resolute in marrying Bellario-turned-woman off to Trasiline at the last moment (thus both evacuating and repeating the love of this woman still dressed as a boy unto a lord).[57] And the Bellario Quarto—still harping on boys in its dialogue if not in its stage directions and speech prefixes[58]—leaves Euphrasia (called still Bellario) unmarried but as a chaste servant to the Princesse and Philaster.

For a Euphrasia Quarto, we might well turn to the 1628 third quarto (Q3), which begins with a list of "*The persons presented*" that is followed in all subsequent texts. This list for the first time divides the characters by gender as well as social class, moving Euphrasia to the bottom of the group of women characters: "EVPHRASIA, Daughter of *Dion*, but disguised like a Page, and called *Bellario*."[59] Here we have the girlhood of Beaumont and Fletcher's boy heroine set out, though again, still, I would want to notice that a reader would have confronted a hybrid approach to this figure. Even as the dramatis personae list marks the arrival here of a notion of gender-stabilized character that seems to precede, govern, and potentially outlast the fiction, it sits in considerable dissonance with the text itself as a reader must have experienced it,[60] for this "person presented" continues in all other respects to be presented by the text as "Bellario" (in dialogue, speech prefixes, and stage directions). Not only is Euphrasia "called Bellario" by the play's characters but she/he is also consistently called Bellario *by the edition*, including (again, still) at and after the moment of her disclosure as Euphrasia.

The folio of 1679 and all but the last of the subsequent seventeenth-century quartos (1634, 1639, 1652, two editions c. 1661, 1687[61]) follow this hybrid or dissonant presentation of the character. Even as Turner saw the "inevitable" "progressive degeneration of the text" in these editions, we can see that, at least with regard to this figure of the boy/woman, something more complicated is happening. On the one hand, in the dramatis personae lists, this process looks like a straightening out of gender and the idea of character across the texts, and thus *potentially* of the erotic plot of this play. On the other, this process registers the persistence of a boy-centered eroticism that has extended well past the modes of production in the early seventeenth-century theater that it emerged from and may in part have represented.

It may not be beside the point at all that the text in which Euphrasia first appears in a dramatis personae list (Q3, 1628) is also a quarto that begins to acknowledge, however tentatively, a difference between a performance audience experiencing plays in the theater and a reading public consuming plays in print—something set out in a new preface, "The Stationer *to* the Vnderstanding Gentrie": "This Play so affectionately taken, and approoued by the Seeing Auditors, or Hearing Spectators, . . . hath receiued (as appeares by the copious vent of two Editions,) no lesse acceptance with improouement of you likewise the Readers" (Q3, sig. A2).[62] One might then hypothesize, however tentatively, the linking here of (1) a more literate idea of the playtext quarto, related to but increasingly separable from the playhouse; (2) the straightening out, however rudimentary, of character gender and erotic trajectories in ways that depart from the ways of or available in early seventeenth-century performance; and (3) the simultaneous persistence of and tolerance for those erotic possibilities, such that they did not appear to require the full-scale reediting or reconfiguration of the text. (In the last scene of *As You Like It*, analyzed at the end of Chapter 1, Rosalind is still joining "his hand" with Orlando's until the third folio edits out the remaining boy in 1664.[63])

The next step on this route, which I will not take up in detail here, would be the last seventeenth-century quarto in 1695. Its title page says it is "Revis'd, and the Two last Acts new Written," and it contains a dramatis personae list that perhaps clarifies—which is to say, reconstitutes under a new regime of production in the Restoration—the relationship of the actor and the boy the play represents.[64] It reads, quite simply:

Bellario.   **Mrs. Rogers.**

FIGURE 25. Excerpt from the dramatis personae list in *Philaster* (Q10), sig. A4ᵛ.
By permission of the Folger Shakespeare Library.

To recast Turner's "progressive degeneration" this way—that is to say, as a movement toward a more modern sense of gender normativity (never fully accomplished) and as a movement toward a straightening out, in the modern sense, of the play's man-boy, woman-boy love—is also to remind ourselves that these things we tend to speak of as "shifts" in the history of sexuality and of early modern drama are incremental rather than instantaneous or immediately realized. There are, that is to say, persons whose experience included two different sets of performance practices in *Philaster* (the unknown, earliest, boy-acted Bellarios, through Mrs. Rogers) and who experienced as well a reading practice that confronted various of the hybrid or dissonant texts that I have examined. Take Samuel Pepys, for example, a contemporary of quartos 4–10 of *Philaster*, who notes on May 30, 1668, after seeing a performance of the play, "it is pretty to see how I could remember almost all along, ever since I was a boy, Arethusa's part which I was to have acted at Sir Rob. Cooke's; and it was very pleasant to me, but more to think what a ridiculous thing it would have been for me to have acted a beautiful woman."[65] If Pepys has seemed in some other respects the very model of a modern, privatized heterosexual subject,[66] his statement here seems a wonderfully apt account of living across the boy-actor divide of the seventeenth century, recording simultaneously, as it does, the nostalgic pleasure he takes in reliving, reciting, an earlier practice of theatrical cross-gendering, and the pleasurable (if potentially proto-modern) self-discipline he enacts in finding this memory now somehow ridiculous.

The Boy/friend

If we return to the moment of *Philaster*'s and *Twelfth Night*'s first writing and staging in the first decade of the seventeenth century, we can see a number of parallel structures in these boy plays, including but not limited to the following:

1. The definitional struggle over the figure of the boy, an instability that is both connected to cross-gendering (in each case, the boy is, within the narrative of the play, "really" a girl) *and in excess of that*;
2. The boy as an erotic negotiator between two adults (Orsino and Olivia, Philaster and Arethusa);

3. The boy as a switchpoint or catalyst for the multiplication of erotic possibilities (staged or fantasized, and including female-female eroticism) over the course of the play;

4. A conclusion in which a "lord," who has in some sense declared his love for a boy, insists that he will continue to call the boy, who is now a woman, by his earlier boy name: "But Bellario— / For I must call thee still so . . ." Or, taking instead Orsino's concluding lines in *Twelfth Night*:

> Cesario, come—
> For so you shall be *while you are a man.*
> But when in other habits you are seen,
> Orsino's mistress, and his fancy's queen. (5.1.375–78)

After this, as if in enactment and further complication of that set of performative fantasies, Feste immediately sings "When that I was and a *little tiny boy*," his concluding song. "A foolish thing was but a toy," he rhymes (5.1.379–81): "If *thing* has the likely overtone of 'penis,' " writes the usually reserved Oxford edition, "then the line roughly means 'a little penis was only a toy'—i.e. was useless—when I was a child" (5.1.381n).[67] Earlier the youth or boy or young gentleman Cesario had opined that "a little thing would make me tell them how much I lack of a man" (3.4.290). The lacking little thing is usually understood to be a penis (of whatever size) and thus to gesture toward Viola's "true" gender, but the line may also (simultaneously) indicate the presumed size difference between younger and older male "things." As the play ends, what manner of toys and things, we might ask, are in use between Orsino and Cesario while (s)he is a man?[68]

I deliberately stress the complexities and multiple valences in this concluding language of Orsino's—and the possibility of seeing Feste's song as oblique commentary on or extension of this plurality—in order to emphasize the way in which the structures or discourses of eroticism here are cross-coupled, even within what we would think of as a "single" relationship. What kind of boys will boys be, being boys? If, in the Orsino/Cesario relationship, that is, *Twelfth Night* had seemed to play with the possibilities of man-boy love—and it is worth recalling that Orsino exclusively hails Cesario in the boyish terms of "youth," "lad," "boy," and "the lamb I love" throughout the play—then, in the play's concluding lines, as Viola becomes her "master's mistress" (5.1.317), Cesario becomes for Orsino "a man."[69] Boys may also be men in *Twelfth Night*, suggesting that we may also need to revise Orgel's sense that boys but not men are objects of adult male attraction.[70]

Similarly, we might consider the distance from our usual, default patriarchal understanding of marriage in this culture that is indicated by the history and conclusion of Olivia's marriage with the boy Sebastian, the union of a countess and gentleman/page. Whatever mutuality is imagined as the basis of their marriage at the end of the play (the priest cites their "mutual joinder of [their] hands" [5.1.153]), this is nevertheless a union that Olivia has desired and negotiated across what she takes to be a difference of degree, if not also of age and actual social status. (As the second-generation Arden edition suggests, in glossing the lines that establish Sebastian and Viola's father's death on *her* thirteenth birthday, either Shakespeare has forgotten the two are twins and his birthday also hers, or "[t]his is possibly a deliberate attempt to suggest that Sebastian is, at least, not younger than Olivia."[71] Deliberate or not, the play's apparent imprecision on this point may be one result of the unconventional reversals of hierarchy spelled out by the Olivia/Sebastian relationship.) Thus, Olivia's earlier resonant line to Cesario/Viola, "I would you were as I would have you be" (3.1.140), often read as the play's knowing performative about gender, may encode other fantasies about age and rank, fantasies that the play *Philaster* puts at the forefront in the imagined sexual relationship between a princess and her serving-boy. There are additional hints of this in *Twelfth Night*: Olivia says, going to the chapel, "we will our celebration keep / According to *my* birth," asserting her rank and possibly age (4.3.30–31). What then are boys, to women, in this play?

To take one additional example—building on Traub's and Mario DiGangi's accounts of this relationship[72]—we can examine Sebastian and Antonio's relationship, conventionally described as an early modern male friendship and marked intermittently by that hierarchy-averse discourse of equality and identicality. (After Olivia's proposal, Sebastian, distrusting his own soul's disputation with itself, desires the conversation of a friend, in terms that seem drawn directly from the discourse of friendship: "His counsel now might do me golden service." Earlier Antonio had urged Sebastian not to go about Illyria "unguided and unfriended" [3.3.10].) Still, and directly at odds with friendship's usual terms,[73] this relation is *simultaneously* structured by the hierarchy of Antonio's intense and explicitly religious devotion and service: "I do *adore* thee so," he says after their first scene (2.1.42, my emphasis), and, at the moment of Sebastian's perceived betrayal (speaking of Sebastian but to Cesario):

> This youth that you see here
> I snatched one half out of the jaws of death,
> Relieved him with such *sanctity* of love,
> And to his *image*, which methought did promise
> Most *venerable* worth, did I *devotion*.
> . . . .
> But O, how vile an *idol* proves this *god*!
> Thou hast, *Sebastian*, done good feature shame. (3.4.350–57)

As DiGangi and Cynthia Lewis remind us, the multiple Sebastians and Antonios of Renaissance drama bear saints' names,[74] and the devotion this Antonio bears his chosen idol, god, and saint named Sebastian seems only further underlined by Sebastian's corporeal description of his own mortification at the moment of their reunion in Act 5: "Antonio! O my dear Antonio," Sebastian exclaims; "How have the hours *racked and tortured* me / Since I have lost thee!" (5.1.211–13). Still, again tracking the crossings and mixtures of discourses and structures in this relation, we could recall the terms of Antonio's denunciation of Sebastian to Orsino moments earlier: "A *witchcraft* drew me hither: / That *most ingrateful boy* there *by your side* / From the rude sea's enraged and foamy mouth / Did I *redeem*." A venerated god, a friend, a saint, a witch, a redeemed boy—pulled out of the water, standing (apparently) beside a duke. Not only is the meaning of the category of boy mobile in this play and this theater, but the structures of affection within which he functions (*they* function?) illustrate a range of relations and internal politics.

Boys in Print

Thinking about boys in the early modern theater, we have been considering printed versions of texts originating in performance for the additional information they provide for understanding the meaning of boys onstage. This has been an important concern for a variety of reasons within theatrical history, feminist scholarship, and, more recently, queer studies. But contemplating the meaning of a repeated speech prefix like the generic "Boy" for the early modern stage also leads me to observe that scholarship has not to this point adequately thought about the erotic energies that the category of "the boy" sometimes also registers specifically in *print* contexts and not simply as print products of the stage. The penultimate section of this chapter works somewhat speculatively, providing a prolegomenon for a larger project I would call "Boys in Print"—a field of inquiry that, as my suggestions will show, requires further investigation.

First, "Boys in Print" might think about the circumstances of print *production*, the overlapping structures of familial relations and affect that may have attended master and/or mistress and apprentice relations in the printing house (as in the playhouse and in other guild-based professions). Chapter 1 argued for skepticism toward the secret lives sometimes imagined for the compositors of the Shakespeare first folio and by extension other early modern books, but whether or not the apprentice "Compositor E" has "imitative tendencies" or "follows copy closely" (and thus recapitulates some of the early modern pedagogical structures for boys noted earlier), the education and relations of apprentice compositors and other laborers in printing and publishing houses are worth examining in greater detail as social structures, and not simply from the perspective of identifying them.[75]

Second, we would want to consider the proliferation of other signs of boys in print culture. As I have mentioned elsewhere, the first two editions of *Philaster* were printed "for *Thomas Walkley*, and [were] to be sold"—strangely enough—"at his shop at the *Eagle and Child* in Brittaines Bursse" (in 1620, also 1622).[76] The Boy Quarto and the Bellario Quarto, that is, were sold at what must have resonated as the sign of the Rape of Ganymede, this story of both pedagogical uplift and homoerotic ravishment and adoption. In the 1620s and early 1630s, Walkley sells at the sign of the Eagle and Child in or near the New Exchange; *Othello* is among his wares, as are catalogs of nobility, the masque *Loves Triumph Through Callipolis*, and some other plays by Beaumont and Fletcher. This is not an unfamiliar sign either before or after him: there are several imprints of Thomas Creed printing and selling at this sign in 1600, "in the Old Change . . . neare Old Fish-streete"; there is a golden eagle and child in Pater Noster Row in 1590; Jasper Emery sells books at the Eagle and Child located in Paul's Churchyard near Watling Street in the 1630s at least through 1642; Thomas Thornicroft sells under this sign "near the little north door" in the 1660s.[77] Given the variety of texts printed and sold at this Ganymedic sign, my point is not that there is some necessary thematic connection or causal relation between the printed text and the sign, though the connection in the case of *Philaster* is a tantalizing one. Rather, I want to gesture toward the ubiquity in this culture of this sign of the Ganymedic child ("sign" in all the senses of that word)—the everydayness of this image, which we, visiting from the twenty-first century, may have difficulty reckoning. Expanding the early modern field of our vision further, we can see the Black Boy, under which sign, near Paul's, a number of imprints are sold in the latter half of the sixteenth century, and then, notably, a flurry of texts in the 1660s through the 1690s and thereafter.[78]

"Boys in Print" would also consider the archive of images of male children and adolescents that adorn Renaissance printed texts. I hardly need to point out the swarms of *putti* that adorn a wide range of Renaissance visual materials. But, without minimizing the differences between painting, sculpture, and printed books, the larger point is to think about the implications of an emergent print culture that thinks of partially clothed boys, youths, and sometimes men not only as *decorative* (though this in itself is not inconsequential) but also as framing, presenting, and emblematizing a wide variety of texts—on title pages, in printed borders, in printers' ornaments, in decorative capitals, in grotesques used as page borders,[79] and, as we will see, in letters themselves. R. B. McKerrow's and F. S. Ferguson's catalogs of printing images, beyond which I will briefly venture at the end of this section, provide an initial survey of the range of uses of boys in these contexts *and*, as in *Twelfth Night*, the range of figures that might be included in this category. Here are five examples, only a small sampling of the possibilities, but these may help us to think about what play readers and other book readers saw when they saw boys in print:

❦ First, naked boys reading in the upper margins of the title page of the 1559 edition of Thomas Elyot's dictionary, the *Bibliotheca Eliotæ* (Figure 26), along with bare-breasted women.[80] This is a book border that, in other contexts, continued to be used through 1579.

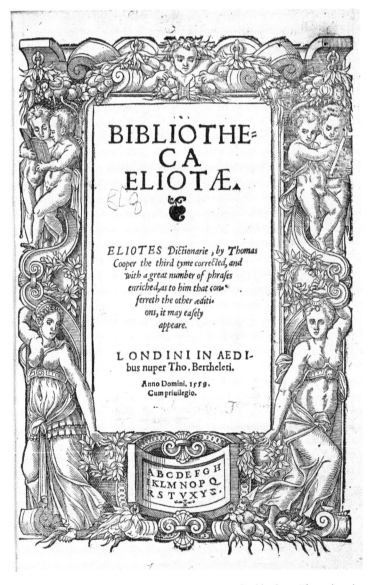

FIGURE 26. Boys and women on the title page of *Bibliotheca Eliotæ* (1559). Reproduced by permission of The Huntington Library, San Marino, California.

Second, a somewhat older and buffer selection of boys (the book's translator's term might have been "striplings") framing—playing musical instruments in the margins of—the title page of Golding's 1565 partial translation of Ovid's *Metamorphoses* (Figure 27), a border in use through at least 1615, where it also appeared on a psalter.[81]

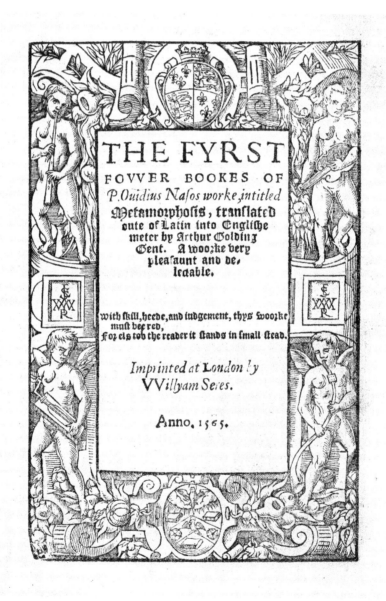

FIGURE 27. Boys on the title page of Ovid, *Metamorphoses* (1565).
By permission of the Folger Shakespeare Library.

❦ Third, an ornament of a boy Triton (Figure 28),[82] with a motto that again brings together the ideas of boys and education.[83] It reads, "IMMORTALITY IS GOTTEN BY THE STVDY OF LETTERS."

FIGURE 28. A boy Triton in a printer's emblem from Iohn Northbrooke, *The poore mans Garden*. Reproduced by kind permission of the Syndics of Cambridge University Library.

❦ And, last, two different versions of a similar printer's ornament, depicting a boy or youth with one winged arm, while the other arm is weighted down (Figures 29 and 30).[84] The younger of these boys (Figure 29) appears in England from 1563 to 1604 and, late in his printed career, on the title pages of some 1597–98 editions of *Richard II* and the 1604 *Dr. Faustus*.[85]

Derived from an Alciato emblem signifying poverty holding talent down, and Englished in Whitney's *Choice Of Emblemes*, these ornaments are notably also the plot of Bellario/Euphrasia's and Cesario/Viola's stories: "My wishe, and will, are still to mounte alofte. / My wante, and woe, denie me my desire."[86] The god who summons from above in these ornaments may resonate with Jove of the Ganymede story, a connection made more emphatic when such a device was sold, as

LONDON

Printed for Thomas Thorpe, and are to be
fold in Paules Church-yard at the figne
of the Crane, by Walter Burre.
1 6 0 4.

FIGURE 29. Printer's ornament on the title page of *A Succinct Philosophicall
declaration of the nature of Clymactericall yeeres*.
Photo courtesy of The Newberry Library.

LONDON

Printed by *W. S.* for *Henry Fetherstone.*
1 6 1 9.

FIGURE 30. Feather and stone ornament, from the title page of Samuel Purchas,
Pvrchas his Pilgrim, Microcosmvs, Or The Historie of Man.
Photo courtesy of The Newberry Library.

Figure 30 was, by Jasper Emery "at his shop at the signe of the Eagle and Childe in S. *Pauls* Church-yard."

These images we conventionally think of as printers' "ornaments," "devices," mere "borders" to the texts proper, but I am urging that we think about the ways in which they visualize, connect with, and rearticulate the signifiers in movable type (e.g., "BOY") that we are more accustomed to reading. Indeed, an entire additional category of "Boys in Print"—the boys who appear in the historiated and decorative woodcut initials that begin sections of hundreds of early modern books—has largely gone unnoticed by modern readers and in the history of English printing. As one would expect, these boy initials do not appear in McKerrow's and Ferguson's catalogs of borders and devices, but they are also absent from Henry R. Plomer's select examples of English decorative initials and from Ruth Samson Luborsky and Elizabeth Morley Ingram's exhaustive *Guide to English Illustrated Books, 1536–1603*.[87] Neither borders, nor devices, nor (in Luborsky and Ingram's definition) "illustrations," these boy initials (and whole boy alphabets) have largely disappeared from view, though they could form a significant part of a text's combined visual and textual impact.

Boy initials persisted as an adopted practice in England, having been widely used in continental printing;[88] like many of the boys on title pages and in printers' devices, they bear a historical relationship to the putti (or *spiritelli*) of Renaissance Italian art (though whether they carry with them into English visual and printed contexts the varied meanings as spirits, "panic phobias," psychological emanations, and spirits of love attributed to them has yet to be established).[89] That the spiritelli's playful escapades, at least in their Italian emergence, are not devoid of multiple levels of erotic meaning is illustrated by Marco Zoppo's remarkable drawings, now at the British Museum, showing in one case apparently playful putti sodomizing each other with a bellows, while adult courtiers look on, one of whom grasps the suggestively placed hilt of his sword (Figure 31).[90]

As in Zoppo (though usually less explicitly erotically), boys within printed initials sometimes appear in groups at play. Like the range of historiated, floriated, and otherwise decorative initials generally, boy initials could range from quite large, like the boys dissecting a boar within the initial capital Q of the dedication page of the Vesalius *Fabrica* (Figure 32)[91] or playing within an O (Figure 33),[92] to small, like a boy reading a book within a Q in a 1541 introduction to grammar in Greek and Latin (Figure 34). Resembling the audience for this text, the latter boy finds himself within, and studying, the circuit of letters: "orthographia."[93]

As these examples also show, these boys in print are not always winged putti or cherubs; further, though the limited historical and critical work on the topic persists in calling them "children initials,"[94] they are invariably alphabets of boys, never girls. In the English context, boy initials and boy alphabets, like other

FIGURE 31. Boys at play in a drawing by Marco Zoppo.
Trustees of the British Museum.

AD DIVVM C

QVINTVM, MAXIMVM,

QVE IMPERATOREM, AN

in suos de Humani corporis fabrica

VANTVMV
dis grauiter ob
tur, minusꝗ fo
clementiſsime
dium quoque
diſciplinarum,
mulantur diuiſ
tis exercitiorur
diſtributionen
unam eius part
ipſum maximc
queunt, relicti
ac propoſitum
artis conſtituti
teras quidem ſilentio præteream, & de ea quæ ſanitati h
monem inſtituam, profectò in hac tametſi reliquarum or
uenit longè cõmodiſsima & imprimis neceſſaria difficilis

FIGURE 32. Boys in a Q dissecting a boar, in Vesalius, *De Humani corporis fabrica*.
Photo courtesy of The Newberry Library.

DE INTENTIONE SVMMAR

caufa intentionis, & libri

MNI
bilis d
puli pı
ditur.
coran
parab:
tates p
rumre
minim
in prin
iam præmiſſa, tranquillitatis ſeu
tates & fructus expreſſit, ut per h

FIGURE 33. Boys dancing in an O, in Marsilius of Padua, *Defensor Pacis*, sig. b[1]ʳ.
Photo courtesy of The Newberry Library.

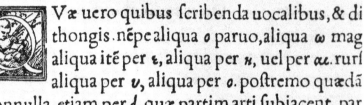

γιας εἰπεῖν, κỳ πὲ̀ ἀφαιρέσεως, κỳ προλήψεως, κỳ ὅλως
ταβολῆς, οὐ τῶ πρόντ῀ σκοπῦ.

DE ORTHOGRAPHIA.

Væ uero quibus ſcribenda uocalibus, & di
thongis népe aliqua *o* paruo, aliqua *ω* mag
aliqua ité per *ε*, aliqua per *η*, uel per *αι*. rurſ
aliqua per *υ*, aliqua per *ο*. poſtremo quædā
ι, nonnulla etiam per *ζ*. quæ partim arti ſubiacent, par
ex etymologia ſumenda ſunt, ut Epirus *o* quidem ex

FIGURE 34. A boy studying letters in a letter, in Theodōros Gazēs, *Introdvctionis grammaticae*. Photo courtesy of The Newberry Library.

woodcuts, circulated among and were passed down between printers. They appear in English books along with, and often apparently unsystematically alongside, other decorated or historiated alphabetic initials, including animals; adults (usually but not always male, often mythological); floriated initials; grotesques; and factotum initials (in which a decorative frame for an initial was temporarily filled with the contextually required letter).[95]

While one would not want to overemphasize the homoeroticism of these boy-letter images in many cases, one would also not want simply to read past or discount it. Their gender exclusivity and their function supplementing, decorating, and initializing texts and sections of texts suggest that they spell a difference between early modern and later printing and culture. Is there an implied or intended connection between the "decorative" initials and the texts they introduce? Does the very ubiquity of boy initials conversely suggest their meaninglessness—a status as unnoticed visual decoration and mere variety? What modes of attachment, identification, and eroticism are intended by, or legible to, a particular or more general set of print producers or readers in these letter figures? (How) do the contexts of their appearances alter the possible meanings of "the same" letter-image woodblock within different books? There has been little sustained work on English historiated initials since some preliminary accounts in the early years of the twentieth century, and those accounts did not answer these questions of meaning production, ideological freight, instrumentality, and reception.[96] In English contexts, boy initials often appear, for example, in bibles, as in the example in Figure 35, from the 1602 edition of the Bishops' Bible, printed by Robert Barker, the Queen's printer. The nude youth seems to grasp at the decorative foliage adorning the initial P for "Paul," at the outset of 2 Thessalonians and again on the following page.[97] In Coverdale's 1537 English Bible, printed in Antwerp, the text is

FIGURE 35. A youth in a letter, the Bishops' Bible (1602), p. 476.
By permission of the Folger Shakespeare Library.

more or less visually divided and structured by several differently sized series of decorative alphabets, many involving boys/putti: initial capitals occupying the height of the first six lines of the blackletter text mark the beginnings of books (including Genesis; see Figure 36).[98] "In the beginnyng," there are naked winged boys, structuring the Bible.

FIGURE 36. Boys in the letter I at the beginning of the Coverdale Bible (1537),
Old Testament, folio i (recto). Photo courtesy of The Newberry Library.

A correspondence between the initials and their context is sometimes legible (though possibly accidental). For example, the same letter O is used in the Coverdale Bible both for 2 Kings (Figure 37) and for the beginning of the Apocrypha's Book of Wisdom (Figure 38), where those same boys are turned 90 degrees and seem to recline on each other as the text begins, "Sett your affeccion vpon wisdome."[99]

¶The fyrst Chapter.
A
Ochoziah the sonne of Ahab be-
ganne to raygne vpon Israel
in Samaria/the.xvij.yere of
Jehosaphat kynge of Juda/&
was kynge ouer Israel two
yere/and dyd euell in the sight
of the Lorde/and walked in the waye of hys
father and in the waye of hys mother/and in
the waye of Jeroboam the sonne of Nabat

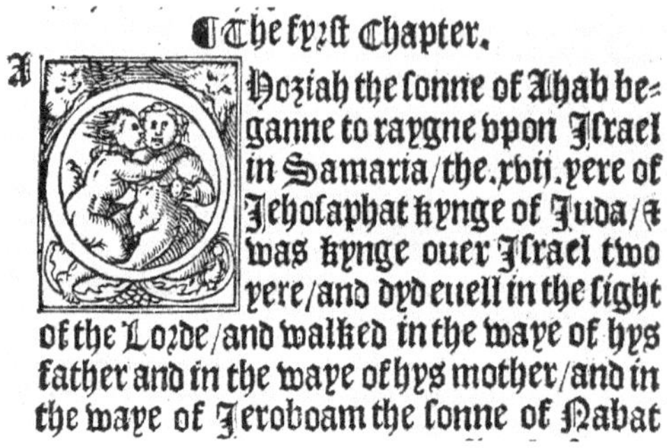

FIGURE 37. Boys embracing in an O, in the Coverdale Bible (1537), Old Testament, folio Cxl^r^. Photo courtesy of The Newberry Library.

¶The boke of
wysdome.
¶How we ought to searche and enquyre after God/
and who be those that fynde hym. Of the holy goost.
We ought to flye from backbityng & murmuring. &c.
¶The fyrst Chapter.
A
Sett youre affeccion
vpon wysdome / ye that be
iudges of the earth. Haue a
good opinion of the Lorde/
and seke hym in the syngle-
nesse of herte. For he wyll
be founde of them that tempte hym not/ and

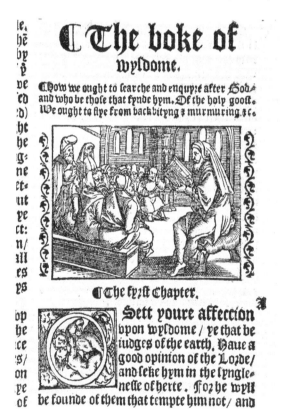

FIGURE 38. "Sett youre affeccion vpon wysdome" (the boys from Figure 37 turned on their side). Book of Wisdom, Apocrypha, folio xxx^r^. Photo courtesy of The Newberry Library.

This is not to say that boy initials always or only appeared in biblical or religious contexts, but that they *also* appeared there, sometimes as angelic putti, sometimes simply as boys. What does a boy signify in these contexts?

Perhaps the most striking example of a boy initial—this one more elaborately historiated—circulates across kinds of books and appears in a 1595 Bible,[100] in the 1602 heraldic work *Honor Military, and Civill,*[101] and in a 1625 *Booke of Common Prayer.*[102] Above a town and landscape, this woodblock C—displacing and matching the height of the first ten to twelve lines of the books' standard fonts—depicts Jove kissing Ganymede within a cloud, accompanied by an eagle that flies into the upper left corner to make the reference explicit. This doubly homoerotic initial—a nude Mercury bearing his caduceus leads the way, perhaps even bearing the message of Jove and Ganymede's love—initiates Thomas Cranmer's preface to the Bishops' Bible (Figure 39), begins the dedication of the heraldic text to Queen Elizabeth (Figure 40), and is the first letter of "Christ" in the gospel to be read the second Sunday after Easter in the *Booke of Common Prayer* (Figure 41).[103]

FIGURE 39. Ganymede, Jove, and Mercury beginning Thomas Cranmer's
"Prologue or Preface," *Holy Bible* (1595), STC 2167, sig. A.ij.
Photo courtesy of The Newberry Library.

Onſidering (
mighty Prince,
Subiect is ,not (
vttermoſt of l.
qualitie , to ad
Prince and Co.
my poore talen
of my duetie, fo.
I holde vnder
moſt Gracious;

courſes concerning Armes, Honor, and the 1

FIGURE 40. Ganymede, Jove, and Mercury in William Segar, dedicatory letter
to Queen Elizabeth, *Honor Military, and Civill*, STC 22164, no sig.
By permission of the Folger Shakespeare Library.

The Goſpel.
Hriſt ſaid, I
herd. A good
life foꝛ the ſhee
and hee whict
(neither the ſi
ſeeth the wolfe
the ſheepe, and
catcheth and l
The hired ſerꝰ
is an hired ſerꝰ

foꝛ the ſheepe. I am the good Shepl

FIGURE 41. C for "Christ," in *The Booke of Common Prayer*,
STC 16364, sig. G5ᵛ. Courtesy of The Rare Book and Manuscript
Library of the University of Illinois at Urbana-Champaign.

What—if anything—do the love of Jove and Ganymede and boy initials more
generally have to do with these contexts, with these texts that they initialize? Does
William Segar's conventionally abasing letter to Elizabeth, averring his "poore
talent," "duetie," and "place of Seruice" as one of the queen's heraldic officials (Nor-
roy), and "prostrat[ing] himselfe, and his Labours, at [her] most Sacred feete," de-

lineate a version of the Ganymede story—a desire to be born aloft into her higher favor?[104] If so, how does a regendering of the Ganymede story (itself enacted if not intended here by another of the queen's servants, her printer Robert Barker) alter or expand our sense of the peculiar homoerotics of the tale and its early modern applications?

Similarly, does Cranmer's letter, "Concerning two sundrie sortes of people," requiring advice and discipline as they approach the biblical text, resonate with Ganymede and Jove? The letter (Cranmer's letter, or Prologue, as well as the C that inaugurates it) certainly is related to the discourses of learning, education, and discipline we have seen in other boy contexts. At the least, in what is an undoubtedly complex text concerning the reading of the scriptures in English, the pedagogical meanings of the Ganymede story resonate with the archbishop's attempt to teach and dissuade "they that refuse to read" the Bible in the "vulgare tongue" and "they which by their inordinate reading, vndiscreet speaking, contentious disputing, *or otherwise by their licentio[u]s liuing*, slander and hinder the Worde of G O D."[105] Is the Ganymede C a letter that recommends learning or warns against license?

Such connections are perhaps most apparent—to a modern reader, at least— in the *Booke of Common Prayer*, for there the recitation of Christ's words—"Christ said, I am the good Shepherd"—recapitulates an aspect of the Ganymede story. But which is the shepherd here, and which the sheep? In the woodblock and the Ganymede story, the shepherd is gathered to the god. Are the commonly praying congregants the Ganymedes, lifted up to heaven? The text of the Epistle that directly precedes this C instructs, "for ye were as sheepe going astray, but are now turned vnto the Shepheard and Bishop of your soules."[106] These are not simply speculative questions emerging from this particular context; as Leonard Barkan and Richard Rambuss have argued, early modern theological understandings of the Ganymede story are not separable from and did not require "a corresponding evacuation of all his original (homo)erotic significances."[107]

The roles and resonances of this inaugurating letter become further complicated in the Gospel that follows, with Christ saying, "I am the good Shepheard, and know my sheepe, and am knowen of mine. As my Father knoweth me, euen so know I also my Father: and I giue my life for the sheepe. And other sheepe I haue, which are not of this fold: them also must I bring, and they shall heare my voyce, and there shall be one fold, and one Shepherd." While the theology of the passage is clear and familiar to those in the Christian tradition, the love of Jove and Ganymede in the letter raises questions that potentially complicate the theology: Who is gathered to whom, who knows whom, who ascends to the Father, in this woodblock C for Christ? (Is the Christ here, as in two of Rambuss's divergent examples, "the true Ganimedes, . . . the fairest among the sons of men," or is he the shepherd who "suffers the little children to come unto [him]"?[108]) Lest we think these religious resonances outside the range of homoeroticisms we read earlier in this chapter (and vice versa), it is worth listening again to Bellario/Euphrasia telling her story at the moment of her discovery:

> I saw *a god,*
> I thought—but it was you—enter our gates.
> My blood *flew out and back again . . .*
> . . . .
> Then was I called away in haste
> To entertain you. Never was a man
> *Heaved from a sheepcote to a sceptre, raised*
> *So high* in thoughts as I. You left a kiss
> Upon these lips. (5.5.156–64, my emphasis)

What does the English Christian reader see, hear, associate, identify with, *become through reading,* when he or she sees this Ganymedic C for Christ on that second Sunday after Easter?

These examples, I know, raise complex questions I have not answered about early modern printed texts: how intentional were the relations between the boy letters and their contexts? Are boy initials (and other decorated initials) best seen as illustrating or structuring, commenting upon or simply decorating, the texts around them? How can we read these image letters in historically attuned ways that account for the changing status and function of illustration in the earlier period, the shifting "relative cultural value of visual and verbal representation" in the years since 1600,[109] the changing status and ideological freight of images and icons more generally—as well as their meanings about boys and early modern homoeroticism? These questions (complex enough for "illustrations" in early modern books) are made more complicated by the fact that we are here reading a letter that is both a letter and a picture (or a little spirit? Renaissance visual culture's version of a psychic emanation? a spirit of love?). Even as boy initials complicate any notion of separating "text" from image—compare the letter Q with which this book began—we can bear in mind James Knapp's contention about more traditionally studied sixteenth-century English woodcut illustrations: "Rather than seeing the words and illustrations as contradictory, one form displacing the other (violently), one can imagine how the movement back and forth—between text and image—might serve to merge the effects of a book's verbal and visual information to produce a tonally complex and hybrid object."[110] We are used to thinking of letters as signifiers and pieces of movable type, but these particular embodied examples suggest an alternative alphabetic episteme—letters, as Jonathan Goldberg suggests, as "simultaneously pictures and characters (in the several meanings of the word)."[111]

We saw in the Introduction, through *Champ Fleury*'s Q and Joseph Moxon's typefaces (their bodies, shoulders, faces, necks, tongues), the embodiment of early modern letters. Along with these boy letters, these accounts may suggest that a printed early modern letter might be seen as something that combines features for which we have no single term: a rebus, a body, a character (with a character's desires, habits, social relations), a pictogram, an ideogram. In this context, is a boy alphabet an alphabet or a boy? Is a boy letter *desired* as an early modern boy? Does the boy let- ter have the desires sometimes, though not always, attributed to boys in this culture? What do letters—and boys in letters—want?

FIGURE 42. Figure bent over in a Q, in [Heinrich Bullinger], *De Origine Erroris Libri Dvo*, sig. G2, p. 118. Courtesy of The Kislak Center for Special Collections, Rare Books and Manuscripts, University of Pennsylvania Libraries.

Title-page borders, printers' devices, boys in/as initial letters: part of the criti- cal and methodological labor, in other words, is to pull these graphics back from their separately numbered entries in musty (if indispensable) bibliographic in- dexes of printers' devices or "children alphabets" and put them back into conver- sation with the texts from which they have been excerpted, and the texts among which they circulated, including plays. Working this way—bringing the larger range of materials in this chapter together—may allow us to think more specifi- cally about the contours, activities, identifications, desires, and aspirations of read- ers in print culture, a readership that intersects with, is sometimes informed by, but is not identical with, the audiences for plays in the theaters. Emblematic print- ers' ornaments, as I have suggested, are not simply ornamental; as emblems, they seek to inspire emulation and identification. As the boy Triton (Figure 28) sug- gests, adult readers (of both genders) and boys are all within the circuit of letters.[112]

Henry Fetherstone sold several books featuring the device shown in Figure 30, and in this context his resonant surname may suggest another kind of identifica- tion with the iconographics of this device and its meanings: does Fetherstone place *himself*, as an aspiring boy with feather and stone, on the title pages of the books he sells? The device's motto (around its edge) is taken from Book 1 of Ovid's *Meta- morphoses*. *Mollia cum Duris*, which might be translated "the soft with the hard," is simultaneously (1) a translation or transliteration of Feather/stone (the name and the rebus/emblem/image); (2) a description of the materials of early modern printing practice: hard type impressed with ink on a mollified surface; and obvi- ously (3) a rhetoric deeply implicated in both early modern gender *and* early mod- ern conceptions of sexual practice (the soft [of whatever genders] with the hard).[113]

Does this Ganymedic emblem spell out and simultaneously, inseparably, visualize Fetherstone's name and boy aspiration? Or does Fetherstone offer his Ganymedic hard-soft emblem to his *readers* as an example of the knowledge they will gain, being taken up by a god to a higher level, by buying and reading his texts? In what contexts do early modern men like Fetherstone and his readers, *though men*, remain "in standing water"—continue, that is, to identify *with or as boys* (the boy of the emblem, the boy in the letter)? "I might be His boy," Thomas Traherne writes, of his Ganymedic relation to Christ.[114]

How do we read early modern boys in books, then—or, in a way that I have suggested may not be separable, in early modern plays onstage, where there, too, they signified as a complex and potentially mobile hybrid of visual, rhetorical, and aural signals? In Ovid's *Metamorphoses* (Figure 27), a text relevant to several of the texts and signs in this chapter, desired boys are at both the centers and the margins. From the upper-right margin of Elyot's dictionary (Figure 26), a boy is made to look out engagingly toward the reader (almost like a boy player, you might say). He is performing, among other things, learning to read and be read.

Coda: Temporal Drag

Though it has certainly been a long time since I *didn't* know that boy actors originally played the roles I have analyzed in this chapter, my consideration of the boy, or youth, or young man in *Twelfth Night* and *Philaster* was nevertheless jump-started by seeing the 2002 Shakespeare's Globe "original practises production" of the play with young, if not boy, actors embodying the roles of Viola/Cesario and Sebastian. The Globe production, which also toured the United States in 2003, gave its audiences at least the simulacrum of a theatrical experience circa 1602, including young men in boys' and women's roles. The kinds of complication of the "boy" category, as well as the intersection and mutual implication of the erotic structures I am analyzing (hierarchical and non-) would be even more evident in a production that went further and staged the play's erotic complications with actual teenagers in these roles—boys "of a certain age," in the elastic term Barbara Hodgdon and I coined in conversation to refer to older boy actors in the established King's Men range of twelve to twenty-one or twenty-two, who would, in modern terms, still be "boys."[115]

Much has been said, in and around the London Globe's productions, of the "authenticity" of theatrical practice attempted there—the authenticity of the building, of the clothing the actors wear, of the all-male staging in some productions.[116] And yet, of course, any "authentic" staging practice brought into the present produces not only a trip (approximating authenticity) into the past but also a set of different and potentially divergent meanings in the present—"temporal drag" in the several senses of Elizabeth Freeman's resonant term. To put younger boy actors in these roles (to marry Orsino to a twenty-first-century boy, to show Antonio's devotion to such a boy, to stage a boy Olivia marrying a boy Sebastian)—what would this now mean for "us," *how* would this mean for us, onstage at the Globe in London, or in the University of Michigan Union ballroom, or at Chicago Shakespeare Theater on Navy Pier, where the production toured?[117] Would such acts seem or even be illegal—would they spur an investigation?[118] (Similarly, how would Jove and Ganymede, framed with naked Mercury in a letter, signify in a modern Bible or prayerbook, or a naked boy reading within a letter in a school grammar text?) Would a more thoroughly boyed theatrical production of *Twelfth Night* or *Philaster* now seem perverse—something Orsino accuses Olivia of, a desire per/verted, "turned" in the wrong direction (5.1.108)? Or would it, to use another discourse, seem simply "not to work" as theater? Contemplating these questions, if not answering them, in the highly charged atmosphere around same-sex eroticism and controversies and discourses of pederasty and sexual abuse in the twenty-first century, may go some way toward indicating the distance the category of the "boy" has gone—its delimiting, but also its reification—since the first performances of these plays in a different/same Globe theater, on a different/same London Bankside, in the first decade of the seventeenth century.[119]

CHAPTER 5

"Amorous Leander," Boy-desire, Gay Shame; Or, Straightening Out Christopher Marlowe

[A]ll they that love not Tobacco & Boies were fooles.
—An opinion of Christopher Marlowe, according
to the testimony of Richard Baines[1]

Cut is the branch that might haue growne ful straight. . . .
—Marlowe, *Doctor Faustus* (1604)[2]

Does it not now seem possible that Christopher Marlowe's homosexuality was just a phase? These developments are, of course, inexact, but we might date the beginning of Marlowe's period of sexual questioning and experimentation to about 1891, the year in which, as Tucker Brooke put it a few decades later, "[a] tasteless memorial to Marlowe at Canterbury was unveiled by Henry Irving."[3] The year 1891: just a few years after the future sexologist Havelock Ellis's "unexpurgated" Mermaids edition appeared in 1887, with a general introduction by John Addington Symonds;[4] and one year before the term *homo-sexuality* was first recorded in English, soon to be followed by its partner, *heterosexuality*.[5] Perhaps Marlowe's gaudy homosexuality—all smoke and minors anyway—has been just a phase.

So it might seem from a set of articles published in the last two decades that have thrown into question Marlowe's same-sex sexuality. Working with the important goal of restricting the speculation, mythologization, and extrapolation from hardly extant data that have been a feature of some work on Marlowe in the twentieth century, essays such as Stephen Orgel's demystification of the Corpus Christi portrait in "Tobacco and Boys: How Queer Was Marlowe?" (2000) and Lukas Erne's "Biography, Mythography, and Criticism" (2005) have emphasized how little we know about Marlowe's sexual practices and desires or, indeed, of his life in general. (This work thus joins skeptical reconsiderations of the available evidence from J. A. Downie, Lisa Hopkins, and J. T. Parnell, all from 2000.[6]) Though I'll return to Erne's problematic essay below, this work as a whole might at least be said to close out a period in which Marlowe's putative homosexual identity (as a person) has run the gamut from "alluded to" (however anxiously) to "taken for granted." So the phase has lasted a good hundred years or so. (Of course a salutary corollary effect of such biographical skepticism is that Marlowe may also have quit smoking.[7])

In part, such skepticism has been enabled by earlier, groundbreaking sexuality scholarship that showed the complexity of applying the identity terms *homosexual* and *heterosexual* to early modern persons.[8] Within Renaissance drama studies, however, this work has also been contemporaneous with a rumored resurrection of "the Author," especially in Shakespeare studies, itself reacting against a range of scholarship historicizing the idea of dramatic authorship in this period. This resurgence includes Erne's *Shakespeare as Literary Dramatist*, Jeffrey Knapp's manifesto on Shakespearean authorship in *Representations* and his related book *Shakespeare Only*, Brian Vickers's *Shakespeare, Co-Author* and some additional attributionist studies, the film *Shakespeare in Love*, and Stephen Greenblatt's biography *Will in the World*. At the same time that hypotheses of Shakespeare's intentions as an "author" on the modern model, his inner life, the ostensible separability of his words from others', and related concepts have apparently been making a comeback in some quarters of the criticism, it is noteworthy that Marlowe (as person, as homosexual) has seemed to be evaporating.

Let me admit to having mixed feelings about these intersecting developments. On the one hand, the fact that much of the evidence we have about the person Christopher Marlowe comes largely from nontheatrical and juridical documents neatly summarizes the historical point that, on balance, early modern English culture was less interested in playwrights in our modern authorial sense than we—or at least the scholars cited immediately above—are. On the other hand, it is clear that—whatever the ferment in scholarship around and against early modern dramatic "authorship" as a concept in the last decades—we now live in a modern institutional and cultural setting that continues in its editions, criticisms, curricula, and performances to organize its work around individual authorial names; and, further, that culture has until relatively recently continued to understand the sexual identities of early modern persons to be (1) identities in the first place and (2) divided along a standard homosexual/heterosexual binary. And so, though perhaps someone such as Vickers will accuse me of inappropriately pressing "the contemporary gay agenda,"[9] I think, in this modern cultural context, that it has been *strategically* useful and indeed intellectually productive for scholarship and pedagogy to experience the generative irritant of at least one playwright from this period who has seemed *in some sense* to cohere with a modern conception of "homosexuality." On yet another hand, if the skeptical biographical work has *now* led some scholars to a point where the unprovability of Marlowe's homosexuality-in-the-modern-sense is eventuating in a sexual cleansing of the texts associated with him—as I argue is the case in the example I analyze here—then it is of crucial importance that we not make this potentially phobic separation between the life and the writing. A queer philology of Marlowe's "amorous" boy, Leander, will be central to this discussion.

Straightening Out Christopher Marlowe

Erne's essay "Biography, Mythography, and Criticism: The Life and Works of Christopher Marlowe" has the stated and laudable intention of breaking the "vicious hermeneutic circle" in which "[m]ythographical readings [of the life] and critical readings [of the texts], both similarly speculative, have come to reinforce each other."[10] As Erne argues, Marlowe's ostensible radicalism underwrites and is underwritten by the ostensible radicalism of the plays; Marlowe's alleged homosexuality underwrites and is underwritten by the alleged homosexuality of the plays (28).

Of course, in Erne's prying apart a playwright and his texts, there is some irony: his book *Shakespeare as Literary Dramatist* begins in its first sentence with a promised "rare glimpse of Shakespeare's inner life,"[11] and it has been widely reviewed as reestablishing the possibility of discerning Shakespeare's literary intentions.[12] Within *Marlowe* studies, however, Erne is conversely arguing *against* the possibility of seeing in Marlowe's texts, in particular, *Edward II*, "a transparent window that gives us access to Marlowe and his intentions" (49). Indeed, though the introduction to Erne's *Shakespeare as Literary Dramatist* isolates "Shakespeare's displeasure" (1), "Shakespeare's attitude toward the emergent printed drama" (10), and ultimately "how Shakespeare intended [his plays] to exist" (23), Erne takes Orgel to task for seeming to know what Marlowe "precisely" intends ("Biography," 47–48). Still, whatever the irony, I would endorse several of Erne's conclusions in the Marlowe essay, for example, that "[o]nce we stop focusing on Marlowe and the mythographic image biographers have created of him and concentrate instead on the material conditions in which plays and playbooks were produced, we become aware that it is precisely impossible to know what Marlowe's intentions were when dramatizing Edward [II]'s death" (49).

Nevertheless, in a sexuality studies context, it is worth pausing for a moment to consider how and why Edward's death functions as the example here. Edward's death—or more specifically, the critical *reading* of Edward's death as a representation or parody of male-male anal penetration—is the essay's final example of three adduced to break the cycle in which critical readings of Marlowe's life feed readings of his texts and vice versa. The first example is a rereading of *Tamburlaine*, against the mythography of an "outrageous and defiant" Marlowe; the second reviews *Dr. Faustus*, against the myth of an always-tragic, never-comic Marlowe. The reading of Edward's death then finally seeks to disconnect "a mythographic understanding of Marlowe the homosexual and Edward, who dies through anal penetration" (45).

However laudable the attempt to disjoin biographical myth from critical reading, it is crucial to ask—and this is not a question for Erne alone—how the death of Edward II has come to stand in for, to be the make-or-break instance of, Marlowe's homosexuality. It is important both to notice that, unlike a number of other instances in the canon available for analysis, this is a moment of incipiently *dead* homoeroticism, as Mario DiGangi has emphasized[13] and also to analyze Erne's accompanying critical rhetoric. Immediately after dispatching with the example of Edward, Erne's essay decries "a mythography that insidiously affects, *and infects*, our understanding of both Marlowe the man and the plays" (49, my emphasis).[14] It is frankly astonishing to see as late as 2005 the casual rhetorical linkage of homosexuality and insidious infection, and the dangers are apparently epidemic—not only implicitly to Marlowe and his plays, but *to us* as well. *Our* understanding is insidiously infected by this myth of alleged homosexuality; the critical formulation here perversely replays *us*, our understanding, through the death of Edward: insidious homosexuality always wants to get inside you; ultimately homosexuality will fuck you over.

In the end, the logic of Erne's essay seems to be that if the red-hot poker isn't required by the *Edward II* script (as Erne, following Orgel in *Impersonations*, argues[15]), or if the printed playtext is incomplete or ambiguous (as so many early modern playtexts are) in not providing a full account of what may have transpired onstage (as Erne now seeks to correct Orgel for not seeing [45–49][16]), that is to say, if Edward does not definitively die through a fatal reenactment of a sodomitical act of anal penetration, then a queer Marlowe cannot be said to exist. (The emphasis of Orgel's reading, by contrast, is that, seen in a larger early modern context, the play seems unusual in potentially *punishing* homoeroticism. For Orgel, the point of the "missing" poker stage direction is not to take homoeroticism *tout court* out of the picture, as it is in Erne's essay, where Edward's death becomes the sole example of Marlovian homoeroticism.)[17]

However powerful the death scene, such an argument sees only with a sodomitical myopia. It fastens on one particular act, one particular stage direction (or its lack), one particular scene, to the exclusion of many. In doing so, it engages a familiar cultural willingness to let one sexual act metonymically stand in (lie down) for male "homosexuality," which is to say, for the full range of same-sex erotics, practices, and affects. (The work of Bray, DiGangi, and Bruce R. Smith in particular has demonstrated this range of practices and affects; Jonathan Goldberg, David M. Halperin, and Valerie Traub have drawn particular attention to interrogating their relation and disjunction.[18])

To the contrary, it seems obvious though important to insist that Edward's death, in all its opaqueness, is neither the beginning nor the end of queerness in this text. Neither is another dead sodomite—whether aptly, ironically, or parodically punished, or not—the end of sodomy or other discourses of homoeroticism in the texts we read as Marlowe's. (If one effect of the biographical skepticism around Marlowe has been to straighten him out, it is quite another thing to straighten out the texts associated with him.) This is true, *whatever* the contingencies in the biographical record of the allegations about tobacco, boys, "the sinners of Sodoma," St. John as "our Savior Christ's Alexis," their "extraordinary love," and so forth.[19]

How might Marlowe remain unstraightened out, even in the absence of definitive biographical evidence of his homosexuality-in-the-modern-sense? My method here will be to turn away from a forensic-authorial mode—let the faux-forensic skull photographs labeled "Marlowe's wound" in Park Honan's recent biography serve as its sign[20]—as if some definitive evidence for Marlowe's sexuality on our terms might come to light. Instead, I will concentrate on the complexities of the universe of discourse in which such evidence circulates. As we shall see, such a method will not mean jettisoning the life for the texts, but rather witnessing their complex interimplication, at the level of language. We must not rephrase Orgel's question to ask simply, "How queer were Marlowe's texts?" but also "How queer was the text of Marlowe's life?"

Such work was brilliantly begun some time ago, in Goldberg's seminal rereading of Baines's testimony.[21] Instead of adjudicating the testimony itself as a truth claim, Goldberg's reading works discursively to illustrate the complex early modern logics connecting sodomy, counterfeiting, atheism, double agency, and so forth; in Chapter 3, I also sought to work in a similar fashion by reading the pervasiveness of Ciceronian friendship discourse, even in Thomas Kyd's denunciation of the playwright he distances himself from as "this Marlowe."[22] But there is more work to do, especially if a critic such as Erne can still cite the tobacco-and-boys allegation (obviously about early modern pederasty) as the "only"[23] biographical bridge to *Edward II*, a text largely focused on *adult* same-sex *friend-*

ship discourse as it shades into or intersects with *adult* sodomy discourse, as Bray has shown.[24] In light of Honan's cranial photography, it seems again obvious though important to insist that the point is to read the biographical textual remains less as "evidence" that would somehow solve the mystery of Marlowe (who killed him and why; whom he slept with, at what ages, in what positions, and how characteristically), less as allusions to be pinned down under the heavy feather-bed or table (as some write) of definitive biographical meaning, and more for the meanings generated in the larger circulation of this discourse.[25]

To do such critical work would be to recite and re-site, in a queer context, some neglected but familiar questions asked by Michel Foucault, noticing how the theorist's resistance to author-centered evidence may also be fruitfully redeployed to resist the application of the modern mystery of the closet to early modern texts and their writers. Foregoing the individuating "author function," Foucault writes, "We would no longer hear the questions that have been rehashed for so long: Who really spoke? Is it really he and not someone else? With what authenticity or originality? And what part of his deepest self did he express in his discourse?"[26] These are questions Foucault associates with attempting to determine authorship, but they are also, as Eve Kosofsky Sedgwick has helped us to see, highly resonant with questions generated by the latter-day structure of the closet.[27] "Instead," Foucault argues, "there would be other questions, like these: What are the modes of existence of this discourse? Where has it been used, how can it circulate, and who can appropriate it for himself? What are the places in it where there is room for possible subjects?"[28] What are the modes of existence of discourses of homoeroticism in Marlowe? Where and how do they circulate within and following upon Marlowe's texts?

Turning away from sodomy per se and attempting to broaden the conversation around "homosexuality" in Marlowe, I take as my central example here the rhetoric and philology of "amorous" passion in Marlowe's erotic narrative poem *Hero and Leander*, first published in 1598.[29] Pursuing the ultimate inseparability of such discourses in the texts and in the life and immediate afterlife, the chapter also analyzes other texts around and after Marlowe. From this other perspective, the chapter works through the famously knotty (but now often ignored) relation of the Marlowe poem (or fragment, or beginning) to the continuation (or conclusion, or excrescence) by George Chapman, published with it in a second edition of 1598 and mostly thereafter.[30] As Chapman and others write in relation to the texts and death of Marlowe, we may begin to see places, even in a discourse centered on amorous boy-desire, where there is room for possible subjects—within the diegesis of the poem(s) and (or *as*) the writing lives of the poets.

Amorous Leander

> [H]ere is caution needed . . . against transferring what
> suits one group to another, such as calling a girl "vener-
> able," an old man "charming," a king "modest," and a
> matron "invincible."
> —Erasmus on "the usual kinds of epithets"[31]

"Amorous Leander, beautiful and young" (1.51).[32] Thus begins the infamous *blason*
of Leander's body and its exceeding beauty and universal desirability fifty lines
into the poem—a blason that, as many have noted, upstages the earlier, opening
blason of Leander's eventual beloved, Hero.[33] We might read right by Leander's
epithet "amorous," but one of my purposes in this chapter is to consider the rhetoric and philology of this passion, the way in which the word and its cognates (like
the frequently appearing *enamoured*) ramify across the surface of the poem, suggesting that we dive deeper into *amor* and what it entails. Indeed, *amorous* is the
first critical term associated with the poem; five years before its publication, the
Stationers' Company register for September 28, 1593, records "a booke intituled
Hero and Leander, beinge an amorous poem devised by Christopher Marlow."[34]

   "Amorous Leander, beautiful and young / Whose tragedy divine Musaeus sung."
From the outset, the epithet *amorous* disturbs the flow of the poem's generally iam-
bic couplets, turning the poem for a moment to trochees and, as David Lee Miller
has noted, giving an extra syllable to the first line describing Leander.[35] But a momentary perturbation in the rhythm should not detain us; surely we know what
amorous means. "I. *actively*," the *Oxford English Dictionary* (*OED*) says; "1. a. Of
persons: Inclined to love; habitually fond of the opposite sex. . . . 2. [Still *actively*]
Affected with love towards one of the opposite sex; in love, enamoured, fond." If the
OED's insistence on "the opposite sex" in these definitions seems somewhat quaint
or even downright oblivious in the context of *this* poem, we can perhaps attribute
this to the word's appearance in the first published fascicle of the *OED* in 1884,[36]
roughly contemporaneous with the introduction of the words *homosexual* and *heterosexual* into English,[37] and apparently not adequately revised since.

   There is eventually a sex opposite Leander, across the Hellespont, but at least
one early modern reader (indeed, the writer of this poem) saw "amorous" passion
in a more diversified light: one man, reading on a letter at the beginning of a history play, remarks the following to his absent friend:

> Sweet prince I come. These, these, thy amorous lines
> Might have enforced me to have swum from France,

And, like Leander, gasped upon the sand,
So thou wouldst smile and take me in thy arms.[38]

But it may not be enough simply to diversify the objects of desire, simply to re-gloss *amorous* as "affected with love towards someone"—of whatever sex, as these opening lines of *Edward II* suggest. For, while Leander is eventually "affected with love *towards*" someone in the course of the poem, it is also the case that the epithet "Amorous Leander" begins or instigates a lengthy blason in which all the fondness and affect is directed *toward* Leander, *from* multiple subjects, most of them male:

> His dangling tresses, that were never shorn,
> Had they been cut, and unto Colchos borne,
> Would have allur'd the vent'rous youth of Greece
> To hazard more than for the Golden Fleece. (1.55–58)

In the space of forty lines, amorous Leander is the actual or hypothesized object of the affections of (in addition to the vent'rous youth) Cynthia (59), Hippolytus (77), "the rudest peasant" (80), "[t]he barbarous Thracian soldier" (81), and an unnamed god "whose immortal fingers did imprint / That heavenly path [down his backside] with many a curious dint" (67–68). Ganymede-like, Leander would have Jove drinking out of the palm of his hand (62). Imprinted, dinted (dented or indented), his hair hypothetically shorn to launch a Jason-revising quest, blazoned forth by the poet's "rude pen," looked over by a catalog of specific and general mythological types mortal and immortal, and tasted or incorporated like Pelops' shoulder (or at least synaesthetically "delicious" to the touch [63–65]),[39] amorous Leander's status as active, desiring agent would initially seem to be somewhat in jeopardy.

The *OED* might have led us here, for the tide does eventually turn in its entry on *amorous*, to include a now "obsolete" definition: "II. . . . *passively*, Of persons and things: Lovable, lovely."[40] Lovable Leander. The meaning is not widely attested even in the sixteenth century, but Henry Cockeram's *English Dictionary* (1623) defines *amorous* as "Louely,"[41] and a primer in use in the decade before Marlowe's birth offers a prayer to "O mother of God moste glorious, and amorous"—a use that apparently suggests Mary as object of worship and veneration, rather than as actively desiring.[42] Indeed, Leander's initial epithet in Musaeus is ἱμερόεις (*himeroeis*): inciting love or desire.[43]

"Amorous Leander" is inclined from the beginning in both directions—and this double status comes to a point at the end of the blason:

> Some swore he was a maid in man's attire,
> For in his looks were all that men desire,
> . . . .
> And such as knew he was a man would say,
> "Leander, thou art made for amorous play:
> Why art thou not in love, and lov'd of all?
> Though thou be fair, yet be not thine own thrall." (83–90)

The lines gesture toward an understanding of cross-sex amorous passion in which only women are its objects but then immediately undo this understanding, for in the following lines there are presumably "such as [know] he [is] a man" who still see in him all that men desire. The following lines don't resolve this; "Leander, thou art made for amorous play" may mean "you are produced for amorous play" (again, *amorous* works potentially in two directions); "you are designed for passion" (actively, passively). The passive meaning is perhaps further activated by the double resonance of *made/maid*.

Further, the poem then asks the question resident in the epithet from the beginning and asks it directly of Leander, thus doubly reinscribing his object status: Leander, "Why art thou not in love, and lov'd of all?" Why art thou not *OED-amorous*-I., *actively*, since thou art *OED-amorous*-II., *passively*? To put this starkly as working across subject/object, active/passive is not to overstate the case, as the last line makes clear: to be in love is to be possessed. "Though thou be fair, yet be not thine own thrall." Be someone else's thrall. As if this had not been the case, promiscuously, for forty lines.

In an important essay, Judith Haber has analyzed Marlowe's poem's resistance to "end-directed sexuality," the consummation and amorous activity on Leander's part that the poem seems otherwise to promise.[44] I want to pursue Haber's provocative queering of heterosexual consummation further, and earlier in the poem, by noticing the way in which the very entry of passionate desire into Leander is registered as a kind of penetration of the subject rendered passively—as literally subject to passion—in ways that may be parallel to or part of the fungible, humoral body as we've come to understand it.

When Leander falls in love with Hero, she is making a sacrifice in the temple of Venus, surrounded by images of the polymorphous "riots, incest[s, and] rapes" of the gods, including Jove "dally[ing] with Idalian Ganymede." Hero looks up: "Thence flew Love's arrow with the golden head, / And thus Leander was enamoured" (1.161–62). Like Leander's epithet "amorous," "enamoured" seems here and elsewhere in the poem to have an objectifying or passive function built into it, recapitulating the standard trope of Cupid's arrow: eros enters in; penetration by the boy the poem calls "the mirthful amorous god" precedes desire. David Halperin has remarked of sex in the premodern period that it almost always relies on hierarchy as the route of eroticism—as he puts it, "hierarchy itself is *hot*"—and the founding penetrations of Cupid might be viewed in this context.[45] Hero is similarly "strook" by Leander's gaze, and the poem provides a sententious summary, again pointing to the meanings of *amorous*: "*Such force and virtue hath an amorous look.*"[46] Sententious, yes, but this statement is again worth thinking through etymologically and rhetorically. With its emphasis on the "force" of the amorous look, and the etymological residue of masculine *vir-* in "virtue," this amorous line may be an early modern articulation of Halperin's point. (Recall Gaveston in *Edward II*: "These, these, thy amorous lines / Might have *enforced* me to have swum from France.")

En-amoured, en-forced. Perhaps I am testing your philological patience, but my interest lies in attempting to revivify the rhetoric of passion—as I have suggested in Chapter 2—"to be more carefully attuned to the ways that etymologies, shorn of their associations with 'origin,' persist in a word and its surrounding discourse as a diachronic record of practice in the midst of language as a synchronic system," a practice that will, I hope, "force us to develop ever-expanding lexicons of erotic and affective terms and their relations."[47] "Leander was enamoured": Leander was en-loved. Perhaps there is a history of sexuality in a preposition, a prefix. Goldberg, Halperin, and others have argued that premodern sexuality is often about "positionality,"[48] and here I want to notice that questions of hierarchy and bodily integrity are implicit in the process of being *en-amoured*. Where is the "in" of *enamoured*?

Love enters in from the outside, its passion working through the fungible body—as any number of period texts on the passions suggest and as the analyses of historians of the passions such as Michael C. Schoenfeldt and Gail Kern Paster have demonstrated.[49] There is also the possibility that *enamoured*, almost always used passively in early modern English and certainly that way in this poem, signifies what the *OED* calls "'to put' what is denoted by the [noun, in this case, *amor*] 'into or on (something).'"[50] Trying to resuscitate this term, we can notice that the noun *amour* was "thoroughly naturalized" into English in the fifteenth through seventeenth centuries in the sense of its Latin and French cognates and was accented on the first syllable.[51] *Enamour*: to put a'mour into something: "Thus Leander was enamoured"; "Had wild Hippolytus Leander seen, / Enamour'd of his beauty had he been."

This is not the end of the prepositionality (pre-positionality) of *amour* in Marlowe or elsewhere; early modern subjects are enamoured *of* but also enamoured *on* someone, something, and this is mostly the case in the poem: "all that view'd [Hero] were enamoured *on* her."[52] Amorous Leander, however, is simply enamoured, in the passive voice, without further comment; he swings, or is swung, both ways: "thus Leander *was enamoured.*"

Orpheus's Melody

I have begun by attempting to open up one possibility for reading an unstraightened Marlowe through the texts themselves—the possibility of seeing in an erotic actor in the narrative of the poem a figure portrayed simultaneously as a passive erotic object for his readers within and beyond the poem. This is a possibility I will call, intending a double valence, boy-desire (an idea to which I will return); it is a possibility distinct from Edward II's death as the "only" link between Marlowe and same-sex eroticism,[53] though, as we will also see, it sometimes intersects with other forms of same-sex eroticism. However, although based in local reading of the text itself, in the case of *Hero and Leander* (and perhaps all cases), it is difficult to keep the texts "themselves" separate from the versions of Marlowe and his work that circulate after his death.[54]

Take Henry Petowe's 1598 continuation of *Hero and Leander*, a poem derided by modern critics for its poor quality, its orthodoxy, and/or its stylistic disjunction from Marlowe.[55] A reading interested in what Marlowe signifies and what Marlowe's texts make possible in 1598, however, would instead notice that Petowe's poem places Marlowe not just in an Ovidian trajectory, as Patrick Cheney has persuasively argued,[56] but also in close conjunction with Orpheus:

> What mortall soule with *Marlo* might contend,
> That could gainst reason force him stoope or bend?
> Whose siluer charming toung, mou'd such delight,
> That men would shun their sleepe in still darke night.
> To meditate vpon his goulden lynes,
> His rare conceyts and sweete according rimes.
> But *Marlo* still admired *Marlo's* gon,
> To liue with beautie in *Elyzium*,
> Immortall beautie, who desires to heare,
> His sacred Poesies sweete in euery eare:
> *Marlo* must frame to *Orpheus* melodie,
> Himnes all diuine to make heauen harmonie.
> There euer liue the Prince of Poetrie,
> Liue with the liuing in eternitie.[57]

Petowe's syntax is ambiguous, but Marlowe is earlier equated in the poem with Apollo, and one reading of the Orphic culmination of this passage would be that "whoever desires to hear the sacred poetry of Marlowe must 'frame' or remake him according to the model of Orpheus."

Alternatively, one might see Petowe implying that, to get back the immortal beauty that was Marlowe—the Marlowe whose sweet poetry moves delight and keeps men up at night, the Marlowe who has gone to Elysium (if not to the underworld)—one must frame one's own[58] singing to Orpheus's melody: sing like Orpheus to get back Eurydicean Marlowe. Whatever the otherwise cross-sexual values of Petowe's poem, the text here may place surviving Elizabethan poets and readers in a distinctly unstraightened relation to admired Marlowe, voyaging to the afterlife to sing like Orpheus. As Golding's rendition voices Orpheus:

> The cause of this my voyage is my wife,
> Whose foot a viper stinging, did abridge her youthful life.
> I would have borne it patiently; and so to do I strave.
> But Love surmounted power.[59]

Elizabethan poets may have striven to bear patiently the loss of Marlowe, but Petowe's and perhaps Chapman's continuations, whatever their other apparent orthodoxies, may speak of another love, beyond the grave, a desire to sing with the ever-living dead or to sing him back to life.

Nonetheless, if (as the passage may more straightforwardly suggest) Marlowe himself is to be framed to Orpheus's melody ("shape[d], form[ed], direct[ed]"[60]), then the discourse is queerer still. For, as DiGangi has shown, Orpheus's story "evoke[d in the 1590s] the complex ideological connection between male homoerotic desire, misogyny, and sodomy."[61] In Ovid, of course, the "double dying" of Eurydice leads Orpheus to avoid the company of women entirely (10.69, 88–89); in Golding's rendition, he teaches the Thracians "a stew [= brothel] of males to make / And of the flowering prime of boys pleasure for to take" (10.91–92); and then, as much of the rest of *Metamorphoses* Book 10 illustrates, to devise amorous songs of boy-desire, including the stories of Ganymede, Hyacinthus, and Adonis. Orpheus sings, "But now I need a milder style to tell of pretty boys / That were the darlings of the gods" (10.157–58). And thus he begins the story of Jove and Ganymede. Marlowe's "Amorous Leander" is an Orphic song.

Even with Marlowe as Apollo, the passage remains resonant in its queerness. Orpheus is presented as the son of Apollo in Ovid; Apollo himself is the admirer of the boy Cyparissus ("the fairest wight that ever man did see / in Cea" [10.128–29]), who himself mourns for the death of a beloved stag (whose "back for pleasure [he did] bestride" [X.131]). From Apollo to Orpheus is thus no straightforwardly straight genealogy; it is at the least homosocial and parthenogenic, certainly repeatedly homoerotic, and possibly involving a complex interspecies homoerotic mourning.

In 1598, Marlowe is gone, but he and his texts are in the company of Orpheus, inventor and pedagogue of boy-desire and singer of boy-admiring poetry. Is this evidence of an unstraightened Marlowe?—no "Baines' *libel*," these conjunctions are Petowe's *praise*.

A similar and, I believe, unnoticed queer complexity unfolds from another brief, late 1590s discourse on Marlowe, Phoebe's famous quotation of *Hero and Le-ander* in Act 3, Scene 5, of *As You Like It*, on Rosalind's exit: "Dead shepherd, now I find thy saw of might: / 'Who ever loved that loved not at first sight?' "[62] In his re-consideration of a queer Marlowe, Orgel comments that "this Marlowe is the epit-ome of pastoral innocence and natural wisdom,"[63] but this quotation, this evidence for the meaning of Marlowe, bespeaks a potentially more complicated erotics. Phoebe frames Marlowe to describe her love for a young man. But she expresses through Marlowe her love of a young man whose name is central to mythic peder-asty. (Like Phoebe, Jove loved the first sight of Ganymede, too.) And, of course, Phoebe is, within the fiction of the play, also speaking, through Marlowe, an attrac-tion for a figure who turns out to be a woman at the end of the play—at least until the epilogue, when he again speaks as a boy (actor), like the boy actor playing Phoebe speaking Marlowe. Here then is another continuation of *Hero and Leander*; it, too, circulates in a discursive surround of boy loving and addresses a character celebrated in Orpheus's "milder style." But this is also the context of a woman loving a woman (in death, Orpheus's singing head floated off to Lesbos); it also gives us a woman writer of love poetry (however derided by the play), and, as Orgel himself has helped us to notice, a boy actor speaking desire for another boy. It is worth noting that, at the moment corresponding to Phoebe's Marlowe quotation in Shake-speare's source text, Ganymede is glossed as "the amorous Girle-boy."[64]

Strange Instigation

But what of that other 1598 continuation of *Hero and Leander*? Chapman's conclu-sion, with its division of the larger poem into "sestiads," has most often been re-garded as gravely serious, censorious, circumscribing of Marlowe's humor, flirta-tion, and heterodoxy—and most damningly, in the last several decades, as unnecessary.[65] Maybe so, but it is also the version an early modern audience is most likely to have read, because, unlike the Marlowe-only version, it was re-printed at least eight more times during the seventeenth century.[66] Moreover, if the question is "what does Marlowe make possible, how is he remembered and reembodied, what does he instigate?" or even "What are the places in [Marlowe] where there is room for possible subjects?,"[67] we need not trouble ourselves with the unanswerable question of whether *Hero and Leander* as first published was intended as complete. For, as Petowe and Chapman both suggest, either the poem was not viewed as such, or it instigated a *desire*—and I use the term advisedly—to complete it. (This is a desire that we might describe as being both a desire to have and complete Marlowe, and to *be* Marlowe.)

The desire to keep Marlowe alive is a common one and in remarkably similar terms. Dedicating the first edition of *Hero and Leander* to Sir Thomas Walsingham, the publisher Edward Blunt (or Blount) remarks that

> we think not ourselves discharged of the duty we owe to our friend, when we have brought the breathless body to the earth, for albeit the eye there taketh his ever farewell of that beloved object, yet the *im*pression of the man, that hath been dear unto us, living *in* an after life *in our memory*, there putteth us *in mind* of farther obsequies due unto the deceased. . . . By these meditations (*as by an intellectual will*) I suppose myself executor to the unhappily deceased author of this poem. (MacLure, *Poems*, 3, my emphasis)

Blunt's impression of the man leads to mental and then bibliographic imprinting, drawn by "an intellectual will," or desire.[68] His phrase in this letter (republished in the second edition) resonates in Chapman's preface to *his* part of the poem, a dedication to Lady Walsingham:[69] "I present your Ladyship with the last affections of the first two lovers that ever Muse shrined in the Temple of Memory; being *drawn by strange instigation* to employ some of my serious time in so trifling a subject, which yet made the first Author, divine Musaeus eternal" (MacLure, *Poems*, 42, my emphasis). Chapman's emphasis on Musaeus rather than Marlowe as the first author who draws him "by strange instigation" into this subject, already takes us in a(nother) potentially queer direction. As Gordon Braden and David Riggs have emphasized, Musaeus Grammaticus, the fifth-century C.E. author of the source poem, was often confused with the "first poet" Musaeus, the pupil of Orpheus.[70] Orphean pedagogy leads to "strange instigation";[71] *instigation* derives from the Latin *instigare*, to urge, set on, incite—etymologically, to prick within. (As John Florio translates *instigatore*, in 1598: "an egger on, a prouoker, a pricker forward, an instigator."[72]) Even as Chapman sets up the continuation and completion of the poem as a cross-sex marriage (the dedication to Lady Walsingham, he writes, is "in figure of the other unity betwixt Sir Thomas and yourself" [43]), he gives the poem a potentially pederastic/pedagogic lineage.

This queer pricking forward becomes yet more complex in Chapman's famous invocation 183 lines into the third sestiad:

Then [t]hou most *strangely-intellectual fire*,
That proper to my soul hast power t'*in*spire
Her burning faculties, and with the wings
Of thy unsphered flame visit'st the springs
Of spirits immortal; now (as swift as Time
Doth follow Motion) find th'eternal clime
Of his free soul, whose living subject stood
Up to the chin in the Pierian flood,
And drunk to me half this Musaean story,
*In*scribing it to deathless Memory:
Confer with it, and make my pledge as deep,
That neither's draught be consecrate to sleep.
Tell it how much *his late desires I tender*,
(If yet it know not), and to light surrender
My soul's dark offspring, willing it should die
To loves, to passions, and society.
                    (3.183–98, my emphasis)

We are accustomed to thinking of the inspiration of the Muses in more spiritual terms, but I want to suggest that we read this complex passage in a more embodied sense, potentially intersecting with the discourse of humoral psychology.[73] In keeping with the "strange instigation" of the dedication, the invocation here is preoccupied with the internalization of Christopher Marlowe. If Chapman, like Blunt, emphasizes the "intellectual" quality of his engagement with Marlowe and Musaeus and the Orphean school, he nonetheless remarks again the "strange" quality of such an engagement.[74] Called upon but marked as "strange," the intellectual fire *in*spires, has the power to breathe into Chapman.[75] Switching from hot and dry to moist, the middle section of the passage is a complex drinking game of incorporation, in which Chapman finishes Marlowe's cup of Musaeus, hoping to drink deep, while at the same time Marlowe, like Leander, is up to his neck in the Pierian flood.[76] Announcing of Marlowe "how much his late desires I tender" (which is to say, his late desires I tend to, but also value, and treat tenderly),[77] the passage concludes with an extraordinary moment of Chapman giving birth out of Marlowe and Musaeus's story, willing "his dark offspring" (cryptically) to "die / To loves, to passions, and society."

These lines seem almost indecipherable—the final phrase may mean that Chapman's poem dies under the influence of loves, passions, and society, or that it "cease[s] to be under the power or influence of" these forces.[78] The lines nonetheless set up unusual resonances, with Chapman's deep drinking (a phrase that recalls Neptune's "deep persuading oratory" during Leander's swim in Marlowe's part [2.226]) and the conjunction of "loves, passions, and societie" recalling Leander's seductive argument to Hero that "maids are nothing then, / Without the sweet society of men" (1.255–56). The association of "dies" with orgasm in the period only further complicates the passage. What has Chapman been drinking, and toward—or away from, or in consummation with—what passions, what society, what ends?

These conjunctions—with Chapman taking up a poem he presents as interrupted, taking up Marlowe's offspring and willing it to die to loves—resonate further in the poem as he concludes it. Earlier, in Marlowe's part of the poem, Neptune had attempted to tutor Leander in a passion to which he was oblivious; Neptune's tale of instruction is simultaneously pedagogic (attempting to teach Leander that he need not be a woman to experience love with the god) and pederastic: "then [Neptune] told a tale, / How that a shepherd, sitting in a vale, / Play'd with a boy so fair and kind, / As for his love both earth and heaven pin'd" (2.193–96). Neptune, doing Orpheus, attempts to teach Leander his version of a boy's own story, an attempt to bring the passive and active meanings of *amorous* together. "Ere half this tale [is] done," Leander swims away (2.201). In the concluding moments of his sixth and final sestiad, however, Chapman—recipient of "half [a] Musaean story" drunk to him by Marlowe, willing his "dark offspring" to die—calls upon Neptune to kill off Leander.[79] As Leander drowns and one of the Fates prepares to draw his destiny, Neptune, "burst[ing] with ruth" (sorrow, but also compassion [*OED*]) at Leander's distress, attempts to intervene:

> he hurl'd his marble mace
> At the stern Fates; it wounded Lachesis
> That drew Leander's thread, and *could not miss*
> The thread itself, as it her hand did hit,
> But smote it full and quite did sunder it.
> The more kind Neptune *rag'd, the more he ras'd*
> His love's life's fort, and *kill'd as he embrac'd*. (6.225–31, my emphasis)

Neptune has been the poem's personification of boy-directed amorous admiration and desire (underlining that investment, Neptune initially mistakes Leander for Ganymede). Earlier Marlowe had also briefly collated "us," the implied readers, into Neptune's enamoured viewpoint, and this sixth-sestiad passage is thus an extraordinary re- and unwriting of the poem's treatment of amorous Leander from the beginning.[80] (Here, building on Margaret W. Ferguson's brilliant unfolding of a similarly homoerotically valenced bi- and trilingual nexus of words around *l'amour/amor* and *la mort* in *Hamlet*, it is worth noticing that Leander's epithet has had, from the beginning, the sound of death within it.[81]) Leander "calls" on Neptune, whom he earlier had spurned; he calls him again (6.195, 6.222), but Neptune's inclination toward Leander is in the end responsible for Leander's death, snatching away that act from the Fates themselves. The poem, taken up by strange instigation, concludes by renouncing instigation, Orphean tutelage. "Rage," Neptune's passion here, is legible in this period as both anger and desire: "the more kind Neptune rag'd, the more he ras'd / His love's life's fort."[82] This embrace razes or cuts, and erases; it kills.[83]

In Musaeus's poem, by contrast, there is no killing pederastic-pedagogic embrace at the moment of Leander's death, only this drinking deep: "A great gush of water of itself poured into his throat, / And he swallowed a worthless draught of the irresistible brine."[84] Returning to Musaeus's text later, Chapman translates the same passage as "His throat was turn'd / free channel to the flood, / And drinke went downe / that did him farre from good."[85] In concluding *Hero and Leander*, however—desiring to have and complete and perhaps be Marlowe—Chapman stages in Neptune a killing pederastic, pedagogic embrace.

Boy-desire, Gay Shame

Pricked on by the work of Orgel and Smith on boys in early modern culture, by Emily Bryan's analysis of the complex mixture of agency and chattel in the role of boy actors, by Richard Rambuss's brilliant reading of "what it feels like for a boy" in *Venus and Adonis*, by Halperin's rethinking of what structures precede and inform modern male "homosexuality" in the West, I have been considering, in the two chapters of this "lexicon," the complex case of pederasty and boy-desire in early modern English culture.[86] One way to map this configuration is to see early modern English boys as standing potentially midway between a classical understanding and a modern dispensation. In the classical era, Halperin notes, "Neither boys nor women were thought to possess the sort of desires that would impel them to become autonomous sexual actors in the relations with men, . . . both [groups being considered] sexually inert."[87] In modernity, by contrast, adolescents are deemed by the culture as always-already susceptible to sexualization and sexual agency, even as sexual "innocence" remains a persisting trope and cultural investment.[88]

The early modern period returns repeatedly to the question of boy-desire—a question of not just (1) early modern desire *for* boys and young men, which is taken as a rarely contested universal given, but also (2) the desires of such young men *themselves* (toward a variety of objects).[89] The complex workings of the early modern stage around women who dress as desiring male youths, as well as the boys and young men ("stripling[s]," to use Golding's term) in Ovidian narrative poetry—these cultural forms are constantly confronting the question of boy-desire and its meanings. To paraphrase Rambuss and Freud, what does Boy want? As Rambuss persuasively argues of Shakespeare's erotic narrative poem *Venus and Adonis*, "Adonis' desire can only be rendered [in Shakespeare] in negative terms: 'I know not love, quoth he, nor will know it, / Unless it be boar, and then I chase it.'"[90] But if the space of Adonis's negative desire is also a placeholder for something Rambuss terms "proto-gay,"[91] it is also the case that, in these poems (and unlike the classical cases Halperin considers), adult figures are always attempting to teach the boy, persuade the boy, to a desire of which they assume him fundamentally *to be capable*. Shakespeare's Adonis, Marlowe's Leander, Beaumont's Hermaphroditus—the list is significant and influential.

The texts constantly figure these beautiful "stripling" figures who "seem[] to stand between the state of man and lad" (Golding, 3.437) as the contested place for the imagining, educating, instigation, of desire itself. Why? I do not pretend to have a definitive answer to this question, but I think a possible answer may lie in the intersection of (on the one hand) the conception of the fungible, humoral body, penetrated, at swim in a world flowing with passions and humors, and (on the other) the liminal, structural position of "striplings" in Renaissance English culture: largely disempowered, like many women; not yet fully trained up in the humoral self-discipline that Paster, Schoenfeldt, and others have analyzed; thought potentially to be desire*less*, but also, simultaneously, incipient male subjects—desire-in-training.[92] These figures are regularly positioned as simultaneously active and passive: driven by desire (itself also a penetrative force through which they are enamoured); thus, subjects subject to the force and virtue of the loving look; themselves inciting or instigating desire (*himeroeis*); *and* often the object of such desire.[93] In a word: *amorous*.

In his chapter describing "[w]hat sort of persons be most passionate" (1.10), Thomas Wright, in *The Passions of the Mind in General*, writes that

> young men generally are arrogant, proud, prodigal, incontinent, and given to all sorts of pleasure. . . . Young men's incontinency, boldness, and confidence proceedeth of heat which aboundeth in them, and those whose complexions are hottest are most subject to these affections. They extremely affect pleasure because they spent as boys almost the time of growth in getting of habits alluring and haling to pleasure; for commonly we see all sorts of boys, till they come to the use of reason and discretion, most addicted to pastimes and plays.[94]

This is not by any means to propose a simply cultural-physiological explanation for these poems and plays. Nor is it to ignore the continuing and complex effects of this boy-positioning on *men*—men trained as boys habitually to cross-voice such desires (an effect, as Lynn Enterline has brilliantly argued, of the *prosopopaeia* of the educational system that constantly recited Ovid[95]), men who, for example, tender the late textualized desires of other men. (An "amorous poem," as the Stationers' Company register may suggest, is a poem about but also inciting *amor*.)

The passions raised *by books* are not unknown to Wright, who, in his chapter "The Impediments to Virtue" (6.3), writes that

> [t]he world leadeth us to sin . . . by suggesting unto us many occasions of ill by obscenous and naughty Books, as light and wanton Poets. . . . Indeed, I must confess that these books . . . with a silent persuasion *insinuate* their matter unto the chief affection and highest part of the Soul, and in all good Commonweals are either wholly prohibited or so circumcised that no such hurt followeth. (326–27, my emphasis)

As described in Chapter 2, *persuasion* also etymologically carries into this period a sense of bodily incorporation, often as *sweet persuasion*,[96] and Chapman, as a continuer of Marlowe and translator of Musaeus (and, famously, others), made a career of such insinuation and incorporation. Gordon Braden notes that, in the widely influential Aldine translation of Musaeus's poem, Leander's epithet "*himeroeis* . . . , 'desirable,' becomes 'suauis'"; Braden views this translation as a making-bland of the original, but the constellation of words, at least eventually in their English cognates and translations, may be closer than anticipated: desire-inciting, persuasive, sweet.[97]

For Chapman, at least in the case of *Hero and Leander*'s ending, this discomforting amorous embodiment must be excised, circumcised, cut out—indeed, understood as its own death and punishment: "the more kind Neptune rag'd, the more he ras'd / His love's life's fort." If, as Rambuss argues, Adonis gestures toward the beginnings of proto-gay desire, Chapman's loving, murderous Neptune may be an antecedent of proto-gay shame.[98] Or, as Chapman writes it, in an extraordinarily ambivalent passage that directly addresses his hero (his Hero?) as he introduces his death into the poem:

> O sweet Leander . . .
>
>   . . . I in floods of ink
> *Must drown* thy graces, which white papers drink,
> Even as thy beauties did the foul black seas.
> I must describe the hell of thy disease,[99]
> That heaven did merit. (6.137–41, my emphasis)

Chapman's words here preface and prepare for Neptune's killing of Leander, but they do so in a passage that closely correlates Neptune's action to the materiality of the writing process, Leander's beauties flooded and fouled by Chapman's dark sea of ink.

The term *gay shame* that I have attached to Chapman and/as Neptune's action has recently received significant critical attention, and I use *shame* only provisionally in an early modern context, where, as a complex topic with an extensive analytic history in both cultural studies and psychoanalysis, its applicability requires still more thought. Further, as Halperin and Traub and their contributors discuss in a recent anthology with this title, *gay shame* has become the rallying cry of a movement to resist contemporary gay assimilation to the mainstream, in contrast to *gay pride*.[100] There are, moreover, both the obvious problems of anachronism in using the term *gay* to talk about same-sex practices/identities/desires in the sixteenth and seventeenth centuries and the complexity of reading *shame* even when it is literally present in early modern contexts: "although shame is a very old word (present in medieval and early modern Western cultures)," Halperin and Traub note, "its specific role as an internalized mechanism of discipline is a peculiarly modern invention—part of the 'civilizing' process" (37). I share with Michael Warner "skepticism about universal accounts of the mechanisms of shame, whether psychoanalytic or ego-psychological," and George Chauncey's caution that "we need to attend to [shame's] historicity and cultural specificity . . . and to recall that its production has always been uneven and its modalities varied."[101] Nevertheless, in this context, I hope that *gay shame*, marked as *proto-*, can address some of the tensions and felt imperatives ("I . . . *must drown* thy graces") within which Chapman may have found himself writing/translating: between, on the one hand, shame as an affect that may have adhered in this period to any enactment, fantasy, or expression of desires recognized as sodomitical or as pederastical (in a potentially changing episteme as discussed above) and, on the other, pressures from the received tradition (Orpheus-Musaeus-Musurus-Marlowe) to assimilate to what had been, after all, a mainstream movement within Western culture (an interest in boy-desire).

In citing shame's possible early modern adherence to "any enactment, fantasy, or expression of desires recognized as sodomitical or as pederastical," I am seeking to be both as capacious and as precise as possible with terms here, both because what we might see as "the same" sexual act could have different meanings in Renaissance culture depending on context and because I think we are only beginning to develop appropriate (non-nineteenth- and twentieth-century) models to analyze psychic structures in operation prior to the emergence of the modern subject, modern, identity-based models of sexuality, and "internalized mechanism[s] of discipline."[102] Indeed, (non)internalization may be the very structure that characterizes Chapman assigning Leander's drowning (which he says *he* "must" perform and describe) to another, external figure. Thus, we can ask more broadly, what are the psychic- or subjectivity-effects of the multiple strands/ structures model of premodern male "homosexuality" as set out by Halperin or Smith, or for women by Traub? An understanding of *shame* as a mode of self-discipline with a long (etymological, religious, social, critical) history may be central to such an account. An analysis of the felt imperative to extend and finish a long poem centered on and finally concluded via boy-desire may contribute to the analysis of Chauncey's varied modalities. Chapman says to "sweet Leander" that he "must describe the hell of thy dis-ease," and the modern editorial hyphen (not in the original printing) may serve to highlight for us, through the word's potential double meaning as "discomfort" and a more constitutional sense of "sickness," the tensions around what Chapman simultaneously raises the more he erases here.

Marlowe Affects

Chapman is not Marlowe, and, returning to the questions I raised at the beginning of this chapter, we can ask whether these textual remains, in all their discursive and performative complexity, are a part of the mythographic Marlowe denounced by Erne—not Marlowe but a "Marlowe effect," in Leah S. Marcus's term.[103] Or are Chapman's and others' engagements with Marlowe a part of the biographical record, connected discursively as they are to records we sometimes regard as biographical, like Baines's and Kyd's allegations? Read discursively, philologically, the evidence will not remain within the tidy categories of biographical versus literary, "author" versus "work," external versus internal, documentary versus fictive, even contemporaneous versus posthumous. These "posthumous" rememberings of ever-living Marlowe in Petowe, Shakespeare, and Chapman speak across the same languages, engage the same frames, as some of the biographical evidence and some of the plays, poems, and translations. Marlowe speaks in these languages: if there is a "queer Marlowe," they are part of it; he also seems to instigate these languages and desires in others, even when, as in Chapman, it seems that desire complexly rages and razes simultaneously.

But, as I have been suggesting, it will not be simple or straightforward simply to read this Marlowe. As the complex combinations of active and passive, of gender and age, and of object and subject status in *Hero and Leander* above suggest, part of what is required in this analysis is critical work better informed by scholarship in the history of sexuality and its significant refinements since Bray's first book. Scholarship on "Marlowe and sexuality" will have to read beyond the boundaries of Marlowe scholarship per se; in its attempt to disjoin Marlowe from homosexuality, the Erne essay, for example, cites only work on sexuality that specifically mentions Marlowe (Orgel, Bray) and seems to do so only to take up relatively narrow questions within Marlowe studies. But to understand "Marlowe and sexuality" is to know something more about the broader culture and the multiple ways in which sexuality/eroticism were constituted. The reading and editing of Marlowe's texts and the writing of Marlowe's life (as the judicious example of David Riggs's biography suggests[104]) cannot remain separate from this larger body of scholarship: the history of sexuality and the complexity of its forms, languages, and terms must also come to be regarded as indispensable technical expertise—another philological tool that scholars and editors must engage.[105] As Halperin has persuasively argued, there are at least four often discrete historical discourses or structures during this period that only eventually come together into something like modern homosexuality.[106] Even as they sometimes complexly *cross*, as we saw in Chapter 4, simply to conflate pederasty in Baines with sodomy in *Edward II*, or not to recognize the divergences of both from same-sex friendship or the valences of *amorous* that overlap with but also go beyond the "opposite" sex, is to straighten out the texts in our modern image. At the same time, further attention is required toward more complex instances of queerness within and across Marlowe's texts. Two brief, final examples follow here.

As Orgel has shown, in his final scene, Faustus's line "*O lente lente currite noctis equi*" (run slowly, O horses of the night) is a complex, cross-gendering quotation of Ovid's *Amores*, in which, as Orgel puts it, "Marlowe's textual arabesque provides Faustus with a boy after all" ("Tobacco," 574–75). In the first scene of *Dido*, however, Marlowe puts a translation of this line in the mouth of Jupiter, who already has a boy from the start:

> What is't, sweet wag, I should deny thy youth,
> Whose face reflects such pleasure to mine eyes,
> As I, exhal'd with thy fire-darting beams,
> Have oft driven back the horses of the night,
> When as they would have hal'd thee from my sight?[107]

Here the line from the *Amores* is translated into a clearly homoerotic context. Moreover, it may echo in Petowe's posthumous description of a Marlowe

> Whose siluer charming toung, mou'd such delight,
> That men would shun their sleepe in still darke night.
> To meditate vpon his goulden lynes,
> His rare conceyts and sweete according rimes.[108]

In Petowe, as we saw, Marlowe may be Apollo, or Orpheus, but if this, too, is the *Amores*, Marlowe is here the boy—Aurora's Cephalus, Jupiter's Ganymede, the sweet wag who here produces sweet according rhymes. Marlowe as Ganymede has gone up to Elysium.

Like the classical pattern Halperin has analyzed, boy-desire in Baines's version of Marlowe is unidirectional (all those who love not tobacco and boys are fools). A similar classical, pederastic structure repeatedly emerges in these texts—here in *Dido* most obviously, in ways brilliantly unfolded by Goldberg,[109] but elsewhere in Gaveston's plan to stage for Edward "a lovely boy in Dian's shape," or in "amorous Leander" at swim with Neptune.[110] But, in a way that departs from the blank slate that boy-subjectivity is said to be in classical pederasty, these early modern texts also sometimes give us boys speaking love back. Yes, it's in return for payment, but Ganymede in *Dido* says to Jupiter, "then I'll hug with you an hundred times" (1.1.48).

Once again: is there a history of sexuality in a preposition? The phobic editor of the play's Revels edition does not hesitate over this question,[111] but *hug* is of unknown etymology and arrives into English only in Marlowe's lifetime; while its meaning in certain contexts may be clear enough, "to hug *with*" is a very rare locution[112] and may denote a mutuality and reciprocity that one would not expect a boy to speak in the classical precedents.[113] Getting straight what Ganymede says here requires some queer philology. Mutual affection or not, it seems a moment of Marlovian homoeroticism beyond the death of Edward II.

Concluding again in Orpheus's milder style, here is a final example of the complex mix of same-sex eroticism and affect yet to be engaged in Marlowe's texts. I noted above that Edward II's death is not the beginning or end of queerness in that text. As we have seen, the play begins with Gaveston's Leander-like announcement, "Sweet prince, I come. These, these, thy amorous lines / Might have enforced me to have swum from France" (1.1.6–7) and with his promise to stage "[s]weet speeches, comedies, and pleasing shows" with a lovely boy and the "sportful" hiding of "those parts that men delight to see" (1.1.55–64). Edward for his part similarly speaks a sugary rhetoric that I identified in Chapter 2 with the homoerotic exchange and equity of idealized male-male friendship in the period, telling Gaveston, "Thy worth, *sweet friend*, is far above my gifts" (1.1.160). Given the critical weight that has been placed on the death of Edward as a final antihomosexual statement, or a final homosexualization of Edward in the play, it is somewhat surprising, then, to see the boy king Edward III taking up or resuming this language of male affection, in an apostrophe to his father as he begins his rule:

> *Sweet father*, here unto thy murdered ghost,
> I offer up this wicked traitor's head,

And let these tears, distilling from mine eyes,
Be witness of my grief and innocency. (5.6.98–101)

Edward III's tears of innocency may attempt to perform a new beginning here, in the last lines of the play, but, in one "sweet" word, his rhetoric marks the persistence or inheritance of his father's habitual language of friendly affection in the new regime.[114] The intersections here of boy-desire, friendship, and homosocial filiation are complex: the new king, at once a hierarchically lower son *and* a full copy in name and power of his dead father, addresses that father as an equal, through the by-now familiar language of his own lover. (While this language might initially or in another context seem merely platonic, it occurs here at the end of a play in which it has been continually reinscribed as the language of adult same-sex affection.) "Sweet prince, I come"; "sweet father, I offer up": this play, too, is framed to Orpheus's melody. We may hear this echo, down the road a bit, in James I's equally complex address to Buckingham as "[m]y only sweet and dear child" and "my sweet child and wife."[115]

Such readings, it should be clear, will not bring back a homosexual Marlowe in our terms, nor should we want to. However, no return of the "author" in the modern sense of that term will be necessary to perform this important kind of historical reading; indeed, as I hope I have suggested, the return of a certain conception of the author, with its concentration on the authenticity of the author's expression, what part of his deepest self he expressed, and so forth, may directly impede such analysis. So, too, as I hope I have also shown, no cranial photography, no forensic evidence of whatever exactitude—only a philological reading that is more attentive to the complex striations, the histories of sexuality inscribed in and around these texts—will, if ever, straighten this Marlowe out.

LEXICON 3

SODOMY

CHAPTER 6

Is the Fundament a Grave?
Translating the Early Modern Body

Let's begin with some anatomical considerations. Human
bodies are constructed in such a way that it is, or at least
has been, almost impossible not to associate mastery and
subordination with the experience of our most intense
pleasures. This is first of all a question of positioning.
—Leo Bersani, "Is the Rectum a Grave?"[1]

I haue had a most rare vision. I had a dreame, past the wit
of man, to say, what dreame it was. . . . Me-thought I was,
and me-thought I had. But man is but a patch'd foole, if he
will offer to say, what me-thought I had. The eye of man
hath not heard, the eare of man hath not seen, mans hand
is not able to taste, his tongue to conceiue, nor his heart to
report, what my dreame was. I will get *Peter Quince* to
write a ballet of this dreame, it shall be called *Bottomes
Dreame*, because it hath no bottome.
—*A Midsommer Nights Dreame*[2]

I n an influential and widely cited essay, Leo Bersani has asked whether the rectum
is a grave—the grave of the self, the burial of "proud subjectivity" he sees literal-
ized in, or at least exacerbated by responses to, the AIDS epidemic (222). The present chapter seeks in part to ask whether the rectum—or, as it will be my habit to
write in these next pages, the *fundament*—was, as inescapably as it seems to be for
Bersani, a grave, a loss of subjectivity, in early modern England as well. I want to
make explicit at the outset that my discussion here will be based largely on the fundaments of men.[3] But, in keeping with the more expansive understanding of early

modern sexuality in recent research, as explored in the Introduction and elsewhere in this book, I mean explicitly not to restrict the range of this discussion to "homosexuals"; it will be a contention of this chapter that, in an era before the invention of the homo/hetero divide, a queer-philological consideration of the fundament is relevant to the bodily structures and practices of early modern people more generally.[4]

Was the *fundament* a grave in early modern England? A review of some familiar literary examples would seem to confirm that this was the case. We could begin, for instance, at the "back-gate" to the corporeally imagined castle of Alma in Spenser's *Faerie Queene*, a structure "cleped . . . *Port Esquiline*."[5] The passage thus associates the body part with the gate near Rome's Esquiline Hill, used as a paupers' cemetery in antiquity. Likewise, the Red Cross knight's exit from the House of Pride is via a "priuie Posterne," a "fowle way," strewn with "many corses . . . / Which all through that great Princesse pride did fall / And came *to shamefull end*." There he sees a "donghill of dead carkases."[6] As we saw in Chapter 2, Hamlet imagines tracing the "dust" of Alexander the Great "till he find it stopping a bunghole"—which a 1611 translation dictionary glosses as a *fundament*.[7] Hamlet makes these associations in a graveyard.

As we began to see in Chapter 5, the end of King Edward II is another important site for this conjunction of *fundament* and grave, at least in the famous Holinshed passage now routinely also used to gloss the absence of any stage direction for the "same" scene in Christopher Marlowe's play:

> [T]hey came suddenlie one night into the chamber where he laie in bed fast asleepe, and with heauie featherbeds or a table (as some write) being cast vpon him, they kept him down and withall put into his fundament an horne, and through the same they thrust vp into his bodie an hot spit, or (as other haue) through the pipe of a trumpet a plumbers instrument of iron made verie hot, the which passing vp into his intrailes, and being rolled to and fro, burnt the same, but so as no appearance of any wound or hurt outwardlie might be once perceiued.[8]

In Holinshed's account the fundament becomes, almost literally, the unmarked grave of Edward; a number of the historical accounts remark the unmarked nature of Edward's death.

In a less torturous but no less fatal instance, Aston Cokayne's description of the double burial of the playwrights John Fletcher and Philip Massinger might seem to activate a similar punning conjunction of fundament and grave:

> In the same Grave *Fletcher* was buried here
> Lies the Stage-Poet *Philip Massinger*:

Playes they did write together, were great friends,
And now one Grave includes them at their ends.[9]

In one sense the text seems unambiguous: Cokayne says that Massinger and Fletcher are buried together at the ends *of their lives*, which, as it turns out, ended fifteen years apart: *these* ends, at least, are not coterminous. At the same time, however, the poem also reads sodomitically (*sodometrically*[10]) in its positioning of the two men: laid side to side if not end to end, the two playwrights seem to find (the text suggests, even in apparently valorizing them) that their ends are at an end, that the fundament has become a grave, two ends in one end. Even as Alan Bray's research on same-sex couples buried together during this period would emphasize the friendship of this practice, the line between sodomy and friendship is easily crossed (as Bray's work has also helped us to see), and Cokayne's play with "ends" may emphasize this: here, separated by only a poetic line, sodomy and friendship rhyme: friends at ends; sodomy as fatal attraction.[11]

Such a reading of the conjunction of fundament and grave in early modern England is persuasive, not least for the ways in which the death penalty for sodomy under the laws of the Tudors and Stuarts, itself a version of the conjunction of sodomy and death in Leviticus 20:13,[12] might thus become a default cultural equation played out in less determinedly lethal contexts, like Cokayne's poem— that is to say, even in a context that seems to approve of and publicize homoerotic union. Massinger and Fletcher's lying together might be said to anticipate and preclude the Levitican punishment: lying together in their abominable state, there is no need to kill them; they're already at an end.[13]

But you know from my borrowing of Bersani's question, my re-citing of it *as* an open question, that this cannot be the end of my discussion, and here, via a queer philology, I want to resist the seemingly easy early modern connection between the fundament and the grave, a site of sodomy and the end of subjectivity. Or to give a less determinedly literal but no less critical reading to Bersani's essay: the idea that "the rectum" has any single definitive meaning. This is to ask a question that engages issues of discursive genealogy and philology at the center of this book and to explore what emerges when we read "the body" and its terms as attentively, historically speaking, as critics have read other terms related to sex and gender[14] in the classical, medieval, and early modern periods: what if we do not simply translate, as I have in repeating Bersani's question, the modern *rectum* into the early modern *fundament*? What is lost in translation? What if, instead, we read the rhetoric of the *fundament* itself more critically, more philologically? "This is first of all," to reiterate Bersani, "a question of positioning." But what position?

"*Bottome . . .* Thou Art Translated"

If *sodometries* are, in Jonathan Goldberg's definition, "relational structures pre-
cariously available to prevailing discourses," the prevailing sodometry in analyses
of the early modern period has been horizontal, the structuring of front and
back—more linearly, the beginning and the end. Goldberg and Patricia Parker
have both detailed the anality and circulation of the rhetorical trope *hysteron
proteron*, translated by George Puttenham as "the Preposterous," a disordering
trope that (as Parker writes) "connotes here the reversal of *post* for *pre*, back for
front, after for before, posterior for prior, end or sequel for beginning."[15] The sodomitical meanings of this prominent trope come more fully into view when we
recall with Parker that John Barret's 1580 dictionary glosses *preposterous* as "arsieversie: contrary to al good order";[16] *preposterous*, as both Goldberg and Parker
note, is a period term for sodomy.[17]

Parker makes clear that this horizontal structure of the preposterous—that
which is, in Barret's phrase, "contrary to al good order"—is linked to the overturning of traditional bodily and social hierarchies, top for bottom, head for posterior, the raising of the Bakhtinian lower bodily strata. Gail Kern Paster has emphasized this structure of anal rhetorics in her readings of bodily purgation and
the reversals of Bottom and Titania's relation in *A Midsummer Night's Dream*. For
Paster, too, these structures are related to more general bodily and political structures, "Titania's mastery and Bottom's passivity."[18]

These readings of early modern anal rhetorics are utterly convincing: there in
the text to be analyzed once—alerted by Parker's and Goldberg's tracings of these
complex webs of etymology, rhetoric, and what we would call wordplay—one
begins to see them.[19] But I want to suggest that this structure that has seemed always to characterize the rhetoric of the anus (whether front and back, beginning
and end, [privileged] top and [derogated] bottom, head and ass) is not the only
rhetoric of the anus in early modern culture: there is at least another rhetoric that
is related to, but does not structure itself along the same axes as, the *histeron proteron*, *preposterous*, *arsieversie*. It is a different "positioning" or sodomy: a sodometry of the fundament.

For *fundament*, of course, does not precisely mean "arse" or "posterior" or
"behind"—it does not mean these things if we take seriously its etymology and
the rhetorical surround of related terms, in the sixteenth and seventeenth centuries in England. *Fundament*, also spelled *foundament* and *foundment* (to name
only two of many other forms), is closely related to several words that have re-
mained in circulation in English: *foundation*, to *found*, and, a bit later, *fund*. One
of *fundament*'s meanings, in fact, is "[t]he foundation or base of a wall, building,
etc."[20] Indeed, the word *fundament*, in its three primary meanings of "founda-

tion," "buttocks," and "anus," seems to exist in English for a century before *foundation*, the word that, after several centuries of overlap, eventually takes its place (or, more precisely, *one* of its places). It is worth noticing, however, that, through the end of the seventeenth century, *fundament* means "foundation," and *foundation* is used to refer to the body part. Not only can we not give *fundament* and *foundment* distinct histories, as the *Oxford English Dictionary* (*OED*) notes, but the fundament seems always to be inseparably foundational.[21]

This inseparability is supported by the kinds of hard-word lists and translation dictionaries from the period that the *OED* does not cite. In John Minsheu's *Ductor in Linguas* (1617), for example, the entry for "*to* founde, *or cause to bee built*"[22] overlaps significantly in its translations with the entries for *fundament*. The entries for *fundament* itself translate the word into a group of meanings around *foundation* (German *Grundt*; Greek *Basis*) and then around *seat* (Latin *sedes*; French *siege*; German *gesesz*; etc.).

Such a history will seem obvious to anyone who has contemplated the etymology of the word still with us, *fundamental*. Yet it is important to notice the way in which even the word *fundamental* during this period had not yet been transfigured into dead metaphoricity; at the same time that *fundament* circulated as "buttocks" and "anus,"[23] the word *fundamental* was being used as we would use *foundational* in its most literal sense (meaning "of a foundation"). Texts speak of a building's "fundamentall walls," the "first fundamental stone" of a foundation.[24] John Florio's *Worlde of Wordes* (1598) translates the Italian "*Fondamentale*, [as] fundamentall, that hath or is a ground or foundation."[25] Many uses of this set of related terms seem to have a religious valence: in a 1653 text cited by the *OED*, for example, Christ is described as the church's "fundamental stone." Again, this is perhaps not surprising to those who have considered modern religious fundamentalism's relation to an ostensibly infallible textual foundation; what *is* striking in this context is the coexistence of the ass(hole) and the church's foundation in a complexly interimplicated rhetoric.[26]

What interests me in these texts is the way in which the *fundament* resists what have become the normative ways of talking about the rectum or anus—ways that may begin to suggest, at least in certain contexts, the alterity of this culture's conception of this part and of the body attached to and articulated around it. Or, to be more attentive to the discourse, the body constructed *upon* it. I have already suggested the way in which the rhetoric of the fundament is not preposterous, not bassackwards, or arsieversie. But notice, too, that the fundament is not always necessarily imagined in this cultural context as a passive recipient or receptacle of dominating penetration. Instead, it is "a grounde, a foundation, a building"[27]—it "hath *or is* a ground or foundation."[28] Or, as Florio also translates, "[a]lso an offspring, beginning, or groundworke."[29] This is not a language of passivity; in fact, it seems largely outside or unengaged with an active/passive binary. At the same time, the fundament is imagined as originary: an offspring, beginning—and thus at some distance from the preposterous ends of the other anal rhetorics. Consider Thomas Elyot's description of the function of the fundament in *The Castel of Helth* (1541), in his chapter "Of Euacuation": "there be two sortes of ordure, that is to saye, one digested, which passeth by siege [a word we have seen above, in Minsheu: from *seat*, but also meaning "stool" and thus "shit"], the other vndigested, which is expellyd by vomyte. Where I saye digested, I meane, that it is passed the stomake, and tourned in to another fygure."[30] For Elyot, the mouth and the fundament are equally salubrious sites of evacuation; like the mouth, the fundament produces health through purgation. And perhaps in this sense it is seen as more productive: engaging as it does early modern terms for the productions, turnings, and translations of rhetoric, what the fundament passes has been "tourned in to another fygure."

This is what is perhaps most striking about the rhetoric of the fundament, especially when juxtaposed with the more familiar Bakhtinian model of the bottom, the lower bodily strata; while the fundament, as foundation and seat, may participate in the rhetoric of the low, this is lowliness with a positive valence—the foundational is hardly a negative rhetoric in this culture. Consider, for example, Florio's translation of the Italian "*Fondataménte*, [meaning] from the very foundation, groundedly, vpon good ground or foundation. Also deeply, or profoundly."[31] By this point, it is probably unnecessary to point out pro*fund*ity's etymological relation to *fund*ament.

One might easily extend this hypothesis too far, but I want nevertheless to advance it as an observation that has some explanatory power. First, however, I want to articulate what is at stake theoretically in this observation, through the work of two modern theorists. Lee Edelman has suggested the importance of reviewing the binarism that places in opposition a valued activity and a derogated passivity, in a way that is ultimately tied to the formation and articulation of the subject in culture. Within the modern regime Edelman is critiquing, "the civic authority of subject status" is thought to be "purchased through the projective refusal of the luxurious 'passivity,' . . . that signifies the erotic indulgence of the self that always threatens to undo the 'self.'"[32] Edelman shows in particular how the modern use of an active/passive rhetoric by gay men urging other gay men to activism reenacts and reinscribes the familiar binary that has done the work of oppression (usually from the "outside") in prior cultural moments. Thinking about the early modern rhetoric of the fundament is another (historical) way of resisting that binary, for, as I have been suggesting, the fundament lies productively in a strangely active/passive position: it is the ground and also the groundwork; the seat and also the offspring; the founding and the foundation. The fundamental is that which "hath *or is* a ground or foundation."[33]

As I will suggest in more detail at the end of this chapter, my hypothesis is also a historical attempt to address Guy Hocquenghem's theorization of the anus as the seat of a privately owned subjectivity: "it forms," he says, activating the etymologies at the base of my argument, "the subsoil of the individual, his 'fundamental' core."[34] To think in this way might be to emerge from the more traditional Freudian model Hocquenghem's text itself works to resist, in which (he argues) "the homosexual can only be a degenerate, for he does not generate—he is only the artistic end to a species."[35] The fundament—if not, in Hocquenghem's term, "the homosexual"—might be said to found, to generate, to merge in a (to us) strangely active/passive, object/subject position.

We might indeed take this to be the meaning of another of Elyot's evocations of the fundament, this time not in the *Castel of Helth* (itself an edifice with a fundament), but instead in his 1538 Latin-English dictionary. There, as the other dictionaries have taught us to anticipate, Elyot defines Latin "Fundamen, & fundamentum [as] *a fundacion*," related closely (etymologically and on the page) to "Fundo . . . , *to founde, to make stable*," and to "Fundus, *that whyche is vsed to be callyd lande or soyle*."[36] In the dictionary's "additions," however, "Fundus, *is somtyme taken for a foundation, also for the chiefe authour of a thynge*."[37] Author: itself from Latin *augere* ("to make to grow, originate, promote, increase") and meaning, in period English, to generate, to father, also a creator, a writer, a cause.[38] Julius Casserius's early sixteenth-century anatomical plate (Figure 43) seems visually to register such a conjunction: the phallus, the body, and a tree all seem to grow up from this fundament—the foundation and chief author of this view.[39] Elyot's "chiefe authour" is probably closer to "authority" or "origin" than to modern "authorship," but to read his startling conjunction of fundament and author, and to entertain the possibility that others in this culture might likewise have seen it, is to ask Foucault's familiar question once again, in an unaccustomed position: "What is an author, that it is related to a fundament?"[40]

Obviously, I am indulging in some speculation here, tracing some possible positionings made available by an early modern discourse of the fundament, but I do at the same time want to show that such a discourse may indeed have been available in the sixteenth and seventeenth centuries and that, furthermore, it might have some relevance not simply for thinking about bodies in their particular members (and the uses and functions of bodies), but also for excavating other discursive strata. Take, of all unexpected anatomical sites, the following passage from the preface to the reader of James I's *Works* (1616), a discussion of precedents for James's royal authorship:

FIGURE 43. The fundament as foundation, in Julius Casserius's anatomical
plate from Adriaan van den Spiegel, *De humani corporis fabrica*.
Shelfmark: f Typ 25.27.804, Houghton Library, Harvard University.

[God] wrote, and the writing was the writing, saith *Moses*, of God; . . . the
matter was in Stone cut into two Tables, and the Tables were the worke of
God written on both sides. *Diuines* hold, that the Heart is the principall
Seate of the Soule; which Soule of ours is the immediate worke of God, as
these Tables were the immediate worke of his owne fingers. . . . And cer-
tainely from this little *Library*, that God hath erected within vs, is the
foundation of all our Learning layd.[41]

Is this passage, concluding as it does at the foundation, "about" the early modern anus? Probably not, although as my quotation marks around *about* suggest, I think it is a theoretical problem of some complexity to extricate the body from the building this prose erects.

Does the passage, however, engage the rhetoric of foundationalism that informs the articulation and experience of the anus in early modern England? In this passage, the heart is the "Seate" of the soul; the soul is the work and ground-work of an authorial god, writer of the Decalogue; the Decalogue, a "little *Library*" within us, situated in the seate/soul, is a foundation—the productive foundment of "all our Learning." The body is figured here as a building; indeed, the passage is itself a rhetorical edifice related to the trope of *gradatio*,[42] culminating in a foundation: heart = soul; soul = God's commandments; commandments = foundation. Or perhaps not "culminating," but *delving down to* the foundation and building up the religious subject from this groundwork: to the extent that the passage encodes an early modern notion of readerly interiority or subjectivity, that space is both fundamentally situated and textually articulated. Reading is fundamental.

The edifice of knowledge built on the fundament is not to be found in quasi-religious contexts alone. Consider the following series of medical procedures, detailed in *[A] treatise of the Fistulae in the fundament*, a 1588 translation and publication of a fourteenth-century text by John Arderne:

> Let the pacient be decently layde vppon a bed against a faire light window. . . . Which done, let the chirurgian put the fore finger of the left hand into his fundament, and with his other hand, put the head of the instrument called *Sequere me*, into the hole of the Fistulae that is next to the fundament. If there be many holes, proue with your instrument diligently in euery hole, your finger remaning in the fundament. . . .
>
> Let ye paciêt be laid vpon a bed against a light window, and his legges raised vp with a towell or a corde, which being done, lette the fundament be opened with a paire of Tonges[43] made in such order, that when ye presse the one end together, the other may open, or with some other conuenuent instrument, at your discrecion.
>
> The fundament being opened, and the griefe diligentlie seene, let the hole be filled with [the following medicines].[44]

These passages (and there are more, not for the squeamish) resonate strikingly with the author-surgeon's description of his own project, the opening and publication of medical knowledge:

[I]n hard things students and practicioners should be more busie to seeke out the secrets of nature. . . . Therefore to the honour of almightie God, that *opened knowledge to mee*, that I should *finde treasure within the fielde of knowledge*, that with longe time and panting breast, I haue sweat and trauailed, and full busilie indeuored my selfe as my facultie suffiseth, to *sette foorth* this woorke faithfullie.[45]

In this text, the fundament is assuredly not a grave (the writer claims to have cured the fistulae of nineteen patients, "with many other which it were to long to set downe"[46]); it becomes the foundation or seat of knowledge, which is *set* forth and *set* down (as a foundation, basis, groundwork), and, following the cure, the foundation of a castle of health for its patients. Likewise, in the descriptions of medical procedure, we see an emergent language of knowledge: "*proue* with your instrument diligently." In a culture where knowledge is figured as depth, the fundament may be fundamental. *Prove* and *probe* are etymologically related.

We are witnessing here, in a specifically fundamental form, an important resemblance, articulated in many other locations in early modern culture, between the rhetoric of the body and the rhetoric of bodily knowledge, its pursuit, and its setting forth. This conjunction is most famously on display on the title page to Vesalius's *Fabrica*, a book that makes opening the body analogical to opening the book that displays the opened body.[47] This equation of bodily knowledge and the opened book is made even more graphically (foliarly? tactilely?) in the anatomical "flapbooks" and broadsides of the sixteenth and seventeenth centuries, in which superimposed leaves or flaps of paper could be lifted by a reader to reveal the organs of the body.[48] In a comparatively late English example—*A Survey of the Microcosme: Or, The Anatomy of the Bodies of Man and Woman* (1695)—the plates (called "visions") of male and female bodies are similarly designed to be opened by the reader: paper flaps representing the skin and layers of organs can be pulled back to reveal other layers (still more bodily knowledge). In vision II, figure H (this flap "[r]epresents the Intestines") contains "a. the *Anus*, or Fundament." The fundament here is inside, to be opened out.

Turned into Another Figure

It is perhaps obvious, as I move further astray from any text that has an explicit homoerotic or sodomitical valence, that the discourse of the fundament I have sought here to uncover may hold no great liberatory erotic potential for early modern men (whether engaged in hetero- or homoerotic practices) and/or for women.

As we might expect, the question of gender is neither incidental nor simple. In an earlier version of this chapter, I perhaps too blithely contemplated what had seemed to me the general lack of uses of the term *fundament* in relation to early modern women, a question I broadened to ask whether early modern discourse (often disposed toward seeing men as the exemplary and usually the primary case) could, in seeing the fundament as foundational, think of this body part as similarly foundational in *women,* a question to which Celia R. Daileader has objected.[49] First, to address the more empirical question: at least in some anatomical texts and midwifery manuals, the term *fundament* is used repeatedly in reference to women's bodies.[50] Whether this answers the larger question I posed about gender and foundations is another matter. Daileader compiles an extensive array of examples she terms *gynosodomy* (that is, women positioned as insertee or object in anal sex or eroticism) in popular-culture contexts, but it is important to notice that, at least to my reading, few if any of her examples use the rhetoric of the fundament in describing the bodies, activities, or desires of such represented women—as opposed to the rhetoric of the preposterous, the back and the front.[51] Further, I think it is potentially too simple to suggest that fundaments are understood in the period as foundational for men, but wombs as foundational for women (the anatomy and midwifery texts' attention to *both* in women thus requires further analysis), or that, as Daileader writes, "any figuration of the anus-as-foundational *is bound* to draw its power from analogy with the womb" (317). While not seeking to write off in advance the possible metonymic connections between fundament and womb (for either male or female early modern bodies), I would want to see the analyses before being bound by Daileader's conclusion here.[52] My point is not to dispute that the womb was seen as a "foundational" body part for women in early modern medical discourse (a point Daileader understands me to have missed), but rather to ask: what is the power of the rhetoric of the fundament in differently gendered bodies during this period?[53] How might that rhetoric have intersected with or inflected the rhetoric of sodomy—whether *gynosodomy, androsodomy* (Daileader's terms), or anal eroticism or penetration enacted *by* women? We will read an example of the latter—a configuration for which Daileader's object-oriented lexicon has no term—in Chapter 9's analysis of female "bumbasting" in *Sir Thomas More.*

So, for early modern men and (potentially but not necessarily differently) for early modern women, the fundament's grounding rhetoric may have held no great emancipatory power.[54] On the one hand, after allegorizing the fundament's excretory function, Phineas Fletcher's *The Purple Island, Or The Isle Of Man* suggests obliquely and without further explanation that it is a "gate endow'd with many properties."[55] But, on the other, the poem does so in the context of a text that is also explicitly antisodomitical.[56] I nevertheless think that there is something to be learned from this broader array of materials about (1) the placement of the fundament within mappings of the (at least male) body and the cultural resonances of those mappings and (2) a sodometry that somehow accounts for the foundationalism of the anus, that is to say, an analysis of eroticism that engages with this alternative understanding of the anus-as-foundation in early modern culture.[57]

Reading the rhetoric of the fundament—that is, an asshole that is not the derogated bottom of the lower bodily strata, not the backside of what should "rightfully" be front-sided—may alert us to other unusual sodomitical positionings (sodometries) that we would not otherwise see. Reading Marlowe's *Edward II*, I had always assumed—and my assumption seems, on the basis of Derek Jarman's film version and the stage versions I have seen and read about, to be widely shared—that Edward ends face down, overthrown, arsieversie, bottoms up. But consider a 1626 verse version of Edward's end, published as Francis Hubert's in 1628, quoted here from the manuscript at the Folger Library:

> 583
> But being ouer watcht and wearie too
> Nature asmuch desirous of some rest
> Which gave them opportunitie to doe
> What they desir'd ? for being wth sleep opprest
> They clapt a massie table on my breast
> And wth great waight, so kept me downe wthal
> That breathe I could not, muchles crie or call;

> 584
> And then into my fundament they thrust,
> A litle horne, as I did groueling lie.[58]

Do I need to go on?—you know how this one ends up. Or do you? It does end up, in one sense: Edward ends face up, ass down, the table on his *breast*. (His "groueling" may introduce further indeterminacy.) But it also does not quite end there either. For, strange as it may seem, Edward goes on to narrate another stanza, a kind of moral conclusion or end to his story, and with it there comes the reader's realization that this whole text—spoken in the first-person singular, as these excerpts have suggested—emerges *after*, or on the basis of, his end. The fundament again seems no grave here, at least in a narratological or discursive sense. It seems to produce a long narrative poem, ending in its 584th stanza, then ending finally again a stanza later, with a final "Finis infortunis," an unfortunate end.

We might, finally, think about what subject positionings could be imagined out of the material circumstances of writing, copying, tracing out, reading the manuscript of this poem, the 585 stanzas of the first-person discourse of a (sodomized) sodomite and then of setting all those stanzas in print two years later, to be read more widely. For the persons in this culture who performed these acts of literacy and inscription, what might have been the subjectivity effects of *this* "little Library"—of articulating (copying, reading out, setting forth in type) that resilient "I" for more than four thousand lines? Writing and reading such a text might be foundational, founding, fundamental in quite another way; the sodomite, the fundament, may be turned into another figure: I. "At last they found / That *I was dead*," Edward says of his murderers, "yet seem'd to have no wound."

Psychic Groundwork

By briefly imagining what I have called possible "subjectivity effects," I would not want to claim that this chapter has fully engaged the question of early modern psychic structures built on or in relation to the fundament. A larger consideration of the issues raised here would ultimately want to do so, for it is a central assumption of my argument that what I have been investigating queer philologically and calling "the rhetoric of the fundament" is not *merely* "rhetoric," in the modern, noninstrumental sense of that term. Rather, it participates in the structuring of everyday social, psychic, and affective life, the experience of the body (at least "a body"), by which I mean the experience of the body-in-culture.[59] By connecting the body-in-culture, bodies-in-their-rhetorics, with "psychic structures," I mean not to disavow psychoanalysis as a methodological tool for the analysis of early modern culture, but rather to stress, as my argument above suggests, that the normative structures and understandings of the body (including and inscribed in particular "rhetorics") available to such an analysis will change over time—in ways that may connect with and/or diverge from those of our own time.[60] One place to begin: what would "anality" mean—would it exist—as a psychoanalytic structure within the "fundamental" rhetoric I analyze here?[61] What will be understood as the relation of this re-untranslated body part to desire and sexual practice? Would the fundament be seen as the essential body part—the seat of desire, as it were—of men erotically involved with other men? With some similar cautions about the historicity of traditional psychoanalytic categories, Ben Saunders has brilliantly followed up on such questions in an essay on Iago, "anality," and racism in *Othello*: "the discourses of sodomy and anality, while often mutually implicated in both the Freudian and the popular imaginations, may have a more tangential relation in the Renaissance. It would follow that Iago's anality [i.e., his interest in evacuation, in early modern terms, and not simply retention] need not be an indicator of homosexuality, 'repressed' or otherwise. *But what else might this anality indicate?*"[62]

What else might anality—or, to translate back into my terms, what else might this *fundamentalism*—indicate? To imagine such a postmodern psychoanalysis on an early modern basis or fundacion is to contest Bersani's assertion, articulated in my epigraph and elsewhere, that "[h]uman bodies are constructed in such a way that it is, or at least has been, almost impossible not to associate mastery and subordination with the experience of our most intense pleasures" (216).[63] Dwelling on the foundment has, I hope, at least troubled the notion of "bodies constructed [only] in such a way." But what—to follow Bersani's sentence further—are "*our* most intense pleasures," and are they the same as those experienced by the early moderns? In this passage, Bersani is writing about (heterosexual) penetration, but we should notice that "our" pleasures, even our "most intense" ones, shift around, apparently, even in modernity. Elsewhere, in the context of sadomasochism, Bersani cites "the powerful appeal of those ['authoritarian'] structures, their harmony with the body's most intense pleasures" and—still elsewhere, in a context that becomes but has not yet been articulated as "the experience of masturbation"—he echoes these citations by citing "a man's most intense experience of his body's vulnerability."[64] Is the rectum, even in Bersani's texts, the site of definitive, superlative pleasure?

To dislodge the rectum or anus from any definitive and transcultural meaning—to acknowledge that the fundament might be turned into another and different figure—may be analogically to experience "Bottom's Dream," or at least to read the experience it encodes seriously. Speaking as a historian of the experience of his own body, Bottom reviews his "most rare vision," an experience only legible as a dream that troubles the meaning of subjectivity ("Me-thought I was . . .") and of the body ("me-thought I had . . .") and that imagines (if only in a negative fantasy) a body in parts set loose from their customary meanings and functions: hearing eyes, seeing ears, tasting hands, conceiving tongues, reporting hearts.[65] What is a fundament in this context? What does a bottom do? "The Scriptural allusion [to the Geneva Bible's "bottom of Goddes secretes"], *perverted as it is*," writes Thomas B. Stroup, "nevertheless brings Bottom to his epiphany, his self-recognition."[66] "Bottom's Dream" is, of course, ultimately antifundamentalist; its vision sees no stable ground or groundwork of bodily meaning, no definitive answer to such questions: "it hath no bottome." Like queer philology as described in this book's Introduction, or like Nietzsche's description of philological reading that assigns delicacy to both eyes and fingers, Bottom's dream is open-ended. The rectum—as we have seen Phineas Fletcher note, in his less explicitly synaesthetic, if no less phantasmatic, description of *The Isle Of Man*—is "endow'd with many properties."[67]

CHAPTER 7

When Genres Breed: "Mongrell Tragicomedie" and Queer Kinship

> The relations of exchange that constitute culture as a series
> of transactions or translations are not only or primarily
> sexual, but they do take sexuality as their issue, as it were,
> when the question of cultural transmission and repro-
> duction is at stake. . . . [T]he figure of the child is one
> eroticized site in the reproduction of culture, one that
> implicitly raises the question of whether . . . hetero-
> sexuality will serve not only the purposes of transmitting
> culture faithfully, but whether culture will be defined,
> in part, as the prerogative of heterosexuality itself.
> —Judith Butler, "Is Kinship Always Already
> Heterosexual?"[1]

> A man and a woman
> Are one.
> A man and a woman and a blackbird
> Are one.
> —Wallace Stevens, "Thirteen Ways of Looking
> at a Blackbird"[2]

A queer philology of *sodomy*, I am arguing, will repeatedly take us beyond the investigation of that term so central to historians and literary historians of sexuality from Michel Foucault and John Boswell to Alan Bray, Gregory Bredbeck, Jonathan Goldberg, David Halperin, Cynthia Herrup, Mark Jordan, Bruce Smith, and many others.[3] While it should not surprise us that an "utterly confused category," in Foucault's famous phrase, will not remain within terminological bounds, I argue that it will require us to imagine and analyze an even larger lexicon—a lexicon that will move us outward in multiple directions, toward the rhetoric of bodily parts and practices (as in the previous chapter's *fundamental* terms), and even into the surprising terrain of so apparently unsexy a traditional literary concern as *genre*. Is there a history of sexuality in a genre? Let me count the ways.

1

"The development of species concepts is a complex story," writes Peter F. Stevens, in "Species: Historical Perspectives." "Some taxonomists have insisted that the act of describing species affords no room for conceptualization; taxonomists simply describe nature, a matter not of theory but of direct observation. Others, perhaps the majority, have utilized some reproductive criterion in their species concept— either the species is not fertile when crossed with other species, or at least the characters used to distinguish the species are constant over successive generations. There has been general agreement that species must be readily recognizable."[4]

2

"[B]esides these grosse absurdities," Sir Philip Sidney writes in *The Defence Of Poesie*, "all their Playes bee neither right Tragedies, nor right Comedies, mingling Kinges and Clownes, not because the matter so carrieth it, but thrust in the Clowne by head and shoulders to play a part in maiesticall matters, with neither decencie nor discretion: so as neither the admiration and Commiseration, nor the right sportfulnesse is by their mongrell Tragicomedie obtained. . . . But if we marke them [the Auncients] well, we shall finde that they neuer or verie daintily matche horne Pipes and Funeralls."[5]

3

"[A]s soon as genre announces itself," Jacques Derrida writes in "The Law of Genre," "one must respect a norm, one must not cross a line of demarcation, one must not risk impurity, anomaly or monstrosity."[6]

4

"A tragie-comedie is not so called in respect of mirth and killing," writes John Fletcher, in the preface to his play *The Faithful Shepherdess*, "but in respect it wants deaths, which is inough to make it no tragedie, yet brings some neere it, which is inough to make it no comedie: which must be a re-presentation of familiar people, with such kinde of trouble as no life be questiond, so that a God is as lawfull in this as in a tragedie, and meane people as in a comedie."[7]

5

Something there is that doesn't love a mixture. Something, that is, in genre criticism at least, and the recent history of criticism of early modern English tragicomedy is the history of a resistance to hybridity. Take, as an example, Nancy Klein Maguire's *Renaissance Tragicomedy: Explorations in Genre and Politics* (1987; one of several essay anthologies published on this topic in the last twenty-five years).[8] Describing the genesis of her collection, Maguire comments that, through the conference sessions she organized on tragicomedy, she "found a core of scholars who . . . were . . . irritated by inexact references to tragicomedy and by the lack of definition. They were willing to tackle the definitional task."[9] The result is a volume arguing "that tragicomedy is neither a 'mungrell' mixture of tragedy and comedy nor a decadent offshoot of tragedy but is rather a genre in its own right, full of generic implications and significance."[10] In the same volume, John Shawcross writes, "While tragicomedy may be a product of 'tragic' and 'comedy,' it should not be treated like a child who is seen only to be a replica of his father or his mother or some admixture of the two: it should have a life and personality of its own, for it is itself."[11] I will return to this discourse of kinship and reproduction, but first let us note the transformative aims of this criticism: even those most interested in tragicomedy (that is to say, even those willing to engage with the idea of a mixed genre) seek to homogenize it, to transmute its hybridity into a new and unmixed kind.

In their account of tragicomedy, *The Politics of Tragicomedy: Shakespeare and After* (1992), Jonathan Hope and Gordon McMullan have definitional concerns as well: "Part of the problem for the critic," they write, "is that the word 'tragicomedy' itself seems never to have acquired anything akin to a fixed meaning."[12] Working toward a more theoretically nuanced and historically accurate account, they argue against the unhelpful critical practice of taking Fletcher's brief preface to *The Faithful Shepherdess* as "a considered and coherent definition (or prediction) of tragicomedy across the period" (3). They find Fletcher's comment seriously undermined by its "specific justificatory context" (it prefaced an initially unsuccessful play) and by its unrepresentativeness (it seems not to represent Fletcher's own later practice or the other plays they take to be tragicomedies during the period). On the other hand, they seek, at the least, "a working definition of tragicomedy" (4) and, at most, "a succinct description and definition" (2).[13]

This focus on definitionality—of discerning the thing and providing its appropriate name and description, a concern that extends as well to earlier critical treatments of tragicomedy, such as Madeleine Doran's *Endeavors of Art* and Eugene Waith's *The Pattern of Tragicomedy in Beaumont and Fletcher*—is a reiterated anxiety in genre criticism. Faced with a question of genre, literary critics often become scientists; consider, for example, the almost Linnean classificatory work of Alistair Fowler. After working through fifteen "generic features" (e.g. external structure, metrical structure, size, scale, values, attitude, task[14]), Fowler writes, definitively, "There is a view that the kinds have undergone so many variations and historical changes as to be indeterminate. . . . This view is wrong. The kinds, however elusive, objectively exist."[15]

It is this widely held Fowlerian view—a view implicit even in Hope and Mc-Mullan's sense that there will be a "considered and coherent" early modern definition of tragicomedy that exists outside a particular or restricted context, whether justificatory or not—that this chapter seeks in part to complicate. There are, I will argue, following and attempting to extend Derrida's ruminations on this topic, no unmixed genres in practice, even if there are imagined to be some in theory. From this follows a corollary: it will be productive to give more analytical attention to tragicomedy, for it—though you will have noted that I am arguing that it (per se) does not exist—encodes the practice of all texts: mixture, hybridity.[16] Or, to put this in Derrida's terms, "[A] text cannot be without or less a genre. Every text participates in one or several genres, there is no genreless text; there is always a genre and genres, *yet such participation never amounts to belonging*" (212, my emphasis). Such a view argues strongly against the way criticism of tragicomedy has been conducted: starting from Sidney's or Fletcher's definition, and looking for signs of gods; or mingled kings and clowns; or persons brought near, but not quite put to, death.

6

Indeed, there is another use for Sidney's and Fletcher's statements about tragicomedy, a use quite unlike the template function they have thus far tended to serve: *What are the discourses that trace out and constitute the idea of tragicomedy? What are their associations and contiguities?*

By writing of *mixture*, I have perhaps already been inattentive to the early modern discourses of tragicomedy. We should notice, first, that discussions of tragicomedy are articulated within particular and overlapping discourses of social class, breeding, and cross-breeding. Not that critics have necessarily been inattentive to the presence of multiple social classes in the "definitions" and plays under discussion; rather, the discourses of genre, social class, mixture, reproduction, and kinship are complexly intertwined, in ways that exceed the plotting of plot and character in the playtexts.[17] Sidney's term *mongrell Tragicomedie* is complicated in this sense, bringing with it the idea of a cross-bred genre, but also necessarily, in a culture of endogamy, a mixture that is cross-classed. This sense of *mongrel* has been illustrated by Marjorie Garber's elaboration of Shakespeare's attention to early modern dog hierarchies as a model of human society.[18] Further, a *mongrell* mixture, for Sidney, lacks "decencie" and "discretion"—a mongrel, as the Clown's dog Crab in *Two Gentlemen of Verona* suggests, is in no way discrete: it is neither of one kind, a *discrete* kind (not even named for his kind, but for another: "crab" [a different animal], or even a botanical kind, a "crab-apple"[19]); nor is it *discreet*, able to keep to himself (he eats others' food, he "thrusts me himselfe into the company of three or foure gentleman-like-dogs, vnder the Dukes table," his smell pervades the dining room[20]). The mongrel neither embodies nor conducts himself within the bounds of decorum.

This reproductive valence of *mongrell* resonates in another of Sidney's comments on tragicomedy: "in his [poetry's] parts, kindes, or *species*, as you list to tearme them, it is to be noted, that some *Poesies* haue coupled together two or three kindes, as the *Tragicall* and *Comicall*, whereupon is risen the *Tragicomicall*."[21] "To couple" is, of course, a verb for both marriage and sex acts, and the term thus continues Sidney's interest in the breeding of kinds or species (as you list to term them—there is apparently some room for slippage in Sidney's terms). In early modern English, *species* had begun to mean something like what it does for us today—a "kind," though not as fully articulated within the modern discourse of classificatory science with which I began.[22] At least according to the *Oxford English Dictionary* (*OED*), Sidney's use here is among the earliest to indicate a "distinct class, sort, or kind," preceding, again according to the *OED*, its use in a specifically zoological context (1608),[23] though surely Sidney's use here must bear some relation to its meaning of attributes or essential qualities in logic, well established in earlier sixteenth-century vernacular usage.[24] We are, to return to Sidney's other term, only too apt to hear "mongrel" as a species, or a *coupling* of species/kinds of dog, but as early modern usage makes clear, *mongrel* brought with it other uses, applied to humans, and not restricted to the *class* mixing we have already noted: "A person not of pure race; the offspring of parents of different nationalities," says the *OED*.[25] Sidney's mongrels may themselves be of multiple kinds, mingling and coupling dogs, species, ranks, races, and nationalities,[26] and it is thus not clear whether Sidney's term *mongrell* is a metaphor or figure of mixing (a mixed dog as a figure for a genre) or a "literal" description of interbred kings and clowns. Further pressure on the word *couple* only complicates this mix, for, in addition to referencing (human) marital and sex acts, the word could mean "[t]o tie or fasten (dogs) together in pairs."[27]

But what of *mingling* as opposed to, or supplemental of, *coupling*? Tragicomedy, Sidney writes, "mingles Kinges and Clownes." *Mingling* leads us in the direction of another text sometimes cited in discussions of early modern tragicomedy.

7

"Time hath confounded our mindes, our mindes the matter," says the Prologue in John Lyly's *Midas* (1589–90?), "but all commeth to this passe, that what heretofore hath beene serued in seuerall dishes for a feaste, is now minced in a charger for a Gallimaufrey. If wee present a mingle-mangle, our fault is to be excused, because the whole worlde is become an Hodge-podge."[28] Lyly's terms have by now largely lost their culinary resonances, but all three (*mingle-mangle, gallimaufry*, and *hodge-podge*) refer to dishes made by mixing together odds and ends of food. To serve up a mingle-mangle for a human audience of drama consumers is also to mix species in another sense, because a mingle-mangle was specifically a mixture of food for swine.[29] The very term raises the question of whether *to mingle* (for this period, at least in the contexts we have engaged so far) is also always (at least from certain perspectives) to *mangle*, or as the *OED* puts it, not just "[t]o hack, cut, or lacerate (a person or his members) . . . to a more or less unrecognizable condition," but also "to divide into rough or ragged parts."[30] Indeed, Sidney's engagement with social-class rhetoric (the mingling of kings and clowns) is itself also an engagement with a familiar bodily rhetoric that suggests as much, denouncing not simply the mingling of a clown with a king, but a clown rhetorically dismembered (mangled, minced in this charger of genre), even as he is figured through the display of body parts more "properly" associated with kings: tragicomedy "thrust[s] in the Clowne *by head and shoulders* to play a part in maiesticall matters."[31]

If mingling—within a rhetoric interested in whole bodies properly distributed—thus mangles, we can notice the persistent concern within these rhetorics (particularly Lyly's culinary terms) of the relation of the whole mixture to the ingredient parts and their genealogies; appropriately, the word *gallimaufry* is itself from French "of unknown origin."[32] Simultaneously mixing bodies and parts and food, these terms, too, are never far from a discourse of social class, even in Lyly's kitchen context: *hodge-podge*, itself a transmutation of *hotch-potch*, was also a long-standing legal term related to "[t]he blending or gathering together of properties for the purpose of securing equality of division."[33] Lyly's sense that all the world's a hotch-potch—rather than, say, a stage of many discrete parts—suggests, at a moment of increasing social mobility, just the sort of mingling of ranks and properties (and races and classes and species?) that Sidney's denunciation of a mongrel genre seeks to resist. Mongrel mixtures, then, are not, to cite the term to which Sidney returns repeatedly, "right" in two senses, seeming to move between, or to mean both, "right" in the sense of "correct" and "right" in the sense of "proper" or "discrete": "all their Playes bee neither *right* Tragedies, nor *right* Comedies, . . . so as neither the admiration and Commiseration, nor the *right* sportfulnesse is by their mongrell Tragicomedie obtained." To be "right" is to be both correct and unmixed. Sportfulness (itself a term not unrelated to breeding, or at least erotic play)[34] may be indulged, but it must be of the right sort, the right sport.[35]

8

"[M]angrel, mangrie: see mongrel, mangery." Reading about mongrels in an earlier edition of the *OED*, we can follow this trace of a tantalizing, though probably "spurious" (as we say), instance of mingle-mangle in the great dictionary. Among its variety of sixteenth- and seventeenth-century forms, *mongrel* is sometimes spelled *mungrell*, *mungrill*, or *mangrel*, with apparently an equally wide range of pronunciation. For example, Edward Topsell's monumental *The History of Four-footed Beasts and Serpents* (1658) heads its chapter on mixed canine breeds, for example, "Of the mixt kinde of *Dogs* called in *English MANGRELS* or *MONGRELS*."[36] *Mangrel*, the *OED* had once said, was possibly related to or to be grouped with *mangrie*, meaning "1. A banquet; a ceremonial feast; a series of festivities; 2. Banqueting, luxurious eating." The *OED Online* has now eliminated this brief entry and connection.[37] Call it a now-missing fossil of a web of associations—probably "spurious," possibly only attempting to save space by creating a brief joint entry. Still, the homonymic resonances remain: do breeding, eating, dogs, and genre coincide in "mongrell tragicomedie"? Is tragicomedy a series of mingled, mangled festivities? Is it mangrel tragicomedie? A dog in a manger(y)? And what would spurious (bastard) etymology even mean in this mongrel context? Fittingly, *mongrel's* etymology is only hypotheticized: "probably" from *mung, n.*, or *mang, v.*, meaning, respectively, a "mingling, a mixture; a confusion, a mess" and "to mingle *with*."[38] An utterly confused category.

In a section of his chapter on dogs devoted to "*CVRS* of the *Mungrel* and *Rascal* sort," Topsell, too, mingles discourses (of cooking and breeding, of tantalizing and spuriousness or bastardy), writing that,

> [o]f such Dogs as keep not their kinde, of such as are mingled out of sundry sorts, not imitating the conditions of some one certain spice, because they resemble no notable shape, nor exercise any worthy property of the true, perfect and gentable kinde, it is not necessary, that I write any more of them, but to banish them as unprofitable implements, out of the bounds of my Book; unprofitable, I say, for any use that is commendable.[39]

Spice is, of course, a culinary term; it is also related to *specie*—in the sense of currency, as Patricia Fumerton notes[40]—and also to *species*, or kind. Further, at the moment he draws the boundary or binding of his book, delimiting commentary on those kinds that "keep not their kinde," Topsell also employs a term (*gentable*) that occurs neither as a word entry nor in the full text of the *OED*, 2nd edition, its current online form, or the searchable texts of Early English Books Online.[41] What is the "*gentable* kind"? We can hypothesize that *gentable* may be related to *gentle*, *genteel*, *genitable*, *genital*, and *gental* (= genital).[42] The amount of correction and retranslation of early texts required, in fact, for the *OED* to stabilize the meaning and spelling of *genital* is, for a word we now think of as commonplace and clinically referential, rather extensive.[43] A queer philology of the genital(s) is beyond the scope of this chapter, but this lacunae (or intersection) at the center of Topsell's marginalization of mongrels can begin to demonstrate how such a study might open out into larger issues of kin/kind at the confused and prolific root *gen-* in early modern English, bringing into relation the genus, the gentle/genteel/gentile, the congenital: the discourses, that is, of kinship, kindship, social class/nation/religion, and reproduction.[44] To take a familiar example that could condense some of these issues: Shylock, called "dog" and "cur" repeatedly in Shakespeare's *Merchant of Venice*, though he initially keeps his kind (his daughter does not), is addressed by the Duke in the climactic trial scene with the line "We all expect a gentle answer, Jew."[45] A gentle, not common, answer, yes, but also, as numerous commentators have noted, a "gentile" answer, since the words overlap in spelling and probably pronunciation in the period.[46] Given the resonances that several critics have seen in this play and this scene of the pound of flesh as circumcision, "genital" may hover (somewhat nonsensically) in the Duke's statement as well.[47] But, even if a genital/gentable answer is potentially anticipated here, can a character so derogated as a "stranger cur"[48] "exercise any worthy property of the true, perfect and gentable kinde" here expected of him? In a context suffused with usury (and indeed in which Shylock himself has earlier compared "use" to "the work of generation" and "breeding"[49]), he is, at the end of the trial scene, banished out of the bounds of, if not Venice, the play at least—an unprofitable instrument after this scene, of no commendable use.

9

If Sidney's text seems determined to define (rightly) and anxious to avoid the coupling or mingling that his definition of tragicomedy constantly gives rise to,[50] Fletcher's text seems to resist the principle of definitionality almost entirely. "A tragie-comedie is *not* so called . . . ," begins the most familiar sentence of the passage, and above this (in lines rarely attended to, except as a notation of the play's initial failure on the stage), he protests with apparent sarcasm the people's "singuler guift in defining,"[51] a gift that has led in this case to their apparently believing that a tragicomedy is definable as just such a mixture: "Shepheards, in gray cloakes, with curtaild dogs in strings, sometimes, laughing together, and sometimes killing one another." Instead, after producing a definition of pastoral ("a representation of shepheards and shepheardesses"), Fletcher turns explicitly to tragicomedy and to a complicated exercise in negation: "A tragie-comedie *is not so called* in respect of mirth and killing"; "it *wants* deaths, which is inough to *make it no tragedie*"; it "brings some neere [death], which is inough to *make it no comedie.*" The passage is concerned chiefly not with identifying characteristics of genre, or with the perils of mixing (the mixture of "mirth and killing" is said to be beside the point), but rather with identifying the sufficient causes to remove a play from other generic categories (whatever is inough to make it *not* this thing, or *not* that thing).

If we seek in Fletcher's sentences an articulation of the "rightness" of genres that so occupies Sidney's, we again find Fletcher's ostensible definition undermining definitionality: in tragicomedy, "a God is *as lawful* . . . *as* in a tragedie, and meane people *as* in a comedie." The law of genre in this preface is flexive; indeed, the sentence may seem even to undermine the legalism of generic definitions—may seem to say, "*If* a God is lawful in tragedy, it is *as lawful* in tragicomedy." The law again seeks only to exclude (to describe what may be, but need not necessarily be, included); further, the law, the singuler guift of definition, or the gift of definitions in the singular, is thrown into question.[52] For Fletcher, it is not that tragicomedy "is"; it is that it is *so called*—or rather, more complexly, *not* so called—in this or that respect. Fletcher's preface ends with an again underread resisting of definition: "Thus much I hope will serue to iustifie my Poeme, and make you vnderstand it, to teach you more for nothing, I do not know that I am in conscience bound." Even in this moment of definitional deferral, of pedagogical withholding, another law (of conscience) is again put into epistemic question; its speaker "do[es] not know" that he is "bound" by it. As in Topsell, a definitive discussion of the mongrel is declared out of bounds.

10

A number of queer theorists have emphasized, in Lee Edelman's words, "the historical relationship that has produced gay sexuality within a discourse that associates it with *figures of nomination or inscription*,"[53] as we saw in the Introduction. Noting the traditional designation of sodomy as "the horrible crime/sin not to be named among Christians,"[54] Edelman emphasizes that "homosexual practices have been placed in [a] powerful, and [a] powerfully proscriptive . . . relation to language" (5). While the joining of sameness in modernity and the slippages of metonymy in the homograph are of central interest to Edelman, it is important to note, speaking of tragicomedy, that it is the joining of *difference* that often produces the same representational crisis (associated with problems of nomination and inscription) in early modern England.[55] Take, for example, this passage, from a chapter entitled "An Example of the Mixture [and] Mingling of Seed,"[56] in Ambrose Paré's 1573 text *Des Monstres et Prodiges*. (An incomplete version of the text was translated into English and published in 1634, but, for the moment, let's remain with a more accurate translation of the French text.)

> There are monsters that are born with a form that is half-animal and the other [half] human, or retaining everything [about them] from animals, which are produced by sodomists [Sodomites][57] and atheists who "join together" and break out of their bounds—unnaturally—with animals, and from this are born several hideous monsters that bring great shame to those who look at them or speak of them. Yet the dishonesty lies in the deed and not in words; and it is, when it is done, a very unfortunate and abominable thing, and a great horror for a man or woman to mix with or copulate [se mesler et accoupler] with brute animals; and as a result, some are born half-men and half-animals.
>
> The same occurs if animals of diverse species [diverses especes] cohabit with one another, because Nature always strives to recreate its likeness [tasche tousjours à faire son semblable].[58]

Edelman's concern with sexual nonnormativity and "figures of nomination or inscription" is evident in the passage: the monsters bred by this method "bring great shame to those who look at them *or speak of them.*" Even the immediate disavowal of this shame in naming ("Yet the dishonesty lies in the deed and not in words") can only supplement rather than erase mixing or mingling's "powerfully proscriptive . . . relation to language."[59] There is as well the resonance with Fletcher and Topsell, imagining writing out of bounds, since here the "sodomists and atheists . . . 'join together' and break out of their bounds—unnaturally." (The 1634 English translation of the passage one-ups the French in this regard by adding "Outlawes" to the atheists and sodomites breaking out of bounds.[60]) Further, the joining not of samenesses but of difference raises the problem of nomination, reminding us that what generates representational crisis in this culture is often *heterosexuality* in its most etymological sense: the copulation of difference—a reminder that the boundaries of sameness and difference are often located elsewhere in this culture.[61]

Thomas Johnson's 1634 English translation of this passage, which elaborates significantly on Paré's text in denouncing cross-breeding, returns more emphatically to the question of nomination: "This so great, so horrid a crime, for whose expiation all the fires in the world are not sufficient, though they [the atheists, sodomites, and outlaws], too maliciously crafty, have concealed, and the conscious beasts could not utter, yet the generated mis-shapen issue hath abundantly spoken and declared, by the unspeakable power of God" (982). While, as the Johnson translation attests, "things that are accounted obscene may bee spoken without blame, but they cannot bee acted or perpetrated without great wickednesse, fury and madnesse," there is a noteworthy swerve in this passage from the speaking of the reporter to that of the monstrous breed itself: "the generated mis-shapen issue hath [itself] abundantly spoken and declared, by the unspeakable power of God." Concerned with discourse and ultimately with things acted, we will return to this question: when the cross-breed, hybrid, or mongrel speaks in this culture, what does it say?

11

"[I]f 'species' is defined in terms of interbreeding within the group and lack of interbreeding between groups, then traditionally recognized species in asexually reproducing organisms would not be species," writes the scientist Mary B. Williams, in an essay entitled "Species: Current Usages."[62] This may be to deconstruct a certain notion of *species* as such. But what happens when *genres* breed? Or, to phrase this more precisely, what happens when genres are written, imagined, or understood as breeds that interbreed? Sidney provides one response to this question, the phantasm of mongrels, genres that are not "right"—mixing that produces not (in Shawcross's terms) a child that is an "admixture" of both parents, with traits of both, but, rather, a mix that does not include the "right" versions of traits from either of the parents thus coupled. Comparing these models of breeding, we could notice that the intercourse of genres is both, in Sidney's instance, de-naturalized (the coupling of difference; *hetero*-sexuality in the etymological sense again[63]), and, in Shawcross's, naturalized (reproductive heterosexuality in the modern sense): mother and father produce a child-genre.[64] Still, Shawcross's rhetoric may alert us to some of the queerness reserved (derogatorily) for tragicomedy in Sidney: Is it a boy or a girl? Neither: a third kind, a tragicomedy.

The illustrations that accompanied the Johnson translation of Paré can help us visualize what the early modern English saw when they saw mixture and confusion (Figures 44–45). The title page to Ben Jonson's 1616 *Workes* (Figure 46) produces another version of such mixture. Jonson surrounds himself, or at least his name, with multiple generic figures: ascending from tragedy and comedy through satire and pastoral, to tragicomedy. "SINGVLA QVAEQVE LOCVM TENEANT SOR-TITA DECENTER,"[65] instructs the Horatian inscription on this edifice of genres; in Jonson's own translation, "Each subject should retaine / The place allotted it, with decent thewes."[66] *Thewes* means here qualities or attributes (those appropriate to genre), but also the physical attributes of the figures: "Physical good qualities, features, or personal endowments" (female) and/or "bodily proportions, linea-ments, or parts, as indicating physical strength" (male).[67] As Joseph Loewenstein has discussed,[68] tragicomedy's allotted place is at the top of the edifice: the only species that crosses the middle plane of the engraving, the queer and queerly dressed figure who stands above, perhaps stands for, the author's name and mixed trade. The figurations labeled "TRAGŒDIA," "COMŒDIA," and "TRAGICOMŒDIA" are apparently gendered female in their visual as well as grammatical depiction, though the latter less clearly so. Tragicomœdia's apparel combines or overlays that

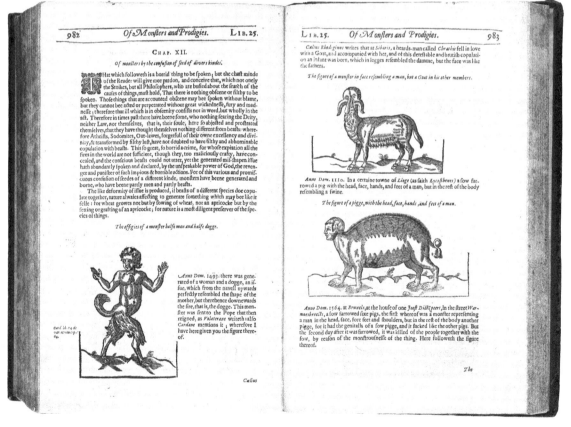

FIGURE 44. "Monsters by the confusion of seed of divers kindes," in Thomas Johnson, trans., *The Workes of that famous Chirurgion Ambrose Parey*. By permission of the Folger Shakespeare Library.

of the other figures; it is also a class mixture. In terms of the bodily hierarchies stressed in Sidney, it is perhaps significant that Tragicomœdia sports the *foot*wear of comedy and the *head*gear of tragedy. The engraving depicts—perhaps only can depict—mixture, rather than a more complete mongrelization, homogenization, or hybridity.

If the Jonson engraving also suggests breeding (the ascent of genre from tragedy and comedy to tragicomedy), it is notably the mixing of women (queer at least in breeding without men). The visual representations in Paré (the English version) and Jonson can gloss and assist us in thinking discursively about kinship discourses in tragicomedy. We have been focusing on the idea of a species as reproduced (a question that potentially has a different answer in evolutionary biology than in taxonomy),[69] but the female familial tree of genres on the Jonson title page may suggest that we will also want to attend to modes of coupling themselves: when it comes to talking about tragicomedies, there are kinds of coupling

FIGURE 45. "Monsters by the confusion of seed of divers kindes," in Thomas Johnson, trans., *The Workes of that famous Chirurgion Ambrose Parey*. By permission of the Folger Shakespeare Library.

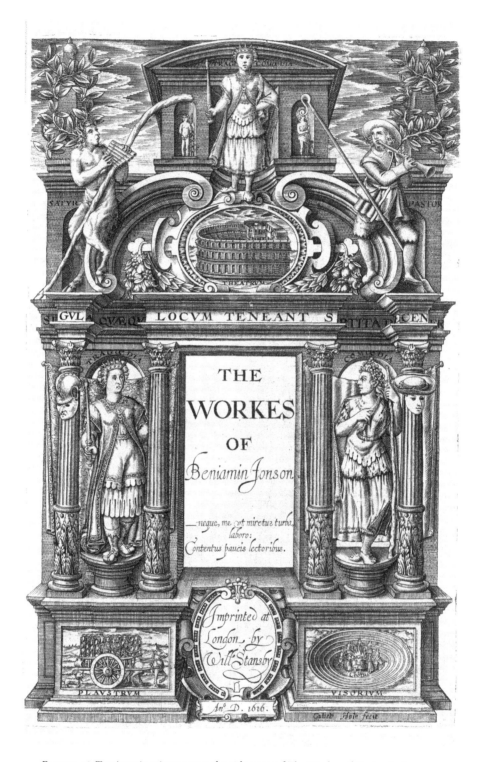

FIGURE 46. Tragicomic mixture atop the title page of *The Workes of Beniamin Jonson*. By permission of the Folger Shakespeare Library.

queerer than those imagined by the modern critics I have quoted.[70] Sidney may be ahead of us here; his ménage imagines the coupling together of "two *or three* kindes."[71] Criticism of tragicomedy, whatever its critical perspective, has instead been attuned to detecting the particular traits of parental genres, of tracing the distribution of ostensibly discrete heritable characteristics, and much less attentive to less orthodox modes of mingling—in the early critical discourse and in the plays themselves. "Kinship," Judith Butler writes, paraphrasing David Schneider, "is a kind of *doing*, one that does not reflect a prior structure but which can only be understood as an enacted practice."[72] Attending to tragicomedy's queer kinship(s), what kinds of enactments, what kinds of couplings, will we find?

12

Few since the Stationers' Register have been willing to call *The Two Noble Kinsmen* a "TragiComedy"[73]—perhaps because the anxieties around this play have been much more about authorial mongrelization than generic—and if one is interested in a strict application of a Fletcherian or Guarinian "definition" of tragicomedy, the play probably is no tragicomedy.[74] Still, a taxonomist (as opposed, say, to an evolutionary biologist[75]) might note the way in which the play repeatedly mixes hornpipes and funerals—first, by staging an opening marriage procession interrupted by an interrupted funeral; or even *pre*-first, staging a prologue that imagines plays as maidenheads on a nuptial first night, interrupted by a brief imagined speech by a dead medieval author; then, second, by ending with (as I have noted elsewhere) repeated reference to the comedic imperative of monogamous marriage finally enacted *simultaneously* with a funeral.[76] In Theseus's concluding terms:

> A day or two
> Let us looke sadly, and give grace unto
> The Funerall of *Arcite*, in whose end
> The visages of Bridegroomes weele put on
> And smile with *Palamon*.[77]

There are, however, more complicated versions of coupling and mixture in this play, and Theseus's speech, this imagined performance as the bridegroom Palamon that is itself a replay of Claudius's auspicious and dropping eyes in *Hamlet*, can serve as a guide. If we are interested in minglings of social class there is no better place to look than the Jailer's Daughter's so-called subplot.[78] Permitted to leap the barrier of class, the Jailer's Daughter might herself make the mixed marriage and funeral of the play's final scene a double marriage, one of them class-mixed. Indeed, the play supplies a version of this marriage in coupling the Jailer's Daughter with a *version* of Palamon acted by the otherwise nameless Wooer, who is of her social rank, unlike the kinsman of her desires. Thrusting in a kind of clown to play a part in majestical (or at least gentable) matters, the play strongly suggests the theatrical construction of social class, its performativity. Giving instructions to this player—"take / Vpon you (yong Sir her friend) the name of / *Palamon*. . . . Sing to her, such greene / Songs of Love, as she sayes *Palamon* hath sung in / Prison"[79]—the Doctor concludes:

> all this shall become *Palamon*, for *Palamon* can
> Sing, and *Palamon* is sweet, and ev'ry good thing, desire
> To eate with her, crave her, drinke to her, and still
> Among, intermingle your petition of grace and acceptance
> Into her favour.[80]

"The visages of Bridegroomes weele put on," says Theseus, and the play thus gestures, with a Wooer in the visage and adopted *habitus* of Palamon, toward class mixing both within the body of this (en)actor *and* in the marriage itself (of a commoner to a noble kinsman): "intermingle your petition of grace and acceptance / Into her favour." The play stages as possible—if only, as the Daughter puts it, at "th end o'th world," where "we shall finde / Some blind Priest for the purpose"[81]—a mongrel marriage fantasized by a lower-class woman. It is not beside the point here that the Daughter's notion of species or kind is itself less than clearly "defined" or out of bounds: she claims to have a horse that can dance a morris, read, and write.[82]

13

Allow me to provide an example of a different kind, but also of mirth in funeral and dirge in marriage: this one about the reproduction and circulation of that familiar template of a genre, *The Spanish Tragedy*. We return to one of the many examples of the recirculation of this play, Hieronimo's Act 3 lament for his dead son:

> Oh eies, no eies, but fountains fraught with teares,
> Oh life, no life, but liuely fourme of death:
> Oh world, no world but masse of publique wrongs.[83]

As we first noted in Chapter 3, this speech is replayed tragicomically at the end of the Middleton, Rowley, et al. collaboration *The Old Law* (1618–19). In the midst of a procession that is simultaneously a funeral and a wedding, Gnothoes (the play's clown) is instructed that, as a result of a change in the laws of Epire, he will lose a two-to-one bet (what he calls his "venter"/venture) because he can no longer have his old first wife put to death and marry a second, younger wife on the same day:

> Oh Musick, no musick, but prove most dolefull Trumpets,
> Oh Bride no Bride, but thou maist prove a Strumpet,
> Oh venter, no venter, I have for one now none,
> Oh wife, thy life is sav'd when I hope t'had been gone.[84]

As for the wedding cake that is a part of the clown's elaborate dual procession—and a slice of which he has just offered to the play's presiding Duke—he adds: "Let it be chip'd and chopt and given to chickens."

This, by no means the only joyful funeral in the play,[85] is *The Old Law*'s *Spanish Tragi-Comedy*, a complicated moment of cross-generic allusion/interbreeding that current definition-directed discussions of tragicomedy cannot account for. The problem is that modern criticism has followed, rather than read critically and contextually, tragicomic discourse in this period, and that discourse (and indeed the discourses of mixture and hybridity at large) features a fluctuation between, on the one hand, a mongrelization or hybridization of forms (the queer reproduction of a new breed) and, on the other, an additive or "admixture" approach that imagines, as in the engravings to the English translation of Paré and in the Jonson folio, the parts of one species attached to the body of another, a play that is half and half, head of a bird with the body of a dog. Both these discourses are available in Sidney. Gnothoes thrusts his head into the Duke's scene here, but he speaks through the culturally high script of tragedy; his mingled discourse is a lament spoken at the bounds of marital monogamy: he has imagined (unsuccessfully) a queer world of two wives in one day.

When we start to move out from the play itself to contemplate as well its modes of production, to think about who is putting on these visages of bridegrooms and dropping eyes, the doubled species model, rather than the mongrel hybridization model, again seems almost impossible to pursue. In this *Old Law* scene, we witness a mirthful/killing clown whose name may have sounded to an English audience like the Greek for "to know" and/or "bastard, false" (*nothos*), written perhaps by a playwright who also played clowns (Rowley),[86] reconstituting the voice of Hieronimo (himself a tragedian), in a speech initiated in a play (*The Spanish Tragedy*, as we saw in Chapter 3) that was continuously revived, rewritten, republished, and transmuted by multiple hands into several plays of similar title and divergent genre, including *The Spanish Comedy* (also known as *The Comedy of Jeronimo*).[87] Who, or what, is the origin of this species? Where in this mix does the head of the man end and the torso of the swine begin? This might be taken as an extreme example, but, insofar as such intertextualities and min-glings of the work of actors and writers are central to textual production in the early modern English theater, Tragicomœdia's centering alignment with the play-wright in the Jonson folio may be especially telling.

There is more kinship trouble in *The Old Law*: Gnothoes's "venter," his bet or venture with his friends on two-to-one odds, is also his *venter*; the word was a legal term for one of two or more wives who produce offspring for the same man—or, more simply, it meant "the womb" or "a mother."[88] Thus, this moment of cross-bred genre (bred with "sporting Kyd") also references breeding; the queer reproductive capacity of this tragicomical scene seems here calculated as double or nothing, a venture that produces no reproducing venter: "I have for one now none."

14

> *Sch[oolmaster].* Couple then
> And see what's wanting; wher's the *Bavian?*
> —*The Two Noble Kinsmen*[89]

In attempting to complicate a "coherent" definition of tragicomedy,[90] I do not mean to argue instead for what might be seen as the logical end of a taxonomical model: the idea that every text is its own genre—individual, unique, not replica-ble.[91] Instead, my fourteen ways of looking at early modern tragicomedy through the lens of queer kinship suggests regarding a playtext as an enactment, rather than as a species. Unable to be fully differentiated or split off either from the the-atrical repertoire and published plays *or* from the complex discourses of the "defi-nitions," a tragicomedy is (i.e., becomes-in-being) a complicated circulation and interaction of generic/genetic encodings, the couplings of sameness and differ-ence, mingling that necessarily exceeds the merely formal or structural and in-cludes the discursive and rhetorical. Such an analysis of tragicomedy will thus be attuned to hybridities of discourse that do not remain within the structural or diegetic bounds of the play and that do not stop at a playhouse door: plays and maidens that desire mixing of kinds and that are themselves (across categories) "near akin," as the prologue to *The Two Noble Kinsmen* has it; the actor playing himself and his desired double, Palamon; the discourse of "tragedy" intermingled within "comedy"; a wedding cake minced in a charger, given (across species) to chickens; the couplings that are inseparably sexual-reproductive and also culi-nary; the queer kinship of kinds that is said to spell danger in the larger culture. This is tragicomedy's queer kinship: a little more than kin, and more than kind.

Because it is discourse—or rather the complex nexus of discourses of cross-breeding, food mixing, genre, and so forth, read through a queer philology—that I have attempted to elaborate in this chapter, I want to conclude by spelling out some implications of my argument. One of my points has been to attempt to revivify what might initially seem to be "merely" metaphoric discussions of genre—to demonstrate not only the complexity of the persistent intermingling languages in Sidney, Fletcher, and others but also the instrumentality of these discourses, the way in which such language is imbricated in rhetorics of social class, sodomy, and so forth, that have effects in the world beyond the play and the early modern literary theories that address it. Punishable by death, sodomy, as we have seen Edward Coke define it, is a coupling of sameness ("mankind with mankind") *and* of difference ("or with brute beast"). In describing the law's hold on the coupling of "womankind with bruite beast," Coke notes that "somewhat before the making of this Act, a great Lady had committed buggery with a Baboon, and conceived by it, &c." In Coke's cryptic "et cetera" we might include the Jailer's Daughter, whose first theatrical appearance is in a morris dance with a "*Bavian*" (baboon) "with long tayle, and eke long tool" (46). Traditional genre criticism's proscription of the queer does not exist separately from the sometimes lethal proscriptions of the culture more generally.

I hope also to have expanded here the mix of texts that are relevant to understanding *kinship* in early modern England—texts as relevant and productive for queer consideration as legal records, sodomy trials, marriage and consanguinity law, parish registries, and other "traces of cultural practices," in Alan Bray's phrase.[92] As this and the preceding chapter have argued, the crucial queer-philological project is to develop a more capacious lexicon or historical translation dictionary of early modern corporeal and kinship terms, terms that will, in their overlaps and interminglings, engage queernesses that are part of kinship's own "breeding" (as a concept)—its own discursive "genealogy." Necessarily, this lexicon will include terms such as *family* (which has not itself been historically self-identical, as Raymond Williams long ago observed[93]) and also such terms as *mongrel* and *sodomy*. These, too, are terms without which early modern kinship (of persons and generic kinds) seems unable to inscribe or describe itself; as Butler observes of modern kinship's definitional struggles, "The sphere of legitimate intimate alliance is established through producing and intensifying regions of illegitimacy."[94] No finite lexicon, a queer philology of kinship and genre necessarily extends to related, intersecting, additive, intermingling terms, like those of food and diet, above: cake and chickens. Early modern tragicomic theories and practices are thus also part of (but part not *only* of) the discourse Laurie Shannon terms *zoography*: "those discourses and modes of writing that are undergirded by animal or broadly taxonomic structures of reference across species." So, too, they help to demonstrate "the broad impact of period practices of animal specification."[95]

As I suggested earlier, this lexicon, the nexus of the terms *tragicomedy, sodomy*, and *mongrel*, brings with it particular "difficult[ies] of nomination and inscription," and the associated rhetoric in the texts we have read cites the dangers of enacting or witnessing such mixture and confusion. Do such dangers attend tragicomedy onstage? Early seventeenth-century acting companies are routinely represented (or at least parodied) as only too willing to mix genres in their repertory. In addition to Polonius's familiar comments in *Hamlet*, Act 2, Scene 2 (a list of genres longer and more mixed in the first quarto and first folio texts), there is the following exchange in Middleton's *Hengist*:

Symo[n]:	. . . now sirs are you Comedians *Enter Cheaters*
2 Chea[ter]:	We are anything sir: Comedians Tragedians
	Tragicomedians, Come-tragedians, pastorallists
	humorists, Clownists & saterists, we haue em sir
	from ye smile to ye laugh; from ye laugh to the handkercher[96]

In this context, we may ask two questions. First, when genres breed, what did an early modern audience hear and see when "the generated mis-shapen issue ha[d] [itself] abundantly spoken and declared"? Second, more speculatively, what were the risks and dangers within tragicomic discourse for the persons who wrote, acted, witnessed, and read these plays in early modern England? A consideration of the perceived audience effects of such plays is beyond the scope of this chapter, but we can at least note their popularity in the Jacobean and Caroline periods onstage, and, during the closure of the theaters, in print—the latter with royalist reading audiences, if the consortium of commendatory verse writers in the Beaumont and Fletcher folio is evidence.[97]

Is the pleasure of danger part of tragicomedy's queer appeal? If, as Johnson explains in the Paré chapter he heads "Of monsters by the confusion of seed of divers kindes," "things that are accounted obscene . . . cannot bee acted or perpetrated without great wickednesse, fury and madnesse: therefore that ill which is in obscenity consists not in word but wholly in the act," then what happens when cross-breeding is staged, acted, witnessed, and read—when the obscene enters the scene? "There we may rehearse most obscenely and courageously," Bottom announces of the forest rehearsal space in *A Midsummer Night's Dream*, preparing to present a play that will, in the end, be described as "very tragical mirth." And, thereafter, as we saw in the first chapter of this lexicon, Bottom is translated, made a gallimaufrey, mixes up his parts (theatrical and corporeal), and cross-couples with a queen.[98]

EDITING PHILOLOGIES

CHAPTER 8

All Is Not Glossed: Editing Sex, Race, Gender, and Affect in Shakespeare

Such is the staggering richness of Shakespeare's language that it is tempting to gloss everything, but there is a law of diminishing returns: *too much explanatory whispering at the margins makes it difficult to enjoy what the reader has come for in the first place.* Our general policy is to gloss only those words that cannot be found in an ordinary dictionary or whose meanings have altered out of recognition. The glosses attempt to be simple and straightforward, giving multiple meanings for words only when the meanings are essential for making sense of the passages in which they appear. . . . [W]e have tried to check the impulse to annotate so heavily that the reader is *distracted from the pleasure of the text*, and we have avoided notes that provide interpretation, as distinct from information.
—Stephen Greenblatt, "General Introduction," in *The Norton Shakespeare Based on the Oxford Edition*[1]

And if you may glosse the Text so farre . . . why should you not glosse it a little farther. . . ?
—William Chillingworth, *The Religion of Protestants a Safe VVay to Salvation* (1638)[2]

Even now, now, very now, an old black ram
Is tupping your white ewe.
—Iago in *Othello* (1.1.88–89)[3]

Tupping

Working via what it has termed a *queer philology*, this book has argued that there can be no nuanced cultural history of what we now call *sexuality* without also working in detail through the history of its languages; examining the meaning of structures of identity, eroticism, sexual practice, the body, affect, and emotion requires dwelling analytically on words, terms, and rhetorics (their etymology, circulation, transformation, and constitutive power), reading closely the history and structure of the languages in which the objects of our study are embedded. At the same time, I have argued, *queer philology* will exert a double action, signifying both a philology *of the queer* (that is, of sexual practices, bodies, affects, and identities that seem nonnormative, whether in their own time or from this historical distance) and a *queer* philology (the traditional and once-hegemonic discipline of philology read and practiced in a way that will highlight its own normativizing categories and elisions). This requires attending to *queer* philologies that have been deemphasized or submerged in more traditional accounts of language—a process that will continue here.

As in previous chapters, one particularly illustrative embodiment of traditional philology will here be the *Oxford English Dictionary* (*OED*). But in the two brief chapters centered on scholarly editing that conclude this study, I also focus on the reliance on and extension of the *OED*'s philology into the glosses, apparatus, and editorial practices of drama editions, specifically in Shakespeare, and on the editorial-philological work—taken to be a central task of philology since at least the Renaissance, as Anthony Grafton and others have argued—that seeks to establish texts and (particularly in Chapter 9) author-organized canons of authentic texts.

Taking up again explicitly the editorial work that is sometimes now, in the academy, seen as the remaining bastion of traditional philological work and expertise, I hope to make explicit here what has been implicit throughout this book: that, even as scholarship in the history of sexuality has begun to make its way into the introductory materials in editions, editors must work harder to think about the broader ramifications of research into the history of sexuality for editing the text "itself," for framing it in canons of particular works, and for how we produce the glosses that incrementally and constitutively underwrite the text and its meanings—perhaps especially for our students and general readers. On the other hand, even after the "New Textualist" interventions of recent decades that have brought bibliographic work more squarely back within the view of interpretive and cultural critics, editorial work has often been regarded as prior to interpretive and cultural study of the text—and has often received less attention from scholars of sexuality.[4] (See also Chapter 1.) To think through these methodological issues—

and to show how they will necessarily engage intersecting histories of sexuality, race, and gender, and require thought about how we register those histories more fully in the editorial work that often becomes the basis of other interpretive and cultural scholarship—I begin with a straightforward glossarial question: in *Othello*, what is *tupping*?

The answer, in Act 1, Scene 1, seems relatively simple: *tupping*, as Michael Neill glosses it, with the support of the *OED*, in his important Oxford Shakespeare edition of the play, means "copulating with (from the northern dialect *tup* = ram . . .)" (203).[5] Tupping is animal sex (made explicitly racial in the color of the animals); it may even get some of its power as a term from the fact that it sounds like "fucking." If the *OED*'s etymology is accurate and *tup* comes from *ram*, the term is also redundant: an old black ram is ramming your white ewe.[6] The line thus economically accomplishes something central to this play: it (re)marks Othello's blackness; it graphically connects power and sex; and, as many have noted,[7] it makes Othello and Desdemona's connection bestial. It may specifically conjure up bodily positionality (penetration from behind, "like" animals), central to analyses of sex throughout this book. "You'll have your daughter covered with a Barbary horse," an Iago line that many have discussed, has a similar discursive economy: bestial sex and/as race (through the pun on Barbary/barbarism), connected with bodily positioning ("covered").[8]

I might not have given *tupping* a second thought, however, if not for a set of changes that Neill makes in the received text of *Othello* later in the play, at two key moments. (Whatever my disagreements with Neill's practice below, his edition is among the most comprehensive accounts of race in a scholarly *Othello* edition.) In Act 3, Scene 3, the long and intense scene in which Iago leads Othello to imagine Desdemona having sex, Iago asks whether Othello really wants evidence of his wife's ostensible infidelity; the 1622 first quarto (and most subsequent editions) reads:

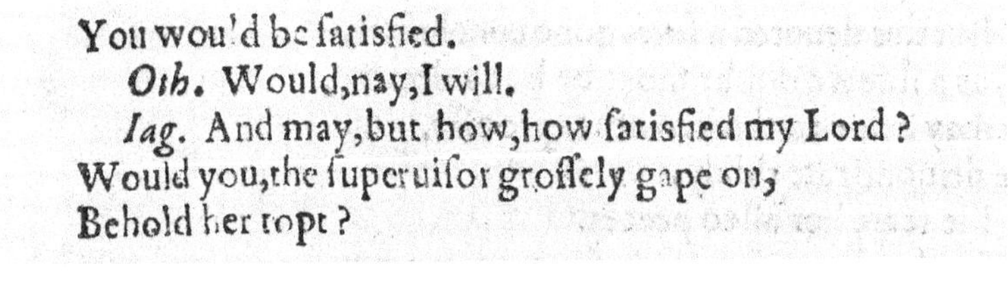

> You wou'd be satisfied.
> *Oth.* Would, nay, I will.
> *Iag.* And may, but how, how satisfied my Lord?
> Would you, the superuisor grossely gape on,
> Behold her topt?

FIGURE 47. *Topt* in the first quarto (Q1), *The Tragœdy of Othello, The Moore of Venice* (1622), sig. H3. By permission of the Folger Shakespeare Library.

For the t-word here, however, Neill's Oxford edition substitutes "tupped" (3.3.398). Leah S. Marcus has made a compelling case for the racial and sexual differences between the quarto and 1623 first folio texts of the play—and, indeed, the folio's more racially charged language[9]—but this is an instance where the texts seem to agree: *tupped* does not appear at this point in the folio text either:

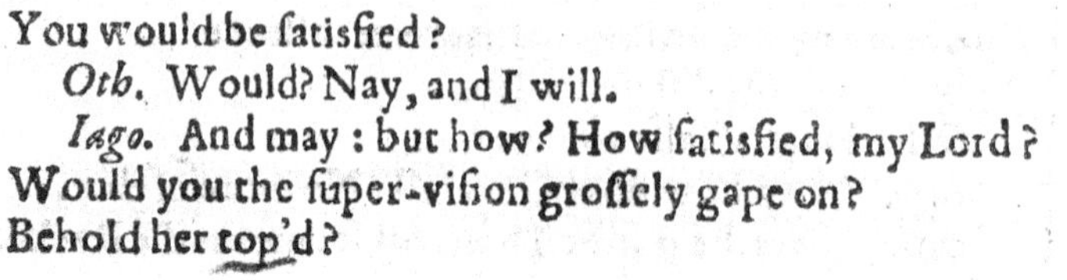

> You would be satisfied?
>   *Oth.* Would? Nay, and I will.
>   *Iago.* And may : but how? How satisfied, my Lord?
> Would you the super-vision grossely gape on?
> Behold her top'd?

FIGURE 48. *Top'd* in the first folio (F1), *The Tragedie of Othello, the Moore of Venice* (1623), in *Mr. VVilliam Shakespeares Comedies, Histories, & Tragedies*, p. 326 of the Tragedies. By permission of the Folger Shakespeare Library.

In supplying *tupped*, Neill is instead following an emendation first made in Alexander Pope's 1728 (second) edition (as *tupp'd*).[10] Neill's note:

> **tupped** Far from representing a "softening" of "topped" (as Rosenberg suggests . . .), Pope's emendation restores the proper connection with 1.1.89. *OED* lists *top* = "copulate with, cover" ($v.^1$ 11), citing this as the earliest example; but it seems likely, as Williams suggests . . . that it is simply a variant of *tup*. The word, with its powerfully animalistic suggestions, is clearly a favourite of Iago's, and it seems important to preserve the echo of 1.1. Cf. also 5.2.136. (306)

What, though, is "the proper connection" with an earlier line, when we are talking about a complex intersection of gender, sexuality, and race? Whatever we might think of an editorial method that imagines characters seeming to exist, in their preferences for favorite words, quite separately from the text that constitutes them, we might also ask: are there particular developments in the histories of sexuality and race that, in 1728, make it seem necessary or possible to reintroduce *tupped* into the play here as the way to stage Iago's imaginary scene of cross-sex sex?[11] Famously criticizing the play in 1693, Thomas Rymer may obliquely highlight the dangers perceived, by the late seventeenth century, of an Othello on top, supplied with the "pre-eminence" of a name and title: "it is an affront to all Chroniclers, and Antiquaries, to top upon 'um a *Moor*, with that mark of renown, who yet had never faln within the Sphere of their Cognisance." A Moor on top is beyond cognizance, threatening to top all historians and scholars. In the next sentence, Rymer also objects to what he sees as the inappropriate class elevation of "the Moors *Wife*" in the play as compared with the source, "dress'd up with her Top knots."[12]

The "proper" relationships among sexuality, gender, race, and hierarchy and also the questions I've raised about these in Neill's emendation are made only more complex by the fact that, in the prestandardization linguistic surround of the early *seventeenth* century, *tup* and *top* may have been near variants of each other; at least in some areas of England and/or Scotland, *tup* was sometimes spelled *toupe, touppe,* or *towpe*.[13] So, given spelling, dialectal, and aural variability during this period,[14] it is possible that where we see the graphic shape *topt* on this page in the quarto or *top'd* in the folio, an early modern actor, audience member, or reader might have heard/read *topt,* or *tupt,* or perhaps both.[15] In the context of a modern edition, choosing *tupped*—and something must be chosen, must it not?—puts the bestial back in Desdemona. It also frames the play with—gives the ruling discursive hand to—the racist Iago. It is *his* echo that is preserved (as Neill puts it). Or, as I would put it: in the service of textual self-consistency, it is his echo that may be *created*.

Indeed, this moment has important ramifications for how we think of the relation of a "crux" to be emended in the text "proper" and the "gloss" that appears (deceptively) below or marginally beside it,[16] for the editorial alteration (presented as textual correction or "restor[ation]") of subsequent instances of *top* to *tup* in the play may be a way of emending the text so that in effect *it appears to gloss itself*: *top*, such emendations argue, should be understood as *tup*. This widely shared editorial (and perhaps readerly) desire for the self-glossing text is, I suggest, part of an ideological formation that values a certain kind of implicitly New Critical aesthetic object: a text with internal echoes, with manifold "connections" between or among scenes, with characters thought to act consistently rather than variably (even as we know that Iago is represented as speaking whatever discourse is necessary depending on context and audience), and so forth.

Whether *topped* or *tupped*, however, what is persistent in these lines is the centrality of hierarchy as inseparable from sexual acts, in a way that Neill's early gloss "copulate with" and our typical commonplace rhetoric of "have sex *with*" or the relatively equitable and recent term "sexual *inter*course"[†] simply don't capture, as it were. (The *Norton Shakespeare*'s *tupping* gloss is also "copulating with" [2102].) As I noted in Chapter 5, David Halperin has remarked that, in premodern systems of sexuality, "hierarchy itself is hot," and Halperin's emphasis on hierarchy carries a valuable reminder of a persistent, if not universal, feature of early sexual discourses (more important in Halperin's view than modernity's predominant focus on a distinction of same-sex/cross-sex).[17] Jonathan Goldberg has likewise emphasized the importance of positionality when speaking of early modern sex.[18] The question of who's on top is for this culture a crucial—one might even say, *fundamental*—question. The final example of *tup/top* in the play underlines

---

[†] **sexual intercourse**   Etymologically, "running between" the sexes, a phrase first used in the latter half of the eighteenth century. See the Coda in Chapter 3.

this as well. In the play's last scene, as Othello tells Emilia what he takes to be the evidence for Desdemona's infidelity, he says, in both the early texts:

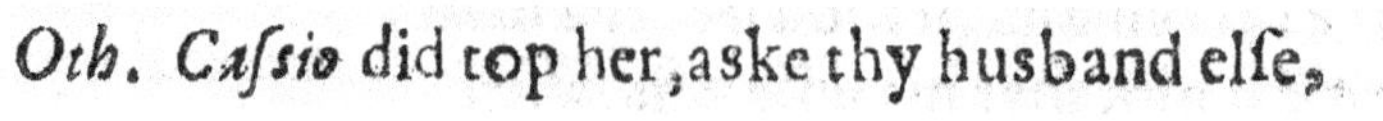

Oth. Cassio did top her, aske thy husband else,

FIGURE 49. *Top* in *The Tragœdy of Othello* (Q1), sig. M3. By permission of the Folger Shakespeare Library.

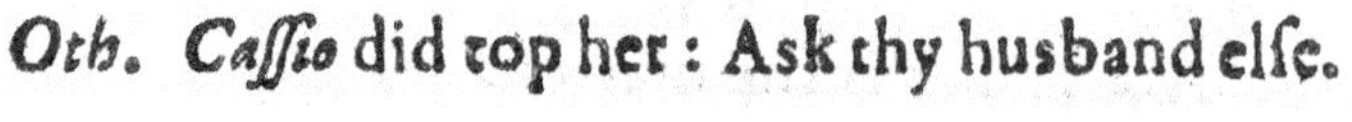

Oth. Cassio did top her : Ask thy husband else.

FIGURE 50. *Top* in *The Tragedie of Othello* (F1), p. 336. By permission of the Folger Shakespeare Library.

Neill again follows Pope's 1728 edition and writes "Cassio did tup her" (5.2.136, p. 382). Neill's Iago's "favourite word" has now become (has been made to become) Othello's. (This is the case even though, within the diegesis, Othello did not hear Iago's original use of the term, and the "black ram" in that original scenario has disappeared from this imagined scene.)

The early texts' insistence on positionality may allow us to see how sexual positioning is constantly at issue in these and other lines, in ways that intersect with the play's minute calibrations of class and service hierarchies, as well as its sexual and racial ones. "Would you, the supervisor, grossly gape *on*?" Even the rhetoric of looking, so persistent in this play, gets tied into the hierarchies of sexual positioning: looking on sex, gaping on it—literally, *super*vising, looking *upon* it—is as hierarchical as the acts themselves. I may seem to be pressing too hard on prepositions, but part of my point here is that understandings of sexuality in these lines and during this period may actually dwell in those syntactical markings of positioning that we less often attend to or bother to gloss: pre-positionality.[19] If Lara Bovilsky is correct that *gross* is "the play's name for the materiality of sexuality as well as of race,"[20] then "grossly gap[ing] on" replays visually the corporeal materiality encoded in the terms of sex "itself." Seeing is (like) enacting.

The rhetoric of position is present back in Act 3, Scene 3, when Iago, having offered to Othello's super-vision the possibility of Desdemona topped by Cassio, graphically supplies not *that* scene of cross-sex topping, but another—what he claims, in a much-discussed passage, is a dream of Cassio's in which he was a participant observer when he "lay with Cassio lately":

In sleep I heard him say, "Sweet Desdemona,
Let us be wary, let us hide our loves";
And then, sir, would he gripe and wring my hand,
Cry "O, sweet creature!", and then kiss me hard,

As if he plucked *up* kisses *by the roots*
That grew *upon* my lips, then laid his leg
Over my thigh, and sighed, and kissed, and then
Cried "Cursèd fate that gave thee to the Moor!"
                    (3.3.420–27, my emphasis)

Reading this scene that stands in (lies in) for that of Cassio and Desdemona having sex, Arthur Little has emphasized the lines' orality;[21] I want to stress positionality. Kisses plucked *up*, leg *over* thigh: to illustrate Desdemona topped, Iago bottoms for an imaginary Cassio, whom, in the military/service hierarchy of the play,
it is ultimately his desire to top. "O monstrous! Monstrous!" Othello says.

I have been moving rapidly across a number of complex problems here: How
can we begin to understand sexuality, in all its historical difference as positionality
in the earlier period? How can we begin to think about the entanglements of European notions of "race," of animality, and of sexuality across time—in 1602–3, 1623,
1728, and (even) an edition of 2006?[22] How are the rhetorics of sexual positioning
in cross-sex and same-sex relations potentially not discrete but in fact related to or
interchangeable with each other in the earlier period? But part of my point is the
need (though I have done so very quickly here) to think through these problems
together—to continue, intensify, and further build sexuality into the intersectional
analysis of the play undertaken along lines especially of gender and race by critics
in recent decades—and to insist that editors accept the challenge of inscribing the
complexity of these intersecting rhetorics in our glossings and related emendings of
the Shakespearean text.[23] Building on earlier gender analyses, for example, Bovilsky
emphasizes "the overlapping terminology of these various discursive fields" and
unpacks "the association between gendered morality and color [that] often goes
unremarked"—"the centrality of racial concepts in policing [female] chastity."[24] As
my example suggests, we should not imagine that we can somehow calibrate the
discourses of sexuality without also confronting the intersecting rhetorics of race
and related racist discourses of power-related positioning and animality; nor should
we think that matters of sex are somehow more easily glossed than other aspects of
these texts, or simply a matter of more or less euphemism, more or less candor
(though that is, of course, often also at stake in editions).

One way to understand the relation of these crossings is by returning once
again to the early modern conception of *sodomy*, returning in editing this text to
the work that Little, Bruce Smith, Goldberg, and others have done on the connection the culture made between some forms of same-sex sex and bestiality, returning again to sodomy as Foucault's "utterly confused category."[25] Not so much be-
fuddlement as *confusion*'s etymological "pouring together," as I noted in the
Introduction, sodomy's apparent "confusions" in this context are potentially ex-

pansive and analytically productive for understanding what Pope, Neill, and others have seen as a crux in need of emendation. What seem to us as modern readers to be the "confusions" of early modern sodomy might lead us to ask: is all the sex in *Othello*—or at least all the sex in *Othello* as imagined and framed by Iago—sodomitical? (In a way that we will philologically contextualize further in Chapter 9, *Othello* is even earlier associated with a "*bumbast* circumstance.") Once again Edward Coke's summary of English sodomy law in the third part of his *Institutes Of The Laws Of England* (1644) is instructive: "Buggery is a detestable, and abominable sin, amongst Christians not to be named, committed by carnall knowledge against the ordinance of the Creator, and order of nature, by mankind with mankind, or with brute beast, or by womankind with bruite beast."[26] "Your daughter covered with a Barbary horse . . . you'll have coursers for cousins and jennets for germans." "O sweet *creature!*" "O monstrous!"—Othello's reply to Iago's suggestive imaging—is one of sodomy's key words. English sodomy law and its meanings, confusions, and effects have been amply discussed by Bruce Smith, Janet Halley, Valerie Traub, and Cynthia Herrup, but an avenue we have not yet fully explored is how to think through the relation during this period of same-sex sodomy and bestiality, man- and womankind with brute beast.[27] Though, as Bovilsky notes, the "old black ram tupping your white ewe" formulation also produces a species *likeness*,[28] it simultaneously plays on other sodomitical linkages, compressing (through the play on "your white *you*") a hint of Othello "tupping" Brabantio himself ("your *you*"), as well as an age difference and a cross-species connection (ram/daughter): as Little has emphasized, the line connects the rhetoric of race to sodomy ("homosexuality" is his term) through bestiality.[29] These connections that we might read swiftly past as merely "discursive" may have had shockingly real effects (indeed, that is one way to summarize the plot of *Othello*): Alan Bray cites a 1647 sodomy case in which "Domingo Cassedon Drago a negro is . . . to be tried . . . for a buggery by him committed [with/on/in view of] a poor boy named William Wraxall."[30] As so often with sodomy in these cases, it is difficult to know which crossings of category are being surveyed and adjudicated through this accusation—whether of class, age, race, nation, religion, and/or species.

As Michael Warner has noted, sodomy, even in its very name, is said to come from elsewhere, never *here*;[31] Coke says it was brought into England by the Lombards, a locale to which we will return in the next chapter. (Female-female sex/eroticism, unnoticed in Coke's definition, is also, as Traub has shown, often "located somewhere *else*."[32]) Othello's name and the play's title, "Othello, the *Moor* of *Venice*," also play on this uncertain boundary of here or there—even if, in Emily Bartels's analysis, the terms of Othello's epithet are less oppositional, more "dynamic," his relation to Venice more "embedded," than critics have emphasized.[33] Sodomy's association with elsewhere means that any theory of its sexual meanings must also—at least in the context of a nation that wants to see itself in the seventeenth century as a unified racial/ethnic "here" —consider the racial assumptions embedded within sodomy law and its surrounding cultural practices. In this context, it is relevant (if hypothetical) to notice that the word the legal record seems to produce as Drago's name may be his title—his profession or role—since it seems to include an abbreviated English loanword (*dragoman*) borrowed from a Spanish or French version of a Turkish or Arabic word for "translator" or guide.[34] *Drago* or *dragoman*, as a word and as an activity, crosses between Here and There. At least in Roderigo's estimation, Othello, too, is "an extravagant and wheeling stranger" (1.1.135), a foreigner who extra-vagates (wanders outside, beyond the bounds).

As I have argued throughout this book, it seems to me crucial to do this editorial and historical work through a sustained analysis and attention to the particularities of early modern terms, rhetorics, what Goldberg calls "syntax[es] of desire"[35]—in short, through *philology*. Without that, and without thinking about the losses in translation we encounter by simply reading their *sodomy* or *tupping* as our *sexuality*, their *on* as our *with*, we lose crucial information and distinctions in our sense of the culture and of Shakespeare's texts. Bray actually does something similar with race in the Drago case, translating *negar* in the legal document into *negro*. In a brilliant analysis of an early English appearance of *negar* in a multilingual translation dictionary, Susan E. Phillips shows the meanings that are lost when we read *negar* simply as race or color, erasing its associations within the complex hierarchies of the English service economy.[36] Queer philologies must inevitably engage intersecting philologies of class and of race—as David Nirenberg's recent work tracing the early emergence of the very term *race* from animal breeding also suggests.[37]

In thinking about this emendation and gloss in *Othello* (or, as I have suggested, this emendation serving to self-gloss *Othello*), I have emphasized the need for the queer philology that I characterized in the Introduction as a philological approach to studying what seems nonnormative, at least from our historical distance. But I also mean—in trying to keep alive the possibilities of *top* and *tup* and the need to read them together, rather than edit them into tidy echoes of Iago's early line—to emphasize that other sense of queer philology: philology made queer, the study of language not just for a historical answer that it might provide about sexuality in this era, but a study that analytically doubles back and studies itself, highlighting philology's own normalizing categories and oversights. As we have seen throughout this book, the *OED*'s philology likes to keep its *tups* and *tops* in separate entries, pages/screens, meanings, and parts of speech. There are separate entries for *tup* (*n.*) and *tup* (*v.*), as well as three separate noun and four verb entries for *top*. Early modern discourse and Shakespeare's use of it hardly follow such tidy boundaries.

Reading across the *OED*'s divisions may even give us something I have left unmentioned in this discussion: Desdemona and her desires. "Would you . . . [b]ehold her topt?" Iago asks. And the *OED* gives for *topt* the possibility "[m]ade tipsy, intoxicated, drunk."[38] The *OED*'s first cited quotation (before 1632) emphasizes liquor—an association that may well have been audible/legible to *Othello*'s early audiences and readers, given the play's emphasis on (whom but?) Cassio "drunk" in Act 2, Scene 3. (Thus, we can say that Iago both bottoms for and tops Cassio.) However, as much as such a reading might suggest a Desdemona also dispossessed of agency and "reputation," just a bit later, in 1637, the *OED* cites, from Thomas Heywood's dialogue of Vulcan and Jupiter, Vulcan's description of the birth of a "live *Virago*, arm'd" (Minerva) from Jupiter's brain: "She leaps and capers, topt with rage divine."[39] Reading across the *OED*'s careful distinctions, and able to see *rage* as carrying with it both anger and (as it so often did in the sexual discourse of the period) "appetite . . . [v]iolent desire or lust; burning sexual passion,"[40] we can see here a glimmer of another "monstrosity" that those watching this play might have seen in Desdemona "topt." This is the glimmer of something feminism might by contrast welcome identifying in this play: the brief, liberatory possibility of beholding Desdemona intoxicated with her own desires.

Less liberatory for Desdemona, more physiological in imagining her body in a humoral sense, and just as fantasmatically threatening for Othello and perhaps an early modern audience is another resonance potentially registering here: Desdemona *tapt* (a spelling that overlaps with *topt*).[41] In this reading, which may not mutually exclude the others, Iago imagines Desdemona as a vessel from which something is extracted or extractable. The *OED*'s progression of meanings for *tap* moves toward the physiological in a conception of the body as humoral and resonates in this context with Gail Kern Paster's influential account of early modern women's bodies in particular as "leaky vessels":[42] "1. *trans.* To furnish (a cask, etc.) with a tap or spout, in order to draw the liquor from it"; "2. a. To pierce (a vessel, tree, etc.) so as to draw off its liquid contents; to broach; to draw liquid from (any reservoir)"; "b. *spec.* in *Surg.* To pierce the body-wall of (a person) so as to draw off accumulated liquid; to drain (a cavity) of accumulated liquid" (beginning in 1655).[43] However, beginning as early as 1575, the dictionary gives an ostensibly "figurative" meaning that may operate in beholding Desdemona *topt/tapt* and that seems coextensive with rhetoric that regards her as a proprietary resource in the play: "3. *fig.* To open up (anything) so as to liberate or extract something from it; to open, penetrate, break into, begin to use. Also *absol.*" Desdemona "liberated" for whom? The liberation of Desdemona's desire may lead in several contrary directions.[44]

How Dear a Lover

I have emphasized the importance, for Shakespeare editions, of more fully under-standing and deploying scholarship in the history of sexuality, race, and gender, and, as I hope I have made clear, this is work that should not necessarily stay put in or be restricted to the gloss on this or that line, or adhere to this or that modern conception of sexuality, race, gender, or their intersections. In particular with regard to sexuality: even as editions of Shakespeare and other Renaissance texts have laudably begun to take account of queer research in the past decades, I am arguing that we must seek a fuller engagement with the implications of that schol-arship in these editions. This is not only the case in the local instances where it seems to matter; a realization of the different *epistemologies* of desire, affect, "iden-tity," sexual practice (including fantasy and imagination) that queer work has been exploring and that I have been attempting to bring to visibility throughout this book may in the end have the greatest capacity for shifting what is thinkable in the text, in the margin, at the bottom of the page, or across the breadth of a text or texts.

Let me take another example—one centered more on sexuality and affect than on race, though one would not want to discount in advance the likelihood of racial and ethnic dimensions in this play's likewise Venetian and complexly multicul-tural setting. The example derives from the *Norton Shakespeare* edition, a useful case to analyze because (1) it is probably the Shakespeare text now taught to the most college students (and therefore is widely influential) and (2) it is arguably the most feminist and the *least* homophobic complete-works edition of Shake-speare ever produced,[45] but (3) there are still moments in the larger edition where queer possibilities are actively foreclosed. (The example is treated identically in the first, second, and third editions of the *Norton* [1997, 2008, 2015].)

At the beginning of Act 3, Scene 4, of the *Norton* version of *The Merchant of Venice*, Lorenzo is praising Portia for her patience in "bearing thus the absence of [her] lord" Bassanio, who has left her to aid Antonio:

> But if you knew to whom you show this honour,
> How true a gentleman you send relief,
> How dear a lover of my lord your husband,
> I know you would be prouder of the work
> Than customary bounty can enforce you. (3.4.4–9)

In describing Antonio as a "dear . . . lover of my lord your husband," the text cites three Bassanio relationships—two described socially ("my lord" and "your hus-

band") and one described more affectively ("How dear a *lover*" of Antonio). Three
and a half acts into the play, the editorial gloss the *Norton* gives to the same-sex
affective relation "lover" is, in the margin, a single word.

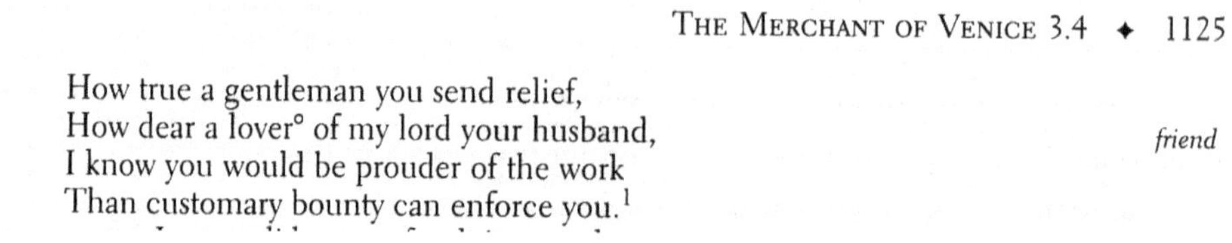

THE MERCHANT OF VENICE 3.4 ✦ 1125

How true a gentleman you send relief,
How dear a lover° of my lord your husband,   *friend*
I know you would be prouder of the work
Than customary bounty can enforce you.[1]

FIGURE 51. Marginal gloss for *The Merchant of Venice*, in *The Norton Shakespeare*,
1st ed., p. 1125. Image courtesy of Northwestern University Library.

Friend is certainly accurate, and in the preceding scenes readers have had the
opportunity to witness the ways small and large in which Antonio and Bassanio's
relationship participates in the protocols of Renaissance male friendship. "My
purse, my person, my extremest means," Antonio had said to Bassanio in the
play's first scene, "[l]ie all unlocked to your occasions" (1.1.138–39), and that line
is itself virtually a gloss of Michel de Montaigne's essay on friendship, first published in English in 1603. As we saw in detail in Chapters 2 and 3, Renaissance
same-sex friendship has been a centerpiece of recent scholarly work on the history of sexuality in early modernity: revaluation, historical investigation, and
rhetorical analysis of what was once dismissively called "the cult of male friendship" have become central concerns of the field.[46] In his posthumous masterwork
The Friend, Alan Bray analyzed in detail and also unearthed (nearly literally)
male friends who were joined in Renaissance liturgy and buried together in the
churchyard tombs he rediscovered, and his scholarship on the intensity of Renaissance male-male friendship resonates throughout this play. So the *Norton*'s
gloss—*lover* means *friend*—is, in this sense, correct.

But when I teach the play in my university's large "Introduction to Shakespeare" course—that is, when I attempt to describe to mostly beginning students
what is so interesting and complicated about friendship and marriage in this
play—I am struck again and again by how much damage even a quick gloss like
this can do to the more complex reading of the history of the idea of friendship
and the history of friendship's affect—what a setback it can be for an understanding of friendship's historical queerness and its relation to the meaning of cross-sex
marriage in Shakespeare's time. So, too, as we will see in a moment, the gloss
potentially undercuts a more complex understanding of female power and agency
in the play. "Oh" (a student, or a general reader of the *Norton*, might say, three

acts into the play, and understandably perhaps a bit perplexed by having wandered into the markedly different erotic and affective setup of Shakespeare's time), "oh, 'lover' just means 'friend.'" The problem is, as I suggested in Chapter 2, that our word *friend* must be regarded in many ways as a false cognate of the early modern term—as we used to say in French class, it is a "false friend" to the earlier word. Our *friend* is related, certainly, but also highly inadequate, or narrowing, as a translation of the early modern word spelled the same way.

Recall Stephen Greenblatt's words as general editor: "Our general policy is to gloss only those words that cannot be found in an ordinary dictionary or whose meanings have altered out of recognition." When we are speaking genealogically of the history of sexualities—when we are tracing social structures that have altered, certainly, since Shakespeare's time, but that are, as Halperin has persuasively argued, still discursively *present* as threads making up modern sexuality[47]—where will we agree that we have left behind the bounds of recognition? Should we in fact agree to do so? More practically, how might we invent a historically attentive editorial practice that can adapt not only to a now-unfamiliar term like *tup*, but also to the problem of the false cognate like *friend* or *top*—terms whose meanings have altered out of *some, but not all*, recognition? Here's a radically conservative tactic: an editor could attempt not to gloss over but instead preserve the historical meaning and the textured alterity of Antonio and Bassanio's relation by emending the text: inserting a new placeholder word or a character chosen to denote linkage. This would mark the term's strangeness (to us); it would produce a graphic shape on the page that, unlike *lover*, would not be fully or partially misrecognizable; and it would force a reader to act more self-sufficiently to produce potential meanings from context:

How dear a & of my lord your husband.

Now gloss *that*.

The *Norton*'s narrowing gloss on a male-male "lover" occurs at a moment in the play potentially even more important for thinking about the productive friction of queer and feminist understandings of the play, for it is the moment in which Bassanio's relation to Antonio begins most strongly to be in tension with his relation to Portia, and it is the beginning of her own expanded power in the play. Interestingly, Bassanio's "love" for Antonio is not seen to require a gloss when it is first announced in Act 1, Scene 1 ("To you, Antonio, / I owe the most in money *and in love*, / And *from your love* I have a warranty to unburden all my plots and purposes" [1.1.130–33, my emphasis]). Nor does it, even in the reading in Act 3, Scene 2, of Antonio's letter asking Bassanio to visit him before his impending death ("Sweet Bassanio, . . . If *your love* do not persuade you to come, let not my letter" [3.2.314–19, my emphasis]). These "loves" are left unremarked, but the appearance of the potentially identitarian and active term "lover" (applied to two men) *in the presence of Portia* is what produces a gloss in the edition. Or that is what seems to *necessitate* a gloss; *lover* is after all a familiar word in most ordinary dictionaries, but it apparently crosses here the editors' threshold of a "meaning[] essential for making sense of the passage[]." On the one hand, glossing this particular instance of *lover* is understandable: a reader might mistake the sixteenth-century word *lover* for our word *lover* (again, false cognates), and, reading now—in the present, in a world where we think of intense same-sex and cross-sex relationships as mutually exclusive—he or she might see this instance of *lover* as antithetical to Bassanio's simultaneous status as a lover *of Portia*. On the other hand, *lover*, of course, *already* describes what Antonio is to and toward Bassanio (i.e., one who loves), and the gloss as realignment and substitution does not do justice to the simultaneity and tension of the relation to Portia. Put another way, the *Norton*'s gloss seems compactly designed to leave (or at least has the effect of leaving) the *philos* standing while deleting *eros*, the possibility of eroticism or sexual acts between men, especially if these are regarded as mutually exclusive of erotic, sexual, or marital union with women. Although it does not intrude in the text "proper," the gloss functions as an editorial emendation.

As I have hinted, the substitution in the *Norton*'s margin of *friend* for *lover* also further solidifies, in a way that seems historically inaccurate, the identitarian associations a modern reader would have for this term: what might look like a sexual-identity term in Shakespeare (*lover*) is presented as simply exchangeable with a modern term (*friend*), even though early modern *lover* might signify a more action-based, verbal identity, "one who loves" (with whatever acts or actions). The gloss thus potentially simplifies a general epistemic shift around the relation of eroticism and identity between that period and ours (whether same-sex or cross-sex), emphasizing identities over actions.

I am not going to worry this one word in the margin of a large book much further, but I do want to emphasize that, however unintentionally, the *Norton*'s gloss is not only narrowing, but also potentially *prophylactic,* protective—and not only locally, at the site of the particular semiotic "crux." More generally, the gloss defends and solidifies in advance a certain (I think *modern*) reading of the play's marital conclusion: in this reading, Bassanio and Antonio are friends (in the modern, less intense sense); Bassanio and Portia are married spouses; and the end of the play valorizes marriage over friendship. But struggling with this mid-play gloss might help us to see that the play ends *not* with Antonio "alone"—as the 2006 Michael Radford film memorably situates Jeremy Irons's Antonio—but rather with Antonio entering explicitly into a *renewed* bond for Bassanio, this time with Portia rather than Shylock:

ANTONIO   I once did lend my body for his wealth

. . . .

        I dare be bound again,
  My soul upon the forfeit, that your lord
  Will never more break faith advisedly.
PORTIA   Then you shall be his surety. (5.1.248–53, my emphasis)

This final bond of the play builds friendship between men (which is to say, lovers) into the structure of marriage between men and women (which is to say, lovers). Friendship guarantees marriage—it is its surety, its collateral. Antonio ends the play in a rebound bond of friendship. Moreover—and this is to stress the potentially feminist angle that this gloss and the larger history of interpretation of which it is a part forestalls—Portia's status as economic power and lender is as much at stake here as the relation of same- and cross-sex relations. To lose sight of this new bond is also to lose sight of Portia's power as mortgage (and marriage) broker.[48]

Reading these glosses through a queer philology, my point is to ask us to think about how the glosses in our editions of Shakespeare can blind us to other, more complex histories of sexuality, gender, and race in these plays and the culture in which they were produced. Issues of race are not outside the question in this case, given the text's insistence on Portia's "fair" appearance (1.2.162), the presence and dismissal of the Prince of Morocco as one of her suitors, Jessica's transit across ethnicity/religion and gender, and Lancelot's sexual/reproductive relationship with a "Moor" apparently in Portia's household (3.5.31–33).

There are, of course, many other such glossarial examples of this kind to follow out, not all of them about forms of identity or relationship. We can, for example, quickly trace the glossing of an affective/somatic term like *wanton* in the *Norton*'s version of *The Two Noble Kinsmen*. There, when used between the two friends and kinsmen Palamon and Arcite in Act 2, Scene 2 (the prison scene in which they pledge their love to each other)—"You have made me— / I thank you, cousin Arcite—almost wanton / With my captivity"—the word is glossed as "delighted" (2.2.95–97). It is left unglossed between Emilia and her serving woman a few lines later (3.2.147), thus eliding the same-sex female eroticism that Laurie Shannon has carefully unfolded in the scene.[49] *Wanton* is later glossed as *lewd* when Emilia, praying to the goddess Diana, uses it in cross-sex context (5.3.12). When Emilia deploys the word to describe Arcite as "just such another wanton Ganymede," the word again carries no gloss at all (4.2.15). Perhaps Ganymede is merely "delighted," but, as we noticed in detail in Chapters 4 and 5, a variety of Renaissance texts and visual depictions suggest that there may be more to Ganymede than that.

Whether in large-scale, complete-works editions designed for undergraduate and general audiences like the *Norton*, or more scholar-oriented, single-text editions like Neill's *Othello*, let me be clear that I do not think editing is easy work. But whatever the inertia that must be overcome to further diversify the already impressive array of technical expertises editors must have, it is important to insist that editorial work steep itself more deeply in the scholarship on, and think more imaginatively about putting into practice, the heretofore seemingly impossible readings of sex and sexuality as they intersect with race, gender, affect, and other categories of modern critical analysis in the texts. Understanding the complex histories of sexuality, what I termed in the Introduction their "textures of alterity," and their relation to race and gender must *also* be understood as part of editorial technique, *as technical*: a set of tools for seeing, producing, allowing, or enabling readings. There is a not-so-surprising tendency in editing to work at the level of the word, the crux, the lemma, the line, the gloss—and obviously I have largely been doing so in this chapter. But it is also the case that a broader, deeper, more polymorphous attention to matters of gender, sex, affect, sexual identity (or its historical lack), and their relation to race as a more global background to an approach to the text is crucial.[50] Larger "syntax[es] of desire" may get lost, and, amid the editorial tendency toward stabilizing the text, we should recall, for the *Norton's* examples in particular, Traub's reminder that for women (and, as I have suggested above, for men) much in this period "exist[s] on the unstable boundary between *philia* and *eros*."[51] Which is to say, "making sense of a passage," to return to the *Norton Shakespeare's* general introduction, may require supplying in the margin, at the bottom or elsewhere on the page, or somewhere on the screen and its links, more multiple meanings than we have yet entertained—inventing a practice of glossing that recognizes that dwelling on that and other unstable boundaries may *also* produce "sense."

Editing *Tupped*

To return to our crux and its glosses in *Othello*: in this set of moments in the play we are confronted with an instance in an early modern linguistic system in which *tupped* and *topped* may be interchangeable in spelling and highly similar in pronunciation (here the very notion of "the word" as a bounded, philological category begins to unravel), in which the rhetorics of sodomy/bestiality/race may have significantly overlapped, in which the rhetoric of sexual positioning inheres in at least one of these spellings, and in which *topt* can also signify intoxication ("Cassio did top/intoxicate her"—is *that* the crime?), as well as the extraction of liquid from a person understood to be like a vessel. At the same time, we know that a modern text of *Othello* cannot, by its very philological protocols of modernization, hope to render in its text "proper" the linguistic complexity of this system of signification prior to standardization. Perhaps, then, the best solution is to confront the constitutive interplay of text and gloss and print a text that sends the reader, hailed now once again as a queer philologist, into the glossarial notes more actively to produce the meaning of the text him- or herself:

> Would you the supervisor grossly gape on?
> Behold her t*pped?[†]

Some will argue that putting an asterisk in the text fails to render it with philological accuracy, but so, of course, does printing simply *topped* or *tupped*, since (a queerer philology will also argue) *neither* graphic shape in a modern edition can render all that an early modern audience might have read or heard in this word/sound.[52] Indeed, I would argue that *t*pped* is clearly the more conservative choice, more faithful to the text of *Othello* (if fidelity must be the rhetoric, particularly in this highly charged marital context, as a queer philologist must remark): while not forcing the text into *tupping*, as Neill's edition does, *t*pped* leaves alive the (currently known) possibilities and resonances. The queer philologist will also be drawn to the asterisk as comparative philology's symbol placed at the beginning of Proto-Indo-European "root" forms that are not actually attested but rather reconstructed from other linguistic evidence: for example, *$h_2$nér (man; power, force). Take *t*pped*, in this sense, as my hypothetical reconstruction of how *tupped/topped* may have worked in early modern English—though you'll have noticed that, practicing queer philology, I have moved the marker of hypothesis (*) inside the "word" itself.

Pedagogically, too, the oddity of an asterisk in the middle of a word—and its suggestion of euphemized or bleeped-out language—might send students and other readers *into the glosses* more forcefully than any † or ° or unmarked lemma or bracketed [crux] may.[53] (That is, at least until my advocated practice here becomes all the rage in editions, at which point I may advocate shifting tactics again.) The jarring unfamiliarity of *t*pped*—putting a nonce character traditionally leading elsewhere in the midst of the smoothed-out, repunctuated, and modernized Shakespearean text, using a character that also serves as a "wildcard" in database searches—leads me to prefer it to another possibility:

> Behold her təpped?

[†] **t*pped** Either "topped" (Q1's "topt" and F1's "top'd," both meaning "fucked by someone on 'top'"); or "tupped" ("fucked like or by an animal," as in Iago's reference to bestial "tupping" in 1.1, with its suggestion of illegal sodomy, which carried a death sentence in England). "Topped" also may mean "intoxicated" (with desire?), and "tapped" (pierced or drained). See also *bumbast* (Chapter 9).
t*pped] MASTEN (conj.); tupped POPE2, NEILL; top'd F1; topt Q1

The latter, however, has the advantage of making readers think about performance, aurality, pronunciation, and the homonymic network of possibilities in
early modern texts and performances that often go unregistered in modernized
editions.[54] Here, too, though, the very method of modernizing spelling serves to
gloss the text (as a whole) as more semantically and phonetically stable than it
historically was; one form of philological and textual accuracy (at the level of the
linguistic system) is lost in the translation of and deference to another (accuracy
at the level of the "word").

I have noted in this consideration both that emendations of a "crux" (*top*
emended to *tup*) can function as a gloss and that glosses (*lover = friend*) can effectively function as a consequential emendation. Even in my proposed queer-
philological editing and/as glossing of this moment in *Othello*, of course, all is not
glossed. Nor, perhaps, could it or will it be—since part of my point here is that an
understanding of sexuality in the text and the conceptions of race and gender that
here inextricably attend it are necessarily produced out of the intersection of our
current historical moment and the received text—whether Shakespearean or otherwise historical. This is an intersection within the history of sexuality that is
(always) a moving target. "Glossed" always has "lost" within it: the world we have
glossed; glossed in translation; loves' labors glossed. Ostensibly, all is not glossed
in the *Norton Shakespeare* because "too much explanatory whispering at the margins makes it difficult to enjoy what the reader has come for in the first place." If
it is not clear that all readers now come to enjoy the *same thing* in the *first place*;
if it is not clear that the role of the editor is to allow those readers to relax unper-
turbed or unchallenged in the comfort of that enjoyment, that default first place;
if, further, recent queer theory has precisely focused on the validity and political
consequences of a historical story that would see a heterosexual or heteronormative "first place" followed by its pale or inconsequential queer imitations and bad
copies;[55] if it is, finally, not clear that "the pleasure of the text," from which the
Norton fears glossing may distract us, is *singular*, I hope I have at least persuaded
you that there might be some benefit in more and different explanatory whispering at the margins and in the notes. That whispering, a queer philology that will
in fact need to speak up, will fundamentally alter our understandings of the text
"itself."

CHAPTER 9

More or Less Queer: Female "Bumbast"
in *Sir Thomas More*

Others there be that fall into the contrary vice by vsing such bombasted wordes, as seeme altogether farced full of winde. . . .[1]	*Bomphiologia,* or Pompious speech.

Queer *More*

I have saved it for last, for, as you will already know and have no doubt been anticipating, the play *Sir Thomas More* is queerer than any of the other texts addressed in this book. Certainly it is queerer than *The Merchant of Venice, Twelfth Night, Two Gentlemen of Verona, Two Noble Kinsmen, As You Like It, Hamlet,* or the *Sonnets*—or any of the other run-of-the-mill queer Shakespearean texts that have made an appearance in this book's analysis. In *Sir Thomas More,* by contrast, the cross-class homoeroticism of the title character's immortal line near the hour of his death—"Sirrah fellow, reach me the urinal" (5.3.22, 58.1751)[2]—has been evident to most, if not all, discerning readers. And, as hardly bears mentioning, More's eloquent Act 3 soliloquy, including his self-admonition to "[f]ear their gay skins" (3.1.18, 79.III.19), has presented a rich vein for critics anatomizing the complexities of early modern queer embodiment and homophobia. Needless to say, More's culminating aphorism in that soliloquy has become a touchstone for early modern queer work: "let this be thy maxim: to be great / Is, when the thread of hazard is once spun, / *A bottom great wound up, greatly [is] undone*" (3.1.19–21, 79.III.20–22, my emphasis).

"As you will know," "needless to say," "hardly bears mentioning": in the emerging canon of early modern queer literary examples as well as in the Shakespeare canon, *Sir Thomas More* is not the familiar play I have invoked. If you are not a Shakespeare scholar, and possibly even if you are, you likely have not read the play, even the bits of it—the allegedly Shakespearean pages of this rare, collaborative play manuscript—often reproduced in current complete-works editions. In this sense, the play could hardly be less queer: hardly noticed.

In the annals of normative-philological scholarship seeking as a fundamental task to establish accurate texts and authorial canons, however, the play's aberrance is well established. It is the only play associated with Shakespeare that survives in manuscript form. Unlike every other play now in that canon, it was not published in the sixteenth or seventeenth centuries. It does not appear in a quarto, good or bad, and it was not included in the 1623 first folio collection of Shakespeare's plays or (unlike *Pericles*) in any of the three subsequent seventeenth-century Shakespeare folios. Like *The Two Noble Kinsmen*, *Cardenio*, and possibly *Henry VIII*, it is collaborative, but unlike those plays, its collaboration is no mere monogamous arrangement of Shakespeare and John Fletcher and indeed seems utterly promiscuous: at least six people seem to have collaborated in its writing and revision. Among these are potentially actors and copyists as well as (or being the same person as) playwrights.[3] One of the writers in the manuscript, Edmund Tilney, Master of the Revels, is the royal censor; *Sir Thomas More* is "the only surviving play indisputably marked with Tilney's own annotations,"[4] and it is the only play in the Shakespeare canon for which there is clear evidence of large-scale government intervention.[5]

In modernity, the play is so queer as hardly to be extant, a play that dare not speak its name. Until the Arden edition published John Jowett's edition of the play in its third series in 2011,[6] the only widely available, modern-spelling, single-play edition of the whole play, Vittorio Gabrieli and Giorgio Melchiori's 1990 Revels edition, had only recently come back into print. The last Shakespeare complete-works edition to print the full text of the play was C. J. Sisson's in 1954;[7] of the prominent U.S. teaching editions, the *Riverside Shakespeare* includes only "The Additions Ascribed to Shakespeare"; the first and second editions of the *Norton Shakespeare* (and the Oxford edition on which it was based) include only "Passages Attributed to Shakespeare."[8] Queerer still, for the *Norton*'s second and third editions, the complete text of the play is available only digitally.[9] As noted, the long-running Arden complete-works series lacked *More* in its first two generations of editions. Another complete-works edition, "The RSC Shakespeare" (2007), includes only what it calls "A Scene for *Sir Thomas More*"; the manuscript transcription and the modernization of the scene comprise the last text of the volume, falling outside the collection's genre-based organization and division of the plays and poems.[10] Because it is a manuscript and wasn't printed until the nineteenth century, *More* is the only extant "Shakespeare" play an early modern version of which cannot be consulted worldwide via Early English Books Online.

There are yet more signs of the play's tendency toward aberrance in editorial philology's protocols. Since the case first began to be built for including *More* in the Shakespeare canon in the early years of the twentieth century—its biggest boost came from the 1923 volume *Shakespeare's Hand in the Play of Sir Thomas More*, with essays by key figures in what would become the dominant movement in twentieth-century Shakespearean editorial theory and practice[11]—Shakespeare's participation in the play's manuscript has been continually under dispute. The second edition of the *Norton Shakespeare* asserts that "a small minority [of scholars] denies" the attribution of part of the play to Shakespeare,[12] but, as Paul Werstine notes, the originally adduced evidence of uniquely Shakespearean spellings (e.g., "scilens") and handwriting features said to resemble the fourteen other known words extant in Shakespeare's handwriting (twelve of them the words "William" and "Shakespeare") has been discredited. As Werstine summarizes, "[T]he case for Shakespearean authorship of the Hand D pages rests chiefly on the analogies that scholars have drawn between the fictional More's plea for civil order and the views attributed to Shakespeare by E. M. W. Tillyard in his long-exploded representation of Shakespeare as the most impassioned and gifted spokesman for the Elizabethan World Picture."[13] If our quarry is queer Shakespeare, what, then, could be queerer than a Shakespeare play not written in whole or in part by Shakespeare?

As this book has already suggested, such an enterprise—the queering of Shakespeare—however strategically laudable, nevertheless seems to me methodologically limiting as well as historically impracticable. Indeed, plays such as *Sir Thomas More* begin to unravel the whole enterprise of a Shakespeare canon understood as queer or queered, as embodied by a volume such as Madhavi Menon's *Shakesqueer*, in which a version of this chapter first appeared.[14] If Shakesqueer, why not Jonsqueer, Marlqueer, Websqueer, Beaumont-and-Fletchqueer? Or, leaving drama, Spensqueer? Why all the bother with queering at the level of the "author" and a circumscribed authorial canon in the first place? Doesn't such a mode of thought and organization simply reproduce the notions of the bounded individual and unitary subjectivity that have been central to queer critique since its advent?[15] Doesn't queering thus organized reproduce the "completeness" fetish of the most traditional complete-works volume?

In this sense, *Sir Thomas More* is either or both more and/or less queer than other Shakespeare plays. On the one hand, possibly—maybe even probably—the play is not by Shakespeare. On the other, passages from it are now routinely included in complete-works volumes—in which, it seems, the more Shakespeare the better, best to include anything he might have touched or retouched, etc. Indeed, as I have argued elsewhere, the manuscript, closely held and carefully protected at the British Library, has achieved a totemic significance, functioning as the "missing link"—the only extant manuscript that potentially connects the writer with the process of playwriting.[16] As such, its function in complete-works editions seems to be as much about providing a photogenic (if not exactly legible) example of Shakespeare's ostensible handwriting as about providing an actual play. In the case of either *Two Noble Kinsmen* or *Henry VIII*, the whole collaborative play is included, no matter who is said to have written each part, but with *More*, we read only the "Shakespeare" bits, plus photographs of the manuscript (and sometimes photos of Shakespeare's few signatures), rather than the edited text of an entire play. As Werstine has noted, the manuscript of the play is "the site upon which the metaphysics of authorship has been centred for most of [the twentieth] century."[17] (And will continue to be erected, if the more recent news of Shakespeare's ostensible hand in *The Spanish Tragedy* is any indication.[18]) Marginal, fragmentary, present-as-absent, materially metaphysical, dubious-but-essential: perhaps this can serve as a provisional working definition of a queer Shakespeare, Menon's "Shakesqueer."[19]

In the context of the interpretatively prolific field of Shakespeare studies, one of the queerer aspects of *Sir Thomas More* is an almost complete absence of critical analysis of the play. The only play known for certain to be from Shakespeare's hand (if it is Shakespeare's hand), metaphysically central to the very conception of Shakespeare as a working playwright and to a twentieth-century editorial practice that seeks to found its treatment of early printed texts on Shakespeare's otherwise hypothetical manuscripts—the basis, that is, for every modern edition quoted in this book and nearly all others in this century and the last—the play has nevertheless evaded commentary in a field that annually cranks it out. With few exceptions, critical discussion of the play has been occluded by, or in the service of, discussions of authorship, manuscript bibliography, and attribution.[20] There is, to my knowledge, no queer criticism of this play if we do not include what you are about to read. Which is to say, in this case, "scilens" equals death. "[W]hat is striking about 'Silence = Death' as the most widely publicized, gay-articulated language of response to the 'AIDS' epidemic," Lee Edelman writes, "is its insistence upon the therapeutic property of discourse without specifying in any way what should or must be said."[21] Taking up Edelman's suggestion in a very different register, I hope to suggest, in the case of *Sir Thomas More*, that the remedy is not simply more discourse, any discourse—for there has been perhaps enough of that, at an impasse, in authorial and attributional registers already, with ostensibly Shakespearean spellings like "scilens" spelling out a dearth, if not a death, of interpretation—but rather a specifically queer philology to address both editorial *and* (and *as*) critical practice around this most disputed "Shakespearean" play.

Strange Roots

> Incorporated into the structures of socialized desire,
> Amazons expose that desire as a system of roles that might
> always be detached from the bodies they exist to
> regulate. . . . Is every amazonian dream a wish fulfillment?
> —Kathryn Schwarz, *Tough Love*[22]

"Whither wilt thou hale me?" says Doll Williamson to the foreigner Francis de Bard in the opening line of *Sir Thomas More* (1.1.1, 1.4), which in its first set of scenes stages the "Ill May Day" riots of 1517, embroidering and sometimes quoting Edward Hall's and Raphael Holinshed's chronicle histories of Henry VIII's reign.[23] A response of urban Londoners to their grievances against immigrants in their midst, the riots stage the "strangers" stealing various forms of what the play presents as English property: jobs, commerce, food, wives. (The strangers are sometimes specified as "Frenchmen" or "Lombards," on which more later.) "How now, husband?" says Doll. "What, one stranger take thy food from thee, and another thy wife?" (1.1.31–32, 2.28–29).

If one point of the play seems to be to stage the resistance of the English to strangers (a resistance also being restaged in the streets of London in the years directly preceding the likely date of the play's composition, in the circulation of xenophobic "libels" against foreigners in the 1590s[24]), it simultaneously stages—from its first line, as we have seen—a specifically *female* resistance that exceeds the anti-alien movement. Even earlier, the play's opening stage direction describes Doll as "*a lusty woman*" (1.1.s.d., 1.3), and it is worth noting that *Sir Thomas More* is one of only three or possibly four plays associated with Shakespeare that begins with a woman/boy actor speaking.[25] The opening scenes of the play return relentlessly to Doll's militancy—a resistance described as resolute marital fidelity to her English husband but also repeatedly threatening female rule and the world upside down: "Hands off proud stranger. . . . [I]f men's milky hearts dare not strike a stranger, yet women will beat them down, ere they bear these abuses" (1.1.56–58, 3.44–46). A moment later, calling for the return of stolen pigeons, Doll imagines an unruly female army supplying male lack: "deliver them back to my husband again or I'll call so many women to mine assistance, as we'll not leave one inch untorn of thee. If our husbands must be bridled by law, and forced to bear your wrongs, their wives will be a little lawless, and soundly beat ye" (1.1.63–68, 3.50–53).[26] At the end of the scene, Doll vows to "make [herself] a captain among ye, and do somewhat to be talk of for ever after" (1.1.134–35, 4.99–100). If the allusion to being talked of in the chronicle histories sets up Doll as an overreacher—she is not a figure named, at least, in the multiple accounts of these events[27]—she does become a captain in the play: the later scene staging the riots begins with a stage direction for "DOLL *in a shirt of mail, a headpiece, sword and buckler, a crew attending*" (2.1.s.d., 14.410–11).

The play thus represents what Kathryn Schwarz has called an "amazon encounter," but Doll stages not precisely Schwarz's Amazons brought from afar and domesticated—in all the queerness such an encounter unleashes in Schwarz's readings—but instead an already-English Amazon whose fierce, outspoken feminism and overturning of patriarchal pieties of silence and obedience are themselves produced out of the encounter with strangeness. "I have no beauty to like a husband," Doll says—and the text probably means "please a husband," though it is ambiguous—"yet whatsoever is mine scorns to stoop to a stranger" (1.1.5–7, 1.7–8).[28] Doll's militantly faithful rebellion threatens to change May Day into "midsummer," instituting what we might call "queer time": "we'll alter the day in the calendar, and set it down in flaming letters" (2.1.36–38, 70.II.28–29).[29] Doll would revise the ecclesiastical calendar, establishing a new red-letter saint's day of riot. If Doll ultimately seems redomesticated by the events of the play—she is nearly hanged for her role in the insurrection, but royal power, acting (unhistorically) through Thomas More, intervenes to pardon her as she concludes her scaffold speech[30]—she nevertheless seems to replay the "double move" that Schwarz sees in Amazon narratives, "which project an image into an antisocial condition of sexual identity only to bring it back again. Back, that is, into articulations of male homosocial power and its perpetuation through domesticated heterosexuality, articulations that the intervention of 'Amazon' can only disconcert" (5). "Now let me tell the women of this town," she says on the scaffold, "No stranger yet brought Doll to lying down" (2.4.127–28, 24.684–85). Stressing fidelity to her husband and the "two little babes" they would leave behind in death (2.4.116, 23.673), Doll nevertheless raises the specter of female sexual resistance.

And, even earlier, female *penetration*: in the riot scene, Doll threatens, "we'll drag the strangers out into Moorfields, and there bombast them till they stink again" (2.1.42–43, 15.432–33). The Revels edition glosses *bombast* as "lit[erally] 'to stuff,'" and this meaning of the verb derives from the noun *bombast* (from *bombase* or *bombace*), meaning "cotton-wool used as padding or stuffing for clothes."[31] But, during the period, *bombast* is spelled interchangeably with *bumbaste/bumbast*[32]—indeed, *bumbast* is the spelling in the manuscript, which the Revels edition "modernizes" to *bombast*.[33] The interchangeable spellings, together with the additional meaning the *Oxford English Dictionary* (*OED*) assigns *bumbast* during the period, suggest that Doll's threatened action against the strangers might run the gamut from spanking to stuffing or fucking; for *bumbast(e)*, the *OED* gives "[t]o beat on the posteriors; hence, to flog, beat soundly, thrash." The *OED*'s exemplary quotation comes from a 1616 husbandry text, describing the cure for a "restie," obstinate horse: "if it be . . . a Gelding, you must bumbast his buttocks with a good long sticke taken hot out of the fire, and burnt at the end, for it will make him goe: . . . if you vse the same course in his rearings, it will correct him, and make him leaue them."[34] Pardon my bombasted philological detail here, but the queer philology of the *OED*'s etymology for the verb *bumbast(e)* is irresistible: "apparently [from] BUM *n*.[1] [i.e., buttocks] + BASTE *v*.[3]: [i.e., beat] but *bum* might be a meaningless intensive or reduplicative prefix."[35] To whom, queer philologists, is *bum* a "meaningless intensive"? Furthermore, *bum* as "reduplicative prefix"— *bum* as a *poster*ior that (re)doublingly *pre*fixes something—seems only to reinscribe the inversions of before and behind, the "preposterous" trope of *hysteron proteron*, the beast with two backs, long associated with sodomy discourse during this period.[36] (Indeed, about eighty lines before the sodomitical "tupping" lines analyzed in Chapter 8, Othello is associated with "a bombast circumstance, / Horribly stuffed with epithets of war"; in *Othello*, the word is spelled *bumbast* in both Q1 and F1 but is now routinely modernized [translated?] in editions without comment.[37]) Writing in 1592 (that is, at about the same time as scholars' best estimate of the date of *Sir Thomas More*'s first writing), Robert Greene makes precisely this sodomitical association, in a dialogue where a native Englishman says to another stranger, "him may wée curse that brought thée first into *Englande*, for thou camest not alone but acompanied with multitude of abhominable vices, hanging on thy bumbast nothing but infectious abuses, and vaine glory, selfeloue, sodomie, and strange poisonings, wherewith thou hast infected this glorious Iland."[38]

Sodomy hangs on and about *bumbast/bombast* and other abominations. Jowett's Arden edition gloss seems to separate *bombast* and *bumbaste*, but the effect of *More* and Greene seems to be to collate or conflate them: Doll's threat is to take the strangers out beyond the city walls[39] and stuff or spank them, or reduplicatively double-spank them before and behind, bumbast them rhetorically and otherwise, until, it seems, they shit themselves.[40] (As Greene's passage suggests, there are significant intersections among rhetorical bumbast/bombast, sodomy, and anality. George Puttenham describes "*Bomphiologia*, or Pompous Speech" as a "contrary vice," "using bombasted words, as seem altogether farced full of wind."[41] Puttenham links a "contrary" or preposterous "vice" stuffed ["farced"] with flatulent, anal "wind.")[42]

Perhaps you will feel I am going too far in unstuffing the meanings of Doll's *bumbast* here, but her lines moments later seem only to emphasize these sexual possibilities, as well as the underlying threat to husband, domestic heterosexuality, and patriarchy: "If thou beest afraid, husband, go home again and hide thy head, for by the Lord *I'll have a little sport now I am at it*" (2.1.60–62, 15.443–44, my emphasis). "Sport" sometimes means "sex" during the period,[43] and though it also means "fun" or "riot" here, Doll's line efficiently associates riot with female sexual availability, the issue around which the riot (dis)organized itself in the first place.[44] "No stranger yet brought Doll to lying down," she says, but the play may well imagine the reverse.

Further, whether the play was ever acted or not,[45] Doll's part was designed to be played by a boy actor, and the specter here of a boy bumbasting foreigners (in whatever senses) is an additional reversal of the period's usual hierarchies, whether in pedagogical beating of schoolboys or in the stock positionings of pederasty.[46] (Compare Domingo Cassedon Drago and the poor boy, William Wraxall, in Chapter 8.) The play does not evade this potential homoeroticism; in the later allegorical play within the play, one boy player plays three female parts, "Dame Science, Lady Vanity, / And Wisdom, she herself," to which Sir Thomas More comments, "And one boy play them all? By'r Lady, he's loaden" (3.2.75–77, 32.935–37). There follows much bawdy play in the flirtation of the male character Wit and Lady Vanity, played by the boy, as Wit comes to her "a stranger" who (encouraged by the Vice-character Inclination) quickly becomes "familiar" (3.2.211–16, 36.1073–77): "I could find in my heart to kiss you in your smock," Wit says. (The line may signify "kiss you in parts covered by your undergarment," but also "kiss you while you're in your boy-actor's lady-costume."[47]) Lady Vanity's/the boy's rhyming reply is even more explicit: "My back is broad enough to bear that mock" (3.2.237–38, 37.1098–99). Doll's earlier line, "*Hands off* proud stranger," is thus here reversed by a boy playing Lady Vanity "singing and beckoning *with her hand*": "Come hither, come hither, come hither, come: / Such cheer as I have, thou shalt have some" (3.2.219–21, my emphasis; 36.1080–82). As Scott McMillin notes, the doubling of actors' parts makes it likely that the same boy would have played Doll and Lady Vanity.[48]

Beyond these antipatriarchal, sodomitical, and erotic resonances around Doll and the boy who may have played her, there is another way in which queer discourses might cohere in their incoherence in the play. As I noted, the play sometimes uses the term *Lombards* to refer to strangers; indeed, this has been a fine point in the discussion of the censorship of the play, because at one point in the manuscript, Tilney crosses out the words "straunger" and "ffrencheman" and replaces them with "lombard" (Greg, 13.364, 368).[49] In a discussion of 1590s anti-alien unrest and this play, James Shapiro has noted the association of Lombards with Jews, and the names of both groups are used during this period as metonyms of "money-lender,"[50] but it is worth exploring further associations of the Lombards. In the scholarship on the play, Tilney's manuscript intervention here is typically understood as a depoliticization of the text: the Crown would not have wanted to offend the French ambassador, Richard Dutton argues, and there would likely have been fewer Lombards than French to offend in 1590s London.[51] But Lombards may have loomed larger, or at least differently, in the cultural imaginary.[52] Here is the Jacobean Chief Justice Edward Coke doing a little queer philology (or at least xenophobic etymology) in his systematic description of English felonies, again in the chapter "Of Buggery, or Sodomy": "*Bugeria* is an Italian word . . . , *Pæderastes* or *Paiderestes* is a Greek word, *Amator puerorum* [lover of boys], which is but a Species of Buggery, and it was complained of in Parliament, that the Lumbards had brought into the Realm the shamefull sin of Sodomy, that is not to be named."[53] Doll, resisting a Lombard, imagines "bumbasting" the Lombards, who brought in sodomy—which always arrives from elsewhere. In Greene, too, the linkage we saw of "abhominable" sodomy, self-love, and bumbast comes from a distinctly Italian elsewhere; the character Clothbreeches, representing "*the old and worthie customes of the Gentilitie and yeomanrie of* England,"[54] says to Velvet-breeches, "borne in *Italy*":[55] "so hast thou beene the ruine of the *Romane* Empire, and nowe fatally art thou come into *Englande* to atempte heere the like subuersion."[56]

Coke's definition, as we saw in Chapters 7 and 8, describes buggery as "a detestable, and abominable sin, amongst Christians not to be named, and committed by carnall knowledge against the ordinance of the Creator, and order of nature, by mankind with mankind, or with brute beast, or by womankind with bruite beast" (58). Doll, fighting off the Lombard who says, "Go with me quietly, or I'll compel thee," responds, "Compel me, ye dog's face?" (1.1.8–9. 1.9–10).[57] In its engagement of these discourses and its simultaneous xenophobic celebration and near-hanging of Doll, the play teeters between Doll as sodomite (woman with brute beast), rape target, and antiroyal subversive; though Coke notes that the authorities "differ in the manner of the punishment" for sodomy, it is a "crime of majesty, against the heavenly King,"[58] and "the judgement . . . is that the person attainted be hanged by the neck, untill he, or she be dead." The condensation of these discourses in the opening scenes of the play is made more resonant through the very structure of Coke's attempt to encode the law, suggesting the culture's associative logic for these crimes; among his enumeration of English felonies, chapter 10, "Of Buggery, or Sodomy," is followed by chapter 11, "Of Rape," and chapter 12, "Felony for carying away a woman against her will, &c." The associative logics are at once analogical (both buggery and rape require, he says, not "*emissio seminis*" but "*penetratio, that is, res in re*" [59]) and intertextually structured, in ways that may also animate the play: "We have thought good next after Buggery and Rape, to speak of the stealing of women, because the Apostle doth rank, after the Sodomite, him that is *Plagiarius*" (61). Plagiarism hasn't yet become fully figurative during this period; it still carries its etymological meaning "kidnapping." As Coke suggests, 1 Timothy associates "whoremongers, . . . buggerers, . . . menstealers, . . . [and] lyers."[59] Doll, at first resisting being carried away against her will ("Whither wilt thou hale me . . . ye dog's face?"), also later imagines carrying away and bumbasting the beasts. It is important to note, among other differences with the sources, that the play, via Doll, personalizes and gives agency to a woman about to be "carried away"—as opposed to the woman in Hall's and Holinshed's accounts, who remains unnamed and her desires/resistances unimagined while she is kept by de Bard.

What are the dangers of the English consorting with strangers and Lombards? "Freres des Lombards," Randle Cotgrave notes in the entry for *Lombard* in his French-English dictionary (1611): "Moles, Moonecalues, monstrous birthes; tearmed so, because the women of Lombardie by much feeding on hearbes, fruites, and other crudities, bring forth sometimes those monsters in stead of children."[60] Or, as the play has it, cataloging the allegations against the strangers and the effects of their diet of roots, potatoes, and parsnips: "They bring in strange roots, which is merely to the undoing of poor prentices" (2.3.10–11, 73. II.130–31). Are we now speaking of vegetables; of monstrous crossbreeds; of sodomy, brought by the Lombards from elsewhere; or of etymological roots? "*Bugeria* is an Italian word."

Queer Philologies' Intersections

Perhaps it goes without saying that there will be no easy alignment in this play or, more generally, between queerness, feminism, class struggle, and antixenophobic and antinationalist critique—though a queer philology will help to identify and analyze these intersections. The challenge was made starkly clear to me as I watched the Royal Shakespeare Company perform *Sir Thomas More* as a part of its "Gunpowder [Plot] Season," on August 1, 2005. Three weeks after the London subway bombings, the attendant attention to "strangers" among "us," and a reaction that included the killing of an unarmed Brazilian immigrant living in London by the police, it seemed impossible not to feel progressive politics drawn in multiple directions by a production in which Doll led a working-class riot against foreigners made obviously Other—played by black, if not visibly Muslim, actors.[61] Thomas More famously quiets the riot by constructing a rhetoric in which the lower-class English must imagine themselves as wandering, mistreated "strangers" in exile, and I witnessed an apparently British white woman near me in the audience enthusiastically applaud More's success, only to look sheepishly at her disapproving husband. Was she embarrassed by her endorsement of state authority, by her empathy with the foreigners in the current political context, or by her opposition to a riot leader of her own gender—or was she simply ashamed of her momentary lack of reserve, her suspension of disbelief? The play pits social-class, feminist, national, royalist, and queer interests continually against each other.[62]

To see this fracturing and dwell in its complex interstices (reading the overlaps and analogies, rather than the chapter *divisions* in Coke's account) is to resist the default treatment of this play as essentially a *de casibus* tragedy of one man, and the riot scenes as merely in the service of More's progress from Sheriff to Sir Thomas and eventual martyrdom in defying Henry VIII. Like the work of the play's revisers, who, for reasons we don't understand at a date we cannot pinpoint, seem to have ignored the demands of censorship, a queer-philological reading would dwell within the complexities of the riot rather than delete or submerge them, as Tilney requires in his edict on the manuscript's first page:

> Leaue out . . . yᵉ insurrection wholy wᵗ yᵉ Cause ther off & begin wᵗ Sʳ Th: Moore att yᵉ mayors sessions wᵗ a reportt afterwards off his good servic' don being' Shriue off Londō vppō a mutiny Agaynst yᵉ Lūbards only by A shortt reportt & nott otherwise att your own perilles. (Revels, 17)

> [Leave out . . . the insurrection wholly, with the cause thereof, and begin with Sir Thomas More at the Mayor's sessions, with a report afterwards of his good service done, being Sheriff of London, upon a mutiny against the Lombards—only by a short report and not otherwise, at your own perils.] (my modernization)

In the space of a brief chapter, I'm keenly aware of the difficulties of mapping the insurrection and resisting a reading that would center only on eventually-Sir Thomas. Indeed, as I have argued elsewhere, the play, even in its later, narrowing focus on the events of More's life, resists a reduction to great-man history in its many redoublings (even "queerings") of More, played in one scene by his servant Randall to fool Erasmus, in More's later stepping into the play-within to supply the role of Good Counsel, and, throughout, in his frequent punning on the supplementarity of his own name. Forgoing office and title near the end of his life, he says, "[M]y title's only More" (4.2.71, 45.1360).

Queer theory and a queer-philological approach might, further, spur us to revisit critically the bibliographical and attributive work that, as I have noted, has scilensed, or at least occluded, almost all critical, interpretive discussion of this play, where Doll scarcely makes an appearance. Such a strategy of reading would interrogate approaches to the play that apprehend/analyze/evaluate the text only then to short-circuit back to authorship, a notion implicit in a different audience member's account of the 2005 production: "I might add that in the Royal Shakespeare Company's 2005 production of *Sir Thomas More* the sudden surge of poetic and dramatic power as the performance reached the 'Shakespearean' scenes was obvious."[63]

To employ the play to perform briefly, though inadequately, a critique here: queer theory's interrogation of identity, identification, their performativity, and the complexities of identity-over-time can help us begin to develop a more critical account of authorial attribution in the *More* manuscript and of what it has meant for something to be "by Shakespeare" more generally. Such ideas have rested on a number of imbricated essences: for example, the idea of a surging "poetic and dramatic power" that is manifest in performance, rather than created in a complex relation with it; or the notion of an author whose "attitude" toward crowds and royal authority does not change over time and who is thus identifiable. "[I]t is . . . no accident," writes Alfred W. Pollard, stating the early case for Shakespeare's hand in *More* in the first folio anniversary year of 1923, "that in these three pages we find the attitude to mobs, the attitude to the crown, and the deep humanity, which are recurrent features in the work of William Shakespeare."[64] (Authentic, surging, Shakespearean "poetic and dramatic power" is incompatible with, and indeed quells, bumbasting/bombastic female riot: discuss.)

Or, recalling the analysis of early modern spelling and compositors in Chapter 1, a queer-philological approach could consider the ostensible essence of Shakespeare said to inhere in what turn out to be widely shared and variant spelling habits, in a linguistic system prior to standardization. Or the ostensible essence of handwriting: "The problem" in identifying handwriting, writes Pollard again, "is thus first to visualize how a handwriting after a *lapse* of some twenty years and in totally different circumstances will show the *natural effects* of these and yet *preserve its identity*, and secondly, to make the process thus *visualized* intelligible to others not specially equipped to deal with it."[65] A queer philology—a philology energized by queer theory, but also a philology whose resident queerness is itself available to be mobilized—can at least help us draw analytical attention to what goes under the sign of "natural effects," to the ostensible continuities of (authorial and other modes of) identity, and to criticism's habit of visualizing things both into and out of intelligibility, providing, as well, a possible vantage point for those ostensibly not "specially equipped."

At the same time, Pollard's words may carry an uncannily productive reminder for a queer theory that would, after a lapse of several centuries, produce a queer Shakespeare somehow separate from, or queerable without, the detailed peculiarities of historical evidence, material artifacts, philological detail, and discursive analysis that may themselves lead to a queer retheorization of the period, its authors, and its texts—what I called in the Introduction the complex textures of alterity. Part of what is queer in Shakespeare, in other words, will only emerge by wrestling with spelling Shakespeare (or whoever wrote these lines in this play)—wrestling, that is, with the continuities and textured alterities of *b*mbast*, among other terms. *Bombast* is, after all, a word still with us, in some but not all of its early modern senses; it lacks, apparently, the thread and threat of sodomitical rape and/or beating, though perhaps it retains a genealogical strand or echo of that danger in its current association with inauthenticity: in Edelman's words, its problems of "nomination and inscription."[66] Is that bombast, or are you really saying something? Do you speak upon your Q, and is your voice imperial?[67]

The effects of such an approach are here represented by my admittedly short-hand analysis of the complexly intertwined discourses around sodomy, insurrection, rape, social class, xenophobia, and nationalism. How else will we, not necessarily "specially equipped" in these latter times to inhabit the queerness of these early modern intersections, account for what is, in *More*, queer, even "Shakesqueer"? How can a queer philology move us beyond Pollard's admirable expertise and its visualizing blind spots—adding to our special equipment? These questions—for Shakespeare studies, for early modern studies more generally, and for queer theory—are, more or less, where, in conclusion, I would want next to begin, if I were not at my own peril in going beyond a shortt reportt.

NOTES

INTRODUCTION

1. Adam Smith, *An Inquiry into the Nature and Causes of the Wealth of Nations*, 358.

2. *A Midsommer Nights Dreame*, in *Mr. VVilliam Shakespeares Comedies, Histories, & Tragedies*, as reproduced in Charlton Hinman, ed., *The Norton Facsimile: The First Folio of Shakespeare*, TLN 883–87.

3. Samuel Johnson, *A Dictionary Of The English Language: In Which The Words are deduced from their Originals* . . . (1755), vol. 2, sig. 20 Y. The *OED* citation includes a minor mistranscription.

4. *OED*, *cue*, *n*.¹, 1.; also quoted at *O*, *n*.¹, 3. Unless otherwise indicated, all citations of the *OED* are to the online edition.

5. *OED*, *Q*.

6. To my knowledge, the first use of the term *queer philology* appears in the title of Carla Freccero's essay "Practicing Queer Philology with Marguerite de Navarre."

7. Maistre Geofroy Tory de Bourges, CHAMP FLEVRY. *Au quel est contenu Lart & Science de la deue & vraye Proportiō des Lettres Attiques, quō dit autremēt Lettres Antiques, & vulgairement Lettres Romaines proportionnees selon le Corps & Visage humain* (1529), as reprinted in Gustave Cohen, ed., *Champ Fleury* (facsimile, 1931 [rpt., 1973]). References to *Champ Fleury* are to the *feuillets* of the facsimile and appear parenthetically. There are some minor differences among the 1529 editions that I have examined at the Bibliothèque nationale de France (BnF) (two of four copies), British Library, Huntington Library, Newberry Library, and Library of Congress, including a press variant on f. XXXV, corrected by hand in BnF copy Res M-V-142, that to my knowledge has not been discussed. For *Champ Fleury*'s significance and sources, with corrections of earlier scholarship (including within the facsimile), see Barbara C. Bowen, "Geofroy Tory's *Champ Fleury* and Its Major Sources."

8. My translations attempt to produce versions that are nondisambiguating (thus, alternatives are occasionally provided) and historicized (thus, the translations are made via a period French-English translation dictionary; see note 11). I am grateful to Marc Schachter for his assistance and querying of some important details. In transcriptions, "q'" (with apostrophe) indicates "q" with a macron in Tory's text—a practice that, Schachter notes (personal correspondence), inscribes a performative version of Tory's topic here: "q" is only alone in abbreviations and must be marked as such. Schachter remarks that the *futur proche/futur périphrastique* in the penultimate clause of the sentence quoted here may serve to emphasize the immediacy or intention of the desire and agency ascribed to the letters.

9. Tom Conley, "The Letter and the Grid: Geoffroy Tory," chap. 2 in *The Self-Made Map*, 63. Subsequent references appear parenthetically.

10. *Coq* and *cinq* are early modern exceptions to the companionate-Q rule. Thus far, within early modern printing, I have been unable to locate any record of a "qu"-type ligature. For an

early type-specimen broadsheet (c. 1565?) with altered q types presumably used for abbreviations, see the Folger Library's STC 7758.3, vol. 3, no. 6.

11. Randle Cotgrave, comp., *A Dictionarie Of The French And English Tongves*, sig. Z.iᵛ.
Subsequent references appear parenthetically. Cf. "*Culot: m.* A little arse, a small taile; (and by
metaphor, a lad, or yong bodie)" (Z.ii). As I suggest later, the question of translation is itself of
interest to this discussion. Because, as this book argues, we should attend to what may be "lost
in translation" from early modern to modern English, there is in effect an act of double translation in moving from early modern French to a modern English critical treatment. My citations of Cotgrave signify an attempt to produce some possible, historically attentive, early
modern English translations.

On the power of the *Q/cul* homonym in mid-twentieth-century Québec, see Miguel Tremblay, "Le Q des vieux": "Je me souviens, lorsque j'étais un jeune Miguel, ma mère était très drôle
lorsqu'elle épelait des mots avec la lettre 'Q.' Elle ne disait pas 'cul' ([ky] en phonétique) pour
prononcer cette lettre mais bien 'que' ([ke]). . . . [L]a lettre Q était considérée trop vulgaire. . . .
En France, les écoles bien-pensantes disait plutôt 'qué' ([ké])." Thanks to Roger Chartier for this
reference.

12. Here and later, by *structures*, I mean historically and culturally located, contingent structures (ultimately alterable, contestable, changing) that are nonetheless experienced as real by
those living within them: structures, that is, in a poststructuralist sense. I am grateful to Steven
Epstein for asking me to clarify this point. See also Chapter 1 on *habitus*.

13. Alan Bray, *Homosexuality in Renaissance England*; Alan Bray, "Homosexuality and the
Signs of Male Friendship in Elizabethan England"; Mario DiGangi, *The Homoerotics of Early
Modern Drama*, esp. 3–12; Jonathan Goldberg, *Sodometries*; Jeffrey Masten, *Textual Intercourse*;
Bruce R. Smith, *Homosexual Desire in Shakespeare's England*; Valerie Traub, *The Renaissance of
Lesbianism in Early Modern England*. For an important summary and synthesis of this histori-
cal work in relation to the modern category, see the title essay in David M. Halperin, *How to Do
the History of Homosexuality*.

14. The most canonical early modern example of friendship discourse is Michel de Montaigne's essay "De L'Amitié" and its English translations and analogues. On early modern
friendship, see especially Alan Bray, *The Friend*; Marc D. Schachter, *Voluntary Servitude and the
Erotics of Friendship*; Laurie Shannon, *Sovereign Amity*. Jacques Derrida, *Politics of Friendship*,
traces this legacy largely without discussion of its erotic associations.

15. When Q is referred to as "la lettre," it/he is, of course, feminine in the immediate grammar of the sentence; cf. f. LIIIᵛ.

16. Cotgrave: "*Par dessus . . . vpward*," sig. Mmm.vᵛ.

17. In the notes to his 1931 photographic reprint of Tory, *Champ Fleury*, Cohen glosses "*incontinent* = après (localement); *joignant après soy* = accolé" (notes, p. 35). On Cohen's limita-
tions, see Bowen, "Major Sources."

18. As glossed by Goldberg and discussed below, the early modern term *sodometry* could
mean both structures and positions of sodomy *and* a "false argument . . . a denial of those socially constructed hierarchies that are taken to be natural"; *Sodometries*, 122.

19. Goldberg, *Sodometries*, esp. 180–81; Patricia Parker, "Preposterous Reversals," esp. 435–36.

20. There are both anal and phallic valences to the English *tail*; see, e.g., the play on the
bavian/baboon's *tail/tool* in John Fletcher and William Shakespeare's *The Two Noble Kinsmen*,
Act 3, Scene 5.

21. In my transcriptions, r̄ and q̄ indicate r and q with macrons in the original. Tory's plac-
ing of a marked and unmarked q/Q next to each other suggests he may again be stressing visually Q's inability to appear alone except in abbreviations.

22. Tory's term is "lettres Attiques"; however, the title page of the volume glosses these as letters that one "dit autremēt Lettres Antiques, & vulgairement Lettres Romaines."

23. Conley, *Self-Made Map*, 81. See also Bowen, "Major Sources," 16–17, 24–25.

24. On bodily hierarchies in the period in relation to the anal, see chap. 3 in Gail Kern Paster, *The Body Embarrassed*.

25. The modern editor of *Champ Fleury* has difficulty with these alignments: "Que le Q représente le lieu à décharger le ventre, soit, mais Euterpe, c'est plus difficile à expliquer; de même aussi embarrassant est le cas de Thalie," i.e., because Thalie represents the penis, site of urination (notes, p. 18).

26. This is not to assume that French and English are utterly separate communities of discourse at this point in history, through translation, immigration, bilingualism, travel, book circulation, and so on—not to mention the French embedded in English, often through the paths of Anglo-Norman etymology. Indeed, one of my interests in this book is in keeping productively alive the possibility of reading the relative permeability of English in this period and its susceptibility to interaction with other languages. Terms like linguistic *borrowing* and *loan-words* hardly address the complexity of the historical situation (and when is a borrowed word ever given back?). What, in other words, are the borders of a language that is so polyglot in its vocabulary, history, and other features? Our ability to see this is undoubtedly hampered by our separation of languages into discrete "families" of language (and distinct university departments). On the family mode of language organization, see note 72 below.

For a history and analysis of cultural transmission between early modern French and English, see Juliet Fleming, "Dictionary English and the Female Tongue." For an important discussion of multilingual translation dictionaries, the European book trade, and cross-cultural language transmission along vectors of race and gender, see Susan E. Phillips, "Schoolmasters, Seduction, and Slavery: Polyglot Dictionaries in Pre-Modern England."

Champ Fleury had English readers: the British Library copy of the 1529 edition is twice inscribed by Thomas Knyvett ("Knyuett") on its title page in sixteenth-century secretary and italic hands; a later note indicates that it belonged to "the Knyvets Family at Ashwellthorpe in Norf." If that note is accurate, the book inscriber is likely Sir Thomas Knyvett (1539–1616?), not the more prominent Thomas, Baron Knyvett (1545/6–1622). A 1549 edition of *Champ Fleury*, also at the British Library, includes marginalia that translate French into English (f. 65ᵛ). *Champ Fleury* is referenced in the first extant English translation of Rabelais's works (1694).

27. Richard Huloet, ABCEDARIVM ANGLICOLATINVM, sig. Bb.i.

28. Iohn Higgins, *Hvloets Dictionarie, newelye corrected, amended, Set In Order And Enlarged*, sig. Ll.iijᵛ. The larger passage: "Q, A mute almost vnneadfull as is K, because yt C, maye supplie bothe their places, and semeth to serue none other purpose, than to ioyne the vowell V, that alwayes foloweth hym, with an other vowel in the same syllable (whiche otherwise can not be ioyned) and maketh a more oblique and grosser sounde. Q, is chaunged into C, as Loquor, locutus, &c."

29. John Baret, *An Alvearie Or Triple Dictionarie, in Englishe, Latin, and French*, sig. Xx.iiiiᵛ. This is an instance in which the alternation of the original blackletter (or "English letter") typeface with roman emphases may have conveyed some significance. The end of the entry reads "it appeareth that Q is no single letter, but compounded of K and V, which soundeth Q."

30. On an early modern "ideology of superfluous things [that] holds the status quo in place by locking identity into property, the subject into the object," see Margreta de Grazia, "The Ideology of Superfluous Things," 31.

31. Cotgrave's entry for the French word *empestrer*. On *pester*, see *OED* (*v.*¹); as a substantive meaning "obstruction; encumbrance," *pester* seems to be an opposite of *void*; a 1589 text de-

scribes a "very fayre entrance or passage . . . altogether voyde of any pester of yce" (qtd. in *OED, pester, n.,* 1).

32. See *OED* (*cross-row*) and Andrew W. Tuer, *History of the Hornbook,* 1:62–82. Expanding on Tuer, Eric Wilson notes that the cross at the beginning of the cross-row "was part and parcel of the articulation [of the alphabet] . . . at once acoustic and graphic" and analyzes the relation of the hornbook to the inculcation of religious ideology; Wilson, "London's ABCs," 2. Patricia Crain makes some related comments about the cross-row in chap. 1 in *The Story of A.*

33. 1 Corinthians 6:9, in *The Holy Bible . . . Newly Translated out of the Originall tongues* (1611), sig. Q4, as reproduced in A. W. Pollard, ed., *The Holy Bible: A Facsimile in a reduced size of the Authorized Version published in the year 1611.* The Geneva text reads: "ne[i]ther fornicatours, nor idolaters, nor adulterers, nor wãtons, nor bouggerers"; *The Bible And Holy Scriptvres* (1560), 78ᵛ (NT), sig. VV.iiᵛ, as reproduced in Lloyd E. Berry, ed., *The Geneva Bible: A Facsimile of the 1560 Edition.*

34. *An answer vnto Sir Thomas Mores dialoge made by VVillyam Tindale* (1531), f. xcviij. I have modernized the original for legibility: "abuse mēs wiues and sofereth sodomitrie."

35. Benjamin Jonson, "Of the Consonants," in *The English Grammar,* in *The Workes of Benjamin Jonson. The second Volume,* 47.

36. On slippages between "natural" and grammatical gender (including the epicene), see Elizabeth Pittenger, "Dispatch Quickly."

37. "The Translators to the Reader," in *The Holy Bible* (1611), sig. A6ᵛ.

38. In the *OED, enfranchise, v.* (6) gives the sense of naturalized (like an alien).

39. Alexander Hume, *Of the Orthographie and Congruitie of the Britan Tongue,* 13. Subsequent references appear parenthetically; I have silently retained the editor's expansion of manuscript abbreviations.

40. *OED, speer, v.*¹

41. This phrase probably means "clear me space in the contentious discussion to say my syllogism."

42. The modernization/translation that follows is mine, with additions in brackets.

43. See note 41.

44. On the conjunction of shame and bodily confusion, see Paster, *Body Embarrassed.*

45. Hume, dedication ("*To the maest ecellent in all princelie wisdom, learning, and heroical artes, JAMES . . .* "), 2. On the relation of *foundation* and *fundament,* see Chapter 6.

46. E.g., Goldberg, *Sodometries*; David M. Halperin, *One Hundred Years of Homosexuality and Other Essays on Greek Love.* On *tribade,* see Stephen Orgel, "Gendering the Crown," 161; Valerie Traub, "The Psychomorphology of the Clitoris"; DiGangi, "Fulfulling Venus," chap. 2 in *Sexual Types.* For the early modern Italian verb "to sodomize," used for the insertive position in anal sex but also the receptive position in fellatio (i.e., cutting across our current default definitions of active/passive), see Michael Rocke, *Forbidden Friendships,* 92–93.

47. The book is thus indebted to the model of Raymond Williams, *Keywords: A Vocabulary of Culture and Society,* as well as William Empson, *The Structure of Complex Words,* and the brilliant analysis of early modern "verbal networks" in Patricia Parker, *Shakespeare from the Margins.* Though aspects of our approaches differ, *Queer Philologies* shares many of the methodological concerns and goals articulated in the introduction to a "critical semantics" in Roland Greene's *Five Words,* 1–40.

48. The question of premodern sexual identities—the nonexistence of which was an article of faith in much of the work that initially followed upon Michel Foucault's *History of Sexuality* (vol. 1)—has reemerged as a matter of contention and reexamination. See especially Halperin, "Forgetting Foucault," in *How to Do the History of Homosexuality,* 24–47; Jonathan Goldberg and Madhavi Menon, "Queering History"; Carla Freccero, *Queer/Early/Modern*; DiGangi, *Sex-*

ual Types. See also the discussion of alterity and continuity in sexuality studies below, and Valerie Traub, "The New Unhistoricism in Queer Studies."

49. Stephen G. Nichols, "Introduction: Philology in a Manuscript Culture," in *The New Philology*, 1. For a detailed example of the intersection of philology and the history of sexuality, see Martin G. Eisner and Marc D. Schachter, "*Libido Sciendi*: Apuleius, Boccaccio, and the Study of the History of Sexuality." Much discussion of a "new" philology has taken place within medieval studies; in addition to the other essays in *The New Philology*, see Anne Middleton, "Medieval Studies"; Louise O. Fradenburg and Carla Freccero, "Introduction: The Pleasures of History"; Louise O. Fradenburg and Carla Freccero, "Caxton, Foucault, and the Pleasures of History." For a brief discussion of the relation of "theory" and "philology," see Christopher Cannon, *The Making of Chaucer's English*, 1–6. On the rise and critiques of "new philology" in medieval studies, see Jan M. Ziolkowski, "Metaphilology."

50. On the rhetoric of castigation and its relation to chastity and rape/violation, see Stephanie H. Jed, *Chaste Thinking*.

51. See *OED*, guess, get.

52. Erich Auerbach, *Introduction Aux Études de Philologie Romane*, 9; Seth Lerer, *Error and the Academic Self*, 221.

53. Lerer, *Error*, 5; Gregory Nagy, "Death of a Schoolboy: The Early Greek Beginnings of a Crisis in Philology," 37–47.

54. Ferdinand de Saussure, *Course in General Linguistics*, 5, 3.

55. Hans Aarsleff, *The Study of Language in England, 1780–1860*; Anthony Grafton, *The Culture of Correction in Renaissance Europe*; Anthony Grafton, *Worlds Made by Words*; Anthony Grafton, *Defenders of the Text*; Geoffrey Galt Harpham, "Roots, Races, and the Return to Philology"; Jed, *Chaste Thinking*; Lerer, *Error*. Grafton in particular credits the development of textual-analytical techniques associated with later Germanic philology to Renaissance humanists (*Defenders*, 4, passim).

56. René Wellek and Austin Warren, *Theory of Literature*, 29.

57. Roberta Frank, "The Unbearable Lightness of Being a Philologist," 488; Aarsleff, *Study*, 4 and passim.

58. Aarsleff, *Study*, 6.

59. In *Introduction Aux Études de Philologie Romane*, Auerbach's chief divisions for philology's "different forms" are critical editing of texts, linguistics, literary research, and explication of texts (7, my translation).

60. Freccero, "Practicing," 120.

61. Dedication and "To the great Variety of Readers," in *Mr. VVilliam Shakespeares Comedies, Histories, & Tragedies*, sigs. A2ᵛ–A3. See Margreta de Grazia's reading of lineal rhetoric in the volume in "The 1623 Folio and the Modern Standard Edition," chap. 1 in *Shakespeare Verbatim*.

62. Aarsleff, *Study*, 152.

63. James Ingram, *An Inaugural Lecture on the Utility of Anglo-Saxon Literature*; see Aarsleff, *Study*, 172.

64. Franz Bopp, "Analytical Comparison of the Sanskrit, Greek, Latin, and Teutonic Languages, Shewing the Original Identity of their Grammatical Structure," 20–21.

65. Lerer, *Error*, 6–7.

66. Raymond Williams, *Marxism and Literature*, 25–26.

67. Lerer, *Error*, 140.

68. Ibid., 6 (my emphasis).

69. Saussure, *Course*, 192. Wade Baskin adds a translator's note to mark (and distance) the multiple meanings in the term that Saussure employs repeatedly for communication across languages: "In his lectures Saussure used the English word *intercourse* [Tr.]" (205n6).

70. Jed, *Chaste Thinking*, 8, 8n7.

71. Contrast the method described in Hans Ulrich Gumbrecht, *The Powers of Philology*: "in different ways, all philological practices generate desires for presence" (6). For a skeptical review of Gumbrecht's pronouncements on philology, see Ziolkowski, "Metaphilology." Gumbrecht apparently confuses sexuality and gender in his account of the "gender component of [Lorca's] identity" in relation to editorial practice (39–40).

72. For a brief summary of the "tree model" versus the "wave model" of mapping language "families," see R. L. Trask, *Historical Linguistics*, 181–87. Though not from a perspective of queerness or a critique of heteronormativity, Harpham discusses the importance of language families in traditional philology, particularly insofar as "family" became interchangeable with notions of race and nation and entangled in the myth of Aryan distinction and superiority ("Roots, Races," 43–49). Synchronic, translinguistic crossings are but one aspect of language transmission and history occluded by the family model of language; on early modern French and English, see note 26 above.

73. Nichols, "Introduction," 1.

74. Jonathan Culler, "Anti-Foundational Philology," 52. See also Stephen Owen, "Philology's Discontents."

75. Frank, "Unbearable Lightness," 488; Lerer, *Error*, 230. On "material for an immanent critique" "[i]n the very bowels of classical philology," see Sean Alexander Gurd, *Iphigenia at Aulis: Textual Multiplicity, Radical Philology*, 4–5.

76. "[I]l veut préserver des ravages du temps les oeuvres qui constituent son patrimoine spirituel" (Auerbach, *Introduction*, 9).

77. Harpham, "Roots, Races," 43–49, and note 73 above; Lerer, *Error*, 147 (emphasis in the original). See also Edward Said's discussion of Islamic philological tradition, *Humanism and Democratic Criticism*, 58.

78. Work on the Q volume of the *OED* was begun around 1901, about 150 years after Johnson; see John Willinsky, *Empire of Words: The Reign of the OED*, 49. Throughout this book, I take note of moments when the *OED* edits or prophylactically comments upon its evidence. For an astonishing example, see Peter Stallybrass, "Shakespeare, the Individual, and the Text."

79. "Les haulteur en toutes & par toutes [les lettres], *excepte le Q*, veult tousiours estre egalle entre deux lignes equidistantes côtenans entre elles en espace dix corps. . . . Encore icelle lettre Q. a sa teste de dix corps commes les autres lettres, & sa queue de quatre corps qui sôt oultre les susdit dix corps *hors & dessoubz* les dit tes deux lignes equidistantes" (Tory, *Champ Fleury*, f. XXIIII, my emphasis).

80. Hume, *Orthographie*, dedication, 2. The word does not appear in the *OED*.

81. Ibid., editor's errata sheet inserted after 3.

82. P. G. W. Glare, ed., *Oxford Latin Dictionary*, 1698.

83. Because it never caught on, *skaiography* would be known as a neologism, an "artificial," coined (as opposed to a "naturally" occurring) word. It is thus a piece of language that appears initially to be "outside" language. As once was *orthography*: see Chapter 1.

84. This point is indebted to Jonathan Goldberg, *Writing Matter: From the Hands of the English Renaissance*, 194–95, 208–22, a book that first directed me to the potential perversity of letters. Following Goldberg, Wilson also emphasizes the historical contingency of the alphabet: "Elizabethan alphabets are not only constituted by an alternative set of graphic figures, but collected in a range of distinctive visual formats" ("London's ABC's," 1). Some period hornbooks in blackletter-type print both forms of lowercase r and s: how does one pronounce this alphabet? (See Figure 7 in this book, as well as the facsimile hornbook 2, in Tuer, *Hornbook*, vol. 1.) The word *alphabet* is first recorded in English in the late fifteenth and early sixteenth century (*OED*, alphabet, n.).

85. Thomas Morley, *A Plaine And Easie Introdvction To Practicall Musicke*, 36. See Tuer, *Hornbook*, 1:31. On *tittle/title*, see *OED*, *tittle, n.*

86. This is not to say that Q is the only pestering letter; Baret writes of C: "This letter troubleth me woorst of all, & maketh me most to woonder howe it got this third place of honour, or howe it hath so absurdly thus long vsurped that dignitie" (sig. L.iii, in blackletter type). See Goldberg, *Writing Matter*, 194. The letter W (and its relation to U/V) is a whole 'nother early modern story; see the following note.

87. For example, Huloet's *ABECEDARIVM* intercollates its dictionary entries for not only all V and U words, but also W words—so that words beginning "Wa-" directly follow those beginning "Va-," and are followed by words beginning "Vd-," [i.e., "ud-"], and so on—*even though* the book announces that "there is a diuersitie betwene the single V. and the dowble W" (n.p.). Wilson notes that the modern American alphabet song produces the sense for some students that there is a letter named *elemenopee*.

88. For a recent discussion of queer etymology reacting to this work, though more invested in distinguishing between "false or folk etymologies and correct ones," see Paula Blank, "The Proverbial 'Lesbian': Queering Etymology in Contemporary Critical Practice," esp. 117–18. On the emergence of more "empirical" and "scientific" etymologies in reaction to the connections made by Horne Tooke and others, see Aarsleff, *Study*, chaps. 2–4.

89. See Empson's chap. 21, "Dictionaries," in *Structure of Complex Words* (391–413), for an analysis of the *N.E.D* (*OED*) division of words into distinct senses.

90. Grafton, *Defenders*.

91. Lee Edelman, *Homographesis*, 4. Subsequent references appear parenthetically.

92. "[P]*eccatum illud horribile, inter christianos non nominandum*" Blackstone, qtd. in Edelman *Homographesis*, 5.

93. Clearly the notion of the *homograph* must work differently, in a period prior to lexical standardization: in a culture of nonstandardized orthography, where many words have overlapping spellings, is the *homograph* everywhere, or nowhere—nonlegible?

94. Philology's ability to unsettle was closely linked to literary theory by Paul de Man, in a brief essay whose influence may account for whatever renewed cachet philology has enjoyed in the last several decades of literary study; see "The Return to Philology," in de Man, *The Resistance to Theory*. Said's conception of a philology that attends to political resistance seems at points less revolutionary and oppositional than he seems to have intended, particularly in its devotion to the presumption of authorial meaning; see "The Return to Philology," chap. 3 in Said, *Humanism and Democratic Criticism*, 57–83.

95. Joseph Moxon, *Mechanick Exercises: Or, the Doctrine of handy-works. Applied to the Art of Printing*, 182 (emphasis in the original). Moxon calls Q (in italic type) a "Swash-Letter": "Yet Swash-Letters, especially *Q*, whose Swashes come below the Foot-Line, and whose Length reaches under the Foot-Line of the next Letter, or Letters in Composing, ought to have the Upper shoulder of that Swash Sculped down straight. . . . Because the Upper Shoulder of the Swash would else be so broad, that it would ride upon the Face of the next letter" (118). On anthropomorphic and reproductive rhetoric in Moxon, see Margreta de Grazia, "Imprints: Descartes, Shakespeare, Gutenberg," and Lisa Maruca, "Bodies of Type." For a reading of the mechanized body in Moxon, see Chapter 1.

96. Benjamin Kahan (private correspondence) points out that the "monogamy" of Q/q differs depending on the use of upper and lower case in early modern printing: QV, Qu, qu, but not qv.

97. *The Life of Henry the Fift*, in *Mr. VVilliam Shakespeares Comedies, Histories, & Tragedies*, TLN 1573.

98. *The Cronicle History of Henry the fift* (1600), sig. D2.

99. Iohn Minsheu, *The Guide into the Tongues* (1625), 591.

100. Charls [*sic*] Butler, *The English Grammar, Or The Institution of Letters, Syllables, and Words, in the English tongue*, sig. c1ᵛ. I have silently translated Butler's reformed spelling into something more closely resembling early modern conventions.

101. There is a slight possibility of another submerged anal meaning in the passage; the 1653 Thomas Urquhart translation of Rabelais in English glosses a "montjoy" as a "heap of ordure and filth" (Francis Rabelais, *The Urquhart-Le Motteux Translation of the Works of Francis Rabelais*,1:429), which may resonate with one of Cotgrave's meanings: "barrow; a little hill, or heape of stones, layed . . . in remembrance of some notable act performed, or accident befallen, in that place" (sig. Hhh.iijᵛ).

102. *Henry the Fift*, TLN 1589–90 (my emphases).

103. The story of Q, as Alexandra Owen (private conversation) has pointed out to me and as the Scottish incident quoted earlier from Hume suggests, is often a story especially marked by nationalism. In Shakespeare's *2 Henry VI*, Jack Cade, for example, glosses "the Dauphin of France" as "Mounsieur Basimecu" (Sir Kiss-my-ass) (4.7.24).

104. *The Merry Wiues of Windsor*, in *Mr. VVilliam Shakespeares Comedies, Histories, & Tragedies*, TLN 1381–82.

105. *Much adoe about Nothing*, in *Mr. VVilliam Shakespeares Comedies, Histories, & Tragedies*, TLN 704.

106. *Midsommer Nights Dreame*, in *Mr. VVilliam Shakespeares Comedies, Histories, & Tragedies*, TLN 912–14.

107. Ibid., TLN 1728–29.

108. Ibid., TLN 1986–87.

109. John Fletcher and William Shakspeare, Gent., *The Two Noble Kinsmen*, sig. G3.

110. Minsheu, *Ductor in Linguas*, 112.

111. *The Life of Henry the Fift*, TLN 1367–74.

112. On the fraught boundary between "hieroglyphs" and alphabetic "writing" in Western culture and its accounts of non-Western inscription since the Renaissance, see Byron Ellsworth Hamann, "How Maya Hieroglyphs Got Their Name." On hieroglyphs and Renaissance humanism, see Brian A. Curran, *The Egyptian Renaissance*. While Hamann makes clear the political stakes in constructing non-European inscription against/below alphabetic writing, my point is to raise the possibility that a notion of the hieroglyph—the character as idea or thing—may exist within European alphabets, in a way that then largely disappears except in satire (see Gulliver's visit to the academy in Lagado).

113. *Loues Labour's lost*, TLN 1784–86.

114. Parker, *Shakespeare from the Margins*, 30.

115. William Hornbye, *Hornbyes Hornbook*. Subsequent references appear parenthetically.

116. Elizabeth Pittenger, "'To Serve the Queere': Nicholas Udall, Master of Revels"; Alan Stewart, "'Traitors to Boyes Buttockes': The Erotics of Humanist Education," chap. 3 in Alan Stewart, *Close Readers*, 84–121; Wendy Wall, "'Household Stuff': The Sexual Politics of Domesticity and the Advent of English Comedy."

117. The young gentlemen are Sir Robert Carr, Baronet, described "Though in the Teenes you scarce haue enterd yet" (sig. A4); Sir Thomas Grantham, Esquire, "Sonne and Heire to Sir Thomas Grantham, Knight," described as "a Lilly" placed "Betwixt two Roses" (A5); and Mr. Rochester Carre, a "Copartner, for to patronize / This little Orphant of my braines conceite" (A6).

118. Hornbye also translates his name into Latin as "*Cornu-apes*" as a signature to the poem "To the Reader" (sig. A8).

119. Roger Ascham, "*A Præface to the Reader*," in *The Scholemaster Or plaine and perfite way of teachyng children* (1570), sig. B.ii.

120. Stewart, "'Traitors to Boyes Buttockes'"; see the further discussion in my review of Stewart, *Close Readers* and in Alan Stewart, "Boys' Buttocks Revisited."

121. I am grateful to Bonnie Honig for the conversation that led to this paragraph.

122. Eve Kosofsky Sedgwick, "Introduction: Axiomatic," in *Epistemology of the Closet*, esp. 47–48. On heterosexuality, see Chapters 8–9, and Rebecca Ann Bach, *Shakespeare and Renaissance Literature Before Heterosexuality*.

123. Vin Nardizzi, Stephen Guy-Bray, and Will Stockton, eds., chap. 1 (introduction), in *Queer Renaissance Historiography: Backward Gaze*, 1. See also Madhavi Menon's assertion of "the impossibility of using historicism for studying either the past or desire" (*Unhistorical Shakespeare*, 6). For Will Stockton's reevaluation of the earlier position, see "Shakespeare and Queer Theory."

124. On "unhistoricism," see Goldberg and Menon, "Queering History," and Menon, *Unhistorical Shakespeare*, 3–4, 16–18; on "compulsory heterotemporality," see Goldberg and Menon, "Queering History," 1616, and Menon, *Unhistorical Shakespeare*, 2. For a critique of "the concepts of homo and hetero as linchpins to suture together diverse phenomena," see Traub, "New Unhistoricism," esp. 30–31.

125. See also Traub, "New Unhistoricism," 31.

126. Jonathan Goldberg, ed., *Queering the Renaissance*. Mario DiGangi, "Queer Theory, Historicism, and Early Modern Sexualities," suggests additional alternatives (142n12).

127. Sedgwick, *Epistemology*, 47; B. Smith, *Homosexual Desire*, 20; Halperin, "How to Do the History of Male Homosexuality," 90; Valerie Traub, "The Present Future of Lesbian Historiography," 126; Traub, *Renaissance of Lesbianism*; Goldberg and Menon, "Queering History," 1609; DiGangi, *Sexual Types*, 1–13.

128. Michel Foucault, *Histoire de la sexualité, Volume 1: La volonté de savoir*, 134; *confus(e)*, *confondre*, *Le Grand Robert de la langue française* (online); *OED*, *confuse, v.*; *confound, v.*

129. Goldberg and Menon, "Queering History," 1610.

130. Goldberg, *Sodometries*, 31 (my emphasis). See also Chapter 1's discussion of the expansive limitedness indicated by Bourdieu's term *habitus*.

131. For a criticism of the citation of dates of literary publication as central to (some varieties of) historicism, see Christopher Lane, "The Poverty of Context," 452–53, and Menon, *Unhistorical Shakespeare*, 12–13. For historical reasons (the ways in which the *OED* gathered its original evidence) as well as theoretical ones (At what point does a word, or a new meaning of an old word, become "coined" or exist? How or in what cases does time lag between oral usage and a word's emergence in written evidence that is citable by the *OED*?), it is my assumption throughout this book that dates of forms and first appearances in *OED* entries and citations must be understood to be approximate ranges, with the distinct possibility that similar or related usages may subsequently be found in earlier texts.

132. Elizabeth Freeman, *Time Binds*, xxii (my emphasis). Cf. Freccero's account of Derridean spectrality and haunting as historical practice in *Queer/Early/Modern*, 8, and chap. 5.

133. Freeman, *Time Binds*, xxi. On asynchrony and queer temporalities, see also Carolyn Dinshaw, *How Soon Is Now?*, 5–6, 33–34. On etymology, see Blank, "Proverbial 'Lesbian'" (discussing an earlier version of this book's Chapter 2). As the above discussion suggests, historiographical writing about the past(s) and theoretically enabled queerings of the present will not function antithetically in this analysis: it is worth noting that Edelman's *Homographesis*, Goldberg's *Sodometries* and *Writing Matter*, and Sedgwick's *Epistemology of the Closet*—influential models for this study and each in its own way advocating the suffusion of synchronic language with destabilizing pluralities of meaning—all set their deconstructively enlivened, elaborative meaning-making within particular historical contexts. From another direction, Traub's archivally rich readings of early modern "lesbian" figures and body parts like the tribade's clitoris

eventuate in an equally theory-rich unfixing of the presumed modern relation between body part, "embodied desire," and "erotic identity" (*Renaissance of Lesbianism*, 225–28).

134. Frank, "Unbearable Lightness," 491.

135. Roland Barthes, "Michelet, Today," in *The Rustle of Language*, 204–5 (initial emphasis added).

136. Friedrich Nietzsche, *Daybreak: Thoughts on the Prejudices of Morality*, 5.

137. For an account of Nietzsche that reintegrates the philologist and the philosopher, see James I. Porter, *Nietzsche and the Philology of the Future*. De Man emphasizes Nietzsche the philologist in his discussion of the emergence of theory in literary studies through philology ("Return to Philology," 24). Nietzsche's identification with philology is famously also countered in his often lacerating comments on classical philology in *Wir Philologen* with its outline of a new/reformed philology; see William Arrowsmith, trans., "Nietzsche: Notes for 'We Philologists,'" and Lerer, *Error*, 13.

CHAPTER 1. SPELLING SHAKESPEARE

1. Alice Walker, *Textual Problems of the First Folio*, 164 (my emphasis).

2. James Gleick, "Crasswords," 20 (emphasis in the original).

3. Charlton Hinman, "Principles Governing the Use of Variant Spellings as Evidence of Alternate Setting by Two Compositors," 79 (my emphasis). Subsequent references appear parenthetically.

4. I borrow the term from Pierre Bourdieu, while noting that (in a way discussed further below) his usage refers to a poststandardization linguistic situation; see "The Production and Reproduction of Legitimate Language." Compare to English the earlier, more prescriptive, and more centrally institutionalized relation to the lexical standardization in France, for example, with the formation of the Academie Française in 1634–35. Geofroy Tory (see the Introduction) is often attributed a central role in the movement of early modern French toward standardized spelling.

5. *OED*, *spell*, *v.*^{2} As a verb, *spell* entered English in a highly generalized way, meaning "[t]o discourse or preach; to talk, converse, or speak" (current to about 1450) and (transitively) "[t]o utter, declare, relate, tell" (current to about 1509); see *spell*, *v.*^{1} The dating in *OED* must often be regarded as providing an approximate range.

6. *OED*, *spell*, *v.*^{2}, 2.a.–2.c.

7. Kenelm Digby, *Two Treatises*, 172.

8. *Mr. VVilliam Shakespeares Comedies, Histories, & Tragedies*, as reproduced in Charlton Hinman, ed., *The Norton Facsimile: The First Folio of Shakespeare*, sig. A3.

9. An exception to my general description here is the manuscript of the *Ormulum* (c. 1180); though its readership and influence were minimal, the manuscript demonstrates that the idea of regularized orthography, understood as producing spellings, is at least locally thinkable in English much earlier than the period under discussion here, at least within (and in the service of) a particular theological context and practice; see Christopher Cannon, "Spelling Practice."

10. See also the illustrative quotations that the *OED* provides for *spell*, *v.*^{2}, 6.a.–b., which *OED* positions on the border of "[t]o form words . . ." and "[t]o read off. . . ." On *spell* in Middle English, see Cannon, "Spelling Practice," 230–31.

11. De Grazia, "Homonyms Before and After Lexical Standardization." See also Peter Stallybrass, "Shakespeare, the Individual, and the Text."

12. Juliet Fleming, "Dictionary English and the Female Tongue," 301–2.

13. The idea of an English grammar on the classical model is also (only) emergent in this period; see, for example, Jonson's attempt at an English grammar, in which orthography is extra-grammatical: "*Prosodie*, and *Orthography*, are not parts of *Grammar*, but diffus'd, like the blood, and spirits through the whole"; *The English Grammar*, 35. On the vernacularization of classical rhetoric in English, see Jenny C. Mann, *Outlaw Rhetoric*.

14. De Grazia, "Homonyms," 152–53; see also de Grazia, "Shakespeare and the Craft of Language." On dictionaries, see Fleming, "Dictionary English."

15. Thomas Clayton, *The "Shakespearean" Addition in the Booke of Sir Thomas Moore*, 39.

16. W. W. Greg, ed., *The Book of Sir Thomas More*, 75 (line 168).

17. Philip Gaskell, *A New Introduction to Bibliography*, 359n37.

18. The scholarship disputing the identities of the *Sir Thomas More* manuscript (especially the Hand D pages) is extensive. For some skeptical reviews of the evidence for Shakespeare's participation, the relation between spelling and individual playwrights, and the manuscript's larger role in Shakespeare editorial theory and practice, see Scott McMillin, "Hand D," chap. 7 in *The Elizabethan Theatre and "The Book of Sir Thomas More"*; Paul Werstine, "Shakespeare, *More* or Less"; Jeffrey Masten, "*More* or Less"; and Paul Werstine, "Close Contrivers."

19. Thomas Smith, *De recta & emendata Lingvæ Anglicæ Scriptione, Dialogus . . .* , in a Latin facsimile with an English translation, in *Sir Thomas Smith: Literary and Linguistic Works*; John Hart, *An orthographie, conteyning the due order howe to write thimage of mannes voice*; William Bullokar, *Bullokars Booke at large, for the Amendment of Orthographie for English speech*.

20. Jonathan Goldberg, *Writing Matter*, 192–93, 196–97, 205–6.

21. Henry George Liddell and Robert Scott, et al., comps., *A Greek-English Lexicon*, 1248–49. On the ideological (in this case, theological) force behind "right writing" in the earlier case of the *Ormulum*, see Cannon, "Spelling Practice," 235.

22. Alexander Hume, "To the maest ecellent in all princelie wisdom, learning, and heroical artes, JAMES . . . ," dedication in *Of the Orthographie and Congruitie of the Britan Tongue*, 2.

23. Hume, *Orthographie*, editor's errata sheet inserted after 3.

24. P. G. W. Glare, ed., *Oxford Latin Dictionary*, 1698.

25. "Yes yes," the Page (Moth) says about him, "he teaches boyes the Horne-booke: / What is A b speld backward with the horn on his head?" (*Loues Labour's lost*, in *Mr. VVilliam Shakespeares Comedies, Histories, & Tragedies*, TLN 1785–86). My reading of this passage as sodomitical and cuckolding follows Patricia Parker's "Preposterous Reversals," 461–65. On the relation of hornbooks and pedagogical beating, see the Introduction.

26. Phil. Massinger, Tho. Middleton, and William Rowley, *The Old Law*, 29. The play may also be referring to *An English Expositor*, a hard-word list by Bullokar's son John. On the play's date and writers, see Gary Taylor and John Lavagnino, gen. eds., *Thomas Middleton: The Collected Works* and *Thomas Middleton and Early Modern Textual Culture: A Companion to the Collected Works*.

27. *Much Adoe about Nothing*, in *Mr. VVilliam Shakespeares Comedies, Histories, & Tragedies*, TLN 851–55. Actually, the folio text reads "turu'd ortho-graphy," and I have myself "righted" the writing here, effacing what is possibly a compositor error (the turning of the letter n) or a compositor's joke (to turn a letter in *turn*, especially when it is followed immediately by *orthography* seems particularly overdetermined). As I hint above, the word *turn* turns up with some regularity in discussions of orthography; Benedick's "conuerted" is itself an etymological relative of *turn*.

28. Cf. *Much Adoe*: "I neuer yet saw man, / How wise, how noble, yong, how rarely featur'd. / But she would *spell him backward* . . . / So *turnes* she euery man the wrong side out . . ." (TLN 1149–58, my emphasis).

29. On French lessons, see Juliet Fleming, "The French Garden." On sex/gender and scenes of early modern (Latin) pedagogy, see Elizabeth Pittenger, "Dispatch Quickly," and "'To Serve the Queere'"; Alan Stewart, "'Traitors to Boyes Buttockes,'" chap. 3 in *Close Readers*, 84–121.

30. Goldberg notes that a number of pedagogical writers resist sixteenth-century spelling reform (e.g., Richard Mulcaster [*Writing Matter*, 195–97]). Shakespeare is perhaps among the resistant—though, by citing plays mentioned above as early examples of *spell* in the modern sense, the *OED* implies that he invents or is at least co-incident with the emergence of modern spelling.

31. Read a few lines of Bullokar's orthography and you may well find it strange and fantastical; the "foreignness" effect might have been redoubled for an early modern reader, because not only the peculiar forms of words, but also the fact that the words *have* set forms, might have signaled its foreignness, its likeness to Latin and Greek.

32. In his description of English, William Camden may register an exception to this statement, though it is not clear that he does so for reasons other than demonstrating the superiority of English to Welsh. While contending that many English write alike, he also admits that "[t]his variety of pronuntiation [in English] hath brought in some diversitie of Orthographie"; *Remaines of a Greater Worke*, 23–24.

33. Richard Mvlcaster, *The First Part of the Elementarie*, 100.

34. Goldberg, *Writing Matter*, chap. 4, passim.

35. Bullokar, *Bullokars Booke at large*, sig. B1 (my emphasis).

36. Stallybrass, "Shakespeare, the Individual, and the Text."

37. *The Autobiography of Thomas Whythorne*, lvii, lxvi. For a reading of Whythorne's text, including a different account of his "eccentric" spelling, see Meredith Skura, *Tudor Autobiography*, 98–125, esp. 112, 115, 260n8. For Bullokar and others, the production of orthographical consent/consensus is linked to forms of political organization; his is a nationalist project (as his prefatory address "Bullokar to his Countrie" suggests), and he says his reform of consenting sound and writing is for the benefit of rich and poor within a nation containing "[i]n one houshold (of diuers sorts) ech one in his degrée" (sig. C2). Further, "The welth and strength of our country, is chéefly maintained by good letters" (40). Likewise, Spenser, in a question quoted repeatedly and with apparent approval in Richard Helgerson's book on the rise of a national culture in late sixteenth-century England, asks, "Why a God's name may not we, as else the Greeks, have the kingdom of our own language?" (qtd. in *Forms of Nationhood*, 1). The rhetoric of nationalism and right-ness that inheres in the debate between a phonetic spelling practice and "our customarie writing" is not incidental to the larger concerns of this chapter. This debate may suggest that spelling practice itself (on whichever side of the debate) adheres with a model of period subjectivity articulated by Francis Barker and others as the location of the early modern subject within the larger spectacle of royal power (*The Tremulous Private Body*, 14–41). Or, adjusting the model here, within the larger system of either a phonetic orthography *or* "our customarie writing"—the kingdom, either way, of "our own language." Within the larger frame of subjection to *either* model of linguistic practice, there is no attention to the questions that loom large for a modern spelling investigator like Hinman: individualized spelling practices, spelling choice, and preference.

38. Bullokar, *Bullokars Booke at large*, sig. D1.

39. Elizabeth Eisenstein, *The Printing Press as an Agent of Change*, 1:117.

40. D. G. Scragg, *A History of English Spelling*, 71.

41. Alfred W. Pollard, "Elizabethan Spelling as a Literary and Bibliographical Clue," 6 (my emphasis).

42. Randall McLeod has also shown that spellings are made to vary to avoid the breakage of certain kinds of types; see "Spell-bound."

43. Richard Hodges, *A Special Help to Orthographie*, title page.

44. Ibid., 1.

45. *The Tragedie of Hamlet*, in *Mr. VVilliam Shakespeares Comedies, Histories, & Tragedies*, TLN 4–7.

46. Charlton Hinman, *The Printing and Proofreading of the First Folio of Shakespeare*, 1:183. Citations will appear parenthetically (*PPFFS*).

47. At the end of his project, Hinman tries to assign actual persons' names to compositors; see below.

48. D. F. McKenzie, "Stretching a Point." There have been several important critiques of compositor analysis. McKenzie's earlier work has shown with devastating logic that Hinman's work is based on erroneous assumptions about attitudes toward labor and efficiency in the printing house ("Printers of the Mind"). Peter W. M. Blayney has demonstrated that the analysis of the production of any one book requires the analysis not only of other books produced contemporaneously in the printer's shop but also of *all* books produced by other shops with which the particular printer may have shared work (*The Texts of King Lear and Their Origins*). The importance of these critiques of bibliographic assumptions and the logic of bibliographic methods lies in revising our notions of printing-house "efficiency," the fallacy of systematic/normal procedures, and, as de Grazia has shown, our notion of jobs, labor, and wages in the preindustrial workshop ("Soliloquies and Wages"). Though enabled by and largely congruent with this work, this chapter attempts a different kind of critique.

49. Or to be more faithful to the metaphors of the field: "to recover from behind the veil of compositor's spellings . . . a clearer impression of the manuscript, or other [printer's] copy, with a view to elucidating textual problems." Alice Walker, "Compositor Determination and Other Problems in Shakespearian Texts," 9. Subsequent references appear parenthetically. Erich Auerbach cites the editorial establishment of authentic texts as one of the key forms of philological practice; see *Introduction aux Etudes de Philologie Romane*; for the historical beginnings of this link in the Renaissance, see Anthony Grafton, *Defenders of the Text*.

50. Alice Walker, "The Folio Text of *1 Henry IV*," 53.

51. Gary Taylor, "The Shrinking Compositor A of the Shakespeare First Folio," 112.

52. See, for example, Harold Jenkins, ed., *Hamlet*, 54.

53. Gaskell, *New Introduction*, 348.

54. In a way to which I will return, I am alluding to a well-known sentence in Michel Foucault, *The History of Sexuality, Volume I*, 43.

55. Fredson Bowers, *Bibliography and Textual Criticism*, 34.

56. T. H. Howard-Hill, "New Light on Compositor E of the Shakespeare First Folio," 178.

57. Andrew S. Cairncross, "Compositors E and F of the Shakespeare First Folio," 395–96.

58. In a reconsideration of Hinman's and Walker's work on Compositor B, Werstine confronts this problem: "perhaps an editor must conclude that compositor variability is so high, as Compositor B's is between the comedies and *1H4*, that compositor identification is a useless tool." "Compositor B of the Shakespeare First Folio," 260.

59. If variability can produce E's potential ubiquity, it may also produce, within this paradigm of individuation, the multiplication of discrete individuals. As Taylor puts it, "if C changed this habit between *King John* and *1 Henry IV*, then the later C might as well be another man" ("Shrinking," 110). This is a larger problematic for the methodology, for, if habits disclose individuals, what if the habit is only a phase? In the decades since Hinman set to work, the history of compositor study (with the possible exception of the treatment of Compositor E) has often favored reading the discovery of changed habits as evidence of new individuals, rather than variable old ones: where, in the beginning, there were only A and B, Hinman found C, D, and E. Howard-Hill discovered F, and Taylor more recently located H, I, and J. On this, see

Blayney, who notes that Hinman's method was originally introduced to differentiate only two (*not* "more than one") compositors (*Texts of King Lear*, 152). See also McKenzie's comments on the dangers of "division as a function of analysis" ("Stretching," 116–17). In the 1940–41 essay, Hinman emphasizes that spelling study must rely on variations, discard evidence of continuities among parts of texts (he labels this evidence "non-significant spellings"), and continue to search for more evidence that will support the discovery of difference.

60. Hill, "Spelling and the Bibliographer," 3.

61. Qtd. in Lee Edelman, "Tearooms and Sympathy," in *Homographesis*, 151.

62. Thomas Satchell, "The Spelling of the First Folio," 352; Ronald B. McKerrow, *An Introduction to Bibliography for Literary Students*; Edwin Eliott Willoughby, *The Printing of the First Folio of Shakespeare*.

63. G. Thomas Tanselle, "The Life and Work of Fredson Bowers," 32. Subsequent references appear parenthetically.

64. Hinman was Bowers's first doctoral student, completing his degree in 1941 (Tanselle, "Life and Work," 72).

65. The relation of cryptanalysis, espionage, and literary studies is productively explored in Shawn James Rosenheim, *The Cryptographic Imagination*, and in forthcoming work on modern and early modern intelligence by William H. Sherman.

66. David K. Johnson, *The Lavender Scare*, 9. Since the original publication of this chapter, Johnson's book has amply documented the extraordinary extent of the antigay investigations, resignations, and dismissals in the federal government and their effects, beginning in the late 1940s and continuing into the 1950s (and beyond). Subsequent references to this important study appear parenthetically.

67. *Employment of Homosexuals and Other Sex Perverts in Government*. Subsequent references appear parenthetically. On the report's widespread effects, see Johnson, *Lavender Scare*, 115–16.

68. On the effects of the publication of the Kinsey report, see Johnson, *Lavender Scare*, 53–54.

69. For a detailed discussion of events that led to the investigation, see ibid., chaps. 1, 3, 4; on the report, see chap. 5. The Austrian example is debunked by Johnson (108–9).

70. John D'Emilio, *Sexual Politics, Sexual Communities*, 43; subsequent references appear parenthetically. On the perceived overlap between signs of communism and homosexuality, see Johnson, *Lavender Scare*, 37.

71. Edelman, "Tearooms and Sympathy."

72. If the virulence of this surveillance did not directly derive from the military's similar surveying of the sexual practices and identities of troops and recruits during the Second World War, the discourse would nevertheless have been familiar to those in the armed services. See Allan Bérubé, *Coming Out Under Fire*.

73. In general, see ibid., 149–74, esp. 152–53; see also *Employment of Homosexuals*, 12; Johnson, *Lavender Scare*, 73 and passim.

74. These sentences cite what were only the most *explicit* forms of surveillance. On the extension of techniques used by the federal government into other arenas, see also Johnson, *Lavender Scare*, 167–69. On universities, see Robert K. Martin's discussion of the investigation (1953–54) and dismissal (1960) of Newton Arvin at Smith College in "Newton Arvin: Literary Critic and Lewd Person"; Jay Grossman's contextualization of F. O. Matthiessen's death at Harvard in 1950, "The Canon in the Closet"; and Barry Werth, *The Scarlet Professor: Newton Arvin*. For additional readings of the links between communism and homosexuality, see David Savran, *Communists, Cowboys, and Queers*, esp. 1–9; and Marjorie Garber and Rebecca L. Walkowitz, eds., *Secret Agents*.

75. On the "as many as five thousand" persons who resigned or were dismissed from federal employment in the early Cold War period because they were under suspicion of being gay or lesbian, see Johnson, *Lavender Scare*, 166–67. This number includes more than four hundred between January 1947 and November 1950 and over eight hundred between May 1953 and June 1955 (166). For examples of the language of "tendencies," see Johnson, *Lavender Scare*, 16, 75, 107, 104.

76. Fredson Bowers, "Whitman's Manuscripts for the Original 'Calamus' Poems." Subsequent references appear parenthetically.

77. I do not mean to suggest that this hesitation I locate in Bowers's prose between acts/behaviors and identities is necessarily intended or foreseen by Bowers. As George Chauncey (*Gay New York*) and David Johnson show (*Lavender Scare*, 61–62), and, as the Kinsey report registered, the idea of a discrete "homosexual" identity on the predominant late twentieth-century model has not solidified even in the 1950s—though arguably the Lavender Scare is a major vehicle of its reification.

78. Walker, "Folio Text of 1 *Henry IV*," 58.

79. Stanley King, *Recollections of the Folger Shakespeare Library*. The 30,000 volumes were stored secretly at Amherst from January, 15, 1942, through November 11, 1944.

80. Charlton Hinman, "The Proof-Reading of the First Folio Text of *Romeo and Juliet*," 61n1. Hinman dates this footnote to April 1953, and the Korean War may have been the specific impetus for concern, though thus far I have been unable to ascertain when or where the books were moved. I am indebted to Elizabeth Walsh and her staff at the Folger Library for assistance in attempting to track the moving books.

81. On the citation of this essay, see note 84.

82. My argument follows the account published in the university newspaper; this account was reprinted almost verbatim in the Charlottesville and Richmond newspapers. I am grateful to Eric Wilson and Steve Wilson for assistance in locating these accounts.

83. See note 86.

84. Readers of this essay will here expect, but will not find, a note citing Bibliographer B's essay, but the perceived necessity of a citation for this text and of the newspaper account of Bibliographer B's death quoted above must be seen within a larger set of citational imperatives: the competing demands of intellectual property (Bibliographer B's), scholarly accountability (mine), and the closet (his?). I have chosen not to cite B's text because to do so would have the effect of disclosing a homosexuality that I do not know he lived or identified with, and it would provide too easily an answer to more complicated questions I hope this chapter asks: What would it mean to "know" that Bibliographer B was gay? What would constitute knowledge of this fact—especially, but not only, in the 1950s U.S. context? To pursue such knowledge, furthermore, is to participate, however sympathetically, in the very activities and discourses of detection/scandal we are analyzing. This is thus the place to record the larger debt of this chapter to the work of D. A. Miller, in particular *Bringing Out Roland Barthes*.

85. English Institute, "A Classified List of Topics, Chairmen, and Speakers, 1939–1963," 3. Walker's paper was apparently read in absentia.

86. On the suicides of suspected gays and lesbians in this period under threat of firing and exposure, see Johnson, *Lavender Scare*, 158–59. Since I first began research on Bibliographer B, I have learned that two sets of documents related to Bibliographer B and his death have been destroyed. Special Collections, University of Virginia Library, once housed a catalogued item including "50 items" in "Papers relating to the death of" Bibliographer B, dated March 1955, and attributed to the "Office of the [University] President" (MSS 7252), as well as "Committee reports pertaining to the cases of [Person C], and [Bibliographer B] and [Professor D]" dated December

11, 1956 (MSS 4137-y, my substitution of bracketed pseudonyms). The latter item, in "two sealed envelopes," was "[n]ot to be used without permission of the President." Both items have since been "destroyed . . . according to the records management guidelines enacted by the Commonwealth of Virginia" (Edward Gaynor, UVA Library, Special Collections, email correspondence). As a result of my inquiry, the items have now also been deleted from the public catalog. I would be grateful to hear from anyone with additional information about these sets of documents.

87. John Milton, *Areopagitica*, 4.

88. Exceptions are Margreta de Grazia's essay on the reproductive discourses of the press and imprinting in Moxon and more generally in the seventeenth century ("Imprints: Descartes, Shakespeare, Gutenberg") and Lisa Maruca's detailed cultural analysis of Moxon's manual (*The Work of Print*).

89. de Grazia, "Imprints."

90. My paraphrases of *OED* definitions 1–2, 4–5.

91. See Maruca, *Work of Print*.

92. Joseph Moxon, *Mechanick Exercises: Or, the Doctrine of handy-works. Applied to the Art of Printing*, 2:220. Subsequent references appear parenthetically.

93. Pierre Bourdieu, *The Logic of Practice*, 53. Subsequent references appear parenthetically.

94. On etymology, see Chapter 2, pp. 76–78.

95. The mechanick exercises of the compositor ("his Thoughts run no faster than his Fingers") resemble, rather than distinguish themselves from, the mechanicks of authorship: "His mind and hand went together," the actors write of Shakespeare's compositional process ("To the great Variety of Readers," in Hinman, *Norton Facsimile*, sig. A3).

96. Cyrus Hoy, "The Shares of Fletcher and His Collaborators in the Beaumont and Fletcher Canon (I)," and "The Shares of Fletcher and His Collaborators in the Beaumont and Fletcher Canon (III)"; Jonathan Hope, *The Authorship of Shakespeare's Plays*. Hoy's methods have been elaborated and extended by a number of scholars working more recently on attribution. For a critique of some assumptions underlying these methods, see Jeffrey Masten, "Beaumont and/ or Fletcher," and "*More* or Less."

97. Philip Edwards, "An Approach to the Problem of *Pericles*," 31, 32. For a review of the evidence, see Suzanne Gossett, ed., *Pericles*, 18–20, 27–28.

98. Barbara A. Mowat, "Theatre and Literary Culture."

99. Except in the reproduction in Figure 14, *As You Like It* is cited by the through-line numbers provided in Hinman, *Norton Facsimile*.

100. I first discussed this folio line in Masten, "Textual Deviance"; the following paragraphs are based on this discussion.

101. Two recent editions retain the folio reading: Frances E. Dolan, ed., *As You Like It* (2000), and Leah S. Marcus, ed., *As You Like It* (2012). The new *Norton Shakespeare*, 3rd ed. (2015), again emends to "her." The folio reading has been advocated by Maura Slattery Kuhn, "Much Virtue in If." For Kuhn, the importance of the reading lies in its raising of the theatrical question of whether Rosalind resumes women's clothes for her final entrance in 5.4; Kuhn's essay is largely uninterested in issues of homoeroticism that motivate my reconsideration of the line.

102. Richard Knowles, ed., *As You Like It*, 293.

103. Gary Taylor, "Textual and Sexual Criticism," 217.

104. The stage direction of the Oxford edition at 5.4.105, in Stanley Wells and Gary Taylor, gen. eds., *The Complete Works*, 732 (and Stephen Greenblatt et al., eds., *The Norton Shakespeare Based on the Oxford Edition*, 2nd ed., 5.4.96).

105. Kuhn also quotes this line in support of her interpretation: "The final stage picture of these two boys holding hands should mirror the earlier scene" ("Much Virtue," 43). But Kuhn's

larger argument suggests that the idea of male-male marriage she, too, sees figured in the play is part of the larger "unreal condition of the play itself," figured and facilitated by "if."

106. Alan Bray, *The Friend*, 88–89, 234–35, 238. The 1641 edition of Richard Brathwait's *English Gentleman* uses an image of a handfast to signify "acquaintance" (male friendship).

107. Taylor, "Textual and Sexual Criticism," 223n17. Taylor's citation of the *As You Like It* instance as a transparent case suggests that we may need to return to the other instances of presumed *his/her* confusion.

108. Gaskell, *New Introduction*, 348.

109. "Textual Note," *As You Like It*, in Greenblatt et al., *Norton Shakespeare*, 2nd ed., 1623; based on the Oxford Shakespeare editors' analysis in Stanley Wells and Gary Taylor, with John Jowett and William Montgomery, *William Shakespeare: A Textual Companion*, 392.

110. See G. E. Bentley's suggestion on revision, given time between first performances and print, in *The Profession of Dramatist in Shakespeare's Time, 1590–1642*, 263.

111. There is the remote possibility that this line is the site of a press variant not yet observed/recorded. Hinman did not exhaustively collate all copies of the folio for his study (or even all the Folger copies), and others have found further variants. For a discussion of additional variants and the utility of this pursuit, see Paul Werstine, "More Unrecorded States," 47–51.

112. Cairncross, "Compositors E and F," 378–80.

113. Fredson Bowers, "The Folio *Othello*: Compositor E" (lecture delivered 1959, published 1964), 357.

114. See also Wells and Taylor, *Complete Works*, original-spelling ed.

115. Richard Helgerson, "Note on the Text," in *Forms of Nationhood*, xi. I do not mean to single out Helgerson's modernization protocols as unusual; though he is significant for raising the notion of national language/culture, there are many other examples.

116. On the bonds between acting-company sharers and their apprentices, see the discussion of actors' wills in Chapter 3.

CHAPTER 2. "SWEET PERSUASION"

1. Louis Althusser, "Ideology and Ideological State Apparatuses," 118.

2. Desiderius Erasmus, "On the Writing of Letters / *De conscribendis epistolis*," 58–59 (my emphasis).

3. Clifford Leech, ed., *The Two Gentlemen of Verona*, 41.

4. David Bergeron, ed., *King James and Letters of Homoerotic Desire*, 147–78.

5. Jacques Derrida, *Politics of Friendship*, 1.

6. Harold Jenkins, ed., *Hamlet* (5.2.364–65), 416. While making reference below to other *Hamlet* editions, including the second quarto and first folio texts, I have elected to cite *Hamlet* from Jenkins's conflated-text, modern-spelling edition; subsequent parenthetical references are to its line numbers.

7. See, e.g., Roland Mushat Frye, *Shakespeare and Christian Doctrine*; and Stephen Greenblatt, *Hamlet in Purgatory*, esp. 51–64.

8. Horace Howard Furness, ed., *Hamlet, A New Variorum Edition of Shakespeare*, 1:470. The Variorum does gloss *sweet* in Horatio's "sweet lord" (3.2.48) as "[a] common style of address in Elizabethan times" (1:231).

9. Jenkins, ed., *Hamlet*, 416, 290. The third-generation Arden edition does not annotate these uses of the word in Act 3, Scene 2, or in Act 5, Scene 2; Ann Thompson and Neil Taylor, eds., *Hamlet*, 299, 460.

10. *The Two Gentlemen of Verona*, dir. Penny Metropolous, Chicago Shakespeare Theater on Navy Pier, fall 2000.

11. Jeffrey Masten, *Textual Intercourse*, chap. 2.

12. *The Two Gentlemen of Verona*, in *Mr. VVilliam Shakespeares Comedies, Histories, & Tragedies*, as reproduced in Charlton Hinman, ed., *The Norton Facsimile: The First Folio of Shakespeare*, TLN 14–16.

13. The issue is not—or at least not for me—the fidelity of any given edition or performance to the canonical text, but the way in which that text sits, comfortably or uncomfortably, in our modern regimes of affect, for audiences, editors, and performers alike. In other words, why, in a modern mainstream Shakespeare production, might this moment seem not to "work"?

14. The whole of *Two Gentlemen of Verona* might be seen as an enactment of this process, through the migrations of the word *sweet*. See esp. Proteus's comparison of Valentine to Sylvia as "a sweeter friend" (TLN 930–73). As a further example, see Mary Bly's work on the gender mobility of puns around *sweetmeats* (*Queer Virgins and Virgin Queans on the Early Modern Stage*, 65, 73–74). Bly argues that *sweetmeat* passes from a pun about (commodified) female genitalia to a male pun.

15. Shakespeare, *The most excellent Historie of the Merchant of Venice*, sig. F3ᵛ. The folio text is nearly identical. Tiffany Stern argues, on the basis of the typical presentation of letter texts within manuscript and printed playtexts, that Portia "snatch[es] the letter out of Bassanio's hands (as she must do to read it herself)," a version of the text she regards as more bibliographically accurate and "undoubtedly more theatrically satisfying" ("Letters, Verses and Double Speech-Prefixes in *The Merchant of Venice*," 231–33). Whatever the ambiguity of the letter's readership in the early printed texts, it seems to me that the question of theatrical satisfaction is historicizable and potentially dependent on one's interpretation of the renegotiated bonds of friendship and marriage in the last scene of the play (see Chapter 8). I'm grateful to M. J. Kidnie for bringing this question to my attention.

16. *The Life of Henry the Fift*, in *Mr. VVilliam Shakespeares Comedies, Histories, & Tragedies*, TLN 725–26, 755–56. The rhetoric of this speech seems to echo and cross-reference a number of the terms discussed elsewhere in this book: "counsailes" may intersect through a homonymic prefix with *conversation* (Chapter 3); "the very bottome of my soule" with *fundament* (Chapter 6) and with the Montaigne passage discussed later in this chapter.

17. Chri. Marlow, *The troublesome raigne and lamentable death of Edward the second*, sigs. A2, A4ᵛ.

18. Philip Sidney, *The Countess of Pembroke's Arcadia (The Old Arcadia)*, 15, 17. Musidorus: "Your words are such, noble cousin, so sweetly and strongly handled in the praise of solitariness, as they would make me likewise yield myself up unto it, but the same words make me know it is more pleasant to enjoy the company of him that can speak such words than by such words be persuaded to solitariness. And even so do I give you leave, sweet Pyrocles" (15).

19. Laurie Shannon, *Sovereign Amity*, 11. See also Alan Bray, "Homosexuality and the Signs of Male Friendship in Elizabethan England"; Alan Bray, *The Friend*; Mario DiGangi, *The Homoerotics of Early Modern Drama*; Bruce R. Smith, *Homosexual Desire in Shakespeare's England*; Alan Stewart, *Close Readers*; Masten, *Textual Intercourse*; and Valerie Traub on female-female friendship in *The Renaissance of Lesbianism*, esp. chaps. 4, 6, and 7.

20. Arden's and other editions' punctuation and modernization of this passage may already have separated and normalized the interchanging identities here. In the second quarto: "I am glad to see you well; *Horatio*, or I do forget my selfe" (*Tragicall Historie of Hamlet*, sig. C1ᵛ). In the first folio: "I am glad to see you well: / *Horatio*, or I do forget my selfe" (*The Tragedie Of Hamlet*, in *Mr. VVilliam Shakespeares Comedies, Histories, & Tragedies*, TLN 346–47).

21. Michel de Montaigne, "Of Friendship," in *Essayes or Morall, Politike, and Millitarie Discourses*, 92. Reacting to an earlier version of this chapter, Elizabeth Hanson ("Fellow Students") emphasizes the persistence and centrality of class distinction between Hamlet and Horatio (which I would not seek to deny), but underestimates what I would call the *aspirational* indistinguishability or substitutability the play registers both characters intermittently seeming to seek, as my discussion here and below will suggest—even while the friends continue to register some conventional class markers ("prince," "lord," etc.): "Horatio's repeated use of 'sweet' to address Hamlet, which is the object of Masten's analysis, is itself a sign of deference, a gracious if standard recognition of the value of a superior" (224). Hanson's reading thus reconventionalizes the epithet (stripping it of affect) in ways discussed above.

22. On the "syntax" of "sexual possibilities," see Jonathan Goldberg, *Sodometries*, 22. On *conversation* as a key word in male-male friendship, see Chapter 3.

23. For a detailed discussion of "cop'd" in this line, including meanings resonant with this chapter, see Karen Newman, "Two Lines, Three Readers: *Hamlet* TLN 1904–5."

24. Kim F. Hall, "Culinary Spaces, Colonial Spaces: The Gendering of Sugar in the Seventeenth Century." See also Wendy Wall, *Staging Domesticity*, 48. My thinking about sugar and food generally in this chapter is indebted to this book and to conversations with Wall. For another reading of the relation of sugar, slavery, power, and affect, see Roland Greene's account of *Astrophil and Stella* in *Unrequited Conquests*, 185–87.

25. Richard Barnfield, *Cynthia. VVith Certaine Sonnets*, sigs. B6–C7ᵛ, sonnets 19, 20, 14, and 8, respectively.

26. *Shake-speares Sonnets* (1609), as reproduced in Stephen Booth, ed., *Shakespeare's Sonnets*, 9. "Beautits" is usually emended to "beauty's."

27. Jeffrey Masten, "Gee, Your Heir Smells Terrific."

28. In such a reading, line 4's threat of self-killing may then carry with it a resonance and reminder of the punishment for sodomy in early modern England, while also registering the killing of the self through the loss of legacy/storage in an heir.

29. John Harington, *A Nevv Discovrse Of A Stale Svbiect, Called The Metamorphosis of Aiax*. Paster's reading, which repeatedly notices Harington's invocation of sweetness, highlights the way in which *Ajax* "places evacuation alongside the action tendencies of desire" ("The Epistemology of the Water Closet"). Following Paster, one might say that Harington's text is in fact legible as an extended meditation on transvaluing the sweet and the sour; the Folger copy of *The Metamorphosis* is bound with a related water-closet treatise "declar[ing], explan[ing], and eliquidat[ing] . . . how vnsauerie places may be made sweet, noysome places made wholesome" (John Harington and T.C., *An Anatomie Of The Metamorpho-sed Aiax*, title page). For a reading of Harington with some intersecting concerns, see Will Stockton, *Playing Dirty*, 14–23. On the rhetorics of the early modern fundament (anus), see Chapter 6.

30. Marlowe, *Edward the second*, sig. D1.

31. Randle Cotgrave, comp., *A Dictionarie Of The French And English Tongves*, sig. Iiii.vi. In entries for both *cul* and *posterol*, Cotgrave writes that the red nettle (sea anemone) "resembl[es]" or is "not much vnlike to a mans bung-hole" (sigs. Z.iᵛ, Rrr.iii). The *OED*, which cites one of Cotgrave's entries to establish the transferred sense of "the anus" (*bung, n.*¹, compounds, C3), also gives a late seventeenth-century quotation (Defoe, 1691) in support of the "Obs. Rare" meaning "bum" (*bung, n.*¹, 5). As Chapter 6's analysis of *fundament/foundation* suggests, Hamlet's "base uses" may further register a cluster of (not entirely sensical) anal resonances: *base, bung-hole*, even *use* (in the sense of sexual use, or possibly even usury, in its association with sodomy). On the latter, see Will Fisher, "Queer Money," and Jody Greene, "'You Must Eat Men.'" Further, the passage may associate sodomy, a base use, with class

transgression (as Bray suggests it often was): to associate "Noble" Alexander with beer barrels is ignobling.

32. Plutarch, "The Life of Alexander the Great," 723. The text includes an emphatic marginal gloss: "*Alexanders body had a maruelous sweete sauor.*" Montaigne's essay "Of smells and odors" begins with the sweetness of Alexander's sweat: "It is reported of some, namely of *Alexander*, that their sweat, through some rare and extraordinarie complexion, yeelded a sweet-smelling savour; whereof *Plutarke* and others seeke to finde out the cause. But the common sort of bodies are cleane contrarie, and the best qualitie they have, is to be cleare of any smel at all" (in Montaigne, *The Essayes*, 170).

33. On the difficulty of smell recall in relation to other senses, see Lewis Thomas, "On Smell." For cross-disciplinary research on smell and memory and a review of the scholarship, see the papers in section 4, "Memory," of Catherine Rouby, ed., *Olfaction, Taste, and Cognition*.

34. Cf. Paula Blank's reaction to an earlier version of this chapter in her "The Proverbial 'Lesbian,'" 125, 131.

35. *OED*, *sweet*, *n.* and *adj.*; *suave*, *adj.*; *suade*, *v.* For early modern connections among *sweet*, *suave*, and *suade*, contemporaneous with instances of *sweet* discussed above, see the extensive list of *suau*- entries in Thomas Cooper's expansion of *Bibliotheca Eliotæ*, sig. Xxx.viii^v.

36. Angel Day, *The English Secretorie*, passim.

37. Ralph Bathurst, "On the Death of Mr. William Cartvvright, and the now publishing of his Poems," in William Cartwright, *Comedies, Tragi-comedies, With other Poems*, sig. **2^v.

38. Sidney W. Mintz, *Sweetness and Power: The Place of Sugar in Modern History*.

39. Patricia Fumerton, *Cultural Aesthetics*, 134.

40. See Gail Kern Paster, *The Body Embarrassed*; Gail Kern Paster, Katherine Rowe, and Mary Floyd-Wilson, eds., *Reading the Early Modern Passions: Essays in the Cultural History of Emotion*.

41. Bray, *The Friend*, 88–89 (my emphasis).

42. Cotgrave, *Dictionarie*, sig. Ooo.iv^v (my emphasis).

43. Margreta de Grazia, "Words as Things"; Juliet Fleming, *Graffiti and the Writing Arts of Early Modern England*.

44. Lynne Magnusson, *Shakespeare and Social Dialogue*, 3.

45. Montaigne, "Of Friendship," 93. See also Masten, *Textual Intercourse*, 35.

46. Montaigne, "Of Friendship," 93.

47. The early printed texts of the play differ on whether Hamlet's voice draws "on" or draws "no" more (1623 folio and 1604 quarto, respectively). Both texts work within friendship discourse: Hamlet's voice draws Horatio's further; Hamlet's voice, which had hitherto drawn forth Horatio's, will draw it no more. The earlier instance of Hamlet's mouth as Horatio's is in the speech structured around the phrases "Not from his mouth, / . . . But . . . / let me speak . . ." (5.2.377–91).

48. Peter Jaros, in an unpublished essay on Horatio, Hamlet, and Ben Jonson, explores both Horatio's classical writer's name and the way in which Horatio is both more antique Roman than Dane and yet the voice of the play's future ("Unnatural Acts").

49. Qtd. in Goldberg, *Sodometries*, 78.

50. Francis Meres, *Palladis Tamia*, 281^v–282.

51. Thomas Blount, *Glossographia: or A dictionary, Interpreting all Such Hard VVords . . . as are now used in our refined English Tongue*, sig. Bb4; Cotgrave, *Dictionarie*, sig. Ff.iv^v.

52. Ben Jonson, "To the memory of my beloued, The Avthor Mr. VVilliam Shakespeare: And what he hath left vs," in *Mr. VVilliam Shakespeares Comedies, Histories, & Tragedies*, no sig.; John Milton, "L'Allegro," in *Poems of Mr. John Milton*, 36.

53. Erasmus, "On the Writing of Letters," 50, quoted from sec. 13, "On the Salutation." The bracketed text is Lisa Jardine's translation of the phrase: "The *epistola* is a kind of mutual exchange of speech between absent friends" (*Erasmus, Man of Letters*, 150).

54. Stewart, *Close Readers*, 156.

55. Jonathan Goldberg, *Writing Matter*, 250.

56. For an alternative reading of the bonds transmitted by and entailed in this letter, see Alan Stewart, *Shakespeare's Letters*, 187–89.

57. *OED*, confection, *n.*, esp. 5.b. and 5.d.

CHAPTER 3. EXTENDED "CONVERSATION"

1. Thomas Newton, trans., *Fovvre Severall Treatises of M. Tvllivs Cicero*, sigs. A2ᵛ, A3.

2. John Lyly, *Euphues*, in *The Complete Works of John Lyly*, 1:199.

3. *OED*, converse, *v.*, 1.

4. Philippians iii:20, *The Holy Bible* (1611), as reproduced in *The Holy Bible: A Facsimile in a reduced size of the Authorized Version*, sig. T3.

5. The 1881 Revised Standard Version gives "citizenship," with the marginal gloss "Or, *commonwealth*"; the 1952 revised RSV, "commonwealth." See *The Parallel Bible . . . Being the Authorised Version Arranged in Parallel Columns with the Revised Version* (1885), 233; and *The Holy Bible, Revised Standard Version* (1952), 223.

6. *The Two Gentlemen of Verona*, in *Mr. VVilliam Shakespeares Comedies, Histories, & Tragedies*, as reproduced in Charlton Hinman, ed., *The Norton Facsimile: The First Folio of Shakespeare*, TLN 712–13.

7. [John Bullokar], *An English Expositor*, sig. E2ᵛ.

8. Iohn Minsheu, [*Hegemon eis tas glossas*] *Ductor in Linguas, The Guide into the tongues*, 95.

9. Iohn Florio, *A Worlde of Wordes, Or Most copious, and exact Dictionarie in Italian and English*, 85.

10. *OED*, conversation, *n.*, 7.a. For reasons relevant below, it is instructive that the *OED*'s first quotation for this meaning appears in a same-sex (female sibling) context in Sidney's *Arcadia*.

11. *OED*, conversation, *n.*, 11.

12. *OED*, converse, *v.*

13. *OED*, conversation, *n.*, 3.

14. Juliet Fleming, "The Ladies' Man and the Age of Elizabeth," 160.

15. *OED*, converse, *n.*[1], 1.a., quoting *Pseudodoxia epidemica*.

16. Mr. John Fletcher and Mr. William Shakspeare Gent., *The Two Noble Kinsmen* (1634), 21. The punctuation of the passage may be misleading for a modern reader; I would suggest reading "[t]he poyson of pure spirits" as a parenthetical phrase set off by commas.

17. *OED*, converse, *v.*, 2.b. (my emphasis).

18. *OED*, converse, *n.*[1], 1.a. The classic discussion of this idea is Stephen Orgel, "Nobody's Perfect," 14–15.

19. Michel de Montaigne, *The Essayes Or Morall, Politike and Millitarie Discourses*, 91 (my emphasis).

20. For Marie de Gournay's attempt to introduce herself into this male-male conversation, see Marc D. Schachter, *Voluntary Servitude and the Erotics of Friendship*.

21. See Alan Bray, *The Friend*; Jeffrey Masten, *Textual Intercourse*, chap. 2; Laurie Shannon, *Sovereign Amity*; Schachter, *Voluntary Servitude*.

22. William Bullokar, *Bullokars Booke at large*, sig. E2ᵛ (my emphasis).

23. *OED*, *converse*, *v.*, etymology; see also Wendy Wall, *The Imprint of Gender*, 33–34.

24. Harley MS 6849, f. 218^r; for this and other transcriptions of manuscripts related to this case, I have compared the original, but, with minor changes noted below, I quote the transcriptions in C. F. Tucker Brooke, *The Life of Marlowe and The Tragedy of Dido Queen of Carthage*, 104, silently retaining the edition's expansion of MS abbreviations. In Harley MS 6849, the sentence (and paragraph) ends with a light virgule followed possibly by a period.

25. Jonathan Goldberg, "Sodomy and Society: The Case of Christopher Marlowe," 78.

26. Thomas Heywood, *An Apology For Actors*, sig. E3^v.

27. [Thomas Kyd,] *The Spanish Tragedie: Or Hieronimo is mad againe*. And in the 1623 edition: "*Newly Corrected, Amended, and Enlarged with new* Additions, as it hath of late been diuers times Acted."

28. Philip Henslowe, *Henslowe's Diary*, 1:168. Cf. an earlier entry: "Lent vnto m^r alleyn the 25 of septmb[er] 1601 to lend vnto Bengemen Johnson vpon his writtinge of his adicians in geronymo the some of . . . xxxx^s" (1:149).

29. Much of the discussion of this question has been taken up by arguments about whether or not the additions eventually printed in the text of the play are "characteristic" of Jonson; W. W. Greg writes, "[I]t has often been remarked that [the printed additions] are quite unlike any authenticated work of his" (Henslowe, *Henslowe's Diary*, 2:154). That additions and revisions of playtexts might cohere more with the play under revision/augmentation than they would disclose the ostensibly characteristic hand of their authentic writer is one of the arguments of the present chapter. James R. Siemon notes that Jonson both mocked and "adapted the play's dialogue without comment" over the course of his career (Siemon, "Sporting Kyd," 553n2), and it is well known that Jonson probably once acted the part of Jeronimo himself (see Philip Edwards, ed., *The Spanish Tragedy*, lxvi–lxvii).

30. See Scott McMillin, *The Elizabethan Theatre and "The Book of Sir Thomas More."* Since Cyrus Hoy's pioneering attempts to discern the authorial "shares" in the Beaumont and Fletcher plays by counting linguistic features of the texts (e.g., "The Shares of Fletcher and His Collaborators in the Beaumont and Fletcher Canon [I]"), there has been a (now-computer-assisted) explosion of analyses premised on the separability of playwrights. For an exposition of a stylometric method that seeks to separate Marlowe and Shakespeare texts but cannot (by its inventors' own admission) adjudicate texts that may be collaborative or of mixed authorship, see Thomas V. N. Merriam and Robert A. J. Matthews, "Neural Computation in Stylometry II." Their stylometric analysis assigns *The Jew of Malta* to Shakespeare, and they hypothesize that this may be a result of "the state in which the text . . . has reached us," of mixed authorship, or of a "possible attribution to Kyd" (3–4).

31. Harley MS 6849, ff. 218–218^v, with address-cover sheet, ff. 219–219^v.

32. Harley MS 6848, f. 154.

33. Harley MS 6848, ff. 187–89. The tract itself appears on recto folia only, with f. 189^v containing the inscription. Though they are usually taken to have been written by the same person on the basis of content, the first two letters are not indisputably of identical handsmanship, though they do resemble each other in the style of secretary hand. It is possible that the signature of the second letter has been cropped. Arthur Freeman's assertion that "these papers [presumably the fragments] are almost certainly *not* in Kyd's handwriting" but "are in a professional hand—a copyist's—but not Kyd's" almost certainly deconstructs itself, given Kyd's father's, and possibly Kyd's, professional training as a scrivener; see *Thomas Kyd: Facts and Problems*, 27, 27n5.

34. Brooke, *Life of Marlowe*, 56.

35. There is a disputed manuscript fragment of *The Massacre at Paris* at the Folger Library as well (Folger MS J.b.8).

36. See the helpfully skeptical reading of biographical documents in Edwards, *Spanish Tragedy*, xviii–xix.

37. The point is not necessarily that the italic interspersed in Kyd's letter to Puckering is precisely identical to the italic in the fragments (there are differences as well as similarities; cf. the initial As of "And," "Allexandriæ," and "Angels" in the manuscript copy of the tract, Harley 6848, f. 188, and "Atheisme" and "Atheist" in the letter), but that, for a person (and possibly persons) who writes at least two hands, handwriting and identity potentially exist in a more fluid relation, even before one factors in the question of elapsed time between the writings/copyings. (If the Folger manuscript is Marlowe's, he, too, could write with two hands, though "his" italic script seems much more rudimentary than "Kyd's," or "his own" default secretary.)

38. My resistance to paleographic evidence as a conduit of identity in the modern sense is indebted to Jonathan Goldberg's demonstration in *Writing Matter*, highly relevant here, that the hand that is writing does not so much disclose as *structure* identity and identification.

39. Brooke, *Life of Marlowe*, 55.

40. I understand that this statement—and the movement from local to general that it describes—represents an important methodological crux, and some readers may contest it. Some questions that have been asked of this argument include the following: Is Marlowe and Kyd's relation typical of early modern male relations? Can this episode, with its set of complications, which might range from writerly competition to government intervention, be representative of such relations? If a reading of the evidence in this case (as I am about to argue) is complexly layered, are there not more straightforward cases (as it were) that might more clearly demonstrate the history of male relations and affect in early modern England? Are the materials in this case not extraordinary (letters to the Privy Council, a case possibly related to espionage, etc.), and are there not more ordinary, quotidian categories of evidence that might allow us to be more certain of the generalizing points I seek to make? My response is that, though we cannot know in advance, I think it is unlikely that we will ever find the typical case; that, given the discursive attention they deserve, all such cases will be complexly layered; and that all of our evidence of homoeroticism (and of course heteroeroticism as well) is mediated by the contexts in which it appears and by the materials in which it is transmitted.

41. Brooke, *Life of Marlowe*, 104. Italics here represent italic handwriting, which I have restored from the original, with some minor adjustments in the transcription (e.g., "Loue" for "loue").

42. Newton, *Fovvre Severall Treatises*, sig. E2. Though there are modern translations that we would see as adhering more closely to the original, the point here is to register how the text was translated (and thus interpreted and transmitted) in(to) the early modern context.

43. Ibid., sig. E1. Compare a modern translation: "there is a sort of disaster in connexion with breaking off friendships" (Cicero, *De Senectute, De Amicitia, De Divinatione*, 185).

44. Newton, *Fovvre Severall Treatises*, sig. E2.

45. "The time of the present dialogue is 129 B.C., just a few days after the mysterious death of Scipio Minor"; William Armistead Falconer, "Introduction to the *Laelius*," in Cicero, *De Senectute, De Amicitia, De Divinatione*, 104.

46. Ibid., 105.

47. Brooke, *Life of Marlowe*, 107; italics represent italic handwriting, restored from the original. For legibility, I offer a translation into modern orthography: Marlowe "would report St. John to be our savior Christ's Alexis (I cover it with reverence and trembling)—that is, that Christ did love him with an extraordinary love." The very run-on quality of the original may itself function as a reverent, trembling cover.

48. Chri. Marlow, *The troublesome raigne and lamentable death of Edward the second*, sig. D1.

49. Walter J. Ong, "Latin Language Study as a Renaissance Puberty Rite."

50. "The exercises of Learning in Corpus Christi Colledg in Cambridge every daye in the weke," qtd. in Richard F. Hardin, "Marlowe and the Fruits of Scholarism," 388.

51. Kyd apparently did not attend university; on his education and its method and content, see Freeman, *Thomas Kyd: Facts and Problems*, 6–10; and Siemon, "Sporting Kyd." Lynn Enterline notes the importance of Cicero to Lily's grammar; see "Rhetoric, Discipline, and the Theatricality of Everyday Life in Elizabethan Grammar Schools," 183.

52. See Jonathan Goldberg, *Sodometries*, 63–81; Bruce R. Smith, *Homosexual Desire in Shakespeare's England*, 81–93; Stephen Guy-Bray, *Homoerotic Space*, esp. 6–7, 14–18. Smith's attention to Cicero's dialogue removes it from discussions of homoeroticism (36, 40–41), but see Smith, *Homosexual Desire*, 84, and Goldberg, *Sodometries*, 79, for an example of bedfellows reading "De Amicitia." Alan Stewart discusses this example and the Ciceronian text at length in *Close Readers*, 122–60, esp. 126–31.

53. "Erroneously for: Conversation, discourse," *eclogue, n.*, 2; the citation quotes Robert Cawdrey's *A Table Alphabeticall* (1604). On the etymology of *eclogue* in a homoerotic context, see Guy-Bray, *Homoerotic Space*, 37–38.

54. Fredson Bowers, ed., "The Passionate Shepherd to His Love," in *The Complete Works of Christopher Marlowe*, 2:537 (my emphasis). I quote Bowers's six-stanza version; in a way that this chapter tries to resist, Bowers is interested in stripping away the highly conversational history of this text, eliminating the "non-Marlovian," "spurious" stanzas. On this poem as a provocation to response, imitation, and parody, see Arthur F. Marotti, *Manuscript, Print, and the English Renaissance Lyric*, 167; Wall, *Imprint of Gender*, 189–90; and forthcoming work by Christopher Shirley.

55. Alan Bray, "Homosexuality and the Signs of Male Friendship in Elizabethan England." On sodomy and its related discourses in these texts, see Goldberg, "Sodomy and Society"; and Will Fisher, "Queer Money."

56. Brooke, *Life of Marlowe*, 99.

57. Ibid. (my emphasis).

58. Bowers, *Complete Works of Christopher Marlowe*, 2:537.

59. Brooke, *Life of Marlowe*, 105 (my emphasis). I have restored the italics for the names, as well as some punctuation from the manuscript. The other Kyd letter (unsigned) begins by citing "marlowes monstruous opinions."

60. Richard Brathwait, "A Draught of the *Frontispice*," in *The English Gentleman*.

61. The period meanings of *consent* and *consort* are closely related and overlap in varying degrees with the meanings of *conversation* and *converse* discussed above; see the *OED*.

62. For a reading of the Kyd and Baines texts that sees the allegations of Christ-as-sodomite as so unusual that they guarantee the texts' *other* allegations of Marlowe's atheism, see Nicholas Davidson, "Marlowe and Atheism," 141–42. For a contextualization of the complexities of Marlowe's death, see Charles Nicholl, *The Reckoning*.

63. E. A. J. Honigmann and Susan Brock, eds., *Playhouse Wills 1558–1642*, 70–71. I have not transcribed this edition's notations of expanded abbreviations, illegibilities, and deletions.

64. Ibid., 73.

65. See Peter Stallybrass, "Worn Worlds."

66. Following Diana Fuss, *Identification Papers*, I use *identification* to indicate *identity* as at least partly formed or informed through *identifying-with*.

67. Honigmann and Brock, *Playhouse Wills*, 98–100.

68. Ibid., 100.

69. See Thomas Whitfield Baldwin's attempt to map the residences of the members of the King's Men on the basis of available evidence in *The Organization and Personnel of the Shakespearean Company*, 148–61.

70. Paul S. Seaver, *Wallington's World*, 49.

71. For a working definition of habitus on which I rely here, see Pierre Bourdieu, *The Logic of Practice*, 53–54; also see the Introduction and Chapter 1.

72. Lyly, *Complete Works of John Lyly*, 1:197.

73. Stephen Greenblatt, *Renaissance Self-Fashioning*; Emily C. Bartels, *Spectacles of Strangeness*. Cf. Goldberg, "Sodomy and Society." Lars Engle's "Oedipal Marlowe, Mimetic Middleton" also resonates with this model. See also Leah Marcus's discussion of a "Marlowe effect" (*Unediting the Renaissance*, 42).

74. Harry Levin, *The Overreacher*.

75. Engle raises the possibility of a "mimetic" schema of desire and subjectivity in Marlowe, alongside what he sees as the more strongly articulated "oedipal" model ("Oedipal Marlowe," 434). Both models strongly feature a competitive rivalry, whether generationally horizontal or vertical. In attempting to maintain a homoerotic/homosocially valenced Marlowe in ways that are not simply equivalent to Marlowe as sodomite/other, I'm advocating a different perspective from Lukas Erne's attempt ("Biography, Mythography, and Criticism") to de-queer Marlowe, discussed within this book in Chapter 5.

76. *As You Like It*, in *Mr. VVilliam Shakespeares Comedies, Histories, & Tragedies*, TLN 1853–54. See also Chapter 5.

77. My sense that one of these things is not like the Other emerges from reading Bartels's otherwise persuasive list of Marlowe's alien characters and landscapes (3). My point about friendship in *Edward II* is closely related to Goldberg's analysis in *Sodometries* (see esp. 119–26). Lawrence Normand analyzes a remarkable set of parallels between *Edward II* and an early episode of favoritism between a king who would later rule England (James VI of Scotland) and the Frenchman Esmé Stewart in "'What Passions Call You These?': *Edward II* and James VI."

78. Edwards, *Spanish Tragedy*, xviii–xix. I don't mean to suggest a simple, modern, binary reading of this evidence (i.e., that Kyd was "homosexual" because there is no evidence of his "heterosexuality"), especially since it is clear that there were players and playwrights involved in intimate male relations while married, in a way that resists modern hetero/homo distinctions. See also the quotation from Seaver, *Wallington's World*, cited above.

79. Edwards, *Spanish Tragedy*, 44 (note to 2.5.67–80).

80. Henslowe, *Henslowe's Diary*, 2:150.

81. Ibid., 1:13–15. This is not to mention the many other performances of the two plays *not* on consecutive days. Henslowe's records for these months suggest, too, the ways in which the plays might have been closely related, in the experience of actors, audiences, and playwrights, to Marlowe's *The Jew of Malta*, as a result of frequent repertory performances.

82. There has been much debate, on problematic stylistic grounds. See Freeman's tentative chronology for these various related Spanish plays (*Thomas Kyd: Facts and Problems*, 177).

83. [Thomas Kyd,] *The Spanish Tragedie . . . Newly corrected and amended*, sigs. E1^v–E2.

84. Phil. Massinger, Tho. Middleton, and William Rowley, *The Old Law: Or A new way to please you*, sig. K4^v.

85. On linguistic sorting, see note 30 above.

86. Ben Ionson, *The Alchemist*, sig. K4^v, 4.7.67–71.

87. Jonson was famously attentive to textual/intellectual property, but there is ample evidence that he also dwelled within the more conversational/collaborative paradigm I am attempting to describe; see, for example, Mark Bland, "Jonson, 'Biathanatos' and the Interpretation of Manuscript Evidence."

88. In the parish register of St. Mary Colchurch: "Thomas Kydd the sonne of ffrauncis Kydd was buried the 15 day of August 1594" (qtd. in Freeman, *Thomas Kyd: Facts and Problems*, 38).

89. Ben: Ionson, "To the memory of my beloued, The Avthor Mr. VVilliam Shakespeare: And what he hath left vs," in *Mr. VVilliam Shakespeares Comedies, Histories, & Tragedies* (emphasis in the original; underscoring added).

90. Cf. Edmund Spenser, *The Faerie Qveene* (1596), 1.6.14.4: "Leaping like wanton kids . . . ." As an adjective, *kid* or *kyd* could also mean, in a way that may be relevant though not syntactically sensical here, "well-known; famous; notorious" (*OED, kid, kyd, adj.*).

91. Thomas Dekker, *A Knights Coniuring*, sig. K4ᵛ.

92. For a reading of "incongruities" in *The Spanish Tragedy* that also takes off from Jonson's naming and then traces conflicting figurations of style, *sprezzatura*, and *decorum* in the play, see Siemon, "Sporting Kyd." Siemon's reading goes some way toward demonstrating the multivalency of Kyd's writing in *The Spanish Tragedy*, and he shows in particular its possible relation to pedagogical practices at the Merchant Taylors' School; my point is to assert Kyd's polyvocality not as simply characteristic of Kyd (if "characteristic" and polyvocal are not in some sense already impossibly oxymoronic), but as implicated in the larger institutional practices of writing. Greene's famous naming of Shakespeare as "an absolute *Johannes fac totum*" can be usefully re-viewed in this context.

93. Marjorie Garber, " 'Infinite Riches in a Little Room,' " 20.

94. Ibid., 21.

95. Henry Abelove, "Some Speculations on the History of 'Sexual Intercourse' During the 'Long Eighteenth Century' in England," 337, 340. On the increased incidence of "intercourse," see also Thomas W. Laqueur, "Sexuality and the Transformation of Culture," 419; and Laqueur, "Sex, Gender, and Desire in the Industrial Revolution."

96. Fleming, "Ladies' Man," 160.

97. I will leave aside the question of "seminal emission uninterrupted" in Abelove's definition. Although I understand why the qualification is necessary in Abelove's reliance on birthrate data, uninterrupted emission opens up larger questions of both sexual practice and meaning during the earlier period. Seventeenth-century rape and sodomy law, for example, turned on the question of "emission" and/vs. "penetration" (Edward Coke, *The Third Part Of The Institutes Of the Laws of England*).

98. *OED, intercourse, n.*

99. *OED, sexual, adj.* and *n.*, S2., in the phrase *sexual intercourse*, cross-checked against *Eighteenth Century Collections Online*.

100. See John Palmer, *An examination of Thelyphthora, on the subject of marriage*, 11.

101. E. Sibly, *Magazine of natural history. Comprehending the whole science of animals, plants, and minerals*, 140. See also "the sexual intercourse," in John Herdman, *An essay on the causes and phenomena of animal life*, 218.

102. William Godwin, *Enquiry concerning political justice*, 1:74. A slightly earlier example of "the sexual intercourse" that also refers to humans appears in John Whitaker, *Mary Queen of Scots vindicated*, 3:57, 82.

103. T. R. Malthus, *An Essay on the Principle of Population . . . A New Edition, Very Much Enlarged*, 77. Subsequent references appear parenthetically.

104. In the 1798 edition, Malthus uses the term twice: "an unshackled intercourse" (184) and "a promiscuous intercourse" (183). My understanding of Malthus is indebted to Christopher Herbert's reading in *Culture and Anomie*, chap. 2, esp. 105ff. Herbert glosses "promiscuous intercourse" in Malthus as "extramarital and unprocreating sex" (108).

105. *OED, intercourse, n.*, 3.

106. *OED, sexual, adj.* and *n.*, 1.

107. I would not, on the basis of the available evidence, attempt to trace when "sexual" ceases to mean something like "narrowly reproductive" and begins to mean "erotic" or "genital" (no

matter the genders involved). As the *OED*'s illustrative quotations for this meaning suggest (see esp. *sexual*, 4.a.–c., as well as 3), it is often difficult to determine in any one instance whether something like sex = eroticism or sex = reproduction is operating.

108. *OED, sexual, adj.* and *n.*, 2.a. On the Latin etymology of *sex* from "cut or divide" (and, thus, originally, the "sharpness and cleanness of the division between natural categories of male and female" now "blunted by historical shifts and rearrangements in the concepts and forms of sexual life," see David M. Halperin, *How to Do the History of Homosexuality*, 136. The etymology is also hypothesized in *OED, sex, n.*[1]

109. Indeed, the subsequent invention of the terms *homosexual* and *heterosexual* may suggest a felt need in the culture for further refinement of *sexual*, once the term ceased to mean simply "cross-sex and involving reproduction" and broadened to include something like "sex as sexual feeling, eroticism, or desire potentially cut loose from gender difference per se." For related philological and semantic questions around the words *sex* and *sexual*, published while this book was in the final stages of preparation, see Will Stockton and James M. Bromley, "Introduction: Figuring Early Modern Sex," in *Sex Before Sex*, 11. On the emergence of the terms *homosexuality* and *heterosexuality* in English, see David M. Halperin, *One Hundred Years of Homosexuality*.

110. Cawdrey, *Table Alphabeticall*, sig. F1ᵛ; [Bullokar], *English Expositor*, sig. I5.

111. Minsheu, *Ductor in Linguas*, 175.

112. Florio, *Worlde of Wordes*, 187.

113. For a brilliant review and analysis of the historiography and critique around Lawrence Stone's "companionate marriage" hypothesis, see Valerie Traub, *The Renaissance of Lesbianism*, 261–70. Traub's preferred term, *domestic heterosexuality*, may best describe what I hypothesize here, because it encodes the perceived necessity of mutual passion/desire/affection in the cross-sexual marital-reproductive relationship as imagined and idealized in this period: "Under the regime of domestic heterosexuality [as it begins to emerge in the seventeenth century], erotic desire for a domestic partner, in addition to desire for a reproductive, status-appropriate mate, became *a requirement for* (not just a happy byproduct of) the bonds between husband and wife" (265, emphasis in the original). The process I see as eventuating potentially in a more equitable term for cross-sex insertive/receptive sex, in other words, may begin in the long evolution that Traub locates as beginning in the mid-seventeenth century: "By the mid-seventeenth-century, marital desire had begun to be viewed not as the imposition of the husband's desire onto his wife, but as a mutual sharing" (267).

114. Thomas Laqueur, *Making Sex*, 35, 42.

115. Fletcher and Shakspeare, *Two Noble Kinsmen*, 21.

116. http://books.google.com/ngrams/ (consulted in 2015).

117. Florio, *Worlde of Wordes*, 137.

118. *OED, fuck, v.*, 1.b.

119. On *occupation* and *occupy*, see Patricia Parker, *Shakespeare from the Margins*, 8, 268–69, 316n19.

120. Fletcher and Shakspeare, *Two Noble Kinsmen*, 24.

121. Minsheu, *Ductor in Linguas*, 174.

122. Ibid., 376.

123. I remain puzzled by an earlier usage of male-male "intercourse" that seems potentially "sexualized" by context and that I have speculated about elsewhere (*Textual Intercourse*, 197n41): a 1647 reference to Francis Beaumont and John Fletcher's "strange unimitable Intercourse"; see Jo. Pettus, "Upon the Works of Beaumont, and Fletcher," in Beaumont and Fletcher, *Comedies and Tragedies*, sig. a4. Although the passage seems to bespeak a spiritual or "intellectual" intercourse/interchange/conversation between Beaumont and Fletcher in their collabora-

tion, the poem nevertheless associates this intercourse both with strangeness (and thus potentially verges on sodomitic discourse) *and* with reproduction (the playwrights' "Volume springs" from this interchange).

124. I'm suggesting that *buddy* marks not only (1) the connection between this term and the historically long discourse of friendship (i.e., *buddy = friend*), bringing with it friendship's resistance to hierarchy in a way that is also in tension with earlier senses of *fuck*, but also potentially (2) a perceived need further to masculinize a sexualized friendship (*buddy* as a term from a certain class-marked discourse that connotes masculinity, and a term of nonintimate intimacy). Apparently of gay-male origin (see *OED*, *fuck buddy*, *n.*; Jonathon Green, *Green's Dictionary of Slang*; and Jesse Sheidlower, *The F-word*, 117), the term has subsequently been taken up in lesbian and straight communities of discourse as well—a fact that may differently inflect the original "masculinity" I'm speculatively attributing to it here, whatever the "actual" sex of the bodies to which it refers.

CHAPTER 4. READING "BOYS"

Special thanks to Richard Preiss for his editorial assistance with an earlier published version of sections of this chapter.

1. Ovid, *The.xv.Bookes of P. Ouidius Naso, entytuled Metamorphosis*, 3:35ᵛ–36.

2. William Shakespeare, *The Tragicall Historie of Hamlet, Prince of Denmarke*, sig. C4. Thanks to Coleman Hutchison, who first brought the sense-making possibilities of this line to my attention.

3. Stephen Orgel, *Impersonations: The Performance of Gender in Shakespeare's England*, 1–2.

4. This is a question prompted for me by Emily D. Bryan's research on the treatment and representation of boys in early modern theater: "In the Company of Boys: The Place of the Boy Actor in Early Modern English Culture"; and Bryan, "The Government of Performance: *Ignoramus* and the Micropolitics of Tutor-Student Relations."

5. Unless indicated otherwise, subsequent parenthetical references are to William Shakespeare, *Twelfth Night*, ed. Roger Warren and Stanley Wells.

6. Viola is apparently the subject of the stage direction "*Enter Uiolenta.*" William Shakespeare, *Twelfe Night, Or what you will*, in *Mr. VVilliam Shakespeares Comedies, Histories, & Tragedies*, as reproduced in Charlton Hinman, ed., *The Norton Facsimile: The First Folio of Shakespeare*, TLN 461. I share with Laurie E. Osborne's account ("The Texts of *Twelfth Night*") a sense that much is to be learned from even the "least problematic" of folio texts, though I would argue that even the "Violenta" moment carries potential import for an analysis of gender in print.

7. Orsino's practice continues after the identity disclosure: "Boy, thou hast said to me a thousand times . . ." (5.1.261).

8. Building on the proverbial craftiness of foxes, editions typically gloss *cub* as "fox cub," but the term may also suggest a bear cub and thus a diminutive or young version of Orsino ("little bear") himself—or an equivalent. See the somewhat self-contradictory evidence of *OED*, *cub*, *n.*¹, 1–3.

9. On the name Cesario ("belonging to Caesar," and thus "cut"), see Orgel, *Impersonations*, 53–54; and Mario DiGangi, *The Homoerotics of Early Modern Drama*, 38–42.

10. See also 3.4.54–55.

11. *OED*, *squash*, *n.*¹, 1. For the gloss, see Warren and Wells, *Twelfth Night*, 110.

12. William Shakespeare, *A Midsommer nights dreame* (1600), sig. D3ᵛ.

13. On gender transitivity in the play, see esp. Stephen Greenblatt, "Fiction and Friction," in *Shakespearean Negotiations*; Jean E. Howard, "Crossdressing, the Theatre, and Gender Struggle in Early Modern England"; Lisa Jardine, *Still Harping on Daughters*; Orgel, *Impersonations*. For revisionary treatments of gender, sameness, and homoeroticism in the play, see Valerie Traub, *Desire and Anxiety*; Laurie Shannon, "Nature's Bias"; and Lisa Jardine, "Twins and Travesties," chap. 4 in *Reading Shakespeare Historically*, 65–77.

14. I mean no simply idle pun here, but rather to illustrate the ways in which such metaphoric, classificatory terms potentially open up in multiple relevant directions and meanings: "apricocks" (a seventeenth-century spelling of the fruit) plays on the fused sense of prematurity (from Latin, *praecox*) and erotics (cocks), senses typically lost when modernized (see John Webster, *The Duchess of Malfi*, 2.1.136).

15. W. Roy Mackenzie, "Standing Water."

16. The gloss appears in *Twelfth Night*, ed. J. M. Lothian and T. W. Craik, in the Arden Shakespeare, 29; Stephen Greenblatt et al., eds., *The Norton Shakespeare Based on the Oxford Edition*, 2nd ed., 1802; Warren and Wells, *Twelfth Night*, 110; G. Blakemore Evans et al., eds., *The Riverside Shakespeare*, 414.

17. Psalms 107:33, 114:8 (Bishops) and 107:35, 114:8 (AV). The Geneva Version's translations, "hee turneth the wildernesse into pooles of water, and the drie lande into water springs" (107:35), and "waterpooles" (114:8), also clearly suggest pools rather than transitional tides.

18. Qtd. in Mackenzie, "Standing Water," 290.

19. Qtd. in ibid., 289; cited in *OED* (*fat, adj.* and *n.*[2], 7). See William Harrison, *The description of England*, in Raphael Holinshed, *The first and second volumes of Chronicles*, 1:170.

20. On boys' vocal ambiguity and flexibility, see Gina Bloom, *Voice in Motion*; and Bruce R. Smith, *The Acoustic World of Early Modern England*, 226–30.

21. Ilana Krausman Ben-Amos, *Adolescence and Youth in Early Modern England*, 36.

22. Ibid., 32. "In England as a whole the mean age of first marriage for both men and women was in the mid- to late twenties, with males generally marrying somewhat later than females," summarizes Martin Ingram, in *Church Courts, Sex and Marriage in England, 1570–1640*, 129.

23. See Bruce R. Smith, *Homosexual Desire in Shakespeare's England*, 194–96. On the trial of Richard Cornish in colonial Virginia (1624–25), see Jonathan Ned Katz, *Gay American History*; and H. R. McIlwaine, ed., *Minutes of the Council and General Court of Colonial Virginia*.

24. Advanced search on Google.com, July 2015. The *OED* gives 1770 as the date of its first example of the phrase (*boy, n.* and *int.*, P1). There is no equivalent for the proverb in the sixteenth and seventeenth centuries, according to Morris Palmer Tilley, *A Dictionary of the Proverbs in England in the Sixteenth and Seventeenth Centuries*. For "Lads (Boys) will be men," see Tilley, L24 (366).

25. In this, I follow Traub's early work on homoeroticism in Shakespearean comedy, in particular, her contention that "the boy actor works . . . as the basis upon which homoeroticism can be safely explored" (*Desire and Anxiety*, 118).

26. Orgel, *Impersonations*, 70.

27. On the affective link between women and boys/youths, see Wendy Wall, "Tending to Bodies and Boys," chap. 5 in *Staging Domesticity*, 161–88.

28. David M. Halperin, "How to Do the History of Male Homosexuality," chap. 4 in *How to Do the History of Homosexuality*, 104–37.

29. Alan Bray's "Homosexuality and the Signs of Male Friendship in Elizabethan England" first began to theorize this overlap among apparently discrete discourses.

30. Unless otherwise indicated, citations refer to Francis Beaumont and John Fletcher, *Philaster, or, Love Lies A-Bleeding*, ed. Suzanne Gossett (Arden). As I suggest below, there are a

number of reasons to resist modern editions' privileging of the second quarto text, as well as the implications of quarantining in an appendix the first quarto's first and last scenes, as both the Revels edition and the Regents Renaissance Drama edition do. Gossett helpfully edits "parallel pages" from the quartos in an appendix.

31. For a summary of the conventional directions of and assumptions about affect within the ancient Greek sexual system, see David M. Halperin, "One Hundred Years of Homosexuality," in *One Hundred Years of Homosexuality and Other Essays on Greek Love*, 35–36. In an essay on the "strangeness" of sexuality in *Philaster*, Laura Williamson Ambrose has analyzed the effeminately marked cross-sex eroticism of Pharamond, the "stranger" prince in the play; see "Domestic Strangers and the Circulation of Desire in Beaumont and Fletcher's *Philaster*."

32. Bryan, "In the Company of Boys," brilliantly explores the widespread rhetoric of "taking up" boys (educating them, but also impressing them into service, including theatrical performance), together with some implications for reading *Philaster*.

33. Elizabeth Pittenger, "'To Serve the Queere': Nicholas Udall, Master of Revels"; Alan Stewart, "'Traitors to Boyes Buttocks': The Erotics of Humanist Education," chap. 3 in Alan Stewart, *Close Readers*; Wendy Wall, "'Household Stuff': The Sexual Politics of Domesticity and the Advent of English Comedy."

34. On pedagogy and the figure of the young page, see Elizabeth Pittenger, "Dispatch Quickly: The Mechanical Reproduction of Pages." On the sexually available page and the Ganymede story, see Mario DiGangi, "Queering the Shakespearean Family."

35. "No children vnder the age of one and twentie yeeres complete, shall contract themselues, or marrie without the consent of their Parents, or of their Guardians and Gouernours, if their Parents be deceased"; H. A. Wilson, ed., *Constitutions and Canons Ecclesiastical 1604*, sig. Q3ᵛ. See Ingram, *Church Courts, Sex and Marriage*, 128, 135–36; on the received presumptions around marital consent, see Frederick Pollock and Frederic William Maitland, *The History of English Law Before the Time of Edward I*, 2:387–88. Further ambiguity was introduced in 1604 by the fact that "marriages made in contravention of these regulations were not declared invalid" (Ingram, *Church Courts, Sex and Marriage*, 136). I am grateful to Stephen Orgel for suggestions regarding marriage law.

36. R. A. Foakes, "Tragicomedy and Comic Form," 83.

37. See Orgel's comment on this passage; whether Bellario/Euphrasia "decides" that this will be his/her ultimate position is, I think, unclear (*Impersonations*, 163n8). On the resonance of the Ganymede myth for erotic rivalry within early modern households, see DiGangi, "Queering the Shakespearean Family," 281–82.

38. See below on the difference in the gender discovery in the first and second quartos.

39. The closing down of homoerotic possibility in the play is emphasized by Nicholas F. Radel in one of the few readings exploring homoerotic valences: "Homoeroticism . . . is revealed as an absurdity that does not exist. . . . *Philaster* almost uncompromisingly deflects the play of sexual energy around Bellario toward the heterosexual"; Radel, "Fletcherian Tragicomedy, Cross-dressing, and the Constriction of Homoerotic Desire in Early Modern England," 65. Radel's detailed reading is part of a larger account of the shutting down of polymorphous sexual possibility on the road toward modern bourgeois sexual normativity, at the moment of earliest emergence.

40. Leonard Barkan, *Transuming Passion: Ganymede and the Erotics of Humanism*.

41. On the power of clothes to determine gender in the theater at any particular moment, despite what we might consider evidence to the contrary, see Orgel, *Impersonations*, 32–35.

42. Ibid., 163n8.

43. On "chaste femme love," see Valerie Traub, *The Renaissance of Lesbianism in Early Modern England*, esp. chap. 6.

44. See pp. 61–65 of Chapter 1 above; Jeffrey Masten, "Textual Deviance"; Orgel, *Imperson-ations*, 32–33. Traub remarks about the end of *Twelfth Night*: "Despite its closure, then, *Twelfth Night*'s conclusion seems only ambivalently invested in the 'natural' heterosexuality it imposes" (*Desire and Anxiety*, 138).

45. On the "sadomasochistic frisson" of the hunting/wounding scenes, see Radel, "Fletche-rian Tragicomedy," 68.

46. On boy's bodies onstage, see Peter Stallybrass, "Transvestism and the 'Body Beneath.' " Also Ann Rosalind Jones and Peter Stallybrass, *Renaissance Clothing and the Materials of Memory*.

47. Leo Kirschbaum, "A Census of Bad Quartos," 43.

48. Robert K. Turner, "Textual Introduction," 371.

49. Andrew Gurr, "Introduction," lxxv–lxxvi. For a review of editorial arguments about the relation of Q1 and Q2 and a new composite hypothesis of their origins, see Suzanne Gossett, "Textual Introduction," in Gossett, *Philaster*, 76–102.

50. Gossett, *Philaster*, 79.

51. Francis Beaumont and Iohn Fletcher, *Philaster. Or, Loue lies a Bleeding*, "The second Impression" (1622), sig. A2. All subsequent references will appear parenthetically as Q2.

52. My renaming of the quartos is indebted to the groundbreaking textual work of Randall McLeod [Random Cloud], esp. "The Marriage of Good and Bad Quartos."

53. Francis Baymont [Beaumont] and Iohn Fletcher, *Phylaster. Or, Loue Lyes a Bleeding* (1620), 14 and passim. Subsequent references appear parenthetically as Q1. "Prestatements" because of its chronological priority in print; Gossett, along with other editors who see Q2 as preceding or existing as a more complete version of the text from early performances, would differ.

54. It is true, however, as Scott McMillin notes, that the boys' roles in later scenes of Q1 have been substantially curtailed; McMillin, ed., *The First Quarto of Othello*, 28.

55. See Valerie Traub, "Introduction: 'Practicing Impossibilities,' " in *Renaissance of Lesbi-anism*, 1–35.

56. Gurr argues that "Q1 was printed from a clumsy, dictated transcript of the central part [of the play from] authorial foul papers, by a scribe familiar with the play in performance" (lxxvii). The authority of this hypothesized transcript aside, a text produced by such a process would nonetheless potentially capture some aspects of performance *more faithfully* than an authorially authorized transcript of the text that "never reached the actors" (and is similarly hypothetical): the former may represent what one or more persons thought they saw onstage in performance—here, the representations of boys, or the apparent importance of the category over a personal name. Gossett's edition admirably does more than previous editions to bring the "boy" aspects of the text into an edition of Q2.

57. In a queer-philological context, it is important to note the overlap between modern bibliographic rhetoric and languages of (derogated) sexuality, however inadvertent—for exam-ple, the use of Q1 to edit Q2 cruxes, "either to find the possible source of [Q2's] *corruption* or as *a back-door way* of ascertaining when the Q2 compositor may have nodded" (Gurr, "Introduc-tion," lxxxiii, my emphasis).

58. There are several interesting emphases of "Boy" in the dialogue via capitalization: 74, "*Ki.* Beare away that Boy / To torture"; and 77, [Bel:] "drest my selfe / In habit of a Boy."

59. Francis Beaumont and Iohn Fletcher, *Philaster, Or Loue lies a Bleeding*, "The third Im-preßion" (1628), sig. A3. Subsequent references appear parenthetically as Q3.

60. For a discussion of printed dramatis personae lists ("identification tables") in the six-teenth and seventeenth centuries, see Gary Taylor, assisted by Celia R. Daileader and Alexan-dra G. Bennett, "The Order of Persons," in *Thomas Middleton and Early Modern Textual Cul-ture*. Taylor writes, "[I]dentification tables are designed to appeal to a new specialist submarket

of readers—readers who read plays. Moreover, unlike other paratextual materials, these tables immediately impinge upon the reading of the play text. . . . [I]dentification tables inevitably summarize or characterize the play, affecting our assumptions about its fictional persons, and unlike other paratext they are often consulted or cross-referenced during reading, potentially interposing themselves at any point in the text" (54). I am particularly interested here in the tensions that may have been generated by such cross-referencing.

61. Q10 (1695) gives a simplified cast list; see below.

62. This is also the first edition to describe its authorship explicitly as such: "*The Authors being* {Francis Beaumont, *and* Iohn Fletcher} Gentlemen." Q1 and Q2 describe a text "[w]ritten by" the playwrights.

63. See also Masten, "Textual Deviance"; Orgel, *Impersonations*, 33.

64. I focus here on the tensions between text, paratext, and performance. For an alternative view of this change in dramatis personae lists, see Taylor, "Order of Persons": "Gender triumphed [in such lists], becoming the most significant of all possible distinctions between persons, an absolute of difference and distance which overcame proximity in every other dimension, genealogical, social, or economic. . . . To the extent that tables in printed plays made the distinction between men and women foundational and natural, the theatrical blurring of that distinction, when boys played women, began to seem unnatural. Conventions of writing altered performance conventions" (69–70).

65. Samuel Pepys, *The Diary of Samuel Pepys*, 9:217–18. The note on p. 218 suggests that the earlier episode must have taken place between 1639 and 1653 (with Pepys's age between six and twenty).

66. For a persuasive account of Pepys's modernity, see Francis Barker, *The Tremulous Private Body*.

67. The lines may also trope on the proverb "Boys will have toys" (Tilley C337, 98).

68. Earlier, Orsino's comment comparing "thy small pipe" and "the maiden's organ," while nominally about Cesario/Viola's voice, may also carry a resonance comparing young male penises and women's clitorises (1.4.32–33). On Viola/Cesario's phallic "lack," see also Traub, *Desire and Anxiety*, 132.

69. Other contradictions and complexities in Orsino's rhetoric include, for example, the father/son resonance of the sacrificial lamb rhetoric versus the possible equality suggested if Cesario as "cub" somehow reflects or reproduces a version of Orsino ("little bear").

70. Orgel, *Impersonations*, 70.

71. Lothian and Craik, *Twelfth Night*, 144n (5.1.242–43).

72. Traub, *Desire and Anxiety*, 132–38; DiGangi, *Homoerotics*, 20, 38, 41.

73. Traub astutely observes that Antonio's "vocalization of desire is caught uncomfortably between the only two discourses available to him: platonic friendship and sodomy" (*Desire and Anxiety*, 137). My brief reading attempts to expand the discourses engaged by the text here to include the (intersecting) discourse of homoerotic religious adoration and devotion, as explored by Richard Rambuss in *Closet Devotions*.

74. DiGangi, *Homoerotics*, 20, 167n61; Cynthia Lewis, " 'Wise Men, Folly-Fall'n': Characters Named Antonio in English Renaissance Drama."

75. In addition to Joseph Moxon's invaluable late-century discussions in *Mechanick Exercises . . . Applied to the Art of Printing*, see the data collected in D. F. McKenzie, ed., *Stationers' Company Apprentices, 1605–1640*, and *Stationer's CompanyApprentices, 1641–1700*. See also Gary Taylor's description of a scene in the bookseller's shop in "Making Meaning Marketing Shakespeare 1623."

76. For a discussion of this and some other printers' shop signs, see Jeffrey Masten, "Ben Jonson's Head."

77. Information derived from the *English Short Title Catalogue*, online edition. See also the comprehensive account of shops and signs in Peter W. M. Blayney, *The Bookshops in Paul's Cross Churchyard*.

78. *English Short Title Catalogue*, online edition. On the cultural meanings attached to young black servants in early modern England, see Kim F. Hall, *Things of Darkness: Economies of Race and Gender in Early Modern England*; and Susan E. Phillips, "Schoolmasters, Seduction, and Slavery."

79. For examples of head-pieces, see Henry R. Plomer, *English Printers' Ornaments*, 193, 227.

80. R. B. McKerrow and F. S. Ferguson, *Title-page Borders Used in England & Scotland, 1485–1640*, #98.

81. Ibid., #121.

82. Ronald B. McKerrow, *Printers' and Publishers' Devices in England and Scotland 1485–1640*, #166, misdescribed as "a boy seated on a dolphin" (60). (I mistakenly followed McKerrow's description in Masten, "Editing Boys," here corrected.) The device reworks the identically titled Alciato emblem ("Ex litterarum studiis immortalitatem acquiri") showing an adult Triton encircled by a snake consuming its own tail. Some English uses of the device leave the space of the motto blank, including a number of other books printed by Williamson and others (e.g., *The General Practise Of Physicke* [1617]; *The rewarde of Wickednesse* [1573–74?]; and *Certayne newes Of The whole discription, ayde, and helpe of the Christian Princes and Nobles* [1574?]). Williamson's monogram appears at the bottom of the version of the device pictured.

83. On boys and pedagogy, see Lynn Enterline, "Rhetoric, Discipline, and the Theatricality of Everyday Life in Elizabethan Grammar Schools."

84. McKerrow, *Printers' and Publishers' Devices*, #142 and 393.

85. The device was used by Valentine Simmes from 1597 to 1604.

86. Geffrey Whitney, "Paupertatem summis ingeniis obesse ne prouehantur," in *A Choice Of Emblemes*, 152.

87. Plomer, *English Printers' Ornaments*, 239–47; Ruth Samson Luborsky and Elizabeth Morley Ingram, *A Guide to English Illustrated Books, 1536–1603*. The list of Luborsky and Ingram's exclusions from the category of "illustrations" is extensive (1:10), though there are strong reasons, explored briefly below, to question the historicity of a firm distinction between "illustration" (even "image") and "text" in early modern print.

88. For a broad survey organized by locale, see Oscar Jennings, *Early Woodcut Initials*.

89. See Charles Dempsey, *Inventing the Renaissance Putto*.

90. Hugo Chapman, *Padua in the 1450s: Marco Zoppo and His Contemporaries*, 38, 65–66. Chapman believes that the "homosexual imagery" suggests that the drawings were a private commission, but the proliferation of interacting putti in even English printed contexts may suggest a broader range of possible meanings for images in wider circulation. I am grateful to Stephen Campbell for suggesting this material.

91. Andreas Vesalius, *De Humani corporis fabrica Libri septem*, sig. *2. For an online edition, see http://archive.nlm.nih.gov/proj/ttp/flash/vesalius/vesalius.html.

92. Marsilius of Padua, *Opvs Insigne Cvi Titvlvm Fecit Avtor Defensorem Pacis*, sig. b[1]^r.

93. Gazēs, *Theodori Gazae Introdvctionis grammaticae*, 190, also used on 250.

94. See, e.g., Jennings, *Early Woodcut Initials*, 35, 60–61.

95. For some early and often basic exploratory work, see Charles Sayle, "Initial Letters in Early English Printed Books"; Jennings, *Early Woodcut Initials*; A. W. Pollard, "Some Pictorial and Heraldic Initials"; A. J. Butler, "The Initial Blocks of Some Italian Printers"; Giuseppe Boffito, *Iniziali Istoriate e Iniziali Fiorite o Arabescate*; Douglas C. McMurtie, *Initial Letters*; Hellmut Lehmann-Haupt, *Initials from French Incunabula*.

96. Exception are Peter Stallybrass's 2011 essay, cited below; Jonathan Goldberg, *Writing Matter*, 164–67, and "Letters Themselves" (chap. 4).

97. *The Holy Bible containing the Old Testament and the New* (1602), 476–476ᵛ (STC 2188, consulted in the Folger copy).

98. *The Byble, which is all the holy Scripture* (1537), Newberry and Folger copies consulted. Smaller four-line initials from a similarly mixed decorative alphabet mark chapters (putti, other human and animal forms, grotesques, etc.).

99. The possibilities of meanings intended by the printer or compositor or legible to an early modern reader are elsewhere intriguing; for example, a four-line C with winged putto is used in Ephesyans fol. lxxxi, where chapter 6 begins with "Chyldren obey youre fathers and mothers in ye Lorde: for so it is ryght." On the same page, the previous chapter reads: "Be ye followers of God as dere childrē / & walke in loue euē as Christ loued vs & gaue hym selfe for vs." At the same time, the passage proceeds to denounce "ye worshypper of ymages."

100. "Prologue or Preface made by Thomas Cranmer," in *The Holy Bible . . . appoynted to be read in Churches* (1595), STC 2167, sig. A.ij.

101. "To the Most High, Most Mighty, and Most Excellent Soueraigne Princesse Elizabeth," dedicatory letter in William Segar, *Honor Military, and Civill* (1602), STC 22164, no sig., Folger STC 22164, copy 1, consulted.

102. *The Booke of Common Prayer*, STC 16364, sig. G5ᵛ.

103. I am grateful to Peter Stallybrass for bringing this initial to my attention. It is part of a series of mythological, historiated initials used by Christopher Barker and then his son Robert, and previously used by Cawood, Berthelet, and John Day; usually containing an engraver's monogram likely signifying "A.S." (visible in the lower right corner), the initials were probably the work of the Antwerp engraver Anton Sylvius, and include other Ovidian stories, for example, an I in which Daphne pursued is transformed into a tree. See Pollard, "Some Pictorial and Heraldic Initials," 244–46. Stallybrass discusses this and related Ovidian letters in "Visible and Invisible Letters: Text Versus Image in Renaissance England and Europe." On similar mythological initials in the 1611 Authorized Version, see Paul C. Gutjahr, "The Letter(s) of the Law: Four Centuries of Typography in the King James Bible," 21–25.

104. Segar, *Honor Military, and Civil*, no sig. (emphasis in the original).

105. "Prologue or Preface made by Thomas Cranmer," sig. A.ij (my emphasis).

106. *Booke of Common Prayer*, sig. G5ᵛ.

107. Rambuss, *Closet Devotions*, 56. Barkan brilliantly unfolds the hermeneutic complexities of reading between/across theological and erotic meanings of the myth in *Transuming Passion*, 26.

108. Rambuss, *Closet Devotions*, 56.

109. See James A. Knapp, "The Bastard Art: Woodcut Illustration in Sixteenth-Century England," esp. 163–65, qtd. at 164. See also Stallybrass on the meaningfulness versus opacity of decorative initials in "Visible and Invisible Letters," 87–96.

110. Knapp, "Bastard Art," 165.

111. Goldberg, *Writing Matter*, 227.

112. On the inculcation of writers and readers via early modern literacy training, see Goldberg, *Writing Matter*.

113. Softness and its antonyms have an extensive history in classical rhetoric and poetics; the influence of that tradition and of the gender and sexuality valences of its terms on early modern conceptions of writing have been traced in Patricia Parker, "Virile Style," esp. 204–5; Patricia Parker, "Gender Ideology, Gender Change: The Case of Marie Germain," esp. 348–50, 354–56; and Jenny C. Mann, "Marlowe's 'Slack Muse': *All Ovids Elegies* and an English Poetics of Softness," esp. 50–54.

114. See Rambuss, *Closet Devotions*, for a reading of Traherne's poem (54–58).

115. Barbara Hodgdon, private conversation in preparation for "Queer Eye for the Straight Play: Roundtable on *Twelfth Night*" (Shakespeare's Globe [London] and Institute for Research on Women and Gender, University of Michigan, Ann Arbor, November 2003). In his survey of the evidence for the ages of pre-Restoration boy actors, David Kathman concludes that "until the early 1660s, female roles on the English stage ... were played by adolescent boys, no younger than twelve, and no older than twenty-one or twenty-two, with a median of around sixteen or seventeen" ("How Old Were Shakespeare's Boy Actors?" 220). On the ages of boy actors in the boy companies, where the age range is somewhat younger, see Shen Lin, "How Old Were the Children of Paul's?"

116. See Orgel's brief comments about "authenticity" in "What's the Globe Good For?"

117. To take another widely known example: at the time of the U.S. release of *Shakespeare in Love* (1998), the actor (Daniel Brocklebank) playing the Chamberlain's Men boy actor Samuel Gosse/Juliet was eighteen going on nineteen. My quotation marks around "us" mean to register the complexity and multiplicity of this modern, global audience.

118. For a brief, provocative survey of contemporary U.S. culture's simultaneous investment in and disavowal of eroticism in relation to children, see James R. Kincaid, "Producing Erotic Children."

119. As Gossett notes, it is not certain whether the 1610 first performances of *Philaster* occurred at the Globe or elsewhere (58), though the Boy Quarto indicates the Globe.

CHAPTER 5. "AMOROUS LEANDER"

1. C. F. Tucker Brooke, ed., *The Life of Marlowe and The Tragedy of Dido Queen of Carthage*, 99.

2. Ch. Marl., *The Tragicall History of D. Faustus*, sig. F3.

3. Tucker Brooke, "The Reputation of Christopher Marlowe," 404–5.

4. Havelock Ellis, ed., *Christopher Marlowe*. Will Fisher first mentioned to me the connections among Ellis, Symonds, and Marlowe; see "The Sexual Politics of Victorian Historiographical Writing About the 'Renaissance,'" esp. 53. See also the discussion of the indebtedness of modern conceptions of Marlowe to Symonds, Ellis, and other "aesthetes" in Thomas Dabbs, "Marlowe Among the Aesthetes."

5. David M. Halperin, "One Hundred Years of Homosexuality," in *One Hundred Years of Homosexuality and Other Essays on Greek Love*, 15–18.

6. J. T. Parnell, "Introduction"; J. A. Downie, "Marlowe: Facts and Fictions"; Lisa Hopkins, *Christopher Marlowe: A Literary Life*, esp. "Introduction."

7. That is, insofar as critics have recently emphasized the highly mediated nature of the Baines allegations; see, e.g., Hopkins, *Christopher Marlowe*, 4. I have no fresh information on the question of Marlowe's actual appetites and addictions.

8. Alan Bray, "Homosexuality and the Signs of Male Friendship in Elizabethan England," and *The Friend*; Jonathan Goldberg, *Sodometries*; Stephen Orgel, *Impersonations*; Mario DiGangi, *The Homoerotics of Early Modern Drama*; Bruce R. Smith, *Homosexual Desire in Shakespeare's England*; Valerie Traub, *The Renaissance of Lesbianism*.

9. Brian Vickers, "Appendix II: Abolishing the Author: Theory *Versus* History," in *Shakespeare, Co-Author*, 535; see also 539, 541.

10. Erne, "Biography," 28, 47. Subsequent references appear parenthetically.

11. Erne, *Shakespeare as Literary Dramatist*, 1. Subsequent references appear parenthetically.

12. E.g., Nicholas Robins, "The Script's the Thing"; James Fenton, "Shakespeare, Stage or Page?"; Dympna Callaghan, "Recent Studies in Tudor and Stuart Drama." For a skeptical view of Erne's thesis, see Jason Scott-Warren, "As It Is Writ."

13. See Mario DiGangi, "Marlowe, Queer Studies, and Renaissance Homoeroticism," 202.

14. Prior to the discussion of the *Edward II* example, the essay's phrase for this process is "affects and disturbs" (38).

15. Orgel, *Impersonations*, 47–48.

16. For an earlier questioning of Orgel's reading of the possible lack of stage direction, see the previously published version of Chapter 6 in Jeffrey Masten, "Is the Fundament a Grave?," 141n6.

17. See also Christopher D. Shirley, "Sodomy and Stage Directions in Christopher Marlowe's *Edward(s) II*."

18. See Bray, "Homosexuality and the Signs"; Mario DiGangi, *Sexual Types*; Smith, *Homosexual Desire*; Goldberg, *Sodometries* (esp. the introduction); David M. Halperin, "How to Do the History of Male Homosexuality"; Traub, *Renaissance of Lesbianism* (esp. 226–28). On the centrality of the anus in cultural formulations of "homosexuality," see Guy Hocquenghem, *Homosexual Desire*.

19. For a full transcription of Baines's and Kyd's allegations about Marlowe, see Brooke, *The Life of Marlowe*, 98–100, 103–8.

20. Park Honan, *Christopher Marlowe*, 353, figure 32, "Marlowe's wound." The photograph thus labeled shows, "in a modern skull," that "the point of a dagger barely impinges on the internal carotid artery."

21. Jonathan Goldberg, "Sodomy and Society: The Case of Christopher Marlowe."

22. See Chapter 3.

23. See Erne, "Biography," 43: "The only evidence the biographical record contains to support [Lisa Hopkins's] view" that *Edward II* is "openly based on [Marlowe's] own sexual preferences" "is Marlowe's flippant statement, according to the Baines note, 'that all they that loue not Tobacco & Boies were fooles.'"

24. Bray, "Homosexuality and the Signs."

25. See Goldberg's objective of "the sites of sexual possibilities, the syntax of desires not readily named" (*Sodometries*, 22).

26. Michel Foucault, "What Is an Author?," 119.

27. Eve Kosofsky Sedgwick, *Epistemology of the Closet*.

28. Foucault, "What Is an Author?," 119–20.

29. Christopher Marloe, *Hero And Leander*.

30. Christopher Marloe and George Chapman, *Hero And Leander*.

31. Erasmus, "On the Writing of Letters" / *De conscribendis epistolis*, 25:58–59 (my emphasis). On homoerotic epithets, see also Chapter 2.

32. Unless otherwise indicated, quotations from the Marlowe-Chapman poem are from Millar MacLure, ed., *The Poems: Christopher Marlowe*. Subsequent references appear parenthetically, citing sestiads and line numbers. I will identify problems with the edited text in the course of the chapter; see, for example, note 99 below. See also the old-spelling edition in Fredson Bowers, ed., *Hero and Leander*, in *The Complete Poems of Christopher Marlowe*.

33. As will become clear, my reading of Leander builds on the groundbreaking work of Nancy Vickers on the blason tradition in early modern poetry, as well as important homoerotic readings of the poem, particularly Gregory W. Bredbeck, *Sodomy and Interpretation*, esp. 110–34; and Smith, *Homosexual Desire*, esp. 132–36. Though our ultimate concerns are divergent, I

find myself often in agreement with Clark Hulse's prescient reading of the poem in his chapter, "Marlowe, the Primeval Poet," in *Metamorphic Verse*.

34. Qtd. in W. W. Greg, "The Copyright of *Hero and Leander*," 165.

35. David Lee Miller, "The Death of the Modern: Gender and Desire in Marlowe's 'Hero and Leander,'" 763.

36. That is, the first serial publication of the *OED* (*a* through *antyteme*), published in January 1884. See John Willinsky, *Empire of Words: The Reign of the OED*, 3.

37. On the emergence of these terms in 1892, see Halperin, "One Hundred Years of Homosexuality," esp. 15–17. Halperin notes that the 1933 edition of the *OED* is "ignorant of (if not willfully blind to) 'homosexuality'; the word appears for the first time in the *OED*'s 1976 three-volume Supplement" (17).

38. Christopher Marlowe, *Edward the Second*, 1.1.6–9.

39. On this reference to Pelops' shoulder as attempting to "arouse[ ] a desire cannibalistic in its intensity," see Matthew Greenfield, "Christopher Marlowe's Wound Knowledge," 235.

40. *OED*, *amorous*, adj. and *n.*, 5.

41. [Henry Cockeram] H.C., *The English Dictionarie: Or, An Interpreter of hard English Words*, sig. B4ᵛ. John Bullokar defines *amorous* as "Louing, or giuen to loue" in *An English Expositor*, sig. B6ᵛ.

42. *OED*, *amorous*, adj. and *n.*, 5, cites "1557 *Primer Sarum* Diij," apparently *The prymer in Englysshe and in Latin after the vse of Sarum* 1555 (1557). I have thus far been unable to locate the quotation cited. I continue to search for instances of "passive" *amorous* beyond those few that the *OED* cites between 1400 and 1611, though, as my argument suggests, "Amorous Leander," a phrase published at least ten times between 1598 and 1637 in a poem much cited, should be added to the list.

43. Musaeus, *Hero and Leander*, 346–47 at line 20. The Loeb editor Cedric Whitman translates as follows: "He was Leander, quickener of desire." "Inciting" is my term; Henry George Liddell and Robert Scott, comps., *A Greek-English Lexicon*, give as their entry for *himero-eis* "A. *exciting desire, lovely, charming*, in Hom. always *of things*." In his extensive discussion of the noun *himeros*, from which *himeroeis* derives, James Davidson makes clear that the term is applied to persons (including boys) as objects, glossing it as "a sudden urge" and "a kind of emanation from the object" and describing a kind of reversal of subject and object deeply relevant to the discussion below (*The Greeks and Greek Love*, 13–14). Martin Mueller (private communication) describes *himeroeis* as an "'aura' word," associated with motion and ambience. On the Musurus translation of the Greek, available to Marlowe and Chapman, see MacLure, *Poems*, xxv–xxvi and n1, and Baldwin, "Marlowe's Musaeus." Gordon Braden, in *The Classics and English Renaissance Poetry*, notes that Baldwin "assumes that Marlowe's 'amorous' is a translation of Mousaios's *himeroeis*; if so, it is further evidence of Marlowe's direct recourse to the Greek" (127).

44. Judith Haber, "'True-Loves Blood': Narrative and Desire in *Hero and Leander*." Haber incisively describes the interpretive implications raised by the editorial transposition in most twentieth-century editions of lines 2.279–300. For further discussion of nonconsummating eroticism in the poem, see James M. Bromley, "Intimacy and Narrative Closure in Christopher Marlowe's *Hero and Leander*," in *Intimacy and Sexuality in the Age of Shakespeare*.

45. Halperin, "How to Do the History of Male Homosexuality," 99 (emphasis in the original).

46. My underscoring.

47. See p. 76 above.

48. Goldberg, *Sodometries*; Halperin, "How to Do the History of Male Homosexuality." On sexual positions and prepositionality, see also Chapter 8.

49. Michael C. Schoenfeldt, *Bodies and Selves in Early Modern England*; Gail Kern Paster, *The Body Embarrassed*. To be sure, the *OED* also gives multiple examples of English words operating during this period in which the prefix *en-* means "to bring into a certain condition or state" (*OED, en-, prefix*[1], 2).

50. *OED, en-, prefix*[1].

51. *OED, amour, n.*[1]

52. Cf. the description of Mercury and the country maid: "On her this god / Enamour'd was." On the basis of this very slight sample, one might argue that, at least in Marlowe, passively enamoured men are nevertheless actively or hierarchically enamoured *on* women, while men are enamoured *of* other men.

53. Erne, "Biography," 43.

54. Though Bredbeck's reading usefully sets aside the question of Marlowe's intentions—which will not concern me either—in order to concentrate on "the social forces encoded in and encoding the text as it was produced in its own time" (*Sodomy and Interpretation*, 128n72), his reading does not significantly take up the question of Chapman's or others' continuations, which I take to be a part of the encoding he describes. Smith, *Homosexual Desire*, briefly considers the continuation of the poem (134).

55. E.g., introducing *Marlowe: The Critical Heritage 1588–1896*, Millar MacLure cites "the casual bumblings of Henry Petowe, one of the most minor of minor versifiers" (5).

56. Patrick Cheney, *Marlowe's Counterfeit Profession*.

57. Henry Petowe, *The Second Part of Hero and Leander. Conteyning their further Fortunes*, sigs. B.ij–B.ij[v] (emphasis in the original, underscoring added).

58. See the reflexive uses in *OED, frame, v.*, 5.a., 6.b. On early modern "framing" discourse, see Rayna Kalas, "The Language of Framing," and *Frame, Glass, Verse*, and her contention that early modern "framing" is conceptualized as integral/structural/constitutive, rather than decorative and separable from the framed object.

59. Ovid, *Ovid's Metamorphoses*, 10.23–26. Subsequent references appear parenthetically.

60. *OED, frame, v.*, 5.a. As this and other meanings in the *OED*'s entry for the verb suggest, in a way potentially illuminating for Petowe's ambiguous syntax and implied objects, the status of grammatical subjects/objects in relation to *frame* (as transitive, passive, reflexive) seems to have been in flux in this period (5.a.).

61. DiGangi, *Homoerotics*, 45. DiGangi's examples, mostly from the 1590s, are contemporaneous with Petowe's poem.

62. *As You Like It*, in Stephen Greenblatt et al., eds., *The Norton Shakespeare Based on the Oxford Edition*, 2nd ed. (3.5.82–83).

63. Orgel, "Tobacco and Boys," 575.

64. "*Phœbe* made no replie, but fetcht such a sigh, that *Eccho* made relation of her plaint: giuing *Ganimede* such an adieu with a piercing glaunce, that the amorous Girle-boy perceiued *Phœbe* was pincht by the heele." [Thomas Lodge], *Rosalynde. Euphues golden legacie*, 49[v]. In the puppet play of *Hero and Leander* in Ben Jonson's *Bartholomew Fair* (ed. E. A. Horsman), Jonson uses the epithet "amorous Leander" three times (5.4.114, 195, 350; also "young Leander," 5.4.153). The final iteration provides Leander with a new epithet, even as the speaker disputes "call[ing] amorous Leander whore-master knave."

65. For a review of the twentieth-century critical reception of Marlowe's poem as complete or fragmentary, see Robert F. Darcy, "'Under My Hands . . . A Double Duty': Printing and Pressing Marlowe's *Hero and Leander*," esp. 29–32.

66. MacLure, *Poems*, xxv. See also the *English Short Title Catalogue*'s "mock poems" and burlesques of *Hero and Leander* in the 1650s and 1660s.

67. Foucault, "What Is an Author?," 120.

68. On the multivalency of *will* in early modern English, including meanings related to desire and sexual anatomy, see Stephen Booth, ed., *Shakespeare's Sonnets*, 466–67.

69. The letter to Lady Walsingham is printed between what have become the second and third sestiads of the poem in the first edition to include Chapman's continuation (Marloe and Chapman, *Hero And Leander*, sigs. E3ᵛ–E4ᵛ).

70. Braden, *Classics*, 55–56, 81–82; David Riggs, *The World of Christopher Marlowe*, 299–300. The "misunderstanding" had been corrected by 1583, "but the news travelled slowly" (Riggs, 299–300). "The history of Mousaios's poem in the literary culture of the Renaissance is almost exactly coextensive with its ascription to the mythical companion of Orpheus, and its popularity and prestige were intricately involved with the Renaissance readers' sense that 'they were communing with the spirit of poetry at its elemental source'" (Braden, 81).

71. "Like Orpheus and Musaeus," Hulse bluntly summarizes, "Marlowe preaches homosexuality and heresy" (*Metamorphic Verse*, 102). On the link between Greek "homosexuality" (i.e., pedagogical pederasty) and "the inspired poets," see *Metamorphic Verse*, 102. Though both critics use the term "homosexuality" more broadly than those currently writing on premodern sexuality would, Cheney's reading relies on a more essential, modern model of sexuality, citing Marlowe's "different sexual orientation" compared to Spenser (*Marlowe's Counterfeit Profession*, 179).

72. Iohn Florio, *A Worlde of Wordes*, 185, sig. Q3.

73. For Hulse's reading of Chapman's invocation of Marlowe, see *Metamorphic Verse*, 124–26.

74. The *OED* (*intellect, n.*) suggests that *intellect* and *intellectual* were not widely used in English before the sixteenth century (2nd ed., 1989).

75. For a reading of this passage that emphasizes Chapman's continuation and relation to Marlowe's poem in relation to Spenser, see Cheney, *Marlowe's Counterfeit Profession*, 256–58.

76. For a possible sexual resonance to "drink deep" as "fellate" in a 1605 text, see Theodore B. Leinwand, "Redeeming Beggary/Buggery in *Michaelmas Term*," 55.

77. Hulse, *Metamorphic Verse*, 127.

78. *OED*, *die*, *v*.¹, 6, "*to die unto* . . . cf. Rom. vi. 2," a meaning with little *OED* documentation.

79. The "dark" quality of Chapman's progeny bears further analysis in the context of early modern "race" as well as "ink." See Kim F. Hall, *Things of Darkness: Economies of Race and Gender in Early Modern England*; Margreta de Grazia, "The Scandal of Shakespeare's Sonnets."

80. On "'us,' the presumed male readers," see Hulse, *Metamorphic Verse*, 108. Though I do not do so in this chapter, one would want to consider carefully the identificatory and erotic effects of this popular poem on female readers, as Phoebe's quotation of it in *As You Like It* may begin to suggest.

81. See Margaret W. Ferguson, "*Hamlet*: Letters and Spirits," 301–5, 308n20. The *Hamlet* passage (4.7.81–9 in Jenkins, ed.), with the multivalent homoeroticisms and identifications (including across species) that Ferguson analyzes, as well as its use of the terms *seat, demi-natur'd*, and *topp'd*, suggests that it may resonate further with the lexicon of early modern sodomy as explored in Chapters 6–9.

82. On *rage* as "lust," "desire," or "passion," see Booth, *Shakespeare's Sonnets*, 154 (note to 13.12), and *OED*, *rage* (*v*., 1.a.–b., and *n*., 5.c.). "Fort" goes unannotated in most modern editions (Bowers, Martin, MacLure, Orgel) and the phrase is not entirely clear (fortress? fortified place? force? "for't"?), especially given the resonances that may appear in the line's unmodernized spelling: "His loues liues fort" (Marloe and Chapman, *Hero And Leander*, sig. N3ᵛ; Bowers, 6.231).

83. David Halperin (private correspondence) has suggested to me the resonant parallels between Pindar's Poseidon, "broken in his wits by *himeros* [longing]" for Pelops (in his first Olympian Ode), and Marlowe's Neptune and Leander.

84. Musaeus, *Hero and Leander*, 327–28.

85. George Chapman, trans., *The Divine Poem Of Mvsæs. First of all Bookes*, sig. G7ᵛ.

86. My understanding of the role and functions of boys in early modern culture has been significantly influenced by Emily D. Bryan's dissertation, "In the Company of Boys," and Bryan, "The Government of Performance: *Ignoramus* and the Micropolitics of Tutor-Student Relations." See also Orgel, *Impersonations*; Smith, *Homosexual Desire*; Halperin, "How to Do the History of Male Homosexuality"; Richard Rambuss, "What It Feels Like for a Boy: Shakespeare's *Venus and Adonis*." For discussion of this question via *Twelfth Night* and *Philaster*, see Chapter 4.

87. Halperin, "One Hundred Years of Homosexuality," 35.

88. On the paradoxes of the modern dispensation, see James R. Kincaid, "Producing Erotic Children." For a contrasting view of the Renaissance male youth, see Smith, *Homosexual Desire*, 136.

89. On the question of young men's desire in relation to age of marital consent, see Chapter 4, note 36.

90. Rambuss, "What It Feels Like," 254.

91. Ibid., 252, 255.

92. See Bryan, "In the Company of Boys." Cf. Hulse: in Marlowe, as well as in Shakespeare and Fletcher, "the pubescent male is the middle term between male and female, between desire and its object" (*Metamorphic Verse*, 108).

93. On *himeros* as "emanation from an object" or "love attack," see Davidson, *Greeks and Greek Love*, 13. For a reading of a boy taking up "numerous, often indeterminate positions," both active and passive, in a dramatic context, see Leinwand, "Redeeming Beggary/Buggery," 67n22 and 61.

94. Thomas Wright, *The Passions of the Mind in General*, 117–18.

95. See Lynn Enterline, "Rhetoric, Discipline, and the Theatricality of Everyday Life in Elizabethan Grammar Schools," esp. 184–87.

96. See Chapter 4.

97. Braden, *Classics*, 87.

98. This is where I differ most fully with Smith, who, in *Homosexual Desire*, briefly discusses Chapman's continuation as "remote indeed from the salacious imagination of Marlowe's narrator" and implicitly "spoiling our pleasure in the [Marlowe] poem's homoerotic fantasy" (134). I do not see Chapman's addition as solely disciplinary in its investments. Darcy also sees "Chapman's reparative additions" as "containing the daring of Marlowe's . . . 'beginning,'" while advancing the novel thesis that "possibly Marlowe's poem needed containment to survive," as a result of its unsettling of gender ("'Under My Hands,'" 47, 49, 50).

99. I have deleted MacLure's hyphen here ("dis-ease") to restore the earliest printed text (Marloe and Chapman, *Hero And Leander*, sig. N2). MacLure's alteration presumably seeks to indicate an assumption that the 1598 edition's "disease" should for a modern reader signify "uneasiness," "trouble," or "cause of trouble," rather than "malady" or "sickness." The unhyphenated spelling was available for both sets of meanings in the sixteenth century (*OED*, *disease, n.*), and an early modern writer/reader might have seen either or both meanings in the graphic shape "disease."

100. David M. Halperin and Valerie Traub, "Beyond Gay Pride," esp. 8–11. The gay shame movement, as Halperin and Traub note, was launched in opposition to celebrations of gay pride, the latter seen as increasingly consumerist and stripped of any real political aspiration or edge; see, for example, the Gay Shame San Francisco site, www.gayshamesf.org. A revaluation of sexual shame is central to Michael Warner, *The Trouble with Normal*, esp. chap. 1, "The Ethics

of Sexual Shame." Among other critical works on shame and sex/sexuality, see Leo Bersani, *Homos*; and Eve Kosofsky Sedgwick, *Touching Feeling*.

101. Michael Warner, "Pleasures and Dangers of Shame," 288; George Chauncey, "The Trouble with Shame," 279.

102. On "the same" act, see Bray, "Homosexuality and the Signs." For multiple and eventually intersecting structures of female same-sex eroticism in this period, see Traub, *Renaissance of Lesbianism*.

103. On a posthumous "Marlowe effect," see Leah S. Marcus, *Unediting the Renaissance*. It seems possible to me, however, in Marcus's analysis of this effect via *Faustus*, that one might more precisely speak of a "Faustus effect."

104. Riggs, *World of Christopher Marlowe*.

105. This argument is extended in relation to textual editing in Chapter 8.

106. Halperin, "How to Do the History of Male Homosexuality."

107. Christopher Marlowe, *Dido Queen of Carthage*, 1.1.23–27. Subsequent references appear parenthetically. The passage reads resonantly with Davidson's discussion of *himeros* (*Greeks and Greek Love*, 13–14).

108. Petowe, *The Second Part of Hero and Leander*, sigs. B.ij–B.ij^v.

109. Goldberg, *Sodometries*, 126–38.

110. Marlowe, *Edward the Second*, 1.1.145; subsequent references appear parenthetically.

111. See Marlowe, *Dido*, xli and 4 (note to 1.1.1–2).

112. See *OED*, *hug*, *v.*, 3.b. I have located only two examples of "hug with" in the period; *OED* cites Shakespeare, *King John*, "hug with swine"; see also Francis Sable, *The Fissher-mans Tale*, sig. E3: "let me goe vnto my wife againe, / Ah my sweet Mepsa, who shall hug with thee."

113. Halperin, "One Hundred Years of Homosexuality."

114. As noted in Chapter 2, *sweet* is not only a same-gendered or male-only term of affection within Renaissance English discourse, but its male-male iteration in this play makes the final turn on this rhetoric significant.

115. See David M. Bergeron, ed., *King James and Letters of Homoerotic Desire*, 173–74; and Bray's masterful reading of this complex letter (*The Friend*, 96–104). On the complexity of James's relation to (older and younger) favorites, see Alan Stewart, *The Cradle King*. On favoritism and its meaning in the play, see also Curtis Perry, "The Politics of Access and Representations of the Sodomite King in Early Modern England."

CHAPTER 6. IS THE FUNDAMENT A GRAVE?

1. Leo Bersani, "Is the Rectum a Grave?," 216. Subsequent references appear parenthetically.

2. William Shakespeare, *A Midsommer Nights Dreame*, in *Mr. VVilliam Shakespeares Comedies, Histories, & Tragedies*, as reproduced in Charlton Hinman, ed., *The Norton Facsimile: The First Folio of Shakespeare*, TLN 1731–42.

3. For a discussion of gender in relation to issues in this chapter, see pp. 186–87 below.

4. For a survey of female anal eroticism and sodomy, particularly in early modern drama, see Celia R. Daileader, "Back Door Sex."

5. Edmund Spenser, *The Faerie Queene*, ed. A. C. Hamilton, 2.9.32.7–8. Hamilton glosses the Esquiline gate as ancient Rome's "anus as it gave passage to the common dump" (253). Reading this passage's Galenic resonances, Michael C. Schoenfeldt emphasizes the healthy elimination of waste, rather than death, in *Bodies and Selves in Early Modern England*, 60–65, 83. In his topographical, quasi-Spenserian surveying of the body as an *island*, Phineas Fletcher likewise

figures the anus as a "port *Esquiline*" that "between two hills, in darkest valley lies" (*The Purple Island, Or The Isle Of Man*, 27 [canto 2.43]).

6. *Faerie Queene*, 1.5.52–53 (my emphasis). "The hinder gate" of the Garden of Adonis through which living forms "returne back" from "mortall state" may also figure this conjunction (3.6.32.8–9) (Kasey Evans, private correspondence). See Harry Berger, "Actaeon at the Hinder Gate," 104–5, 118n26.

7. *The Tragedie Of Hamlet, Prince of Denmarke*, in *Mr. VVilliam Shakespeares Comedies, Histories, & Tragedies*, TLN 3390–92. On French *trou* as "the bung-hole, fundament, nock-androe," see Randle Cotgrave, comp., *A Dictionarie Of The French And English Tongves*, sig. Iiii. vi; and Chapter 2.

8. Raphael Holinshed et al., *Chronicles*, 3:341. On this passage, see Bruce R. Smith, *Homosexual Desire in Shakespeare's England*, 220. My "same" is in quotation marks, for, as Stephen Orgel has pointed out, critics have not been fully attentive to the difference the lack of direction in the printed text might make for the scene's meaning (*Impersonations*, 47–48). A notable exception to this critical blindness is Derek Jarman's film, which stages Edward's death à la Holinshed as (only) a dream/fantasy. Orgel's certainty that the hot spit was *not* used in early modern performance occludes some other possibilities: that, like many other stage directions, it doesn't appear in the printed text (technically speaking, Edward doesn't die either) or that a stage direction used in performance was (for whatever reason, perhaps including censorship) left out of the printed version. On Edward's death and its role in readings of Marlowe's life and texts, see Chapter 5.

9. Aston Cokain, *Small Poems of Divers sorts*, epigram 100, p. 186.

10. This term is Jonathan Goldberg's (*Sodometries*); here and below I mean to engage two of its meanings outlined there: structures and positions of sodomy, and the argument whose logic seems illogical.

11. See Alan Bray, *The Friend*; Alan Bray, "Homosexuality and the Signs of Male Friendship in Elizabethan England."

12. To be precise, the crime in Leviticus 18:22 and 20:13 is "lying with" "man" or "mankind" as with woman, in the Geneva, Bishops', and Authorized Versions, but verse 20:13 is summarized as "Sodomie" in the headnote to the AV, chap. 20. On Tudor/Stuart sodomy laws, see Smith, *Homosexual Desire*, 41–53; Gregory W. Bredbeck, *Sodomy and Interpretation*, 5–10, 18–20; Goldberg, *Sodometries*, 3, 7 (cf. also 238–42 on America); Janet E. Halley, "*Bowers v. Hardwick* in the Renaissance," 15–39; Cynthia B. Herrup, *A House in Gross Disorder*; the numerous contemporary sodomy prosecutions discussed in Bray, *Homosexuality in Renaissance England*; and Chapters 8 and 9.

13. On the collaborative homoerotics of this poem, see Jeffrey Masten, *Textual Intercourse*, 1–4.

14. For especially formative cultural analyses of the gendered body in early modern England, see Nancy J. Vickers's influential essays on the poetic *blason*, the early modern body, and gender ("The Blazon of Sweet Beauty's Best" and "Diana Described"); Gail Kern Paster, *The Body Embarrassed*; Peter Stallybrass and Allon White, *The Politics and Poetics of Transgression*; David Hillman and Carla Mazzio, eds., *The Body in Parts*, in which a version of this chapter first appeared; and Valerie Traub, *The Renaissance of Lesbianism in Early Modern England* (esp. chaps. 2 and 5).

15. Frank Whigham and Wayne A. Rebhorn, eds., *The Art of English Poesy by George Puttenham: A Critical Edition*, 253; Patricia Parker, "Preposterous Reversals," 435–36. The quotation that is the heading of this section of the present book derives from *A Midsommer Nights Dreame*, TLN 935–36.

16. Qtd. in Parker, "Preposterous Reversals," 436.

17. Goldberg, *Sodometries*, esp. 180–81; Parker, "Preposterous Reversals," 479. I also want to acknowledge the influence throughout this chapter of Jonathan Goldberg, "The Anus in *Coriolanus*."

18. Paster, *Body Embarrassed*, 138. For a recent reading of Bottom in relation to both animality and anal rhetorics, see Richard Rambuss, "Shakespeare's Ass Play." Rambuss notes that "anal desire [in *Midsummer*] is principally female in issue, if not aim" (240).

19. On this kind of linguistic activity as structuring early modern English, rather than as linguistic excess or (merely) intentional "wordplay," see Margreta de Grazia, "Homonyms Before and After Lexical Standardization"; Patricia Parker, *Shakespeare from the Margins*, 3.

20. *OED, fundament, n.*, 1.a.

21. The "form *fundament* is directly from the Latin, and is therefore strictly a distinct word < *foundment*, but it is convenient to treat them together on account of the occurrence of mixed forms" (*OED, fundament, n.*, Etymology). For a critique of the *OED*'s anachronistic notion of discrete words, see Chapter 8. On *foundation* as *fundament*, see *OED, foundation*, 5.b.

22. Iohn Minsheu, *Ductor in Linguas, The Guide into the tongues*, 204.

23. Both of these terms were also in use during the period, though *anus* seems to have been restricted to more learned and medical use.

24. *OED, fundamental, adj. and n.*, 1.a.

25. Iohn Florio, *A Worlde of Wordes*, 135.

26. See *OED, fundamental, adj. and n.*, 1.a. A different but related positioning of God (Christ?), fundament, and church is mapped in Richard Rambuss's important rereading of the Donne sonnet "Batter my heart," in "Pleasure and Devotion"; see also Richard Rambuss, *Closet Devotions*, 49–54, 59–60. Many anatomy texts during the period refer to the sacrum as the "holy bone," "not because," in Helkiah Crooke's words, "it containeth in it any sacred and hidden mystery, as some haue fondly imagined, but because of his greatnesse, for it is the greatest of all the bones of the Spine"; Helkiah Crooke, *[Mikrokosmographia], A Description of the Body of Man*, 978.

27. Florio, *Worlde of Wordes*, 135.

28. Ibid. (my emphasis).

29. Iohn Florio, *Qveen Anna's New World of Words*, 192.

30. Thomas Elyot, *The Castel of Helth Corrected and in some places augmented*, 53ʳ.

31. Florio, *Qveen Anna's New World of Words*, 192.

32. Lee Edelman, "The Mirror and the Tank: 'AIDS,' Subjectivity, and the Rhetoric of Activism" in *Homographesis*, 110. Edelman's chapter has been a foundational influence on this discussion; see also his commentary on Bersani's "Is the Rectum a Grave?" (*Homographesis*, 98–99).

33. The fundament as a site of subject-producing activity is articulated by Crooke, in his chapter "Of the muscles of the Fundament, the Bladder, the Testicles and the Yard": "Because Man was a politique creature, made for Action and contemplation, it was not fit that he should either receiue his nourishment, or auoyde his excrements perpetually as plants doe, but at his owne choyce. As therefore in the Chops there are muscles seruing for diglutition or swallowing, so in the end of the guts and the outlet of the vrine, there are muscles set as porters to interclude the passage vnlesse we list to open it" (*[Mikrokosmographia]*, 803).

34. Guy Hocquenghem, *Homosexual Desire*, 100.

35. Ibid., 107. Will Stockton objects that an earlier version of this essay "disallows the same coexistence of anal rhetorics within psychoanalysis" in "address[ing] fundamentalism's queer potential" and "leaves us to assume that the Freudian body is irredeemably homophobic" (*Playing Dirty*, xvii–xviii). For the earlier version's non-disavowal of psychoanalysis in relation to early modern anality, see Jeffrey Masten, "Is the Fundament a Grave?," 145n47; I have at-

tempted to clarify this point here and below. I think Stockton and I would agree that reading plural early modern rhetorics of what has come to be called the anus is a useful corrective to a *doctrinaire* interpretation of (some of) Freud's work that has been (redeemably, one hopes) homophobic—something his, Hocquenghem's, and my texts each seem to seek. On the possibilities of other psychoanalyses that might emerge by taking seriously the rhetoric of the fundament, see the final section of this chapter.

36. Thomas Elyot, *The Dictionary of syr Thomas Eliot knyght*, n.p. My italics signify the blackletter (normative) type in the original.

37. "The additions," in ibid., n.p.

38. Quotation and summary of the *OED*'s entries for *author*.

39. The anatomist Casserius's plates (apparently drawn by a pupil of Tintoretto) were published in both Adriaan van de Spiegel, *De humani corporis fabrica libri decem*; and Guilio Placentini Casseri, *Tabulae Anatomica LXXIIX*. For a review of Casserius's career, see Alessandro Riva et al., "Iulius Casserius (1552–1616)." Thanks to Carla Mazzio for bringing this image to my attention.

40. Michel Foucault, "What Is an Author?," 101–20. On the relation of the early modern term *author* to modern authorship, see Masten, *Textual Intercourse*, 64–73.

41. James I, *The Workes of the Most High and Mightie Prince, Iames*, sig. b3 (emphasis in the original).

42. On *gradatio*, see Thomas Wilson, *The Arte of Rhetorique*, 204; Patricia Parker, *Literary Fat Ladies*, 96.

43. The spelling overlap in early modern forms of the modern words *tongs* and *tongues*—as well as *tongs'* etymological relation to "bite" and "biting"—may have added a momentary orality to this passage for sixteenth-century readers (*OED*, *tongs*, *n.*), though the capitalization of "Tonges" may seek to defend against that possibility. As the *OED* laments, in a brief what-if fantasy imagining a more systematic spelling development for *tongue* in English, "[t]he spelling *tongue* is thus neither etymological nor phonetic, and is only in a very small degree historical" (*tongue*, *n.*, Etymology).

44. John Arderne, *[A] treatise of the Fistulae in the fundament, and other places of the body, translated out of Iohannes Ardern*, 85ᵛ–86, 89ᵛ. The Arderne text is printed as part of a larger volume in 1588 but is internally dated 1349; on Arderne and this text (including illustrations from the MS), see D'Arcy Power, ed., *Treatises of Fistula in Ano, Haemorrhoids, and Clysters by John Arderne*.

45. Arderne, *[A] treatise*, 82 (my emphases).

46. Ibid.

47. My thinking about the relation of the book to dissection in Vesalius has been influenced by Wendy Wall's consideration of "'violent enlargement' and the voyeuristic text" in *The Imprint of Gender*, 169–72, 202–3; Katharine Park's reading of Nero's dissection of his mother and its relation to Vesalius's title page (see esp. "The Empire of Anatomy"); and Marjorie Garber (private conversation). Park persuasively reads the *Fabrica* as associating the opening of a new mode and method of anatomical knowledge with the opening up of the "secrets of women." Another version of this linking (or substitution) of open book/open body is made in Alexander Read's tiny anatomical handbook, *The Manvall of the Anatomy or dissection of the body of Man*, in which the typical title-page cartouche is an opened-up human skin, with hands and feet at the borders and a decorative head at the top; the entire text of the title page is inscribed upon this corpus, as if the book (already a "manual") were to be discovered (literally) in the body.

48. On anatomical flapbooks, see LeRoy Crummer, "A Check List of Anatomical Books Illustrated with Cuts with Superimposed Flaps." On anatomical broadsides or broadsheets, see A. Carlino, "Paper Bodies: A Catalogue of Anatomical Fugitive Sheets 1538–1687." See also Suzanne Karr Schmidt, with Kimberly Nichols, "Printed Scientific Objects," esp. 82–91.

49. Masten, "Is the Fundament a Grave?," 144n43; Daileader, "Back Door Sex," 317.

50. For a general anatomy text, see, for example, Thomas Johnson, trans., *The Workes of that famous Chirurgion Ambrose Parey* (1634). Some midwifery and childbirth texts that follow this practice include [Jacques Guillemeau], *Child-birth or, The happy deliuerie of vvomen* (1612); Jane Sharp, *The midwives book* (1671); Nicholaas Fonteyn, *The womans doctour* (1652); and Nicholas Culpeper, *A directory for midwives* (1651–62). In his translation dictionary, Florio writes of "a disease that comes in the fundament of man or woman" (*A Worlde of Wordes*). See also the example in note 54.

51. As Daileader indicates, there is often an emphasis on "other" ethnicities entering (women, England) through this "back door" practice ("Back Door Sex," 304).

52. Margaret W. Ferguson has alerted me to an example of Rabelais's satirical conflation of a womb and female fundament in Rabelais, where Gargamelle's delivery of Gargantua is represented as caused by or coincident with her "bum-gut . . . or fundament" "slipp[ing] out." (See Francis Rabelais, *The Urquhart-Le Motteux Translation of the Works of Francis Rabelais*, 1:208, 214.) As Ferguson has noted to me (private correspondence), the episode conflates a series of body parts (including womb, fundament, and ear, through which the child eventually "issue[s] forth" [214]), confounds gender divisions (by associating the fundaments of Gargamelle and the reader, as well as the story-writing/birthing capacities of the writer, the "fundamental gospel text" of the Immaculate Conception, and a number of mythological birthing narratives), and reverses "fundamental" directions (the birth of the child by leaping up, through the head).

53. In a text that uses *fundament* to refer to rectum/anus, Stephen Batman, in *Batman vppon Bartholeme his booke*, also uses *fundament* foundationally in a chapter on the genitals to write of the testicles: "other members be ground & fundament of ye vertue of gendring [i.e. reproduction], as ye ballock stones" (61^v).

54. For a rich reading of sodomitical discourse through complex interweavings of economy, homosociality, and social class, see Theodore B. Leinwand, "Redeeming Beggary/Buggery in *Michaelmas Term*." Leinwand's evidence sometimes but not always coheres with the rhetoric of the preposterous (66n17) and seems rarely to intersect with the fundament/foundation.

55. Fletcher, *Purple Island*, 27.

56. See ibid., 90 (canto 7.21–22), where the allegorical figure of Acatharus (glossed as "Sodomie," with biblical citations) is described in pejorative (if extensive) pederastical terms, "sport[ing]," "toy[ing]," "kiss[ing]," and "lean[ing]" upon a boy "in wanton wise," bearing a shield adorned with Jove and Ganymede, encircled by the motto "*Like with his like is coupeled*."

57. The "'Blason du Q [Cul]' ('Blason of the Ass[hole]')" cited by Nancy J. Vickers in a collection of body-part blasons from 1539 and the publications that followed it provide a fascinating trove of rhetoric related to this part in a (sometimes) gendered, French context; see Vickers, "The Unauthored 1539 Volume in Which Is Printed the *Hecatomphile, The Flowers of French Poetry*, and *Other Soothing Things*," 171. Although by no means the only discourse employed by these poems, foundational rhetoric plays a part: "Chascun cognoit, & voit euidemment, / Que de beaulté estes le fondement . . . / Vous sçauez tout, & les secretz celez." See the two "Blason[s] du Cul" included in *Les Blasons Et Contreblasons Dv Corps Mascvlin, & feminin* (n.d.), sig. D8.

58. *The historie of the troublesome Raigne of King Edward the second . . . 1626 Neuer printed. written by* [name obliterated], attributed to Francis Hubert; Folger MS V.a. 234. I am indebted to Laetitia Yeandle for assistance with some difficulties in reading the handwriting. The Folger manuscript is interesting not least for the possible context(s) of transgression, censorship, controversy, and perhaps even "the closet" that might be read out of the seemingly intentional obliteration of the writer's name. Bredbeck discusses the printed version in *Sodomy and Interpretation*, chap. 2, passim. The manuscript stanza quoted above concludes as follows:

And that my violent death might shune mistrust
Through that same horne; a red hot spitt whereby
They made my gutts and bowells for to frie
And soe continued, till at last they found
That I was dead, yet seem'd to haue noe wound

59. See Judith Butler, *Bodies That Matter*, esp. 67–68.

60. On these issues of alterity/continuity, see the Introduction.

61. Stockton, *Playing Dirty*, has recently taken up related substantive questions, as well as some of the methodological issues inherent in thinking about psychoanalysis, "homosexuality," and the early modern period. On the relation of body parts, desire, and (sexual) identity, see Valerie Traub, "The Psychomorphology of the Clitoris," 226–28. Scholarship regarding the role of psychoanalysis in early modern studies is extensive (one controversial place to start being Stephen Greenblatt, "Psychoanalysis and Renaissance Culture"); a very brief list of representative discussions would include Meredith Anne Skura, "Understanding the Living and Talking to the Dead: The Historicity of Psychoanalysis"; Carla Mazzio and Doug Trevor, eds., *Historicism, Psychoanalysis and Early Modern Culture*; Cynthia Marshall, *The Shattering of the Self*; and Lynn Enterline, *The Rhetoric of the Body from Ovid to Shakespeare*.

62. Ben Saunders, "Iago's Clyster," 152 (my emphasis). See also 148n2, 158.

63. An especially important example of such contestation is Traub, "Psychomorphology of the Clitoris," esp. 226–28.

64. Leo Bersani, *Homos*, 90, 102.

65. As many have noted, the passage rewrites I Corinthians 2:9–10, especially in the Great Bible (1540) and early Geneva (1557) versions, which culminate in a *bottom*: "the Spirite searcheth all thinges, yea, the botome of Goddes secretes" (Geneva). For a discussion of the variant versions, see Thomas B. Stroup, "Bottom's Name and His Epiphany." Stroup sees scriptural allusion overriding other possible sources of Bottom's name; this insistence is itself an example of the separation of discourses this chapter attempts to resist (a separation, for Stroup, of the religious [and therefore apparently more meaningful] from the vocational or bodily). For an interpretation employing the bodily resonance, see Jan Kott, *The Bottom Translation*, 31.

66. Stroup, "Bottom's Name," 81 (my emphasis).

67. Fletcher, *Purple Island*, 27n. For a related reading of Bottom's Dream, see Paster, *Body Embarrassed*, 142. On Bottom as somatic "pun," see pp. 125–26 of Paster; on the disputed (a)historicity of *bottom* as bodily term, see Rambuss, "Shakespeare's Ass Play," 244n7; Stockton, *Playing Dirty*, 26; and Mario DiGangi, *The Homoerotics of Early Modern Drama*, 64–65.

CHAPTER 7. WHEN GENRES BREED

1. Judith Butler, "Is Kinship Always Already Heterosexual?," 35.

2. Wallace Stevens, "Thirteen Ways of Looking at a Blackbird," 93.

3. For an eloquent commentary on the complexities of learning to understand the use of the term *sodomy* ("*sodomia* and its siblings") during the medieval period, a preface to its unfolding in early Christian theological and ecclesiastical contexts, see Mark D. Jordan, "A Prelude After Nietzsche: The Responsibilities of a History of Sodomy," in *The Invention of Sodomy*.

4. Peter F. Stevens, "Species: Historical Perspectives," 302.

5. Sir Phillip Sidney, Knight, *The Defence Of Poesie*, sigs. I1–I1ᵛ. On titling and textual variance among the early printed and manuscript versions (including *An Apologie for Poetrie*, also

1595), see *Miscellaneous Prose of Sir Philip Sidney*, ed. Katherine Duncan-Jones and Jan van Dorsten, 65–70.

6. Jacques Derrida, "The Law of Genre," 203–4.

7. Iohn Fletcher, "To the Reader," in *The Faithfvll Shepeardesse*, sig. ¶2ᵛ.

8. Nancy Klein Maguire, ed., *Renaissance Tragicomedy*; Gordon McMullan and Jonathan Hope, eds., *The Politics of Tragicomedy*.

9. Maguire, "Acknowledgments," in *Renaissance Tragicomedy*, vii.

10. Maguire, "Introduction: Towards Understanding Tragicomedy," in *Renaissance Tragicomedy*, 1.

11. John T. Shawcross, "Tragicomedy as Genre, Past and Present," 21.

12. Jonathan Hope and Gordon McMullan, "Introduction: The Politics of Tragicomedy, 1610–50," in *Politics of Tragicomedy*, 1. Subsequent references appear parenthetically.

13. Two recent volumes are more wary of the problem of tragicomic definition: see Verna A. Foster's chronologically broader discussion in *The Name and Nature of Tragicomedy*; and Subha Mukerji and Raphael Lyne, eds., *Early Modern Tragicomedy*.

14. Alistair Fowler, *Kinds of Literature: An Introduction to the Theory of Genres and Modes*, 60–72. For a discussion relying on Fowler's distinctions of genre and mode, see Robert Henke, *Pastoral Transformations*, which shares some of my suspicions of genre-as-biological-classification (31, 39). For an attempt at classification through statistical-linguistic analysis, see Michael Witmore and Jonathan Hope, "Shakespeare by the Numbers."

15. Fowler, *Kinds*, 73. On the existence and meaning of species in modern scientific discussions, see Mary B. Williams, "Species: Current Usages," as well as note 69 below. The apparently scientific discourse of Fowler's discussion of genre theory may also have a political dimension: "The kinds are subject to change; but that does not destroy their coherence, *any more than that of other institutions*" (74, my emphasis).

16. On epic as "a heterocosm or compendium of subjects, forms, and styles" in Renaissance genre theory, see Barbara Kiefer Lewalski, *Paradise Lost and the Rhetoric of Literary Forms*, chap. 1, esp. 4–9; and Rosalie Colie, *The Resources of Kind*, 22–23.

17. For a discussion of class mixing and theories of tragicomedy and the pastoral, see Henke, *Pastoral Transformations*, chaps. 9–10.

18. See Marjorie Garber, "Shakespeare's Dogs," 183–84, 192. Garber's analysis emerges from a discussion of *Macbeth* 3.1.90–94: "Ay, in the catalogue ye go for men, / As hounds and greyhounds, mungrels, spaniels, curs, / . . . are clipt / All by the name of dogs." "Catalogue," the term sometimes used in early modern books to head tables of contents, is closely associated with genre in the first Shakespeare folio's "CATALOGVE of the seuerall Comedies, Histories, and Tragedies contained in this Volume," in *Mr. VVilliam Shakespeares Comedies, Histories, & Tragedies*, as reproduced in Charlton Hinman, ed., *The Norton Facsimile: The First Folio of Shakespeare*. Laurie Shannon discusses the *Macbeth* passage, focusing on its interest in "addition" as distinction within the catalog, in "Poor, Bare, Forked: Animal Sovereignty, Human Negative Exceptionalism, and the Natural History of *King Lear*," 184–85.

19. The latter is the gloss on the name at Act 2, Scene 3 (S.D.), in the second- and third-generation Arden editions; *The Two Gentlemen of Verona*, ed. Clifford Leech, 32; *The Two Gentlemen of Verona*, ed. William C. Carroll, 176.

20. *The Two Gentlemen of Verona*, in *Mr. VVilliam Shakespeares Comedies, Histories, & Tragedies*, TLN 1835–38. Launce's monologue in Act 2, Scene 3, is deeply attentive to the separateness of kinds of species and is, despite this, a complicated mixing, and mixing up, of kinds and species: mother, father, sister, cat, Jew, stone, and (as Garber notes) man, dog. The speech takes up the close connection between species and performativity: "I am the dogge: no, the

dogge is himselfe, and I am the dogge: oh, the dogge is me, and I am my selfe: I; so, so" (TLN 613–15).

21. Sidney, *Defence*, sig. E3ᵛ (emphasis in the original). Italics are used in Ponsonby's text for proper names and place-names as well as foreign phrases and terms, some genre terms, and some important words in the text (e.g., *Poetry, Poeme, Poet, Poesies*, all on sigs. E3–E3ᵛ). It is unclear why *species* is italicized, and the authorial or compositorial agency behind the italics here remains unclear (see Chapter 1). In this passage in the 1595 *Apology* edition, *Species* is both capitalized and in italics, though the other terms are not, perhaps indicating its unfamiliarity as a term to this compositor (as well as Ponsonby's) or indicating Sidney's manuscript's emphasis; see *An Apologie for Poetrie*, sigs. F2–F2ᵛ.

22. *OED, species, n.,* 10. On the flexibility of early modern conceptions of the species/kind, see Shannon, "Poor, Bare, Forked," Laurie Shannon, *The Accommodated Animal*, 6–10, and Brian W. Ogilvie, *The Science of Describing*, 218–28.

23. See *OED, species, n.,* 9.a. and 10, respectively.

24. *OED, species, n.,* 7.a.

25. *OED*, 2nd ed., *mongrel, n.* and *adj.,* 3. In the current online edition, this definition has been updated (as of 2002): "Chiefly *derogatory*. A person of mixed descent; a person whose parents are of different nationalities; †a person whose parents are of differing social status (*obs.*)" (*OED, mongrel, n.* and *adj.,* 2).

26. The relevance to the early modern period of the more modern sense of *race* (particularly in relation to skin color) continues to be the subject of critical discussion. For some key statements, see Kwame Anthony Appiah, "Race," esp. 279; Kim F. Hall, *Things of Darkness*, which maintains the importance of race as a category for the analysis of early modern culture (esp. 3–7); Ania Loomba, *Shakespeare, Race, and Colonialism*; David Nirenberg, "Was There Race Before Modernity?"; and the especially useful summary of recent scholarship in Ania Loomba and Jonathan Burton, eds., *Race in Early Modern England*. Jean E. Feerick has argued for a Renaissance conception that understood the "symbolics of blood" "rather than skin colour to be the somatic referent anchoring this system of race" (*Strangers in Blood*, 12, 10). Étienne Balibar's commentary on the relation of classification and racism resonates with the broader concerns of the present chapter; see "Racism and Nationalism."

27. *OED, couple, v.,* 1.

28. John Lyly, "The Prologve in Pavles," in *Midas*, sigs. A2–A2ᵛ.

29. As Wendy Wall notes, Falstaff in Shakespeare's *Merry Wives* is associated with several "unruly" mixtures, including a "gallimaufry" (2.1.108) and a "hodge pudding" (5.5.150), which associate him with the feminine and the domestic (*Staging Domesticity*, 121).

30. *OED*, 2nd ed., *mangle, v.*¹, 1–2.

31. Cf. Sidney's discussion of poetry's "parts," where "perchance in some one defectuous peece we may finde blemish" (*Defence*, sig. E3ᵛ).

32. *OED, gallimaufry, n.* Lyly's parallel syntax ("what heretofore hath beene serued in seuer-all dishes for a feaste, is now minced in a charger for a Gallimaufrey") suggests diminishment as well as mixture: from a large feast to a kind of dish.

33. *OED, hotchpot, n.*and *adj.,* 3; *hotchpotch, n.,* 3.

34. For eroticized uses of *sport* (*OED, sport, n.*¹, I.1.b.–c.), see, e.g., *As You Like It* (1.2 and 4.3); and Leah S. Marcus, *The Politics of Mirth*, esp. 152–54.

35. There is a close resonance with this passage in the Italian-English dialogue of three men in *Florios Second Frvtes*, 23; the facing-page English translation uses *right* for the Italian *vere*.

> *H.* The plaies that they plaie in England, are not right comedies.
>
> *T.* Yet they doo nothing else but plaie euery daye.
>
> *H.* Yea but they are neither right comedies, nor right tragedies.

G. How would you name them then?

H. Representation of histories, without any decorum.

A sport—a game of tennis—subsequently substitutes for a play in this passage.

36 *OED, mongrel, n.* and *adj.*; Edward Topsell, *The History of Four-footed Beasts and Serpents,* 122.

37. *OED,* 2nd ed. on CD-ROM, *mangery,* 1–2. (It is not clear whether this earlier *OED* entry, quoted at the outset of the section, was intending to associate *mangrel* and *mangrie* etymologically or simply attempting to save space.) On the semiotics of Jacobean banqueting, see Patricia Fumerton, *Cultural Aesthetics,* 111–67.

38. See *OED, mung, n.*¹ and *mang, v.*¹

39. Topsell, *History of Four-footed Beasts,* 139.

40. Fumerton, *Cultural Aesthetics,* 166, 252.

41. *OED,* 2nd ed. on CD-ROM; *OED Online* (accessed July 30, 2015); EEBO Text Creation Partnership (TCP) searchable texts (accessed May 5, 2011).

42. The earlier reference to the word *gental* no longer appears in the *OED,* and it does not come up in an EEBO TCP search.

43. See the corrections and editorial commentary in quotations supporting *OED Online* entries for *genital, adj.* and *n., genitable.*

44. On *genos* as a complex term mediating between (and deconstructing the relation of) nature and culture, nature and history, "nature and the vast lineage of its others," see Derrida, "The Law of Genre," 207–9.

45. *The Merchant of Venice,* in Stephen Greenblatt et al., eds., *The Norton Shakespeare Based on the Oxford Edition,* 2nd ed., 4.1.33.

46. See *OED, gentile, adj.* and *n.,* and *gentle, adj.* and *n.* (forms).

47. See esp. James Shapiro, *Shakespeare and the Jews,* 114–30; Patricia Parker, "Cutting Both Ways."

48. *Merchant of Venice,* 1.3.114.

49. Ibid., 1.3.78–79, 92.

50. The Aristotelian/Horatian view of genre in Sidney (which I have been emphasizing) sits alongside "the inclusionist view of literature as not only representing but as indeed being the *paideia*" (Colie, *Resources,* 76).

51. Fletcher, "To the Reader," sig. ¶2ᵛ. Subsequent citations of Fletcher's preface refer to this page.

52. Derrida's discussion of "the law of genre" begins, "Genres are not to be mixed. I will not mix genres" (202).

53. Lee Edelman, *Homographesis,* 4 (my emphasis). Subsequent references appear parenthetically.

54. "*[P]eccatum illud horribile, inter christianos non nominandum*" (Blackstone, qtd. in Edelman, *Homographesis,* 5).

55. For an extended analysis of this idea, see Laurie Shannon, "Nature's Bias."

56. Ambroise Paré, *On Monsters and Marvels,* 67. The original reads "Exemple de la Commixtion et Meslange de Semence"; Janis L. Pallister translates *et* as "or" here and in a number of other instances.

57. A printed marginal note in the French text reads: "Impieté abominable des Sodomites"; Ambroise Paré, *Des Monstres et Prodiges: Édition Critique et Commentée,* 62. Original French and marginal notes follow this edition, based on the 1585 (fourth) edition of Paré's works (xlvii–viii).

58. Paré, *On Monsters,* 67. The marginal note in the French edition is "Nature tasche tousjours à faire son semblable" (Paré, *Des Monstres,* 62). The 1573 and 1575 editions redouble the simulacra here: "tasche toujours à faire le semblable de son semblable" (62n10).

59. On the ostensible etymological link between *monster* and *monstrate* ("to show"), see Lorraine Daston and Katharine Park, *Wonders and the Order of Nature, 1150–1750*, 200.

60. Thomas Johnson, trans., *The Workes of that famous Chirurgion Ambrose Parey*, 982. Subsequent references appear parenthetically. Pallister stresses the inaccuracy of Johnson's translation (xxviii), but my interest is in its additions and discursive formations.

61. Though criticized for a monolithic account that shuts out other models of Renaissance gender, Thomas Laqueur's "one-sex model" in *Making Sex* may demonstrate that at least in some early modern accounts, what we would think of as "heterosexual" intercourse is a kind of copulation of sameness with a difference. For critiques of Laqueur, see esp. Katharine Park and Robert A. Nye, "Destiny Is Anatomy"; and Valerie Traub, *The Renaissance of Lesbianism*, 191–93. On early modern sameness and difference, see Shannon, "Nature's Bias."

62. M. Williams, "Species," 319.

63. On the etymology and invention of the term *heterosexuality*, see David M. Halperin, *One Hundred Years of Homosexuality*, 15–17.

64. Cf. Shawcross, "Tragicomedy as Genre," 21: "What is the family of tragicomedy, . . . which shows likeness from the Renaissance through the present age, even though specific members of that family are not duplicates of the others?" There is a more subtle familial rhetoric (also implying particular kinds of property relations) underlying Stanley Cavell's discussion of the inherited "features" of genres: "members of a genre share the inheritance of certain conditions, procedures and subjects and goals of composition, and . . . each member of such a genre represents a study of these conditions, something I think of as bearing the responsibility of the inheritance" (*Pursuits of Happiness*, 28). On family resemblance, see also Joseph Loewenstein, "Guarini and the Presence of Genre," 36–37.

65. Beniamin Jonson, *The Workes of Beniamin Jonson*, title page.

66. Ben Jonson, *Horace His Art of Poetrie, Made English by Ben. Iohnson*, in *Ben Jonson*, ed. C. H. Herford, Percy Simpson, and Evelyn Simpson, 8:311, lines 124–25.

67 *OED*, *thew, n.*¹, 3.a., 3.b.; the gendering of these definitions is the *OED*'s.

68. Loewenstein, "Guarini," 33–34. Loewenstein's question about the engraving—"insofar as the literary genetics of tragicomedy constitutes what we might call the 'structural theme' of the illustration, what is the relation of literary genetics to general questions of poetics?" (34)—has been provocative for this chapter at several points. Eugene M. Waith, *The Pattern of Tragicomedy in Beaumont and Fletcher*, 45–46, also discusses the engraving's construction of tragicomedy. For a detailed reading of the page's iconography, see Margery Corbett and Ronald Lightbown, *The Comely Frontispiece*, 145–50. Henke, *Pastoral Transformations*, also provides a commentary on the engraving (13–16).

69. Williams, "Species," 320. Ernst Mayr's work has been particularly significant in this discussion; see esp. "Species Concepts and Definitions"; "Difficulties and Importance of the Biological Species Concept"; and *Populations, Species, and Evolution*. On the shift from early modern descriptive taxonomy to modern models, see Ogilvie, *Science of Describing*, and Shannon, *Accommodated Animal*.

70. Cf. Loewenstein's apparent pun on "raciness" (in the senses of "sexually transgressive" and "of a race/kind") in his discussion of Guarini in "Guarini," 49. See also Shawcross, "Tragicomedy as Genre," quoted earlier.

71. Sidney, *Defence*, sig. E3ᵛ (my emphasis).

72. Butler, "Is Kinship Always Already Heterosexual?," 34.

73. Edward Arber, ed., *A Transcript of the Registers of the Company of Stationers of London, 1554–1640, A.D.*, 4:316.

74. Some important exceptions to my "few": Lois Potter's Arden edition of the play (John Fletcher and William Shakespeare, *The Two Noble Kinsmen*, 1–6) and her "Topicality or Poli-

tics? *The Two Noble Kinsmen*, 1613–34"; and Gordon McMullan's noting of the play's "radical tragicomic conclusion," in *The Politics of Unease in the Plays of John Fletcher*, 105. Jeanne Addison Roberts both notes the play's divergence from Fletcher's statement and writes that, in the play, "tragicomedy . . . has moved beyond the bounds of received definitions": "Crises of Male Self-Definition in *The Two Noble Kinsmen*," 144.

75. See Potter's excellent essay on the evolution of the generic meaning of *The Two Noble Kinsmen* ("Topicality or Politics?").

76. See Jeffrey Masten, *Textual Intercourse*, 49–56.

77. Mr. John Fletcher and Mr. William Shakspeare, Gent., *The Two Noble Kinsmen* (1634), 88 (5.4.125–28). Subsequent references are to the quarto's numbered pages.

78. As a term, *subplot* encodes, in a way that is often taken to be ideology-free, an ostensibly generic division that this play (as I will suggest below) and many others override or efface. On the intertextuality/citationality of the Jailer's Daughter, see Douglas Bruster, "The Jailer's Daughter and the Politics of Madwomen's Language."

79. Fletcher and Shakspeare, *Two Noble Kinsmen*, 69.

80. Ibid. Most editors emend "crave her" to "carve her" (i.e., carve for her); see the Waith (4.3.82) and Potter (4.3.87) editions. However, in this context, note that the standard emendation may be based on the idea that sexual desire and eating would not logically be mixed or conflated. (Dare we serve up a text that is a hodge-podge?)

81. Fletcher and Shakspeare, *Two Noble Kinsmen*, 78.

82. Ibid., 77.

83. [Thomas Kyd], *The Spanish Tragedie*, sigs. E1^v–E2.

84. Phil. Massinger, Tho. Middleton, and William Rowley, *The Old Law*, sig. K4^v.

85. On the mixed and performative nature of funerals in the play, see Jeffrey Masten, ed., *An/The Old Law*, in *Thomas Middleton: The Collected Works*.

86. On Gnothoes's name, see Masten, *An/The Old Law*, 3.1.111n. On the multiple playwrights of the play, see Gary Taylor, "*An/The Old Law*."

87. For a fuller consideration of *The Spanish Tragedy*'s transmutations, see Chapter 3.

88. Most editors emend/modernize the term to *venture*; on the resulting loss of meaning, see Masten, *An/The Old Law*, 3.1.177; and *OED*, venture, n. and v. (forms).

89. Fletcher and Shakspeare, *Two Noble Kinsmen*, 43.

90. Again, we might better use either Roberts's phrase "received definition" or, as I might revise it, "received *in*definition."

91. See Barbara Kiefer Lewalski, "Introduction: Issues and Approaches," 1–2.

92. Alan Bray, "Why Have English Historians Run Away from Kinship?" For related commentary on such "traces," see Alan Bray, *The Friend*, 105, as well as his conception of period friendship as "voluntary kinship."

93. Raymond Williams, "Family," in *Keywords: A Vocabulary of Culture and Society*, 131–34.

94. Butler, "Is Kinship Always Already Heterosexual?," 17.

95. Shannon, "Poor, Bare, Forked," 175; see also Shannon, *Accommodated Animal*, 8, 133.

96. Thomas Middleton, *Hengist, King of Kent; or The Mayor of Queenborough*, ed. R. C. Bald, 79; see also Thomas Middleton, *Hengist*, ed. Grace Ioppolo.

97. On the royalist significance of the folio, see Lois Potter, *Secret Rites and Secret Writing*, chap. 3. The generic hybridity of tragicomedy may have been or has come to be associated with multiplicity of authorship; see Madeleine Doran, *Endeavors of Art*, 186. On the "strange production" attributed to Beaumont and Fletcher's folio, see Masten, *Textual Intercourse*, chap. 4. See also Suzanne Gossett, "Major/Minor, Main Plot/Subplot, Middleton/and."

98. This is to say that it may be productive to see some cross-coupling aspects of tragicomedy in Shakespeare's canon earlier than in the "late plays," where it is usually discussed. Barbara

A. Mowat disrupts the traditional chronology, both by reading the relation of tragicomedy to "the problem plays"/"dark comedies" and by noting that Guarini may have had an influence on English drama a decade or more earlier than typically supposed; "Shakespearean Tragicomedy," 84. On the generic periodization of Shakespeare's "development," see Margreta de Grazia, *Shakespeare Verbatim*, 25n37.

CHAPTER 8. ALL IS NOT GLOSSED

1. Stephen Greenblatt, "General Introduction," in Stephen Greenblatt et al., eds., *The Norton Shakespeare Based on the Oxford Edition*, 1st ed., 74, my emphasis. Subsequent citations of plays in this edition will appear parenthetically.

2. William Chillingworth, *The Religion of Protestants a Safe VVay to Salvation*, 390. Chillingworth's usage of "gloss" in this extensive text arguing with Catholicism seems to me potentially poised directly between the words the *OED* separates into *gloze* and *gloss*, despite their overlapping forms and overlapping period meanings (explanation through annotation, explaining *away*, and deception through smooth talk). See *OED*, *gloss*, *v*.¹, *n*.¹, and *gloze*, *v*.¹, *n*.¹ Chillingworth's text features extensive marginal citations and glosses.

3. William Shakespeare, *Othello, the Moor of Venice*, ed. Michael Neill, 1.1.88–89, p. 203. Unless otherwise indicated, quotations from *Othello* are taken from this edition and follow its line numbering, given parenthetically. Page references to Neill's textual apparatus also appear parenthetically.

4. For earlier discussions and critiques of the relation of editing and interpretation, see G. Thomas Tanselle, "The Varieties of Textual Editing," 14–15; Gary Taylor, "The Renaissance and the End of Editing," 130; Margreta de Grazia and Peter Stallybrass, "The Materiality of the Shakespearean Text"; Leah S. Marcus, "Introduction: The Blue-Eyed Witch," in *Unediting the Renaissance*; and the essays of Random Cloud [Randall McLeod], cited in de Grazia and Stallybrass, "Materiality," headnote, 255.

5. Neill notes that this is the first use of the verb cited in the *OED* (*Othello*, 203). There is actually an earlier instance of (intransitive) "tupping" further down in the *OED*'s entry, dated 1549, apparently referring to human sex (*tup*, *v*., 2.a.). The investment of Shakespeare editions in instances for which Shakespeare can be cited as the first known user of particular words and meanings deserves further scrutiny, at least in part for its effect of underwriting incrementally the generativity/originality/priority of Shakespeare and thus certain conceptions of authorship as well as language change; see, e.g., the headnote to Neill's edition's glossarial index highlighting with an asterisk "citations of first recorded use" (469). On the "loop" between the *OED* and the Shakespearean critical tradition, see Timothy Billings, "Squashing the 'Shard-borne Beetle' Crux."

6. The *OED* (*tup*, *v*., 1.a.) cites the Motteux/Urquhart Rabelais edition of 1694/1737, which reads, as part of the "Pantagruelian Prognostication" of the year to come, "The *Moscovites, Indians, Persians*, and *Troglodytes*, will often be troubld with the Bloody Flux, because they will not be ridden, tupp'd and ram'd by the *Romanists*, considering the Ball of *Sagittarius* Ascendant." *The Fifth Book of the Works Of Francis Rabelais, M.D.* (1694), 5:241; see also Rabelais, *The Urquhart-Le Motteux Translation of the Works of Francis Rabelais*, 2:899. (A reference to an inn called the Sagittary appears shortly after the "tupping" line in *Othello*; see Neill's note [1.1.157; *Othello*, 207] and the association with centaurs, species hybridity, and rape across kind.) The *OED* cites the 1737 Rabelais ("ramm'd," 5:222).

7. On the connections in *Othello* between racially marked sex and bestiality, see Arthur Little, "Witnessing Whiteness," chap. 2 in *Shakespeare Jungle Fever*, esp. 72–87. The scholarship

on "race" in early modern culture published in the last several decades, often addressing *Othello* in particular and often interrogating the historicity of the very notion of modern "race," is extensive; see esp. Kim F. Hall, *Things of Darkness*; Margo Hendricks and Patricia Parker, eds., *Women, "Race," and Writing in the Early Modern Period*; Ania Loomba, *Shakespeare, Race, and Colonialism*; Ania Loomba and Jonathan Burton, "Introduction," in *Race in Early Modern England: A Documentary Companion*; Karen Newman, " 'And Wash the Ethiop White.' "

8. On Barbary/barbarism, see, in particular, Patricia Parker, *Shakespeare from the Margins*, 238–70; and "Barbers and Barbary"; Ian Smith, "Barbarian Errors."

9. Leah S. Marcus, "The Two Texts of 'Othello' and Early Modern Constructions of Race."

10. The *Variorum* edition attributes the emendation to Pope's second edition, 1728, where it appears silently in the text, without note. See Horace Howard Furness, ed., *Othello. A New Variorum Edition of Shakespeare*, 205; Alexander Pope and George Sewell, eds., *The works of Mr. William Shakespear*, 8:382 (also the related emendation, discussed later, at 8:420).

11. For the intersecting meanings of (hetero)sex and race in *Othello* in the later seventeenth and especially eighteenth centuries, see Rebecca Ann Bach, *Shakespeare and Renaissance Literature Before Heterosexuality*, chap. 5. Marcus, in "Two Texts," sees a shift in racial ideology evidenced even within the narrow frame of Q1/F1 chronology (whatever it may have been).

12. Thomas Rymer, *A Short View of Tragedy; It's Original, Excellency, and Corruption* (1693), 87–88 (emphasis in the original). Thanks to Ted Leinwand for this reference. Bach, *Before Heterosexuality*, discusses the contemporary critical contestation of Rymer's view of race in the play (160–61).

13. *OED* gives forms only for *tup, n.*, referring the verb to the noun for etymology: "Forms: ME tope, *Sc.* toupe, ME–15 tupe, ME–16 tuppe, (15 tuepe, touppe, towpe), 15–16 tupp, 15, 17–18 *Sc.* tip, 15– tup; 17–18 *Sc.* and *north. dial.* tuip /tʏp/, teep, teap, toop." I am grateful to Jessie Mathiason for alerting me to the variation in forms. For reasons already explored, it is my assumption that dates of forms and first appearances in the *OED* must be understood to be approximate ranges, with the distinct possibility that similar or related usages may subsequently be found in earlier texts by other writers.

14. On the implications of variability, see Margreta de Grazia, "Homonyms Before and After Lexical Standardization"; de Grazia and Stallybrass, "Materiality," 262–66; and de Grazia, "Shakespeare and the Craft of Language."

15. The recent Folger edition may attempt to have it both ways, at least in its gloss of *topped* in Act 3, Scene 3: "covered, in coition, i.e., 'tupped' "; Barbara A. Mowat and Paul Werstine, eds., *Othello*, 144. *Topped, id est, tupped.*

16. "[W]hat I am defining as the Shakespearean crux is not epistemologically distinct from the critical tradition and is never manifest without a gloss," writes Timothy Billings in "Slubbering the Gloss and Other Crucial Pleasures." For an edition that uses editorial format to question the priority of gloss and text as well as the separation of glossarial and textual notes, see Jeffrey Masten, ed., *An/The Old Law*. For a brilliant discussion of text and gloss in history, practice, and theory, see Lawrence Lipking, "The Marginal Gloss."

17. David M. Halperin, "How to Do the History of Male Homosexuality," in *How to Do the History of Homosexuality*, 118. Halperin's statement is qualified to "[w]ithin the horizons of the male world," but I would see his statement as true more broadly, into the early modern period, at least insofar as it describes what is desirable ("hot") and counts as sexual *from the perspective of adult male subjects* (the latter being a significant caveat).

18. Jonathan Goldberg, *Sodometries*.

19. *Preposition*'s etymological relation to *prosthesis* and to the function of the prefix in Greek and Latin (and as transmuted in English) is worth exploring further (*OED, preposition, n.*).

20. Lara Bovilsky, "Desdemona's Blackness," chap. 1 in *Barbarous Play*, 59–60.

21. Little, *Shakespeare Jungle Fever*, 85. On early modern intercrural sex, see Will Fisher, " 'Wantoning with the Thighs': The Socialization of Thigh Sex in England, 1590–1730."

22. On the possibility that discourses of race shifted over the course of *Othello*'s earliest performance and print history, see Marcus, "Two Texts."

23. Formative intersectional analyses of race and gender in the play include Newman, " 'And Wash the Ethiop White' "; Michael Neill, " 'Unproper Beds' "; and Patricia Parker, "Fantasies of 'Race' and 'Gender.' " See also Bovilsky's intersectional analysis of race and sexual purity, "Desdemona's Blackness"; Emily Bartels, "The 'Stranger of Here and Everywhere': *Othello* and the Moor of Venice," chap. 7 in *Speaking of the Moor*, 182–83; and Little, *Shakespeare Jungle Fever*. Peter Stallybrass's influential account, "Patriarchal Territories," adds social class.

24. Bovilsky, "Desdemona's Blackness," 58.

25. See Little, *Shakespeare Jungle Fever*, 83–84, 86; Bruce R. Smith, *Homosexual Desire in Shakespeare's England*, 174–80; and Goldberg, *Sodometries*, chap. 6.

26. Edward Coke, "Of Buggery, or Sodomy," in *The Third Part Of The Institutes Of The Laws of England*, 58.

27. B. Smith, *Homosexual Desire*, 41–53; Janet E. Halley, "*Bowers v. Hardwick* in the Renaissance"; Valerie Traub, *The Renaissance of Lesbianism in Early Modern England*, 164–68, 276–77; Cynthia B. Herrup, *A House in Gross Disorder*. On animal execution in buggery cases, see Laurie Shannon, *The Accommodated Animal*, 230n34.

28. Bovilsky, "Desdemona's Blackness," 41.

29. Little, *Shakespeare Jungle Fever*, 84–85. On *ewe/you*, see Neill, *Othello*, 203.

30. Qtd. in Alan Bray, *Homosexuality in Renaissance England*, 40. Bray raises a number of evidentiary questions about the passage (40–41), but he assumes that the case involves buggery between Drago and Wraxall. My "with/on/in view of" attempts to loosen that assumption. (Thanks to Ted Leinwand for this point.) The record is not explicit that Wraxall is necessarily a (sexual) participant in the buggery; he is a witness (in some fashion): it is possible that he witnesses a crime with another (unmentioned) person or animal, or that he participates in the buggery but is here being protected by the record (he seems, though not certainly, to be young, since he is under guardianship, and the record is partly about making sure that he is delivered to court to testify). Researching this moment in Bray, it seems possible in the limited Assize records I have examined to hypothesize that "sodomy" may be more typically used between persons, and "buggery" for men with animals. (See J. S. Cockburn, ed., *Calendar of Assize Records: Home Circuit Indictments, Elizabeth I and James I: Introduction*, and the associated Calendar volumes edited by Cockburn.) A more thorough canvass and analysis of these records is desirable, also to compare Coke's definition with provincial usage in legal practice. See also Herrup, *House in Gross Disorder*.

The case raises additional interpretive issues, for example, the overdetermination of "Wraxall" as a signifier that incorporates the confusions of and/or punishment for sodomy—William wracks/wrecks/racks all—and potentially resonates as reassigning some blame to the victim/participant/observer.

31. Michael Warner, "New English Sodom."

32. Traub, *Renaissance of Lesbianism*, 202.

33. Bartels, " 'Stranger of Here and Everywhere,' " 173–74, 189–90. Bartels's conclusion that the play includes grounds "for reimagining as a dynamic and unscripted interaction the relation between Venice and the Moor, the domestic and the strange, the here and the everywhere" (190) nevertheless resonates with the shifting terms of sodomy in the era.

34. *Dragoman*—a word existing in English contexts from the fourteenth century onward, with a wide range of spelling variations and overlapping words, including *truchman* (*OED*)—signified in early modern English usage an interpreter or guide and came to designate an offi-

cial role within the Ottoman Empire and bureaucracy, as well as those of European countries negotiating and trading with the Ottomans, into the twentieth century. Ottoman dragomans were often from non-Muslim (often Greek) ethnic groups. For a historical discussion of the role of the dragoman in the Ottoman Empire and related terms in languages during the period, see C. E. Bosworth, "Tardjumān." On the early modern history, see also Ruth A. Roland, *Interpreters as Diplomats*, 44–46. In a fascinating study of the cluster of early modern English words around *interpreter*, Samuli Kaislaniemi demonstrates that *dragoman* was generally restricted to Middle Eastern contexts; see "*Jurebassos* and *Linguists*: The East India Company and Early Modern English Words for 'Interpreter.'" Thanks to Dagmar Riedel and Rebecca Johnson for assistance with this term.

35. Goldberg, *Sodometries*, 22.

36. Bray, *Homosexuality*, 122n20; Susan E. Phillips, "Schoolmasters, Seduction, and Slavery," esp. 148–52.

37. David Nirenberg, "Was There Race Before Modernity? The Example of 'Jewish' Blood in Late Medieval Spain," esp. 248–53; David Nirenberg, "Pre-Modern Race: Philology, Socio-Theology, History."

38. *top*, *v*.³, 2.

39. Ibid.; Thomas Heywood, *Pleasant Dialogves and Dramma's, Selected Ovt of Lucian, Erasmus, Textor, Ovid, &c.*, 118. This reading's transferability over to what I am calling Desdemona's desires is complicated by the fact that the woman in Heywood is Minerva, "a Virgin vow'd, / Nay, a perpetuall Votary"; however, whatever the other signifiers of her virginity, her intoxicated, warlike dance ("the Matachine") arouses Vulcan's desire to marry (118) or "rape" her (119).

40. *OED*, *rage*, *n*., 5.a. and 5.c.; also *OED*, 2nd ed., *rage*, *v*., 3. and 3.b. See also Chapter 5.

41. *OED*, *tap*, *v*.¹

42. Gail Kern Paster, "Leaky Vessels," chap. 1 in *The Body Embarrassed*. Paster notes Othello's description of Desdemona as "false as water" (47).

43. *OED*, *tap*, *v*.¹

44. On Desdemona as vessel, see also Bovilsky, "Desdemona's Blackness," 62.

45. See, e.g., Jean Howard's elegant introduction to *As You Like It*, with its ample attention to polymorphous desires.

46. See Alan Bray, "Homosexuality and the Signs of Male Friendship in Elizabethan England"; Alan Bray, *The Friend*; Mario DiGangi, *The Homoerotics of Early Modern Drama*; Laurie Shannon, *Sovereign Amity*; B. Smith, *Homosexual Desire*; Alan Stewart, *Close Readers*; and Jeffrey Masten, *Textual Intercourse*. See also Traub's account of female-female friendship in *Renaissance of Lesbianism*, chaps. 4, 6, and 7.

47. Halperin, "How to Do the History of Male Homosexuality."

48. Alan Stewart also analyzes the complexity of Portia's legal and economic role in the final scene; see *Shakespeare's Letters*, 185–86, 191–92.

49. Shannon, *Sovereign Amity*, 118–20.

50. See Valerie Wayne's related argument about the role of feminism in early modern editing, in "The Sexual Politics of Textual Transmission."

51. Traub, *Renaissance of Lesbianism*, 19.

52. On this problem in modernized editions, see Stephen Booth, ed., *Shakespeare's Sonnets*, esp. the Preface and notes to sonnet 129; de Grazia and Stallybrass, "Materiality."

53. Throughout this chapter I have lumped together glosses that appear marginally and those at the bottom of the page; for the historical and theoretical differences, see Lipking, "Marginal Gloss."

54. For the role that early-performance-attentive editing can productively play in modern editions, see Barbara Hodgdon, ed., *The Taming of the Shrew*, 309–27.

55. Judith Butler ("Imitation and Gender Insubordination," 17, 22–24) and Annamarie Jagose have both questioned what Jagose labels "the logic of sexual sequence that govern relations between normal and perverse sexual organization" ("First Things First: Some Second Thoughts on Lesbianism," 28, in *Inconsequence*).

CHAPTER 9. *MORE* OR LESS QUEER

1. [George Puttenham], *The Arte Of English Poesie*, Lib. III, 217.

2. Anthony Munday and others, Revised by Henry Chettle, Thomas Dekker, Thomas Heywood, and William Shakespeare, *Sir Thomas More*, ed. Vittorio Gabrieli and Giorgio Melchiori. Parenthetical citations of the play refer to the act, scene, and line numbers of this edited, modern-spelling edition (cited as "Revels"), followed by cross-references to the page, line, and sometimes Addition numbers in W. W. Greg's edited 1911 transcript: Greg, ed., *The Book of Sir Thomas More*. According to Greg, the "urinal" line is among those no longer legible in the play manuscript but included in what Alexander Dyce "purported to have read there" (xxiii).

3. Most counts put the number of hands at seven; Scott McMillin raises the possibility that C and D may be the same person fulfilling different (but not mutually exclusive) roles. Part of his point is the difficulty of counting/distinguishing identities in such a context ("Hand D," in *The Elizabethan Theatre and "The Book of Sir Thomas More"*). Paul Werstine has brilliantly shown how the default distinction between "authorial" and "scribal" "hands" in discussions of the manuscript breaks down further, to include writers who are (also) actors ("Close Contrivers," esp. 13–14).

4. Richard Dutton, *Mastering the Revels*, 81.

5. An exception may be the deposition scene in *Richard II*; I'm excluding the many smaller interventions involving the performance of profanity and oaths beginning in 1606.

6. John Jowett, ed., *Sir Thomas More* (Arden).

7. C. J. Sisson, ed., *William Shakespeare: The Complete Works*.

8. G. Blakemore Evans et al., eds., *The Riverside Shakespeare*, 1st ed., 1683; Stanley Wells and Gary Taylor et al., eds., *William Shakespeare: The Complete Works*, 889; Stephen Greenblatt et al., eds., *The Norton Shakespeare Based on the Oxford Edition*, 1st ed., 2011. The *Riverside*'s second edition does not substantially change its treatment of the play; for the *Norton* second and third editions, see below.

9. Walter Cohen, introduction to *Sir Thomas More*, in Greenblatt et al., *Norton Shakespeare*, 2nd ed., 2031. Cohen notes that the *Norton* edition treats *Sir Thomas More* as an aberrance, both in printing an "authorial" rather "theatrical" version of the text and in printing only part of the text. The newly published *Norton*, 3rd ed., includes an introduction to the play in the printed book, but no passages or play text, which is "digital-only."

10. Jonathan Bate and Eric Rasmussen, eds., *Complete Works: William Shakespeare*.

11. Alfred W. Pollard, ed., *Shakespeare's Hand in the Play of Sir Thomas More*. On the play's centrality to New Bibliography, see Paul Werstine, "Shakespeare, *More* or Less: A. W. Pollard and Twentieth-Century Shakespeare Editing"; Jeffrey Masten, "*More* or Less: Editing the Collaborative."

12. Cohen, introduction, 2031.

13. Werstine, "Close Contrivers," 17–18.

14. Madhavi Menon, ed., *Shakesqueer*.

15. See, for example, Eve Kosofsky Sedgwick, "Introduction: Axiomatic," in *Epistemology of the Closet*, esp. 51–55.

16. Masten, "*More* or Less," 111.

17. Werstine, "Close Contrivers," 7.

18. See Jennifer Schuessler, "Much Ado About Who: Is It Really Shakespeare? Further Proof of Shakespeare's Hand in 'The Spanish Tragedy,' " *New York Times,* August 12, 2013, reporting on Douglas Bruster's argument in "Shakespearean Spellings and Handwriting in the Additional Passages Printed in the 1602 *Spanish Tragedy.*" Citing the spelling and handwriting in parts of the *More* manuscript as its principal link to Shakespeare, Bruster's argument relies both on Shakespeare's ostensible spelling "preferences," "tendencies," and "habits" to identify him *and* (paradoxically) on "Shakespeare's practice [of] variant spellings" (421–22). On this critical rhetoric in relation to variation and identification, see Chapter 1.

19. For Menon's definition, see "Introduction: Queer Shakes."

20. For example, only three pages (29–32) of the Revels edition's fifty-three-page introduction are devoted to the play's "structure." Another index of interpretive neglect: of the thirty-nine items published in relation to the play between 1997 and 2007 (according to the *World Shakespeare Bibliography Online*), only seven focus substantially on readings of the play beyond matters of authorship and attribution; I suspect the division in criticism prior to that decade is even starker. These seven include Nina Levine's important essay on the play, "Citizens' Games," which engages both the discussion of authorship and a reading/analysis of the play, as does Masten, "*More* or Less." Such figures are necessarily incomplete and approximate, and they do not include analytic or discursive accounts of the play in monographs; see, for example, Will Fisher, " 'His Majesty the Beard': Beards and Masculinity," chap. 3 in *Materializing Gender in Early Modern English Literature and Culture*, 124–28.

21. Lee Edelman, "The Plague of Discourse: Politics, Literary Theory, 'AIDS,' " chap. 4 in *Homographesis*, 87.

22. Kathryn Schwarz, *Tough Love*, 45.

23. On Holinshed and Hall, see Vittorio Gabrieli, "*Sir Thomas More*: Source, Characters, Ideas," and Revels, 7–11.

24. See Levine, "Citizens' Games," 41; Revels, 11, 19, 45, 48.

25. The others are *All's Well* (Countess) and *Macbeth* (First Witch). If one includes boy actors generally, *Two Noble Kinsmen* begins, after its prologue, with a boy singing.

26. Similarly: "if you men durst not undertake it, before God we women [will. Take] an honest woman from her husband!" (1.1.95–96, 3.71–4.72).

27. Levine notes Doll's "unhistorical part"; in my view, Doll both seems to replay, and herself makes reference to, the unnamed wife in Holinshed who is "entised" to de Bard's chamber (qtd. in Revels, 228; see also 11).

28. My argument is not that Doll is an Amazon—she is not named as such—but that her description and dialogue resonate with other attributes associated in the period with Amazons as martial women.

29. For perspectives on queer temporality, see Carolyn Dinshaw et al., "Theorizing Queer Temporalities: A Roundtable Discussion"; Elizabeth Freeman, *Time Binds*; Carolyn Dinshaw, *How Soon Is Now?*

30. See Revels, 11 and 118n145–47. On the complex negotiations enacted in women's scaffold speeches, see Frances E. Dolan, " 'Gentlemen, I Have One Thing More to Say.' "

31. See *OED, bombast, n.; bombase, v.;* and *bombace, n.* On female penetration, see Valerie Traub, *The Renaissance of Lesbianism in Early Modern England.*

32. *OED, bumbaste, v.; bombast, n.*

33. Jowett's recent Arden edition (2011) usefully retains *bumbaste* from the manuscript.

34. Charles Stevens and Iohn Liebavlt, *Maison Rustique, Or The Covntrey Farme*, 146.

35. *OED, bumbaste, v.*

36. On linguistic inversions of before and behind associated with sodomy, see Jonathan Goldberg, *Sodometries*, esp. 180–81; and Patricia Parker, "Preposterous Reversals," esp. 435–36.

37. *Othello, the Moor of Venice*, ed. Michael Neill, 1.1.12–13. Cf. William Shakespeare, *The Tragœdy of Othello*, sig. B1; *The Tragedie of Othello*, in *Mr. VVilliam Shakespeares Comedies, Histories, & Tragedies*, as reproduced in Charlton Hinman, ed., *The Norton Facsimile: The First Folio of Shakespeare*, TLN 17. Neill, *Othello* (196) and the *Norton Shakespeare* (2nd ed., 2119) silently translate/modernize to *bombast*; the *Riverside* retains *bumbast*, presumably as one of its archaic spellings, glossing as *bombast* (1st ed., 1203). On bombastic speech, see Patricia Parker, *Shakespeare from the Margins*, 215–17, 221–28, 346–47.

38. [Robert Greene], *A Qvip For An Vp-start Courtier: Or, A quaint dispute betvven Veluet breeches and Cloth-breeches*, sigs. B2–B2ᵛ. This is an instance in which the text's original black-letter type (also known as "English letter"), with emphases in roman type, may signify in sexually valenced, nationalist terms; see the "Note on Citations and Quotations" in this book and the quotations from *A Qvip* that follow in this chapter.

39. Though the etymology of "Moorfields" (reached by departing the city walls through Moorgate) comes from the "moor" at one time on that site, the name may also resonate with the play's other plays on "More," including, in the context of "strangers," with discourses of race.

40. See Jowett, *Sir Thomas More*, 173.

41. See Frank Whigham and Wayne A. Rebhorn, eds., *The Art of English Poesy by George Puttenham: A Critical Edition*, 345. Puttenham adopts Richard Sherry's coinage here, who glosses *Bomphiologia* as "*Verborum bombus . . .* great gasyng wordes" in *A treatise of Schemes & Tropes*, sig. [Dvii].

42. Greene's "hanging on thy bumbast" may also suggest the solidity or instrumentality of rhetoric as a thing and thus the way in which rhetorical bombast, too, is situated between or across "stuffing" and "bum-beating-with-words." Ryan Friedman first brought the potential sodomitical resonances of rhetorical "bombast" to my attention in "Bombastic Subjects." See also Parker, *Shakespeare from the Margins*, 215–17, 221–28, 346–47.

43. *OED*, *sport*, *n.*¹, 1.c.: "Lovemaking, amorous play; (also) sexual intercourse . . . *Obs.*"

44. Early modern audiences might have heard illicit sexual activity resonating in Doll's name even from its first appearance in the play. "Doll" functions as a prostitute's name in Shakespeare's *2 Henry IV* (Doll Tearsheet) and implies sexual availability in Ben Jonson's *Alchemist* (Doll Common). See also note 48 below.

45. See Revels, 33; Jowett, *Sir Thomas More*, 96–97.

46. On the homoerotics of pedagogical beatings during the period, see Elizabeth Pittenger, "'To Serve the Queere'"; Alan Stewart, "'Traitors to Boyes Buttockes,'" chap. 3 in *Close Readers*; Wendy Wall, "'Household Stuff'"; and the Introduction for this book, pp. 27–29.

47. *OED*, *smock*, *n.*, 1.a., 1.c.

48. McMillin, *Elizabethan Theatre*, 78–79. Intriguingly, in *The Marriage Between Wit and Wisdom*, the play that gives the title (if not the text) to the play-within, there is a lower-class, sexually active character named Doll; the manuscript of the play (which the *More* collaborator Munday probably had seen) specifies that the actor playing Doll also plays the female characters Wantonness and Fancy. See Trevor N. S. Lennam, ed., *The Marriage Between Wit and Wisdom*; and Giorgio Melchiori, "The Contextualization of Source Material." Jowett provides other doubling possibilities in the *More* scene (*Sir Thomas More*, 97–98).

49. Tilney does not always do so; just a few lines before, he has let stand the line "If these hott ffrenchemen needsly will have sporte" (Greg, 13.359), referring to strangers stealing wives/sex.

50. James Shapiro, *Shakespeare and the Jews*, 180–87, esp. 186.

51. Dutton, *Mastering the Revels*, 97, 83. For an attempt to determine the number of strangers in London by country and city of origin on the basis of a 1593 census of foreigners, see Irene Scouloudi, *Returns of Strangers in the Metropolis*, 84–85.

52. Even if Tilney intended his revision as political expediency (Revels, 81n53), the *effects* of the revision, the meanings generated by it, might have exceeded his intentions in unexpected ways, and "Lombard" is in any event used elsewhere in the play (1.1.50).

53. Edward Coke, *The Third Part Of The Institutes Of the Laws of England*, 58. (Again, the printed text's default blackletter/English type may signify.) Coke's marginal note cites a parliamentary roll from the reign of Edward III that banished Lombards (associated with Jews and Saracens) for bringing in (unnamable) sodomy. In a term resonating with Chapter 7, boy love in Coke is a "species" of buggery. On early English sodomy law, see Bruce R. Smith, *Homosexual Desire in Shakespeare's England*; and Janet E. Halley, "*Bowers v. Hardwick* in the Renaissance."

54. Greene, *Qvip*, dedicatory letter, n.p.

55. Ibid., B1ᵛ. See note 38 above on blackletter type.

56. Ibid., sigs. B2–B2ᵛ.

57. On the animal-human nexus and the law, see Laurie Shannon, "'Hang-Dog Looks': From Subjects at Law to Objects of Science in Animal Trials," chap. 5 in *The Accommodated Animal*.

58. My translation from the French (58).

59. 1 Tim. 1:10, Geneva Bible.

60. Randle Cotgrave, comp., *A Dictionarie Of The French And English Tongves*, Lombard: m., sig. Ccc.viᵛ. The entry for *Frere* adds further detail, implying a monstrous twin "ingendered with a liuing child" (sig. Qq.viᵛ).

61. *Thomas More*, dir. Robert Delamere, Swan Theatre, Stratford-upon-Avon, Royal Shakespeare Company, "Gunpowder Season," performance of August 1, 2005. De Bard and Caveler were both played by black actors. Later in the performance the significance of race in casting became less clear, with the Lord Mayor and Lady Mayoress played by black actors.

62. Such fractures are sometimes framed as evidence of insufficiently integrated collaboration; for a relatively recent example, see E. A. J. Honigmann, "Shakespeare, *Sir Thomas More* and Asylum Seekers," which contends that Shakespeare's "much less savage tone" toward foreigners is a result of his association with immigrants, as well as proof of his authorship of the manuscript pages (226–27).

63. MacDonald P. Jackson, "Is 'Hand D' of *Sir Thomas More* Shakespeare's?," n35.

64. Alfred W. Pollard, "Introduction," in *Shakespeare's Hand*, 5–6.

65. Ibid., 12 (my emphasis).

66. Edelman, *Homographesis*, 4. On the association between queer sexualities and concepts of imitation and inauthenticity, see also Judith Butler, "Imitation and Gender Insubordination"; and Annamarie Jagose, *Inconsequence*.

67. See my Introduction, pp. 25–26.

BIBLIOGRAPHY

Authorial attributions in the Bibliography generally follow early modern attributions, but in some cases, for ease of reference, modern attributions have been supplied. Depending on the context in which they are cited, edited texts may in some cases be found under editors', rather than authors', names. On spelling and typography in early modern titles, see Note on Citations and Quotations.

ABBREVIATIONS

RD   *Renaissance Drama*
SB   *Studies in Bibliography*
SQ   *Shakespeare Quarterly*

Aarsleff, Hans. *The Study of Language in England, 1780–1860.* 2nd ed. Minneapolis: University of Minnesota Press, 1983.

Abelove, Henry. "Some Speculations on the History of 'Sexual Intercourse' During the 'Long Eighteenth Century' in England." In *Nationalisms and Sexualities*, ed. Andrew Parker, Mary Russo, Doris Sommer, and Patricia Yeager, 335–42. New York: Routledge, 1992.

Althusser, Louis. "Ideology and Ideological State Apparatuses: Notes Towards an Investigation." In *Lenin and Philosophy, and Other Essays*, trans. Ben Brewster, 85–126. New York: Monthly Review Press, 2001.

Ambrose, Laura Williamson. "Domestic Strangers and the Circulation of Desire in Beaumont and Fletcher's *Philaster, or Love Lies a-Bleeding*." Unpublished paper. University of Michigan, October 2003.

Appiah, Kwame Anthony. "Race." In *Critical Terms for Literary Study*, 2nd ed., ed. Frank Lentricchia and Thomas McLaughlin, 274–87. Chicago: University of Chicago Press, 1995.

Arber, Edward, ed. *A Transcript of the Registers of the Company of Stationers of London, 1554–1640, A.D.* 5 vols. London: privately printed, 1875–94.

Arderne, John. *A treatise of the Fistulae in the fundament, and other places of the body, translated out of Iohannes Ardern.* In *A most excellent and Compendiovs Method of curing woundes in the head, and in other partes of the body, . . . [by] Franciscvs Arcevs, . . . and translated into English by Iohn Read, Chirurgion.* London: by Thomas East, for Thomas Cadman, 1588.

Arrowsmith, William, trans. "Nietzsche: Notes for 'We Philologists.'" *Arion*, n.s. 1, no. 2 (1973–74): 279–380.

Articles vvherupon it was agreed by the Archbishops and Bishops of both Prouinces . . . For the auoiding of diuersities of opinions, and for the stablishing of consent touching true Religion Put forth by the Queenes authoritie. London: by Robert Barker, 1605.

Ascham, Roger. *The Scholemaster Or plaine and perfite way of teachyng children.* London: by Iohn Daye, 1570.

Auerbach, Erich. *Introduction Aux Études de Philologie Romane.* Frankfurt: Vittorio Klostermann, 1965.

Bach, Rebecca Ann. *Shakespeare and Renaissance Literature Before Heterosexuality*. New York: Palgrave Macmillan, 2007.

Baldwin, Thomas Whitfield. "Marlowe's Musaeus." *Journal of English and Germanic Philology* 54 (1955): 478–84.

———. *The Organization and Personnel of the Shakespearean Company*. Princeton, NJ: Princeton University Press, 1927.

Balibar, Étienne. "Racism and Nationalism." In *Race, Nation, Class: Ambiguous Identities*, ed. Étienne Balibar and Immanuel Wallerstein, 87–106. New York: Verso, 1991.

Baret, John. *An Alvearie Or Triple Dictionarie, in Englishe, Latin, and French*. London: by Henry Denham, n.d. [1574].

Barkan, Leonard. *Transuming Passion: Ganymede and the Erotics of Humanism*. Stanford, CA: Stanford University Press, 1991.

Barker, Francis. *The Tremulous Private Body: Essays on Subjection*. London: Methuen, 1984.

Barnfield, Richard. *Cynthia. VVith Certaine Sonnets*. London: for Humphrey Lownes, 1595.

Bartels, Emily C. *Speaking of the Moor: From "Alcazar" to "Othello."* Philadelphia: University of Pennsylvania Press, 2009.

———. *Spectacles of Strangeness: Imperialism, Alienation, and Marlowe*. Philadelphia: University of Pennsylvania Press, 1993.

Barthes, Roland. *The Rustle of Language*. Trans. Richard Howard. Berkeley: University of California Press, 1989.

Bate, Jonathan, and Eric Rasmussen, eds.; Héloïse Sénéchal, chief assoc. ed. *Complete Works: William Shakespeare*. The RSC Shakespeare. New York: Modern Library, 2007.

Bathurst, Ralph. "On the Death of Mr. William Cartvvright, and the now publishing of his Poems." In *Comedies, Tragi-comedies, With other Poems*, by William Cartwright, sigs. **1ᵛ–**2ᵛ. London: for Humphrey Moseley, 1651.

Batman, Stephen. *Batman vppon Bartholome his booke*. London: by Thomas East, [1582].

Baymont, Francis, and Iohn Fletcher. *Phylaster. Or, Loue Lyes a Bleeding*. London: for Thomas Walkley, 1620.

———. *See also* Beaumont, Francis, and Iohn Fletcher; Beaumont, Francis, and John Fletcher.

Beaumont, Francis, and Iohn Fletcher. *Philaster. Or, Loue lies a Bleeding*, "The second Impression." London: for Thomas Walkley, 1622.

———. *Philaster, Or Loue lies a Bleeding*, "The third Impreßion," London: by A.M. for Richard Hawkins, 1628.

[Beaumont, Francis, and John Fletcher]. *Philaster: Or, Love lies a bleeding*, "Revis'd and the Two last Acts new Written." London: for R. Bentley, 1695.

Beaumont, Francis, and John Fletcher. *Philaster, or Love Lies a-Bleeding*. Ed. Andrew Gurr. The Revels Plays. Manchester: Manchester University Press, 1969.

———. *Philaster*. Ed. Dora Jean Ashe. Regents Renaissance Drama. Lincoln: University of Nebraska Press, 1974.

———. *Philaster, or, Love Lies A-Bleeding*. Ed. Suzanne Gossett. Arden Early Modern Drama. London: A&C Black, 2009.

Ben-Amos, Ilana Krausman. *Adolescence and Youth in Early Modern England*. New Haven, CT: Yale University Press, 1994.

Bentley, G. E. *The Profession of Dramatist in Shakespeare's Time, 1590–1642*. Princeton, NJ: Princeton University Press, 1971.

Berger, Harry. "Actaeon at the Hinder Gate: The Stag Party in Spenser's Gardens of Adonis." In *Desire in the Renaissance: Psychoanalysis and Literature*, ed. Valeria Finucci and Regina Schwartz, 91–119. Princeton, NJ: Princeton University Press, 1994.

Bergeron, David M., ed. *King James and Letters of Homoerotic Desire*. Iowa City: University of Iowa Press, 1999.

Berry, Lloyd E., ed. *The Geneva Bible: A Facsimile of the 1560 Edition*. Madison: University of Wisconsin Press, 1969.

Bersani, Leo. *Homos*. Cambridge, MA: Harvard University Press, 1995.

———. "Is the Rectum a Grave?" In *AIDS: Cultural Analysis/Cultural Activism*, ed. Douglas Crimp, 197–222. Cambridge, MA: MIT Press, 1988.

Bérubé, Allan. *Coming Out Under Fire: The History of Gay Men and Women in World War Two*. New York: Penguin, 1990.

The Bible And Holy Scriptvres Conteyned In The Olde And New Testament. . . . Geneva: by Rovland Hall, 1560. Reprod. in *The Geneva Bible: A Facsimile of the 1560 edition*, ed. Lloyd E. Berry. Madison: University of Wisconsin Press, 1969.

Billings, Timothy. "Slubbering the Gloss and Other Crucial Pleasures." Unpublished paper. Modern Language Association Convention, Chicago, IL, December 2007.

———. "Squashing the 'Shard-borne Beetle' Crux: A Hard Case with a Few Pat Readings." *SQ* 56, no. 4 (2005): 434–47.

Bland, Mark. "Jonson, 'Biathanatos' and the Interpretation of Manuscript Evidence." *SB* 51 (1998): 154–82.

Blank, Paula. "The Proverbial 'Lesbian': Queering Etymology in Contemporary Critical Practice." *Modern Philology* 109, no. 1 (2011): 108–24.

Les Blasons Et Contreblasons Dv Corps Mascvlin, & feminin. Composez par plusiers Poëtes auec les figures au plus pres du naturel. Paris: pour la veuve [de] Iean Bonfons, n.d.

Blayney, Peter W. M. *The Bookshops in Paul's Cross Churchyard*. Occasional Papers of the Bibliographical Society, no. 5. London: Bibliographical Society, 1990.

———. *The Texts of King Lear and Their Origins, Vol. 1: Nicholas Okes and the First Quarto*. Cambridge: Cambridge University Press, 1982.

Bloom, Gina. *Voice in Motion: Staging Gender, Shaping Sound in Early Modern England*. Philadelphia: University of Pennsylvania Press, 2007.

Blount, Thomas. *Glossographia: or A dictionary, Interpreting all Such Hard VVords . . . as are now used in our refined English Tongue*. London: by Tho. Newcomb, [for] Humphrey Moseley and George Sawbridge, 1656.

Bly, Mary. *Queer Virgins and Virgin Queans on the Early Modern Stage*. Oxford: Oxford University Press, 2000.

Boffito, Giuseppe. *Iniziali Istoriate e Iniziali Fiorite o Arabescate*. Florence: Tipografia Giuntina, 1925.

The Booke of Common Prayer, and Administration of the Sacraments. London: Bonham Norton and Iohn Bill, 1625.

Booth, Stephen, ed. *Shakespeare's Sonnets*. New Haven, CT: Yale University Press, 1977.

Bopp, Franz. "Analytical Comparison of the Sanskrit, Greek, Latin, and Teutonic Languages, Shewing the Original Identity of Their Grammatical Structure." In *Internationale Zeitschrift für Allgemeine Sprachwissenschaft*, ed. F. Techmer, vol. 4, 14–60. Heilbronn, 1889.

Bosworth, C. E. "Tardjumān." In *Encyclopaedia of Islam*, 2nd ed. Ed. P. Bearman, Th. Bianquis, C. E. Bosworth, E. van Donzel, W. P. Heinrichs. Brill Online, 2012.

Bourdieu, Pierre. *The Logic of Practice*. Trans. Richard Nice. Stanford, CA: Stanford University Press, 1990.

———. "The Production and Reproduction of Legitimate Language." In *Language and Symbolic Power*, ed. John B. Thompson, trans. Gino Raymond and Matthew Adamson, 43–65. Cambridge, MA: Harvard University Press, 1994.

Bovilsky, Lara. *Barbarous Play: Race on the English Renaissance Stage*. Minneapolis: University of Minnesota Press, 2008.

Bowen, Barbara C. "Geofroy Tory's *Champ Fleury* and Its Major Sources." *Studies in Philology* 76, no. 1 (1979): 13–27.

Bowers, Fredson. *Bibliography and Textual Criticism*. Oxford: Oxford University Press, 1959.

———. "The Folio *Othello*: Compositor E." Lecture delivered 1959, pub. 1964, rpt. in Bowers, *Essays in Bibliography, Text, and Editing*, 326–58. Charlottesville: University Press of Virginia, for the Bibliographical Society, 1975.

———, ed. *Hero and Leander*. In *The Complete Poems of Christopher Marlowe*, 2nd ed., vol. 2, 423–515. Cambridge: Cambridge University Press, 1981.

———, ed. "The Passionate Shepherd to His Love." In *The Complete Works of Christopher Marlowe*, 2nd ed., vol. 2, 519–37. Cambridge: Cambridge University Press, 1981.

———. "Whitman's Manuscripts for the Original 'Calamus' Poems." *SB* 6 (1954): 257–65.

Braden, Gordon. *The Classics and English Renaissance Poetry: Three Case Studies*. New Haven, CT: Yale University Press, 1978.

Brathwait, Richard. *The English Gentleman*. London: by Iohn Haviland [for] Robert Bostock, 1630.

Bray, Alan. *The Friend*. Chicago: University of Chicago Press, 2003.

———. "Homosexuality and the Signs of Male Friendship in Elizabethan England." *History Workshop Journal* 29 (1990): 1–19. Rpt. in *Queering the Renaissance*, ed. Jonathan Goldberg, 40–61. Durham, NC: Duke University Press, 1994.

———. *Homosexuality in Renaissance England*. London: Gay Men's Press, 1982.

———. "Why Have English Historians Run Away from Kinship?" Unpublished paper. King's College, London, March 23, 2001.

Bredbeck, Gregory W. *Sodomy and Interpretation: Marlowe to Milton*. Ithaca, NY: Cornell University Press, 1991.

Bromley, James M. *Intimacy and Sexuality in the Age of Shakespeare*. Cambridge: Cambridge University Press, 2012.

Brooke, C. F. Tucker. *The Life of Marlowe and The Tragedy of Dido Queen of Carthage*. London: Methuen, 1930.

———. "The Reputation of Christopher Marlowe." In *Transactions of the Connecticut Academy of Arts and Sciences* 25: 347–408. New Haven, CT: Yale University Press for Connecticut Academy of Arts and Sciences, 1922.

Bruster, Douglas. "The Jailer's Daughter and the Politics of Madwomen's Language." *SQ* 46, no. 3 (1995): 277–300.

———. "Shakespearean Spellings and Handwriting in the Additional Passages Printed in the 1602 *Spanish Tragedy*." *Notes and Queries* 60, no. 3 (2013): 420–24.

Bryan, Emily D. "The Government of Performance: *Ignoramus* and the Micropolitics of Tutor-Student Relations." In *Early Modern Academic Drama*, ed. Jonathan Walker and Paul D. Streufert, 87–114. Farnham, UK: Ashgate, 2008.

———. "In the Company of Boys: The Place of the Boy Actor in Early Modern English Culture." Ph.D. diss., Northwestern University, 2005.

[Bullinger, Heinrich]. *De Origine Erroris Libri Dvo*. Zurich: in Officina Froschouiana, [c. 1550].

[Bullokar, John.] *An English Expositor: Teaching The Interpretation of the hardest words vsed in our Language*. London: by Iohn Legatt, 1616.

Bullokar, William. *Bullokars Booke at large, for the Amendment of Orthographie for English speech. . . .* London: by Henrie Denham, 1580.

Butler, A. J. "The Initial Blocks of Some Italian Printers." *Bibliographia I*, parts I–IV, 418–27. London: 1895.

Butler, Charls. *The English Grammar, Or The Institution of Letters, Syllables, and Words, in the English tongue*. Oxford: by William Turner for the Authour, 1633.

Butler, Judith. *Bodies That Matter*. New York: Routledge, 1993.

———. "Imitation and Gender Insubordination." In *Inside/Out: Lesbian Theories, Gay Theories*, ed. Diana Fuss, 13–31. New York: Routledge, 1991.

———. "Is Kinship Always Already Heterosexual?" *differences: A Journal of Feminist Cultural Studies* 13, no. 1 (2002): 14–44.

The Byble, which is all the holy Scripture. Antwerp: by Matthew Crom for Richard Grafton and Edward Whitchurch, 1537.

Cairncross, Andrew S. "Compositors E and F of the Shakespeare First Folio." *Papers of the Bibliographical Society of America* 66 (1972): 395–96.

Callaghan, Dympna. "Recent Studies in Tudor and Stuart Drama." *SEL Studies in English Literature 1500–1900* 44, no. 2 (2004): 405–44.

Camden, William. *Remaines of a Greater Worke, Concerning Britaine, the inhabitants thereof, their Languages, Names, Surnames, Empreses, Wise speeches, Poësies, and Epitaphes*. London: by G.E. for Simon Waterson, 1605.

Cannon, Christopher. *The Making of Chaucer's English: A Study of Words*. Cambridge: Cambridge University Press, 1998.

———. "Spelling Practice: The *Ormulum* and the Word." *Forum for Modern Language Studies* 33 (1997): 229–44.

Carlino, A. "Paper Bodies: A Catalogue of Anatomical Fugitive Sheets 1538–1687." *Medical History Supplement* 19 (1999): 1–352.

Casseri, Guilio Placentini. *Tabulae Anatomica LXXIIX*. Venice: Evangelista Deuchino, 1627.

Cavell, Stanley. *Pursuits of Happiness: The Hollywood Comedy of Remarriage*. Cambridge, MA: Harvard University Press, 1981.

Cawdrey, Robert. *A Table Alphabeticall, conteyning and teaching the true vvriting, and vnderstanding of hard vsuall English wordes*. London: by I.R. for Edmund Weauer, 1604.

Certayne Newes Of The whole discription, ayde, and helpe of the Christian Princes and Nobles. London: by W. Williamson, [1574?].

Chapman, George, trans. *The Divine Poem of Mvsæs. First of all Bookes*. London: by Isaac Iaggard, 1616.

Chapman, Hugo. *Padua in the 1450s: Marco Zoppo and His Contemporaries*. London: British Museum Press, 1998.

Chauncey, George. *Gay New York: Gender, Urban Culture, and the Making of the Gay Male World, 1890–1940*. New York: Basic Books, 1994.

———. "The Trouble with Shame." In *Gay Shame*, ed. David M. Halperin and Valerie Traub, 277–82. Chicago: University of Chicago Press, 2009.

Cheney, Patrick. *Marlowe's Counterfeit Profession: Ovid, Spenser, Counter-Nationhood*. Toronto: University of Toronto Press, 1997.

Chillingworth, William. *The Religion of Protestants a Safe VVay to Salvation*. Oxford: by Leonard Lichfield [for] Iohn Clarke, 1638.

Cicero. *De Senectute, De Amicitia, De Divinatione*. Trans. William Armistead Falconer. Loeb Classical Library. London: William Heinemann Ltd.; Cambridge, MA: Harvard University Press, 1964.

Clayton, Thomas. *The "Shakespearean" Addition in the Booke of Sir Thomas Moore: Some Aids to Scholarly and Critical Shakespearean Studies*. Vol. 1 of *Shakespeare Studies Monographs Series*, ed. J. Leeds Barroll. Dubuque: Wm. C. Brown Company for Vanderbilt Center for Shakespeare Studies, 1969.

Cloud, Random. *See* McLeod, Randall.

Cockburn, J. S. *Calendar of Assize Records: Home Circuit Indictments, Elizabeth I and James I: Introduction*. London: H.M.S.O., 1985.

[Cockeram, Henry.] H.C. *The English Dictionarie: Or, An Interpreter of hard English Words.* London: for Edmund Weauer, 1623.

Cohen, Walter. Introduction to *Sir Thomas More: Passages Attributed to Shakespeare.* In *The Norton Shakespeare Based on the Oxford Edition,* ed. Stephen Greenblatt et al., 2029–32. 2nd ed. New York: W. W. Norton, 2008.

Cokain, Aston. *Small Poems of Divers sorts.* London: by Wil. Godbid, 1658.

Cokayne, Aston. *See* Cokain, Aston.

Coke, Edward. *The Third Part Of The Institutes Of the Laws of England.* London: by M. Flesher, for W. Lee and D. Pakeman, 1644.

Colie, Rosalie. *The Resources of Kind: Genre-Theory in the Renaissance.* Ed. Barbara K. Lewalski. Berkeley: University of California Press, 1973.

Conley, Tom. *The Self-Made Map: Cartographic Writing in Early Modern France.* Minneapolis: University of Minnesota Press, 1996.

Cooper, Thomas. *Bibliotheca Eliotæ. Eliotes Dictionarie . . . the third tyme corrected.* London: Tho. Berthelet, 1559.

Corbett, Margery, and Ronald Lightbown. *The Comely Frontispiece: The Emblematic Title-page in England, 1550–1660.* London: Routledge and Kegan Paul, 1979.

Cotgrave, Randle, comp. *A Dictionarie Of The French And English Tongves.* London: by Adam Islip, 1611.

Cox, John D., and David Scott Kastan, eds. *A New History of Early English Drama.* New York: Columbia University Press, 1997.

Crain, Patricia. *The Story of A: The Alphabetization of America from "The New England Primer" to "The Scarlet Letter."* Stanford, CA: Stanford University Press, 2000.

Cranmer, Thomas. "Prologue or Preface made by Thomas Cranmer." In *The Holy Bible conteyning the Olde Testament and the Newe. Authorised and appoynted to be read in Churches.* London: by the deputies of Christopher Barker, 1595. STC 2167.

Crooke, Helkiah. *[Mikrokosmographia], A Description of the Body of Man.* London: by W. Iaggard, 1616.

Crummer, LeRoy. "A Check List of Anatomical Books Illustrated with Cuts with Superimposed Flaps." *Bulletin of the Medical Library Association* 20, no. 4 (1932): 131–39.

Culler, Jonathan. "Anti-Foundational Philology." In *On Philology,* ed. Jan Ziolkowski, 49–52. University Park: Pennsylvania State University Press, 1990.

Culpeper, Nicholas. *A directory for midwives, or, A guide for women, in their conception, bearing and suckling their children.* London: by Peter Cole, 1651–62.

Curran, Brian A. *The Egyptian Renaissance: The Afterlife of Ancient Egypt in Early Modern Italy.* Chicago: University of Chicago Press, 2007.

Dabbs, Thomas. "Marlowe Among the Aesthetes." In *Reforming Marlowe: The Nineteenth-century Canonization of a Renaissance Dramatist,* 108–35. Lewisburg, PA: Bucknell University Press, 1991.

Daileader, Celia R. "Back Door Sex: Renaissance Gynosodomy, Aretino, and the Exotic." *ELH* 69, no. 2 (2002): 303–34.

Darcy, Robert F. " 'Under My Hands . . . A Double Duty': Printing and Pressing Marlowe's *Hero and Leander." Journal for Early Modern Cultural Studies* 2, no. 2 (2002): 26–56.

Daston, Lorraine, and Katharine Park. *Wonders and the Order of Nature, 1150–1750.* Cambridge, MA: MIT Press, 2001.

Davidson, James. *The Greeks and Greek Love: A Radical Reappraisal of Homosexuality in Ancient Greece.* London: Weidenfeld and Nicholson, 2007.

Davidson, Nicholas. "Marlowe and Atheism." In *Christopher Marlowe and English Renaissance Culture,* ed. Darryll Grantley and Peter Roberts, 129–47. Aldershot, UK: Scolar Press, 1996.

Day, Angel. *The English Secretorie*. London: by Robert Walde-graue and are to be sold by Richard Iones, 1586.

de Grazia, Margreta. "Homonyms Before and After Lexical Standardization." *Shakespeare Jahrbuch* (1990): 143–56.

———. "The Ideology of Superfluous Things: *King Lear* as Period Piece." In *Subject and Object in Renaissance Culture*, ed. Margreta de Grazia, Maureen Quilligan, and Peter Stallybrass, 17–42. Cambridge: Cambridge University Press, 1996.

———. "Imprints: Descartes, Shakespeare, Gutenberg." In *Alternative Shakespeares*, vol. 2, ed. Terence Hawkes, 63–94. London: Routledge, 1996.

———. "The Scandal of Shakespeare's Sonnets." In *Shakepeare's Sonnets: Critical Essays*, ed. James Schiffer, 88–112. New York: Garland, 1999.

———. "Shakespeare and the Craft of Language." In *The Cambridge Companion to Shakespeare*, ed. Margreta de Grazia and Stanley Wells, 49–64. Cambridge: Cambridge University Press, 2001.

———. *Shakespeare Verbatim: The Reproduction of Authenticity and the 1790 Apparatus*. Oxford: Clarendon, 1991.

———. "Soliloquies and Wages in the Age of Emergent Consciousness." *Textual Practice* 9, no. 1 (1995): 67–92.

———. "Words as Things." *Shakespeare Studies* 28 (2000): 231–35.

de Grazia, Margreta, Maureen Quilligan, and Peter Stallybrass, eds. *Subject and Object in Renaissance Culture*. Cambridge: Cambridge University Press, 1996.

de Grazia, Margreta, and Peter Stallybrass. "The Materiality of the Shakespearean Text." *SQ* 44, no. 3 (1993): 255–83.

Dekker, Thomas. *A Knights Coniuring*. London: by T.C. for VVilliam Barley, 1607.

de Man, Paul. "The Return to Philology." In *The Resistance to Theory*, 21–26. Theory and History of Literature 33. Minneapolis: University of Minnesota Press, 1986.

D'Emilio, John. *Sexual Politics, Sexual Communities: The Making of a Homosexual Minority in the United States, 1940–1970*. Chicago: University of Chicago Press, 1983.

Dempsey, Charles. *Inventing the Renaissance Putto*. Chapel Hill: University of North Carolina Press, 2001.

Derrida, Jacques. "The Law of Genre." *Glyph* 7 (1980): 202–32.

———. *Politics of Friendship*. Trans. George Collins. London: Verso, 1997.

DiGangi, Mario. *The Homoerotics of Early Modern Drama*. Cambridge: Cambridge University Press, 1997.

———. "Marlowe, Queer Studies, and Renaissance Homoeroticism." In *Marlowe, History, and Sexuality: New Critical Essays on Christopher Marlowe*, ed. Paul Whitfield White, 195–212. New York: AMS, 1998.

———. "Queer Theory, Historicism, and Early Modern Sexualities." *Criticism* 48 (2006): 129–42.

———. "Queering the Shakespearean Family." *SQ* 46, no. 3 (1996): 269–90.

———. *Sexual Types: Embodiment, Agency, and Dramatic Character from Shakespeare to Shirley*. Philadelphia: University of Pennsylvania Press, 2011.

Digby, Kenelm. *Two Treatises in the one of which, The Natvre of Bodies; in the other, the Natvre of Mans Sovle*. Paris: by Gilles Blaizot, 1644.

Dinshaw, Carolyn. *How Soon Is Now? Medieval Texts, Amateur Readers, and the Queerness of Time*. Durham, NC: Duke University Press, 2012.

Dinshaw, Carolyn, Lee Edelman, Roderick A. Ferguson, Carla Freccero, Elizabeth Freeman, Judith Halberstam, Annamarie Jagose, Christopher Nealon, and Nguyen Tan Hoang. "Theorizing Queer Temporalities: A Roundtable Discussion." *GLQ: A Journal of Lesbian and Gay Studies* 13, nos. 2–3 (2007): 177–95.

Dolan, Frances E. "'Gentlemen, I Have One Thing More to Say': Women on Scaffolds in England, 1563–1680." *Modern Philology* 92, no. 2 (1994): 157–78.

Doran, Madeleine. *Endeavors of Art: A Study of Form in Elizabethan Drama*. Madison: University of Wisconsin Press, 1954.

Downie, J. A. "Marlowe: Facts and Fictions." In *Constructing Christopher Marlowe*, ed. J. A. Downie and J. T. Parnell, 13–29. Cambridge: Cambridge University Press, 2000.

Dutton, Richard. *Mastering the Revels: The Regulation and Censorship of English Renaissance Drama*. Iowa City: University of Iowa Press, 1991.

Edelman, Lee. *Homographesis: Essays in Gay Literary and Cultural Theory*. New York: Routledge, 1994.

Edward II. Dir. Derek Jarman. British Screen and BBC Films, Fine Line Features, 1992.

Edwards, Philip. "An Approach to the Problem of *Pericles*." *Shakespeare Survey* 5 (1952): 25–49.

———, ed. *The Spanish Tragedy*, by Thomas Kyd. The Revels Plays. Cambridge, MA: Harvard University Press, 1959.

EEBO Text Creation Partnership. ProQuest LLC, University of Michigan, and Oxford University. 2009–12. http://quod.lib.umich.edu/e/eebogroup.

Eisenstein, Elizabeth. *The Printing Press as an Agent of Change: Communications and Cultural Transformations in Early-Modern Europe*. 2 vols. Cambridge: Cambridge University Press, 1979.

Eisner, Martin G., and Marc D. Schachter. "*Libido Sciendi*: Apuleius, Boccaccio, and the Study of the History of Sexuality." *PMLA* 124, no. 3 (2009): 817–37.

Eliot, Thomas. *The Dictionary of syr Thomas Eliot knight*. London: [Thomas Berthelet], [1538].

———. *See also* Elyot, Thomas.

Ellis, Havelock, ed. *Christopher Marlowe*. Unexpurgated edition with a General Introduction by J. A. Symonds. The Mermaids Series. London: Vizetelly, 1887.

Elyot, Thomas. *The Castel of Helth Corrected and in some places augmented*. London: [Thomas Berthelet], 1541.

———. *See also* Eliot, Thomas.

Employment of Homosexuals and Other Sex Perverts in Government. Interim report submitted to the Committee on Expenditures in the Executive Departments by its Subcommittee on Investigations, 81st Congress, 2nd Session, Senate document 241. Washington, DC: U.S. Government Printing Office, 1950.

Empson, William. *The Structure of Complex Words*. Cambridge, MA: Harvard University Press, 1989.

Engle, Lars. "Oedipal Marlowe, Mimetic Middleton." *Modern Philology* 2008: 417–36.

English Institute. "A Classified List of Topics, Chairmen, and Speakers, 1939–1963." Memorandum. The English Institute, [1963?].

English Short Title Catalogue. The British Library and ESTC/North America. 1981–2003. http://estc.bl.uk.

Enterline, Lynn. "Rhetoric, Discipline, and the Theatricality of Everyday Life in Elizabethan Grammar Schools." In *From Performance to Print in Shakespeare's England*, ed. Peter Holland and Stephen Orgel, 173–90. Basingstoke, UK: Palgrave, 2006.

———. *The Rhetoric of the Body from Ovid to Shakespeare*. Cambridge: Cambridge University Press, 2000.

Erasmus, Desiderius. "On the Writing of Letters / *De conscribendis epistolis*." Trans. and annotated by Charles Fantazzi. In *Literary and Education Writings* 3, ed. J. K. Sowards, vol. 25 of *Collected Works of Erasmus*, 1–254. Toronto: University of Toronto Press, 1985.

Erne, Lukas. "Biography, Mythography, and Criticism: The Life and Works of Christopher Marlowe." *Modern Philology* 103 (2005): 28–50.

———. *Shakespeare as Literary Dramatist*. Cambridge: Cambridge University Press, 2003.

Evans, G. Blakemore, et al., eds. *The Riverside Shakespeare*. 1st ed. Boston: Houghton Mifflin, 1974.

Falconer, William Armistead. "Introduction to the *Laelius*." In Cicero, *De Senectute, De Amicitia, De Divinatione*, with trans. by Falconer, 103–7. Loeb Classical Library. London: William Heinemann Ltd.; Cambridge, MA: Harvard University Press, 1946.

Feerick, Jean E. *Strangers in Blood: Relocating Race in the Renaissance*. Toronto: University of Toronto Press, 2010.

Fenton, James. "Shakespeare, Stage or Page?" *New York Review of Books*, April 8, 2004.

Ferguson, Margaret W. "*Hamlet*: Letters and Spirits." In *Shakespeare and the Question of Theory*, ed. Patricia Parker and Geoffrey Hartman, 292–309. New York: Methuen, 1985.

Fisher, Will. *Materializing Gender in Early Modern English Literature and Culture*. Cambridge: Cambridge University Press, 2006.

———. "Queer Money." *ELH* 66, no. 1 (1999): 1–23.

———. "The Sexual Politics of Victorian Historiographical Writing About the 'Renaissance.'" *GLQ: A Journal of Lesbian and Gay Studies* 14, no. 1 (2008): 41–67.

———. "'Wantoning with the Thighs': The Socialization of Thigh Sex in England, 1590–1730." *Journal of the History of Sexuality* 24, no. 1 (2015): 1–24.

Fleming, Juliet. "Dictionary English and the Female Tongue." In *Enclosure Acts: Sexuality, Property, and Culture in Early Modern England*, ed. Richard Burt and John Michael Archer, 290–325. Ithaca, NY: Cornell University Press, 1994.

———. "The French Garden: An Introduction to Women's French." *ELH* 56 (1989): 19–51.

———. *Graffiti and the Writing Arts of Early Modern England*. London: Reaktion, 2001.

———. "The Ladies' Man and the Age of Elizabeth." In *Sexuality and Gender in Early Modern Europe: Institutions, Texts, Images*, ed. James Grantham Turner, 158–81. Cambridge: Cambridge University Press, 1993.

Fletcher, Iohn. *The Faithfvll Sheapeardesse*. London: for R. Bonian and H. Walley, n.d.

———. *See also* Fletcher, John; Baymont, Francis; Beaumont, Francis.

Fletcher, John, and William Shakespeare. *The Two Noble Kinsmen*. Ed. Lois Potter. The Arden Shakespeare, 3rd ser. Walton-on-Thames, UK: Thomas Nelson and Sons, 1997.

Fletcher, John, and William Shakspeare. *The Two Noble Kinsmen*. London: Tho. Cotes, for Iohn Waterson, 1634.

[Fletcher, Phineas]. P.F. *The Purple Island, Or The Isle Of Man*. Cambridge: by the Printers to the Universitie, 1633.

Florio, [Iohn]. *Florios Second Frvtes*. London: for Thomas Woodcock, 1591.

Florio, Iohn. *Qveen Anna's New World of Words, Or Dictionarie of the Italian and English tongues*. London: by Melch. Bradwood, for Edw. Blount and William Barret, 1611.

———. *A Worlde of Wordes, Or Most copious, and exact Dictionarie in Italian and English*. London: by Arnold Hatfield for Edw. Blount, 1598.

Foakes, R. A. "Tragicomedy and Comic Form." In *Comedy from Shakespeare to Sheridan: Change and Continuity in the English and European Dramatic Tradition*, ed. A. R. Braunmuller and J. C. Bulman, 82–86. Newark: University of Delaware Press, 1986.

Fonteyn, Nicholaas. *The womans doctour, or, An exact and distinct explanation of all such diseases as are peculiar to that sex*. London: for John Blague and Samuel Howes, 1652.

Foster, Verna A. *The Name and Nature of Tragicomedy*. Aldershot, UK: Ashgate, 2004.

Foucault, Michel. *Histoire de la sexualité, Volume 1: La volonté de savoir*. Paris: Gallimard, 1976.

———. *The History of Sexuality, Volume I: An Introduction*. Trans. Robert Hurley. New York: Vintage, 1978.

———. "What Is an Author?" In *The Foucault Reader*, ed. Paul Rabinow, 101–20. New York: Pantheon, 1984.

Fowler, Alistair. *Kinds of Literature: An Introduction to the Theory of Genres and Modes.* Cambridge, MA: Harvard University Press, 1982.

Fradenburg, Louise O., and Carla Freccero. "Introduction: The Pleasures of History." *Premodern Sexualities in Europe.* Spec. issue of *GLQ: A Journal of Lesbian and Gay Studies* 1, no. 4 (1995): 371–84.

Fradenburg, Louise, and Carla Freccero. "Caxton, Foucault, and the Pleasures of History." In *Premodern Sexualities,* ed. Louise Fradenburg and Carla Freccero, xiii–xxiv. New York: Routledge, 1996.

Frank, Roberta. "The Unbearable Lightness of Being a Philologist." *Journal of English and Germanic Philology* 96, no. 4 (1997): 486–513.

Freccero, Carla. "Practicing Queer Philology with Marguerite de Navarre: Nationalism and the Castigation of Desire." In *Queering the Renaissance,* ed. Jonathan Goldberg, 107–23. Durham, NC: Duke University Press, 1994.

———. *Queer/Early/Modern.* Durham, NC: Duke University Press, 2006.

Freeman, Arthur. *Thomas Kyd: Facts and Problems.* Oxford: Clarendon, 1967.

Freeman, Elizabeth. *Time Binds: Queer Temporalities, Queer Histories.* Durham, NC: Duke University Press, 2010.

Friedman, Ryan. "Bombastic Subjects: Inauthenticity and Disorder in the Discourse of Renaissance Humanism." Unpublished paper.

Frye, Roland Mushat. *Shakespeare and Christian Doctrine.* Princeton, NJ: Princeton University Press, 1963.

Fumerton, Patricia. *Cultural Aesthetics: Renaissance Literature and the Practice of Social Ornament.* Chicago: University of Chicago Press, 1991.

Furness, Horace Howard, ed. *Hamlet. A New Variorum Edition of Shakespeare.* 2 vols. Philadelphia: J. B. Lippincott, 1877; rpt., New York: Dover, 1963.

———, ed. *Othello. A New Variorum Edition of Shakespeare.* 11th ed. Philadelphia: J. B. Lippincott, 1886.

Fuss, Diana. *Identification Papers.* New York: Routledge, 1995.

Gabrieli, Vittorio. "*Sir Thomas More*: Source, Characters, Ideas." *Moreana* 90 (1986): 17–43.

Garber, Marjorie. "'Infinite Riches in a Little Room': Closure and Enclosure in Marlowe." In *Two Renaissance Mythmakers: Christopher Marlowe and Ben Jonson,* ed. Alvin Kernan, 3–21. Baltimore, MD: Johns Hopkins University Press, 1977.

———. "Shakespeare's Dogs." In *Profiling Shakespeare,* 182–94. New York: Routledge, 2008.

Garber, Marjorie, and Rebecca L. Walkowitz, eds. *Secret Agents: The Rosenberg Case, McCarthyism, and Fifties America.* New York: Routledge, 1995.

Gaskell, Philip. *A New Introduction to Bibliography.* New York: Oxford University Press, 1972.

Gazēs, Theodōros. *Theodori Gazae Introdvctionis grammaticae libri qvatuor.* Basel: Valderiana, 1541.

The General Practise Of Physicke. London: for Thomas Adams, 1617.

Glare, P. G. W., ed. *Oxford Latin Dictionary.* Oxford: Clarendon, 1982.

Gleick, James. "Crosswords." *New York Times Magazine,* April 16, 1995.

Godwin, William. *Enquiry concerning political justice, and its influence on morals and happiness.* 2nd ed. corrected. 2 vols. London, 1796.

Goldberg, Jonathan. "The Anus in *Coriolanus.*" In *Historicism, Psychoanalysis, and Early Modern Culture,* ed. Carla Mazzio and Doug Trevor, 260–71. New York : Routledge, 2000.

———, ed. *Queering the Renaissance.* Durham, NC: Duke University Press, 1994.

———. *Sodometries: Renaissance Texts, Modern Sexualities.* Stanford, CA: Stanford University Press, 1992.

———. "Sodomy and Society: The Case of Christopher Marlowe." In *Staging the Renaissance: Reinterpretations of Elizabethan and Jacobean Drama*, ed. David Scott Kastan and Peter Stallybrass, 75–82. New York: Routledge, 1991.

———. *Writing Matter: From the Hands of the English Renaissance*. Stanford, CA: Stanford University Press, 1990.

Goldberg, Jonathan, and Madhavi Menon. "Queering History." *PMLA* 120, no. 5 (2005): 1608–17.

Google Books. "Google Ngram Viewer." 2015. http://books.google.com/ngrams.

Gossett, Suzanne. "Major/Minor, Main Plot/Subplot, Middleton/and." In *The Elizabethan Theatre XV: Papers Given at the Fifteenth and Sixteenth International Conferences on Elizabethan Theatre*, ed. A. Lynne Magnusson and C. Edward McGee, 21–38. Toronto: P. D. Meany, 2002.

Grafton, Anthony. *The Culture of Correction in Renaissance Europe*. London: British Library, 2011.

———. *Defenders of the Text: The Traditions of Scholarship in an Age of Science, 1450–1800*. Cambridge, MA: Harvard University Press, 1991.

———. *Worlds Made by Words: Scholarship and Community in the Modern West*. Cambridge, MA: Harvard University Press, 2009.

Le Grand Robert de la langue française. Dictionnaires Le Robert. 2013. http://gr.bvdep.com.

Green, Jonathon. *Green's Dictionary of Slang*. Chambers Harrap Publishers and Oxford Reference. 2012. http://www.oxfordreference.com/view/10.1093/acref/9780199829941.001.0001/acref-9780199829941.

Greenblatt, Stephen. "General Introduction." In *The Norton Shakespeare Based on the Oxford Edition*, 1st ed., ed. Stephen Greenblatt et al., 1–76. New York: W. W. Norton, 1997.

———. *Hamlet in Purgatory*. Princeton, NJ: Princeton University Press, 2001.

———. "Psychoanalysis and Renaissance Culture." In *Literary Theory/Renaissance Texts*, ed. Patricia Parker and David Quint, 210–24. Baltimore, MD: Johns Hopkins University Press, 1986.

———. *Renaissance Self-Fashioning: From More to Shakespeare*. Chicago: University of Chicago Press, 1980.

———. *Shakespearean Negotiations: The Circulation of Social Energy in Renaissance England*. Berkeley: University of California Press, 1988.

———. *Will in the World: How Shakespeare Became Shakespeare*. New York: W. W. Norton, 2004.

Greenblatt, Stephen, et al., eds. *The Norton Shakespeare Based on the Oxford Edition*. 1st ed. New York: W. W. Norton, 1997.

———. *The Norton Shakespeare Based on the Oxford Edition*. 2nd ed. New York: W. W. Norton, 2008.

Greene, Jody. "'You Must Eat Men': The Sodomitic Economy of Renaissance Patronage." *GLQ: A Journal of Lesbian and Gay Studies* 1 (1994): 163–97.

[Greene, Robert]. *A Qvip For An Vp-start Courtier: Or, A quaint dispute betvven Veluet breeches and Cloth-breeches*. London: by Iohn Wolfe, 1592.

Greene, Roland. *Five Words: Critical Semantics in the Age of Shakespeare and Cervantes*. Chicago: University of Chicago Press, 2013.

———. *Unrequited Conquests: Love and Empire in the Colonial Americas*. Chicago: University of Chicago Press, 1999.

Greenfield, Matthew. "Christopher Marlowe's Wound Knowledge." *PMLA* 119, no. 2 (2004): 233–46.

Greg, W. W., ed. *The Book of Sir Thomas More*. Malone Society Reprints. Oxford: Oxford University Press for the Malone Society, 1911.

———. "The Copyright of *Hero and Leander*." *The Library*, 4th ser., 24 (1944): 165–74.

Grossman, Jay. "The Canon in the Closet: Matthiessen's Whitman, Whitman's Matthiessen." *American Literature* 70 (1998): 799–832.

[Guillemeau, Jacques]. *Child-birth or, The happy deliuerie of vvomen. VVherein is set downe the gouernment of women*. London: by A. Hatfield, 1612.

Gumbrecht, Hans Ulrich. *The Powers of Philology: Dynamics of Textual Scholarship*. Urbana: University of Illinois Press, 2003.

Gurd, Sean Alexander. *Iphigenias at Aulis: Textual Multiplicity, Radical Philology*. Ithaca, NY: Cornell University Press, 2005.

Gurr, Andrew. "Introduction." In *Philaster, or Love Lies a-Bleeding*, by Francis Beaumont and John Fletcher, ed. Andrew Gurr, xix–lxxxiv. The Revels Plays. Manchester: Manchester University Press, 1969.

Gutjahr, Paul C. "The Letter(s) of the Law: Four Centuries of Typography in the King James Bible." In *Illuminating Letters: Typography and Literary Interpretation*, ed. Paul C. Gutjahr and Megan L. Benton, 17–44. Amherst: University of Massachusetts Press, 2001.

Guy-Bray, Stephen. *Homoerotic Space: The Poetics of Loss in Renaissance Literature*. Toronto: University of Toronto Press, 2002.

Guy-Bray, Stephen, Vin Nardizzi, and Will Stockton. "Queer Renaissance Historiography: Backward Gaze." In *Queer Renaissance Historiography: Backward Gaze*, ed. Vin Nardizzi, Stephen Guy-Bray, and Will Stockton, 1–11. Farnham, UK: Ashgate, 2009.

Haber, Judith. "'True-Loves Blood': Narrative and Desire in *Hero and Leander*." *English Literary Renaissance* 28, no. 3 (1993): 372–86.

Hall, Kim F. "Culinary Spaces, Colonial Spaces: The Gendering of Sugar in the Seventeenth Century." In *Feminist Readings of Early Modern Culture: Emerging Subjects*, ed. Valerie Traub, M. Lindsay Kaplan, and Dympna Callaghan, 168–90. Cambridge: Cambridge University Press, 1996.

———. *Things of Darkness: Economies of Race and Gender in Early Modern England*. Ithaca, NY: Cornell University Press, 1995.

Halley, Janet E. "*Bowers v. Hardwick* in the Renaissance." In *Queering the Renaissance*, ed. Jonathan Goldberg, 15–39. Durham, NC: Duke University Press, 1994.

Halperin, David M. *How to Do the History of Homosexuality*. Chicago: University of Chicago Press, 2002.

———. "How to Do the History of Male Homosexuality." *GLQ: A Journal of Lesbian and Gay Studies* 6, no. 1 (2000): 87–123.

———. *One Hundred Years of Homosexuality and Other Essays on Greek Love*. New York: Routledge, 1990.

Halperin, David M., and Valerie Traub. "Beyond Gay Pride." In *Gay Shame*, ed. David M. Halperin and Valerie Traub. Chicago: University of Chicago Press, 2009.

Hamann, Byron Ellsworth. "How Maya Hieroglyphs Got Their Name: Egypt, Mexico, and China in Western Grammatology Since the Fifteenth Century." *Proceedings of the American Philosophical Society* 152, no. 1 (2008): 1–68.

Hanson, Elizabeth. "Fellow Students: Hamlet, Horatio, and the Early Modern University." *SQ* 62 (2011): 205–29.

Hardin, Richard F. "Marlowe and the Fruits of Scholarism." *Philological Quarterly* 63, no. 3 (1984): 387–400.

Harpham, Geoffrey Galt. "Roots, Races, and the Return to Philology." *Representations* 106 (2009): 34–62.

[Harington, John.] *A Nevv Discovrse Of A Stale Svbiect, Called The Metamorphosis of Aiax*. London: by Richard Field, 1596.

[Harington, John, and] T.C. *An Anatomie Of The Metamorpho-sed Aiax*. London: by Richard Field, 1596.

Harrison, William. *The description of England*. In *The First and Second volumes of Chronicles*, by Raphael Holinshed. London, 1587.

Hart, John. *An orthographie, conteyning the due order howe to write thimage of mannes voice*. London: by William Seres, 1569.

Helgerson, Richard. *Forms of Nationhood: The Elizabethan Writing of England*. Chicago: University of Chicago Press, 1992.

Hendricks, Margo, and Patricia Parker, eds. *Women, "Race," and Writing in the Early Modern Period*. London: Routledge, 1994.

Henke, Robert. *Pastoral Transformations: Italian Tragicomedy and Shakespeare's Last Plays*. Newark: University of Delaware Press, 1997.

Henslowe, Philip. *Henslowe's Diary*. 2 vols. Ed. W. W. Greg. London: A. H. Bullen, 1904.

Herbert, Christopher. *Culture and Anomie: Ethnographic Imagination in the Nineteenth Century*. Chicago: University of Chicago Press, 1991.

Herdman, John. *An essay on the causes and phenomena of animal life*. London, 1795.

Herrup, Cynthia B. *A House in Gross Disorder: Sex, Law, and the 2nd Earl of Castelhaven*. Oxford: Oxford University Press, 1999.

Heywood, Thomas. *An Apology For Actors*. London: by Nicholas Okes, 1612.

———. *Pleasant Dialogves and Dramma's, Selected Ovt of Lucian, Erasmus, Textor, Ovid, &c*. London: by R. O[ulton] for R. H[earne] [for] Thomas Slater, 1637.

Higgins, Iohn. *Hvloets Dictionarie, newelye corrected, amended, Set In Order And Enlarged*. London: [Thomas Marshe], 1572.

Hill, T. H. "Spelling and the Bibliographer." *The Library*, 5th ser., 18, no. 1 (1963): 1–28.

Hillman, David, and Carla Mazzio, eds. *The Body in Parts: Fantasies of Corporeality in Early Modern England*. New York: Routledge, 1997.

Hinman, Charlton, ed. *The Norton Facsimile: The First Folio of Shakespeare*. New York: W. W. Norton, 1968.

———. "Principles Governing the Use of Variant Spellings as Evidence of Alternate Setting by Two Compositors." *The Library*, 4th ser., 21 (1940–41): 78–94.

———. *The Printing and Proofreading of the First Folio of Shakespeare*. 2 vols. Oxford: Clarendon, 1963.

———. "The Proof-Reading of the First Folio Text of *Romeo and Juliet*." *SB* 6 (1954): 61–70.

The historie of the troublesome Raigne of King Edward the second with the liues and deaths of the greate Duke of Cornwall & Sr Hugh Spencer the youngest, the two greate Minions of his time, togither wthe the Conspiracie of the Queene & Mortimer against the Deposinge of the Kinge. 1626 Neuer printed. written by [name obliterated]. Attributed to Francis Hubert. Folger MS V.a. 234.

Hocquenghem, Guy. *Homosexual Desire*. Trans. Daniella Dangoor. Pref. Jeffrey Weeks. New intro. Michael Moon. Durham, NC: Duke University Press, 1993.

Hodgdon, Barbara, ed. *The Taming of the Shrew*, by William Shakespeare. The Arden Shakespeare, 3rd ser. London: A&C Black, 2010.

Hodges, Richard. *A Special Help To Orthographie: Or, The True-writing of English. Consisting of such Words as are alike in sound, and unlike both in their signification and Writing: As also, of such Words which are so neer alike in sound, that they are sometimes taken one for another*. London: for Richard Cotes, 1643.

Holinshed, Raphael, et al. *The First and Second volumes of Chronicles* [*of England, Scotlande, and Irlande*]. 3 vols. in 2. London: [by Henry Denham], 1587.

Holland, Peter, and Stephen Orgel, eds. *From Performance to Print in Shakespeare's England*. Basingstoke, UK: Palgrave, 2006.

The Holy Bible containing the Old Testament and the New. London: by Robert Barker, 1602.

The Holy Bible, Conteyning the Old Testament And The New: Newly Translated out of the Origi-nall tongues. . . . London: by Robert Barker, 1611. Reprod. in *The Holy Bible: A Facsimile in a reduced size of the Authorized Version published in the year 1611.* Intro. A. W. Pollard. Oxford: Oxford University Press, 1911.

The Holy Bible, Revised Standard Version . . . revised A.D. 1952. New York: T. Nelson, 1952.

Honan, Park. *Christopher Marlowe: Poet and Spy.* Oxford: Oxford University Press, 2005.

Honigmann, E. A. J. "Shakespeare, *Sir Thomas More* and Asylum Seekers." *Shakespeare Survey* 57 (2004): 225–35.

Honigmann, E. A. J., and Susan Brock, eds. *Playhouse Wills 1558–1642: An Edition of Wills by Shakespeare and His Contemporaries in the London Theatre.* Manchester: Manchester University Press, 1993.

Hope, Jonathan. *The Authorship of Shakespeare's Plays: A Socio-linguistic Study.* Cambridge: Cambridge University Press, 1994.

Hopkins, Lisa. *Christopher Marlowe: A Literary Life.* Basingstoke, UK: Palgrave, 2000.

Hornbye, William. *Hornbyes Hornbook.* London: by Aug. Math. for Thomas Bayly, 1622.

Howard, Jean E. "Crossdressing, the Theatre, and Gender Struggle in Early Modern England." *SQ* 39 (1988): 418–40.

Howard-Hill, T. H. "New Light on Compositor E of the Shakespeare First Folio." *The Library,* 6th ser., 2, no. 2 (1980): 156–78.

Hoy, Cyrus. "The Shares of Fletcher and His Collaborators in the Beaumont and Fletcher Canon (I)." *SB* 8 (1956): 129–46.

———. "The Shares of Fletcher and His Collaborators in the Beaumont and Fletcher Canon (III)." *SB* 11 (1958): 85–106.

Hubert, Francis. *See The historie of the troublesome Raigne of King Edward the second.*

Huloet, Richard. Abecedarivm Anglicolatinvm. London: Ex officina Gulielmi Riddel, 1552.

———. *See also* Higgins, Iohn.

Hulse, Clark. *Metamorphic Verse: The Elizabethan Minor Epic.* Princeton, NJ: Princeton University Press, 1981.

Hume, Alexander. *Of the Orthographie and Congruitie of the Britan Tongue; A Treates, Noe Shorter Then Necessarie, for the Schooles.* Ed. Henry B. Wheatley. London: Trübner and Co., for the Early English Text Society, 1865.

Ingram, James. *An Inaugural Lecture on the Utility of Anglo-Saxon Literature.* Oxford: Oxford University Press, 1807.

Ingram, Martin. *Church Courts, Sex and Marriage in England, 1570–1640.* Cambridge: Cambridge University Press, 1987.

Ionson, Ben. *The Alchemist.* London: by Thomas Snodham, for Walter Burre, and are to be sold by Iohn Stepneth, 1612.

———. "To the memory of my beloued, The Avthor Mr. VVilliam Shakespeare: And what he hath left vs." In *Mr. VVilliam Shakespeares Comedies, Histories, & Tragedies.* London: by Isaac Iaggard, and Ed. Blount, 1623.

———. *See also* Jonson, Ben; Jonson, Beniamin; Jonson, Benjamin.

Jackson, MacDonald P. "Is 'Hand D' of *Sir Thomas More* Shakespeare's? Thomas Bayes and the Elliott-Valenza Authorship Tests." *Early Modern Literary Studies* 12, no. 3 (January 2007): 1.1–36. http://purl.oclc.org/emls/12-3/jackbaye.htm.

Jagose, Annamarie. *Inconsequence: Lesbian Representation and the Logic of Sexual Sequence.* Ithaca, NY: Cornell University Press, 2002.

James I. "Letters of James and Buckingham." In *King James and Letters of Homoerotic Desire,* ed. David Bergeron, 147–78. Iowa City: University of Iowa Press, 1999.

———. *The Workes of the Most High and Mightie Prince, Iames*. London: Iames, Bishop of Winton, 1616.

Jardine, Lisa. *Erasmus, Man of Letters: The Construction of Charisma in Print*. Princeton, NJ: Princeton University Press, 1993.

———. *Reading Shakespeare Historically*. London: Routledge, 1996.

———. *Still Harping on Daughters: Women and Drama in the Age of Shakespeare*. Sussex, UK: Barnes and Noble, 1983.

Jaros, Peter. "Unnatural Acts: Shakespeare's First Folio, Ben Jonson, and *Hamlet*." Unpublished essay, 2001.

Jed, Stephanie. *Chaste Thinking: The Rape of Lucretia and the Birth of Humanism*. Bloomington: Indiana University Press, 1989.

Jennings, Oscar. *Early Woodcut Initials, Containing Over Thirteen Hundred Reproductions of Ornamental Letters of the Fifteenth and Sixteenth Centuries*. London: Methuen, 1908.

Johnson, Barbara. "Philology: What Is at Stake?" In *On Philology*, ed. Jan Ziolkowski, 26–30. University Park: Pennsylvania State University Press, 1990.

Johnson, David K. *The Lavender Scare: The Cold War Persecution of Gays and Lesbians in the Federal Government*. Chicago: University of Chicago Press, 2004.

Johnson, Samuel. *A Dictionary Of The English Language: In Which The Words are deduced from their Originals. . . .* Vol. 2. London: by W. Strahan, For J. and P. Knapton [et al.], 1755. Rpt., New York: AMS Press, 1967.

Johnson, Thomas, trans. *The Workes of that famous Chirurgion Ambrose Parey Translated out of Latine and compared with the French*. London: by Th: Cotes and R. Young, 1634.

Jones, Ann Rosalind, and Peter Stallybrass. *Renaissance Clothing and the Materials of Memory*. Cambridge: Cambridge University Press, 2000.

Jonson, Ben. *Bartholomew Fair*. Ed. E. A. Horsman. The Revels Plays. Manchester: Manchester University Press, 1960, 1979.

———. *Horace His Art Of Poetrie, Made English By Ben. Iohnson*. 1640. In *Ben Jonson*, ed. C. H. Herford, Percy Simpson, and Evelyn Simpson, vol. 8, 297–355. Oxford: Clarendon, 1947.

Jonson, Beniamin. *The Workes of Beniamin Jonson*. London: by W: Stansby and are to be sould by Rich: Meighen, 1616.

Jonson, Benjamin. *The English Grammar*. In *The Workes of Benjamin Jonson. The second Volume*. London: for Richard Meighen, 1640.

———. *See also* Ionson, Ben.

Jordan, Mark D. *The Invention of Sodomy*. Chicago: University of Chicago Press, 1997.

Jowett, John, ed. *Sir Thomas More*. The Arden Shakespeare, 3rd ser. London: Methuen Drama, 2011.

Kaislaniemi, Samuli. "*Jurebassos* and *Linguists*: The East India Company and Early Modern English Words for 'Interpreter.'" In *Selected Proceedings of the 2008 Symposium on New Approaches in English Historical Lexis (HEL-LEX 2)*, ed. R. W. McConchie, Alpo Honkapohja, and Jukka Tyrkkö. http://www.lingref.com/cpp/hel-lex/2008/paper2167.pdf.

Kalas, Rayna. *Frame, Glass, Verse: The Technology of Poetic Invention in the English Renaissance*. Ithaca, NY: Cornell University Press, 2007.

———. "The Language of Framing." *Shakespeare Studies* 28 (2000): 240–47.

Kathman, David. "How Old Were Shakespeare's Boy Actors?" *Shakespeare Survey* 58 (2005): 220–46.

Katz, Jonathan Ned. *Gay American History: Lesbians and Gay Men in the U.S.A.: A Documentary*. New York: Crowell, 1976.

Kincaid, James R. "Producing Erotic Children." In *Human, All Too Human: Essays from the English Institute*, ed. Diana Fuss, 203–19. New York: Routledge, 1995.

King, Stanley. *Recollections of the Folger Shakespeare Library*. Ithaca, NY: Cornell University Press for the Trustees of Amherst College, 1950.

Kirschbaum, Leo. "A Census of Bad Quartos." *Review of English Studies* 14 (1938): 20–43.

Knapp, James A. "The Bastard Art: Woodcut Illustration in Sixteenth-Century England." In *Printing and Parenting in Early Modern England*, ed. Douglas A. Brooks, 151–72. Aldershot, UK: Ashgate, 2005.

Knapp, Jeffrey. *Shakespeare Only*. Chicago: University of Chicago Press, 2009.

———. "What Is a Co-Author?" *Representations* 89, no. 1 (2005): 1–29.

Kott, Jan. *The Bottom Translation: Marlowe and Shakespeare and the Carnival Tradition*. Evanston: Northwestern University Press, 1987.

Kuhn, Maura Slattery. "Much Virtue in If." *SQ* 28 (1977): 40–50.

Kyd, Thomas. *The Spanish Tragedy*. Ed. Philip Edwards. The Revels Plays. Cambridge, MA: Harvard University Press, 1959.

[Kyd, Thomas]. *The Spanish Tragedie . . . Newly corrected and amended of such grosse faults as passed in the first impression*. London: by Edward Allde for Edward White, n.d. [1592?]

———. *The Spanish Tragedie: Or Hieronimo is mad againe*. London: by W. White, for I. White and T. Langley, 1615.

———. *The Spanish Tragedie: Or Hieronimo is mad againe Newly Corrected, Amended, and Enlarged with new Additions*. London: by Thomas Langley, 1623.

Lane, Christopher. "The Poverty of Context: Historicism and Nonmimetic Fiction." *PMLA* 118 (2003): 450–69.

Laqueur, Thomas W. *Making Sex: Body and Gender from the Greeks to Freud*. Cambridge, MA: Harvard University Press, 1990.

———. "Sex, Gender, and Desire in the Industrial Revolution." In *The Industrial Revolution and British Society: Festschrift for R. M. Hartwell*, ed. Patrick O'Brien and Roland Quinault, 100–123. Cambridge: Cambridge University Press, 1993.

———. "Sexuality and the Transformation of Culture: The Longue Durée." *Sexualities* 12, no. 4 (2009): 418–36.

Lehmann-Haupt, Hellmut. *Initials from French Incunabula*. New York: Aldus, 1948.

Leinwand, Theodore B. "Redeeming Beggary/Buggery in *Michaelmas Term*." *ELH* 61, no. 1 (1994): 53–70.

Lennam, Trevor N. S., ed. *The Marriage Between Wit and Wisdom*. Malone Society Reprints. Oxford: Oxford University Press for the Malone Society, 1966 [1971].

Lerer, Seth. *Error and the Academic Self: The Scholarly Imagination, Medieval to Modern*. New York: Columbia University Press, 2002.

Levin, Harry. *The Overreacher, a Study of Christopher Marlowe*. Cambridge, MA: Harvard University Press, 1952.

Levine, Nina. "Citizens' Games: Differentiating Collaboration and *Sir Thomas More*." *SQ* 58 (2007): 31–64.

Lewalski, Barbara Kiefer. "Introduction: Issues and Approaches." In *Renaissance Genres: Essays on Theory, History, and Interpretation,* ed. Barbara Kiefer Lewalski, 1–12. Harvard English Studies 14. Cambridge, MA: Harvard University Press, 1986.

———. *Paradise Lost and the Rhetoric of Literary Forms*. Princeton, NJ: Princeton University Press, 1985.

Lewis, Cynthia. " 'Wise Men, Folly-Fall'n': Characters Named Antonio in English Renaissance Drama." *RD*, n.s. XX (1989): 197–236.

Liddell, Henry George, and Robert Scott, et al., comps. *A Greek-English Lexicon*. 9th ed. Oxford: Clarendon, 1968.

———, comps. *A Greek-English Lexicon*. Perseus Digital Library. http://www.perseus.tufts.edu/hopper/text?doc=Perseus:text:1999.04.0057.

Lin, Shen. "How Old Were the Children of Paul's?" *Theatre Notebook* 45 (1991): 121–31.

Lipking, Lawrence. "The Marginal Gloss." *Critical Inquiry* 3 (1977): 609–55.

Little, Arthur. *Shakespeare Jungle Fever: National-Imperial Re-Visions of Race, Rape, and Sacrifice*. Stanford, CA: Stanford University Press, 2000.

[Lodge, Thomas]. T.L. *Rosalynde. Euphues golden legacie*. London: by Thomas Orwin for T.G. and John Busbie, 1590.

Loewenstein, Joseph. "Guarini and the Presence of Genre." In *Renaissance Tragicomedy: Explorations in Genre and Politics*, ed. Nancy Klein Maguire, 33–55. New York: AMS, 1987.

Loomba, Ania. *Shakespeare, Race, and Colonialism*. Oxford: Oxford University Press, 2002.

Loomba, Ania, and Jonathan Burton. "Introduction." In *Race in Early Modern England: A Documentary Companion*, ed. Ania Loomba and Jonathan Burton, 1–36. New York: Palgrave Macmillan, 2007.

Luborsky, Ruth Samson, and Elizabeth Morley Ingram. *A Guide to English Illustrated Books, 1536–1603*. 2 vols. Tempe, AZ: Medieval and Renaissance Texts and Studies, 1998.

Lyly, John. *Euphues*. In *The Complete Works of John Lyly*, vol. 1, ed. R. Warwick Bond, 177–326. Oxford: Clarendon, 1902.

———. *Midas*. London: by Thomas Scarlet for I.B., 1592.

Mackenzie, W. Roy. "Standing Water." *Modern Language Notes* 41, no. 5 (1926): 283–93.

MacLure, Millar. *Marlowe: The Critical Heritage, 1588–1896*. London: Routledge and Kegan Paul, 1979.

———, ed. *The Poems: Christopher Marlowe*. London: Methuen, 1968.

Magnusson, Lynne. *Shakespeare and Social Dialogue: Dramatic Language and Elizabethan Letters*. Cambridge: Cambridge University Press, 1999.

Maguire, Nancy Klein, ed. *Renaissance Tragicomedy: Explorations in Genre and Politics*. New York: AMS, 1987.

Malthus, T. R. *An Essay on the Principle of Population: Or, a View of its Past and Present Effects on Human Happiness . . . A New Edition, Very Much Enlarged*. London: for J. Johnson by T. Bensley, 1803.

Mann, Jenny C. *Outlaw Rhetoric: Figuring Vernacular Eloquence in Shakespeare's England*. Ithaca, NY: Cornell University Press, 2012.

———. "Marlowe's 'Slack Muse': *All Ovids Elegies* and an English Poetics of Softness." *Modern Philology* 113, no. 1 (2015): 49–65.

Marcus, Leah S. *The Politics of Mirth: Jonson, Herrick, Milton, Marvell, and the Defense of Old Holiday Pastimes*. Chicago: University of Chicago Press, 1986.

———. "The Two Texts of 'Othello' and Early Modern Constructions of Race." In *Textual Performances: The Modern Reproduction of Shakespeare's Drama*, ed. Lukas Erne and Margaret Jane Kidnie, 21–36. New York: Cambridge University Press, 2004.

———. *Unediting the Renaissance: Shakespeare, Marlowe, Milton*. New York: Routledge, 1996.

Marl., Ch. *The Tragicall History of D. Faustus*. London: by V.S. for Thomas Bushell, 1604.

———. *See also* Marloe, Christopher; Marloe, Christopher, and George Chapman; Marlow, Chri.; Marlowe, Christopher.

Marloe, Christopher. *Hero And Leander. By Christopher Marloe*. London: by Adam Islip for Edward Blunt, 1598.

Marloe, Christopher, and George Chapman. *Hero And Leander: Begun by Christopher Marloe; and finished by George Chapman*. London: by Felix Kingston for Paule Linley, 1598.

Marlow, Chri. *The troublesome raigne and lamentable death of Edward the second*. London: for William Iones, 1594.

———. *See also* Marl., Ch.; Marloe, Christopher; Marloe, Christopher, and George Chapman; Marlowe, Christopher.

Marlowe, Christopher. *Dido Queen of Carthage and The Massacre at Paris.* Ed. H. J. Oliver. The Revels Plays. Cambridge, MA: Harvard University Press, 1968.

———. *Edward the Second.* Ed. Charles R. Forker. The Revels Plays. Manchester: Manchester University Press, 1994.

———. *See also* Marl., Ch.; Marloe, Christopher; Marloe, Christopher, and George Chapman; Marlow, Chri.

Marotti, Arthur F. *Manuscript, Print, and the English Renaissance Lyric.* Ithaca, NY: Cornell University Press, 1995.

Marshall, Cynthia. *The Shattering of the Self: Violence, Subjectivity, and Early Modern Texts.* Baltimore, MD: Johns Hopkins University Press, 2002.

Marsilius of Padua. *Opvs Insigne Cvi Titvlvm Fecit Avtor Defensorem Pacis.* Basel, 1522.

Martin, Robert K. "Newton Arvin: Literary Critic and Lewd Person." *American Literary History* 16, no. 2 (2004): 290–317.

Maruca, Lisa. "Bodies of Type: The Work of Textual Production in English Printers' Manuals." *Eighteenth-Century Studies* 36, no. 3 (2003): 321–43.

———. *The Work of Print: Authorship and the English Text Trades, 1660–1760.* Seattle: University of Washington Press, 2007.

Massinger, Phil., Tho. Middleton, and William Rowley. *The Old Law: Or A new way to please you.* London: for Edward Archer, 1656.

Masten, Jeffrey. "Beaumont and/or Fletcher: Collaboration and the Interpretation of Renaissance Drama." *ELH* 59 (1992): 337–56.

———. "Ben Jonson's Head." *Shakespeare Studies* 28 (2000): 160–68.

———. "Editing Boys: The Performance of Gender in Print." In *From Performance to Print in Shakespeare's England*, ed. Peter Holland and Stephen Orgel, 113–34. Basingstoke, UK: Palgrave, 2006.

———. "Gee, Your Heir Smells Terrific: Response to 'Shakespeare's Perfume' [by Richard Halpern]." *Early Modern Culture: An Electronic Seminar*, no. 2 (2001). http://eserver.org/emc/1-2/masten.html.

———. "Is the Fundament a Grave?" In *The Body in Parts: Fantasies of Corporeality in Early Modern Europe*, ed. Carla Mazzio and David Hillman, 128–45. New York: Routledge, 1997.

———. "*More* or Less: Editing the Collaborative." *Shakespeare Studies* 29 (2001): 109–31.

———, ed. *An/The Old Law.* In *Thomas Middleton: The Collected Works*, gen. ed. Gary Taylor and John Lavagnino, 1331–96. Oxford: Oxford University Press, 2007.

———. "Playwrighting: Collaboration and Authorship." In *A New History of Early Modern Drama*, ed. John D. Cox and David Scott Kastan, 357–82. New York: Columbia University Press, 1997.

———. Review of *Close Readers: Humanism and Sodomy in Early Modern England*, by Alan Stewart. *Shakespeare Studies* 20 (2000): 361–65.

———. "Textual Deviance: Ganymede's Hand in *As You Like It.*" In *Field Work: Sites in Literary and Cultural Studies*, ed. Marjorie Garber, Paul B. Franklin, and Rebecca Walkowitz, 153–63. New York: Routledge, 1996.

———. *Textual Intercourse: Collaboration, Authorship, and Sexualities in Renaissance Drama.* Cambridge: Cambridge University Press, 1997.

Mayr, Ernst. "Difficulties and Importance of the Biological Species Concept." In Ernst Mayr, ed., *The Species Problem*, 371–88. New York: Arno, 1974.

———. *Populations, Species, and Evolution.* Cambridge, MA: Belknap, Harvard University Press, 1970.

———. "Species Concepts and Definitions." In Ernst Mayr, ed., *The Species Problem*, 1–22. New York: Arno, 1974.

Mazzio, Carla, and Doug Trevor, eds. *Historicism, Psychoanalysis, and Early Modern Culture.* New York: Routledge, 2000.

McIlwaine, H. R., ed. *Minutes of the Council and General Court of Colonial Virginia.* Richmond, VA: Colonial Press, 1924.

McKenzie, D. F. "Printers of the Mind: Some Notes on Bibliographical Theories and Printing-House Practices." *SB* 22 (1969): 1–75.

———, ed. *Stationers' Company Apprentices, 1605–1640.* Charlottesville: Bibliographical Society of the University of Virginia, 1961.

———, ed. *Stationers' Company Apprentices, 1641–1700.* Oxford: Oxford Bibliographical Society, 1974.

———. "Stretching a Point: Or, The Case of the Spaced-out Comps." *SB* 37 (1984): 106–21.

McKerrow, Ronald B. *An Introduction to Bibliography for Literary Students.* Oxford: Clarendon, 1927.

———. *Printers' and Publishers' Devices in England and Scotland 1485–1640.* London: Chiswick, 1913.

McKerrow, R. B., and F. S. Ferguson. *Title-page Borders Used in England and Scotland, 1485–1640.* London: Oxford University Press, for the Bibliographical Society, 1932 [for 1931].

McLeod, Randall. [Random Cloud]. "The Marriage of Good and Bad Quartos." *SQ* 33, no. 4 (1982): 421–31.

———. "Spell-bound." In *Play-Texts in Old Spelling: Papers from the Glendon Conference*, ed. G. B. Shand, with Raymond C. Shady, 81–96. New York: AMS, 1984.

McMillin, Scott. *The Elizabethan Theatre and "The Book of Sir Thomas More."* Ithaca, NY: Cornell University Press, 1987.

———, ed. *The First Quarto of Othello.* Cambridge Shakespeare. Cambridge: Cambridge University Press, 2001.

McMullan, Gordon. *The Politics of Unease in the Plays of John Fletcher.* Amherst: University of Massachusetts Press, 1994.

McMullan, Gordon, and Jonathan Hope. "Introduction: The Politics of Tragicomedy, 1610–50." In *The Politics of Tragicomedy: Shakespeare and After*, ed. Gordon McMullan and Jonathan Hope, 1–7. New York: Routledge, 1992.

———, eds. *The Politics of Tragicomedy: Shakespeare and After.* New York: Routledge, 1992.

McMurtie, Douglas C. *Initial Letters.* Pelham, NY: Bridgman, 1928.

Melchiori, Giorgio. "The Contextualization of Source Material: The Play Within the Play in 'Sir Thomas More.'" *Le Forme del Teatro* III, 59–94. Rome: Edizioni di Storia e Letteratura, 1984.

Menon, Madhavi. "Introduction: Queer Shakes." In *Shakesqueer: A Queer Companion to the Complete Works of Shakespeare*, ed. Madhavi Menon, 1–27. Durham, NC: Duke University Press, 2011.

———, ed. *Shakesqueer: A Queer Companion to the Complete Works of Shakespeare.* Durham, NC: Duke University Press, 2011.

———. *Unhistorical Shakespeare: Queer Theory in Shakespearean Literature and Film.* New York: Palgrave, 2008.

Meres, Francis. *Palladis Tamia.* London: by P. Short, for Cuthbert Burbie, 1598.

Merriam, Thomas V. N., and Robert A. J. Matthews. "Neural Computation in Stylometry II: An Application to the Works of Shakespeare and Marlowe." *Literary and Linguistic Computing* 9, no. 1 (1994): 1–6.

Middleton, Anne. "Medieval Studies." In *Redrawing the Boundaries: The Transformation of English and American Studies*, ed. Stephen Greenblatt and Giles Gunn. New York: MLA, 1992.

Middleton, Thomas. *Hengist*. Ed. Grace Ioppolo. In *Thomas Middleton: The Collected Works*, gen. ed. Gary Taylor and John Lavagnino, 1448–87. Oxford: Oxford University Press, 2007.

———. *Hengist, King of Kent; or The Mayor of Queenborough*. Ed. R. C. Bald. New York: Charles Scribner's Sons for the Trustees of Amherst College, 1938.

Miller, D. A. *Bringing Out Roland Barthes*. Berkeley: University of California Press, 1992.

Miller, David Lee. "The Death of the Modern: Gender and Desire in Marlowe's 'Hero and Leander.'" *South Atlantic Quarterly* 88, no. 4 (1989): 757–87.

Milton, John. *Areopagitica; A Speech of M^r. John Milton For the Liberty of Vnlicenc'd Printing, To the Parlament of England*. London, 1644.

———. "L'Allegro." In *Poems of Mr. John Milton, Both English and Latin*. London: by Ruth Raworth for Humphrey Moseley, 1645.

Minsheu, Iohn. *The Guide into the Tongues . . . The second Edition*. London: by Iohn Haviland, 1625.

———. [*Hegemon eis tas glossas*] *Ductor in Linguas, The Guide into the tongues*. London: for Iohn Browne, 1617.

Mintz, Sidney W. *Sweetness and Power: The Place of Sugar in Modern History*. New York: Viking, 1985.

Montaigne, Michel de. *Essayes*. Trans. John Florio. London: Melch. Bradvvood for Edvvard Blovnt and William Barret, 1613.

———. *The Essayes Or Morall, Politike and Millitarie Discourses*. Trans. John Florio. London: by Val. Sims for Edward Blount, 1603.

Morley, Thomas. *A Plaine And Easie Introdvction To Practicall Mvsicke*. London: by Peter Short, 1597.

Motteux, Peter Anthony, trans. *The Fifth Book of the Works Of Francis Rabelais, M.D.* London: for Richard Baldwin, 1694.

Mowat, Barbara A. "Shakespearian Tragicomedy." In *Renaissance Tragicomedy: Explorations in Genre and Politics*, ed. Nancy Klein Maguire, 80–96. New York: AMS, 1987.

———. "Theatre and Literary Culture." In *A New History of Early English Drama*, ed. John D. Cox and David Scott Kastan, 213–30. New York: Columbia University Press, 1997.

Mowat, Barbara A., and Paul Werstine, eds. *Othello*. Folger Shakespeare Library series. New York: Washington Square Press and Folger Shakespeare Library, 1999, 2004.

Moxon, Joseph. *Mechanick Exercises: Or, the Doctrine of handy-works. Applied to the Art of Printing*, The Second Volumne [of the *Exercises*]. London: for Joseph Moxon, 1683.

Mukerji, Subha, and Raphael Lyne, eds. *Early Modern Tragicomedy*. Cambridge, UK: D. S. Brewer, 2007.

Mulcaster, Richard. *See* Mvlcaster, Richard.

Munday, Anthony, and others. Revised by Henry Chettle, Thomas Dekker, Thomas Heywood, and William Shakespeare. *Sir Thomas More*. Ed. Vittorio Gabrieli and Giorgio Melchiori. The Revels Plays. Manchester: Manchester University Press, 1990.

Musaeus. *Hero and Leander*. Ed. Thomas Gelzer, with an English trans. by Cedric Whitman. Loeb Classics 421. Cambridge, MA: Harvard University Press, 1975.

Mvlcaster, Richard. *The First Part of the Elementarie VVhich Entreateth Chefelie of the right writing of our English tung*. London: by Thomas Vautroullier, 1582.

Nagy, Gregory. "Death of a Schoolboy: The Early Greek Beginnings of a Crisis in Philology." In *On Philology*, ed. Jan Ziolkowski, 37–47. University Park: Pennsylvania State University Press, 1990.

Nardizzi, Vin, Stephen Guy-Bray, and Will Stockton, eds. *Queer Renaissance Historiography: Backward Gaze*. Farnham, UK: Ashgate, 2009.

Neill, Michael, ed. *Othello, the Moor of Venice*. By William Shakespeare. Oxford World Classics. Oxford: Oxford University Press, 2006.

——. "'Unproper Beds': Race, Adultery and the Hideous in *Othello*." *SQ* 40 (1989): 383–412.

Newman, Karen. "Two Lines, Three Readers: *Hamlet* TLN 1904–5." *SQ* 62 (2011): 263–70.

——. "'And Wash the Ethiop White': Femininity and the Monstrous in *Othello*." In *Shakespeare Reproduced: The Text in History and Ideology*, ed. Jean E. Howard and Marion F. O'Connor, 141–62. New York: Methuen, 1987.

Newton, Thomas, trans. *Fovvre Severall Treatises of M. Tvllivs Cicero: Conteyninge his most learned and Eloquente Discourses of Frendshippe: Oldage: Paradoxes: and Scipio his Dreame*. London: by Tho. Marshe, 1577.

Nicholl, Charles. *The Reckoning: The Murder of Christopher Marlowe*. London: J. Cape, 1992.

Nichols, Stephen G. "Introduction: Philology in a Manuscript Culture." *The New Philology*. Spec. issue of *Speculum* 65 (1990): 1–10.

Nietzsche, Friedrich. *Daybreak: Thoughts on the Prejudices of Morality*. Trans. R. J. Hollingdale. Ed. Maudemarie Clark and Brian Leiter. Cambridge: Cambridge University Press, 1997.

Nirenberg, David. "Pre-Modern Race: Philology, Socio-Theology, History." Unpublished paper, Shakespeare Association of America, Toronto, March 28, 2013.

——. "Was There Race Before Modernity? The Example of 'Jewish' Blood in Late Medieval Spain." In *The Origins of Racism in the West*, ed. Miriam Eliav-Feldon, Benjamin Isaac, and Joseph Ziegler, 232–64. Cambridge: Cambridge University Press, 2009.

Normand, Lawrence. "'What Passions Call You These?': *Edward II* and James VI." In *Christopher Marlowe and English Renaissance Culture*, ed. Darryll Grantley and Peter Roberts, 172–97. Aldershot, UK: Scolar Press, 1996.

Northbrooke, Iohn. *The poore mans Garden*. London: by VV. VVilliamson, 1573.

Ogilvie, Brian W. *The Science of Describing: Natural History in Renaissance Europe*. Chicago: University of Chicago Press, 2006.

Ong, Walter J. "Latin Language Study as a Renaissance Puberty Rite." *Studies in Philology* 56 (1959): 103–24.

Orgel, Stephen. "Gendering the Crown." In *Subject and Object in Renaissance Culture*, ed. Margreta de Grazia, Maureen Quilligan, and Peter Stallybrass, 133–65. Cambridge: Cambridge University Press, 1996.

——. *Impersonations: The Performance of Gender in Shakespeare's England*. Cambridge: Cambridge University Press, 1996.

——. "Nobody's Perfect: Or, Why Did the English Stage Take Boys for Women?" In *Displacing Homophobia*, ed. Ronald R. Butters, John M. Clum, and Michael Moon, 7–30. Durham, NC: Duke University Press, 1989.

——. "Tobacco and Boys: How Queer Was Marlowe?" *GLQ: A Journal of Lesbian and Gay Studies* 6, no. 4 (2000): 555–76.

——. "What's the Globe Good For?" *SQ* 49, no. 2 (1998): 191–94.

Osborne, Laurie E. "The Texts of *Twelfth Night*." *ELH* 57, no. 1 (1990): 37–61.

Ovid. *The Fyrst Fovver Bookes Of P. Ouidius Nasos worke, intitled Metamorphosis, translated oute of Latin into Englishe meter by Arthur Golding Gent*. London: by Willyam Seres, 1565.

——. *Ovid's Metamorphoses*. Trans. Arthur Golding. Ed. and intro. Madeleine Forey. Baltimore, MD: Johns Hopkins University Press, 2002.

——. *The.xv.Bookes of P. Ouidius Naso, entytuled Metamorphosis, translated oute of Latin into English meeter, by Arthur Golding, Gentleman*. London: by Willyam Seres, 1567.

Owen, Stephen. "Philology's Discontents: Response." In *On Philology*, ed. Jan Ziolkowski, 75–78. University Park: Pennsylvania State University Press, 1990.

Oxford English Dictionary. 2nd ed. CD-ROM. Oxford University Press, 1994.

Oxford English Dictionary. 2nd ed. Oxford University Press, 1989.

Oxford English Dictionary Online. Oxford University Press. 2015. http://www.oed.com.

Oxford Latin Dictionary. Ed. P. G. W. Glare. Oxford: Clarendon, 1982.

Palmer, John. *An examination of Thelyphthora, on the subject of marriage.* Birmingham, 1781.

The Parallel Bible: The Holy Bible . . . Being the Authorised Version Arranged in Parallel Columns with the Revised Version. Oxford: for the Universities of Oxford and Cambridge at Oxford University Press, 1885.

Paré, Ambroise. *Des Monstres et Prodiges: Édition Critique et Commentée.* Ed. Jean Céard. Geneva: Librairie Droz, 1971.

———. *On Monsters and Marvels.* Trans. with an intro. and notes by Janis L. Pallister. Chicago: University of Chicago Press, 1995.

Park, Katharine. "The Empire of Anatomy." In *Secrets of Women: Gender, Generation, and the Origins of Human Dissection,* 207–59. New York: Zone, 2006.

Park, Katharine, and Robert A. Nye. "Destiny Is Anatomy." Review of Thomas Laqueur, *Making Sex. New Republic,* February 18, 1991, 53–57.

Parker, Patricia. "Barbers and Barbary: Early Modern Cultural Semantics." *RD* 33 (2004): 201–44.

———. "Cutting Both Ways: Bloodletting, Castration/Circumcision, and the 'Lancelet' of *The Merchant of Venice.*" In *Alternative Shakespeares,* vol. 3, ed. Diana E. Henderson, 95–118. London: Routledge, 2008.

———. "Fantasies of 'Race' and 'Gender': Africa, *Othello,* and Bringing to Light." In *Women, "Race," and Writing in the Early Modern Period,* ed. Margo Hendricks and Patricia Parker, 84–100. London: Routledge, 1994.

———. "Gender Ideology, Gender Change: The Case of Marie Germain." *Critical Inquiry* 19, no. 2 (1993): 337–64.

———. *Literary Fat Ladies: Rhetoric, Gender, Property.* London: Methuen, 1987.

———. "Preposterous Reversals: *Love's Labor's Lost.*" *Modern Language Quarterly* 54, no. 5 (1993): 435–82.

———. *Shakespeare from the Margins: Language, Culture, Context.* Chicago: University of Chicago Press, 1996.

———. "Virile Style." In *Premodern Sexualities,* ed. Louise Fradenburg and Carla Freccero, 201–22. New York: Routledge, 1996.

Parnell, J. T. "Introduction." In *Constructing Christopher Marlowe,* ed. J. A. Downie and J. T. Parnell, 1–12. Cambridge: Cambridge University Press, 2000.

Paster, Gail Kern. *The Body Embarrassed: Drama and the Disciplines of Shame in Early Modern England.* Ithaca, NY: Cornell University Press, 1993.

———. "The Epistemology of the Water Closet: John Harington's *Metamorphosis of Ajax* and Elizabethan Technologies of Shame." In *Material Culture and Cultural Materialisms in the Middle Ages and Renaissance,* ed. Curtis Perry, 139–58. Turnhout, Belgium: Brepols, 2001.

Paster, Gail Kern, Katherine Rowe, and Mary Floyd-Wilson, eds. *Reading the Early Modern Passions: Essays in the Cultural History of Emotion.* Philadelphia: University of Pennsylvania Press, 2004.

Pepys, Samuel. *The Diary of Samuel Pepys.* Ed. Robert Latham and William Matthews. 11 vols. Berkeley: University of California Press, 1970–83.

Perry, Curtis. "The Politics of Access and Representations of the Sodomite King in Early Modern England." *Renaissance Quarterly* 53, no. 4 (2000): 1054–83.

Petowe, Henry. *The Second Part of Hero and Leander. Conteyning their further Fortunes.* London: by Thomas Purfoot, for Andrew Harris, 1598.

Pettus, Jo. "Upon the Works of Beaumont, and Fletcher." In *Comedies and Tragedies*, by Francis Beaumont and John Fletcher, sig. a4. London: for Humphrey Robinson and Humphrey Moseley, 1647.

Phillips, Susan E. "Schoolmasters, Seduction, and Slavery: Polyglot Dictionaries in Pre-Modern England." *Medievalia et Humanistica* 34 (2008): 129–58.

Pittenger, Elizabeth. "Dispatch Quickly: The Mechanical Reproduction of Pages." *SQ* 42, no. 4 (1991): 389–408.

———. "'To Serve the Queere': Nicholas Udall, Master of Revels." In *Queering the Renaissance*, ed. Jonathan Goldberg, 162–89. Durham, NC: Duke University Press, 1994.

Plomer, Henry R. *English Printers' Ornaments*. London: Grafton and Co., 1924.

Plutarch. "The Life of Alexander the Great." In *The Lives of the Noble Grecians and Romanes*. Trans. Thomas North. London: Thomas Vautrollier, 1579.

Pollard, Alfred W. "Elizabethan Spelling as a Literary and Bibliographical Clue." *The Library*, 4th ser., no. 1 (1923): 1–8.

———, ed. *The Holy Bible: A Facsimile in a reduced size of the Authorized Version published in the year 1611*. Oxford: Oxford University Press, 1911.

———, ed. *Shakespeare's Hand in the Play of Sir Thomas More . . . with the text of the Ill May Day Scenes edited by W. W. Greg*. Cambridge: Cambridge University Press, 1923.

———. "Some Pictorial and Heraldic Initials." In *Bibliographia: Papers on Books and Their History and Art*, vol. 3, parts IX–XII, 232–52. London: Kegan, Paul, Trench, Trübner & Company Ltd., 1897.

Pollock, Frederick, and Frederic William Maitland. *The History of English Law Before the Time of Edward I*. 2 vols. Cambridge: Cambridge University Press; Boston: Little, Brown, 1895.

Pope, Alexander, and George Sewell, eds. *The works of Mr. William Shakespear. In ten volumes. Publish'd by Mr. Pope and Dr. Sewell*. 10 vols. London: for J. and J. Knapton, J. Darby, A. Bettesworth, J. Tonson et al., 1728.

Porter, James I. *Nietzsche and the Philology of the Future*. Stanford, CA: Stanford University Press, 2000.

Potter, Lois. *Secret Rites and Secret Writing: Royalist Literature, 1641–1660*. Cambridge: Cambridge University Press, 1989.

———. "Topicality or Politics? *The Two Noble Kinsmen*, 1613–34." In *The Politics of Tragicomedy: Shakespeare and After*, ed. Gordon McMullan and Jonathan Hope, 77–91. New York: Routledge, 1992.

Power, D'Arcy, ed. *Treatises of Fistula in Ano, Haemorrhoids, and Clysters by John Arderne, from an Early Fifteenth-Century Manuscript Translation*. London: Oxford University Press for the Early English Text Society, 1910.

Purchas, Samuel. *See* Pvrchas, Samvel.

[Puttenham, George]. *The Arte Of English Poesie*. London: by Richard Field, 1589.

Pvrchas, Samvel. *Pvrchas his Pilgrim, Microcosmvs, Or The Historie of Man*. London: W. S. for Henry Fetherstone, 1619.

Rabelais, Francis. *The Urquhart-Le Motteux Translation of the Works of Francis Rabelais*. Ed. with intro., Albert Jay Nock and Catherine Rose Wilson. 2 vols. New York: Harcourt, Brace, 1931.

Radel, Nicholas F. "Fletcherian Tragicomedy, Cross-dressing, and the Constriction of Homoerotic Desire in Early Modern England." *RD* n.s. XXVI (1995): 53–82.

Rainoldi, Joannis. *Orationes Duodecim*. London: William Stansby for Henry Fetherstone, 1619.

Rambuss, Richard. *Closet Devotions*. Durham, NC: Duke University Press, 1998.

———. "Pleasure and Devotion." In *Queering the Renaissance*, ed. Jonathan Goldberg, 271–74. Durham, NC: Duke University Press, 1994.

———. "Shakespeare's Ass Play." In *Shakesqueer: A Queer Companion to the Complete Works of Shakespeare*, ed. Madhavi Menon, 234–44. Durham, NC: Duke University Press, 2011.

———. "What It Feels Like for a Boy: Shakespeare's *Venus and Adonis*." In *A Companion to Shakespeare's Works: Vol. IV, The Poems, Problem Comedies, and Late Plays*, ed. Richard Dutton and Jean E. Howard, 240–59. Malden, UK: Blackwell, 2003.

Read, Alexander. *The Manvall of the Anatomy or dissection of the body of Man, Which usually are shewed in the publike Anatomicall exercises.* 1638.

The rewarde of Wickednesse. London: by William Williamson, [1573–74?].

Riggs, David. *The World of Christopher Marlowe.* New York: Henry Holt, 2004.

Riva, Alessandro, et al. "Iulius Casserius (1552–1616): The Self-Made Anatomist of Padua's Golden Age." *Anatomical Review* 265 (2001): 168–75.

Roberts, Jeanne Addison. "Crises of Male Self-Definition in *The Two Noble Kinsmen*." In *Shakespeare, Fletcher, and "The Two Noble Kinsmen*," ed. Charles H. Frey, 133–44. Columbia: University of Missouri Press, 1989.

Robins, Nicholas. "The Script's the Thing." *Times Literary Supplement*, November 7, 2003.

Rocke, Michael. *Forbidden Friendships: Homosexuality and Male Culture in Renaissance Florence.* New York: Oxford University Press, 1996.

Roland, Ruth A. *Interpreters as Diplomats: A Diplomatic History of the Role of Interpreters.* Ottawa: University of Ottawa Press, 1999.

Rosenheim, Shawn James. *The Cryptographic Imagination: Secret Writing from Edgar Poe to the Internet.* Baltimore, MD: Johns Hopkins University Press, 1997.

Rouby, Catherine, ed. *Olfaction, Taste, and Cognition.* Cambridge: Cambridge University Press, 2002.

Rymer, Thomas. *A Short View of Tragedy; It's Original, Excellency, and Corruption. With Some Reflections on Shakespear, and other Practitioners for the Stage.* London: by Richard Baldwin, 1693.

Sable, Francis. *The Fissher-mans Tale: Of the famous Actes, Life and loue of Cassander a Grecian Knight.* London: by Richard Iohnes, 1595.

Said, Edward W. *Humanism and Democratic Criticism.* New York: Columbia University Press, 2004.

Satchell, Thomas. "The Spelling of the First Folio." Letter, *Times Literary Supplement*, June 3, 1920.

Saunders, Ben. "Iago's Clyster: Purgation, Anality, and the Civilizing Process." *SQ* 55, no. 2 (2004): 148–76.

Saussure, Ferdinand de. *Course in General Linguistics.* Ed. Charles Bally and Albert Sechehaye in collab. with Albert Riedlinger. Trans. Wade Baskin. New York: Philosophical Library, McGraw-Hill, 1966.

Savran, David. *Communists, Cowboys, and Queers: The Politics of Masculinity in the Work of Arthur Miller and Tennessee Williams.* Minneapolis: University of Minnesota Press, 1992.

Sayle, Charles. "Initial Letters in Early English Printed Books." *The Library* 7, no. 1 (1902): 15–47.

Schachter, Marc D. *Voluntary Servitude and the Erotics of Friendship: From Classical Antiquity to Early Modern France.* Aldershot, UK: Ashgate, 2008.

Schmidt, Suzanne Karr, with Kimberly Nichols. "Printed Scientific Objects." In *Altered and Adorned: Using Renaissance Prints in Daily Life*, 73–91. New Haven and London: Yale University Press/Art Institute of Chicago, 2011.

Schoenfeldt, Michael C. *Bodies and Selves in Early Modern England: Physiology and Inwardness in Spenser, Shakespeare, Herbert, and Milton.* Cambridge: Cambridge University Press, 1999.

Schwarz, Kathryn. *Tough Love: Amazon Encounters in the English Renaissance.* Durham, NC: Duke University Press, 2000.

Scott-Warren, Jason. "As It Is Writ." Review of *Shakespeare's Book*, ed. Richard Meek, Jane Rickard and Richard Wilson. *Times Literary Supplement*, August 14, 2009.

Scouloudi, Irene. *Returns of Strangers in the Metropolis 1593, 1627, 1635, 1639*. Quarto Series of the Huguenot Society of London, vol. 57. London: Huguenot Society, 1985.

Schlegel, Friedrich. "Concerning Philology I." In *Theory As Practice: A Critical Anthology of Early German Romantic Writings*, trans. and ed. Jochen Schulte-Sasse et al., 344–49. Minneapolis: University of Minnesota Press, 1997.

———. "Zur Philologie I." In *Kritische Friedrich-Schlegel-Ausgabe*, ed. Ernst Behler et al., vol. 16, ed. Hans Eichner, 33–56. Munich: Ferdinand Schöningh, 1981.

Scragg, D. G. *A History of English Spelling*. New York: Barnes and Noble, 1974.

Seaver, Paul S. *Wallington's World: A Puritan Artisan in Seventeenth-Century London*. Stanford, CA: Stanford University Press, 1985.

Sedgwick, Eve Kosofsky. *Epistemology of the Closet*. Berkeley: University of California Press, 1990.

———. *Touching Feeling: Affect, Pedagogy, Performativity*. Durham, NC: Duke University Press, 2003.

Segar, William. *Honor Military, and Civill*. London: Robert Barker, 1602.

Shakespeare, William. *As You Like It*. Ed. Frances E. Dolan. Signet Classic Shakespeare. New York: Penguin, 2000.

———. *As You Like It*. Ed. Richard Knowles. A New Variorum Edition of Shakespeare. New York: MLA, 1977.

———. *As You Like It*. Ed. Leah S. Marcus. Norton Critical Editions. New York: W. W. Norton, 2011.

———. *As You Like It*. In *The Norton Shakespeare Based on the Oxford Edition*, 2nd ed., ed. Stephen Greenblatt et al., 1615–81. New York: W. W. Norton, 2008.

———. *The Complete Works*. Gen. ed. Stanley Wells and Gary Taylor. Oxford: Clarendon, 1986.

———. *The Complete Works*. Gen. ed. Stanley Wells and Gary Taylor. Original-spelling ed. Oxford: Clarendon, 1986.

———. *Hamlet*. Ed. Harold Jenkins. The Arden Shakespeare, 2nd ser. London: Methuen, 1982.

———. *Hamlet*. Ed. Ann Thompson and Neil Taylor. The Arden Shakespeare, 3rd ser. London: Thompson Learning, 2006.

———. *The Merchant of Venice*. In *The Norton Shakespeare Based on the Oxford Edition*, 2nd ed., ed. Stephen Greenblatt et al., 1111–75. New York: W. W. Norton, 2008.

———. *A Midsommer nights dreame*. London: for Thomas Fisher, 1600.

———. *The most excellent Historie of the Merchant of Venice*. London: by I.R. for Thomas Heyes, 1600.

———. *Mr. VVilliam Shakespeares Comedies, Histories, & Tragedies*. London: by Isaac Iaggard, and Ed. Blount, 1623.

———. *Mr. VVilliam Shakespeares Comedies, Histories, & Tragedies*. London: by Isaac Iaggard, and Ed. Blount, 1623. Reprod. in *The Norton Facsimile: The First Folio of Shakespeare*. Prepared by Charlton Hinman. New York: W. W. Norton, 1968.

———. *Othello, the Moor of Venice*. Ed. Michael Neill. Oxford World Classics. Oxford: Oxford University Press, 2006.

———. *Pericles*. Ed. Suzanne Gossett. The Arden Shakespeare, 3rd ser. London: Thomson Learning, 2004.

———. *Shake-speares Sonnets*. London: By G. Eld for T.T. and are to be sold by William Aspley, 1609. Reprod. in *Shakespeare's Sonnets*. Ed. Stephen Booth. New Haven, CT: Yale University Press, 1977.

———. *The Tragœdy of Othello, The Moore of Venice*. London: by N.O. for Thomas Walkley, 1622.

———. *The Tragicall Historie of Hamlet, Prince of Denmarke*. London: by I.R. for N.L., 1604.

———. *Twelfth Night*. Ed. J. M. Lothian and T. W. Craik. The Arden Shakespeare, 2nd ser. London: Methuen, 1975.

———. *Twelfth Night*. Ed. Roger Warren and Stanley Wells. Oxford World Classics. Oxford: Oxford University Press, 1994.

———. *Twelfth Night*. In *The Norton Shakespeare Based on the Oxford Edition*, 2nd ed., ed. Stephen Greenblatt et al., 1785–1846. New York: W. W. Norton, 2008.

———. *Twelfth Night*. In *The Riverside Shakespeare*, ed. G. Blakemore Evans et al., 403–41. Boston: Houghton Mifflin, 1974.

———. *The Two Gentlemen of Verona*. Ed. William C. Carroll. The Arden Shakespeare, 3rd ser. London: Thomson Learning, 2004.

———. *The Two Gentlemen of Verona*. Ed. Clifford Leech. The Arden Shakespeare, 2nd ser. London: Methuen, 1969.

———. *See also* Fletcher, John, and William Shakspeare.

[Shakespeare, William]. *The Cronicle History of Henry the fift*. London: by Thomas Creede, for Tho. Millington, and Iohn Busby, 1600.

Shakespeare in Love. Dir. John Madden. Miramax, 1998.

Shannon, Laurie. *The Accommodated Animal: Cosmopolity in Shakespearean Locales*. Chicago: University of Chicago Press, 2013.

———. "Nature's Bias." *Modern Philology* 98, no. 2 (2000): 183–210.

———. "Poor, Bare, Forked: Animal Sovereignty, Human Negative Exceptionalism, and the Natural History of *King Lear*." *SQ* 60, no. 2 (2009): 168–96.

———. *Sovereign Amity: Figures of Friendship in Shakespearean Contexts*. Chicago: University of Chicago Press, 2002.

Shapiro, James. *Shakespeare and the Jews*. New York: Columbia University Press, 1997.

Sharp, Jane. *The midwives book, or, The whole art of midwifry discovered*. London: for Simon Miller, 1671.

Shawcross, John T. "Tragicomedy as Genre, Past and Present." In *Renaissance Tragicomedy: Explorations in Genre and Politics*, ed. Nancy Klein Maguire, 13–32. New York: AMS, 1987.

Sheidlower, Jesse. *The F-word*. 3rd ed. New York: Oxford University Press, 2009.

Sherry, Richard. *A treatise of Schemes & Tropes*. London: by Iohn Day, [1550].

Shirley, Christopher D. "Sodomy and Stage Directions in Christopher Marlowe's *Edward(s) II*." *SEL: Studies in English Literature 1500–1900* 54, no. 2 (Spring 2014): 279–96.

Sibly, E. *Magazine of natural history. Comprehending the whole science of animals, plants, and minerals*, vol. 12, no. 149. London: sold by Champante & Whitrow, and at the British Directory-Office, [1794–1808]. *Eighteenth Century Collections Online*.

Sidney, Philip. *An Apologie for Poetrie*. London: for Henry Olney, 1595.

———. *The Countess of Pembroke's Arcadia (The Old Arcadia)*. Ed. Katherine Duncan-Jones. Oxford: Oxford University Press, 1985.

———. *The Defence Of Poesie*. London: for William Ponsonby, 1595.

———. *Miscellaneous Prose of Sir Philip Sidney*. Ed. Katherine Duncan-Jones and Jan van Dorsten. Oxford: Clarendon, 1973.

Siemon, James R. "Sporting Kyd." *English Literary Renaissance* 24 (1994): 553–82.

Sisson, C.J., ed. *William Shakespeare: The Complete Works*. New York: Harper, 1954.

Skura, Meredith. *Tudor Autobiography: Listening for Inwardness*. Chicago: University of Chicago Press, 2008.

———. "Understanding the Living and Talking to the Dead: The Historicity of Psychoanalysis." *Modern Language Quarterly* 54 (1993): 77–89.

Smith, Adam. *An Inquiry into the Nature and Causes of the Wealth of Nations.* Ed. Edward Cannan. Chicago: University of Chicago Press, 1976.

Smith, Bruce R. *The Acoustic World of Early Modern England: Attending to the O-factor.* Chicago: University of Chicago Press, 1999.

——. *Homosexual Desire in Shakespeare's England: A Cultural Poetics.* Chicago: University of Chicago Press, 1991.

Smith, Ian. "Barbarian Errors: Performing Race in Early Modern England." *SQ* 49 (1998): 168–86.

Smith, Thomas. *De recta & emendata Lingvæ Anglicæ Scriptione, Dialogus.* . . . Paris: Robert Stevens, 1568. Reprod. with English trans. in *Sir Thomas Smith: Literary and Linguistic Works,* Part 3, ed. Bror Danielsson. Stockholm: Almqvist & Wiksell, 1983.

Spenser, Edmund. *The Faerie Queene.* Ed. A. C. Hamilton. London: Longman, 1980.

——. *The Faerie Qveene.* London: for VVilliam Ponsonbie, 1596.

Spiegel, Adriaan van den. *De humani corporis fabrica libri decem.* Venice: Evangelista Deuchino, 1627.

Stallybrass, Peter. "Patriarchal Territories: The Body Enclosed." In *Rewriting the Renaissance: The Discourse of Sexual Difference in Early Modern Europe,* ed. Margaret W. Ferguson, Maureen Quilligan, and Nancy J. Vickers, 123–42. Chicago: University of Chicago Press, 1986.

——. "Shakespeare, the Individual, and the Text." In *Cultural Studies,* ed. Lawrence Grossberg, Cary Nelson, and Paula Treichler, with Linda Baughman, and with assistance from John Macgregor Wise, 593–610. New York: Routledge, 1992.

——. "Transvestism and the 'Body Beneath': Speculating on the Boy Actor." In *Erotic Politics: Desire on the Renaissance Stage,* ed. Susan Zimmerman, 64–83. New York: Routledge, 1992.

——. "Visible and Invisible Letters: Text Versus Image in Renaissance England and Europe." In *Visible Writings: Cultures, Forms, Readings,* ed. Marija Dalbello and Mary Shaw, 77–98. New Brunswick, NJ: Rutgers University Press, 2011.

——. "Worn Worlds: Clothes and Identity on the Renaissance Stage." In *Subject and Object in Renaissance Culture,* ed. Margreta de Grazia, Maureen Quilligan, and Peter Stallybrass, 289–320. Cambridge: Cambridge University Press, 1996.

Stallybrass, Peter, and Allon White. *The Politics and Poetics of Transgression.* Ithaca, NY: Cornell University Press, 1986.

Stern, Tiffany. "Letters, Verses and Double Speech-Prefixes in *The Merchant of Venice.*" *Notes and Queries* 46, no. 2 (1999): 231–33.

Stevens, Charles, and Iohn Liebavlt. *Maison Rustique, Or The Covntrey Farme.* Trans. Richard Svrflet, with Gervase Markham. London: Adam Islip for John Bill, 1616.

Stevens, Peter F. "Species: Historical Perspectives." In *Keywords in Evolutionary Biology,* ed. Evelyn Fox Keller and Elisabeth A. Lloyd, 301–11. Cambridge, MA: Harvard University Press, 1992.

Stevens, Wallace. "Thirteen Ways of Looking at a Blackbird." In *The Collected Poems of Wallace Stevens,* 92–95. New York: Vintage, 1990.

Stewart, Alan. "Boys' Buttocks Revisited: James VI and the Myth of the Sovereign Schoolmaster." In *Sodomy in Early Modern Europe,* ed. Tom Betteridge, 131–47. Manchester: Manchester University Press, 2002.

——. *Close Readers: Humanism and Sodomy in Early Modern England.* Princeton, NJ: Princeton University Press, 1997.

——. *The Cradle King: The Life of James VI and I, the First Monarch of a United Great Britain.* New York: St. Martin's, 2003.

———. *Shakespeare's Letters.* Oxford: Oxford University Press, 2008.

Stockton, Will. *Playing Dirty: Sexuality and Waste in Early Modern Comedy.* Minneapolis: University of Minnesota Press, 2011.

———. "Shakespeare and Queer Theory." Review of *Shakesqueer: A Queer Companion to the Complete Works of Shakespeare,* ed. Madhavi Menon. *SQ* 63 no. 2 (2012): 224–35.

Stockton, Will, and James M. Bromley, "Introduction: Figuring Early Modern Sex." In *Sex Before Sex: Figuring the Act in Early Modern England,* ed. James M. Bromley and Will Stockton, 1–23. Minneapolis: University of Minnesota Press, 2013.

Stroup, Thomas B. "Bottom's Name and His Epiphany." *SQ* 29 (1979): 79–82.

Tanselle, G. Thomas. "The Life and Work of Fredson Bowers." *SB* 46 (1993): 1–155.

———. "The Varieties of Textual Editing." In *Scholarly Editing: A Guide to Research,* ed. D. C. Greetham, 11–32. New York: Modern Language Association, 1995.

Taylor, Gary. "*An/The Old Law.*" In "Works Included in This Edition: Canon and Chronology." In *Thomas Middleton and Early Modern Textual Culture: A Companion to the Collected Works,* gen. ed. Gary Taylor and John Lavagnino, 405–8. Oxford: Oxford University Press, 2007.

———. "Making Meaning Marketing Shakespeare 1623." In *From Performance to Print in Shakespeare's England,* ed. Peter Holland and Stephen Orgel, 55–72. Basingstoke, UK: Palgrave, 2006.

———. "The Renaissance and the End of Editing." In *Palimpsest: Editorial Theory in the Humanities,* ed. George Bornstein and Ralph G. Williams, 121–50. Ann Arbor: University of Michigan Press, 1993.

———. "The Shrinking Compositor A of the Shakespeare First Folio." *SB* 34 (1981): 96–117.

———. "Textual and Sexual Criticism: A Crux in *The Comedy of Errors.*" *RD* 19 (1988): 195–225.

Taylor, Gary, and John Lavagnino, gen. eds. *Thomas Middleton: The Collected Works.* Oxford: Oxford University Press, 2007.

———, gen. eds. *Thomas Middleton and Early Modern Textual Culture: A Companion to the Collected Works.* Oxford: Oxford University Press, 2007.

Taylor, Gary, assisted by Celia R. Daileader and Alexandra G. Bennett. "The Order of Persons." In *Thomas Middleton and Early Modern Textual Culture: A Companion to the Collected Works,* gen. ed. Gary Taylor and John Lavagnino, 31–79.

Thomas, Lewis. "On Smell." *New England Journal of Medicine* 302 (March 27, 1980): 731–33.

Thomas More. Dir. Robert Delamere. Swan Theatre, Stratford-upon-Avon, Royal Shakespeare Company, "Gunpowder Season." Performance of August 1, 2005.

Tilley, Morris Palmer. *A Dictionary of the Proverbs in England in the Sixteenth and Seventeenth Centuries.* Ann Arbor: University of Michigan Press, 1966.

Topsell, Edward. *The History of Four-footed Beasts and Serpents.* London: by E. Cotes for G. Sawbridge, T. Williams, and T. Johnson, 1658.

Tory, Geofroy. *Champ Flevry. Au quel est contenu Lart & Science de la deue & vraye Proportiō des Lettres Attiques, quō dit autremēt Lettres Antiques, & vulgairement Lettres Romaines proportionnees selon le Corps & Visage humain.* Paris: par Maistre Geofroy Tory [et] Giles Gourmont, [1529]. Facsimile in *Champ Fleury,* intro. and ed. Gustave Cohen, [1931]. Geneva: Slatkine Reprints, 1973.

Trask, R. L. *Historical Linguistics.* London: Arnold, 1996.

Traub, Valerie. *Desire and Anxiety: Circulations of Sexuality in Shakespearean Drama.* New York: Routledge, 1992.

———. "The New Unhistoricism in Queer Studies." *PMLA* 128, no. 1 (2013): 21–39.

———. "The Present Future of Lesbian Historiography." In *A Companion to Lesbian, Gay, Bisexual, Transgender, and Queer Studies,* ed. George E. Haggerty and Molly McGarry, 124–45. Oxford: Blackwell, 2007.

———. "The Psychomorphology of the Clitoris." In *The Renaissance of Lesbianism in Early Modern England*, 188–228. Cambridge: Cambridge University Press, 2002.

———. *The Renaissance of Lesbianism in Early Modern England*. Cambridge: Cambridge University Press, 2002.

Tremblay, Miguel. "Le Q des vieux." January 25, 2008. http://ptaff.ca/blogue/2008/01/25/le_q_des_vieux.

Tuer, Andrew W. *History of the Hornbook*. 2 vols. London: Leadenhall, 1896.

Turner, Robert K. "Textual Introduction." In *Philaster*, ed. Robert K. Turner, in *The Dramatic Works in the Beaumont and Fletcher Canon*, gen. ed. Fredson Bowers, vol. 1, 369–97. Cambridge: Cambridge University Press, 1966.

T.W. *A Succinct Philosophicall declaration of the nature of Clymactericall yeeres*. London: for Thomas Thorpe, by Walter Burre, 1604.

The Two Gentlemen of Verona. Dir. Penny Metropolous. Chicago Shakespeare Theater on Navy Pier, Chicago, IL, fall 2000.

[Tyndale, William]. *An answer vnto Sir Thomas Mores dialoge made by Uvillyam Tindale*. Antwerp: S. Cock, 1531.

Type-specimen broadsheet. Folger Library STC 7758.3, vol. 3, no. 6, [1565].

Urquhart, Thomas, trans. *The first [and Second] Book[s] Of the Works of Mr. Francis Rabelais*. London: for Richard Baddeley, 1653.

Vesalius, Andreas. *De Humani corporis fabrica Libri septem*. Basel: Ioannis Oporini, 1543. http://archive.nlm.nih.gov/proj/ttp/flash/vesalius/vesalius.html.

Vickers, Brian. *Shakespeare, Co-Author: A Historical Study of Five Collaborative Plays*. Oxford: Oxford University Press, 2004.

Vickers, Nancy J. "'The Blazon of Sweet Beauty's Best': Shakespeare's Lucrece." In *Shakespeare and the Question of Theory*, ed. Patricia Parker and Geoffrey Hartman, 95–115. New York: Methuen, 1985.

———. "Diana Described: Scattered Woman and Scattered Rhyme." *Critical Inquiry* 8, no. 2 (1981): 265–79.

———. "The Unauthored 1539 Volume in Which Is Printed the *Hecatomphile*, *The Flowers of French Poetry*, and *Other Soothing Things*." In *Subject and Object in Renaissance Culture*, ed. Margreta de Grazia, Maureen Quilligan, and Peter Stallybrass, 166–88. Cambridge: Cambridge University Press, 1996.

Waith, Eugene M. *The Pattern of Tragicomedy in Beaumont and Fletcher*. New Haven, CT: Yale University Press, 1952.

Walker, Alice. "Compositor Determination and Other Problems in Shakespearian Texts." *SB* 7 (1955): 3–15.

———. "The Folio Text of *1 Henry IV*." *SB* 6 (1954): 45–59.

———. *Textual Problems of the First Folio: Richard III, King Lear, Troilus & Cressida, 2 Henry IV, Hamlet, Othello*. Cambridge: Cambridge University Press, 1953.

Wall, Wendy. "'Household Stuff': The Sexual Politics of Domesticity and the Advent of English Comedy." *ELH* 65, no. 1 (1998): 1–45.

———. *The Imprint of Gender: Authorship and Publication in the English Renaissance*. Ithaca, NY: Cornell University Press, 1993.

———. *Staging Domesticity: Household Work and English Identity in Early Modern Drama*. Cambridge: Cambridge University Press, 2002.

Warner, Michael. "New English Sodom." *American Literature* 64 (1992): 19–47.

———. "Pleasures and Dangers of Shame." In *Gay Shame*, ed. David M. Halperin and Valerie Traub, 283–96. Chicago: University of Chicago Press, 2009.

———. *The Trouble with Normal: Sex, Politics, and the Ethics of Queer Life*. Cambridge, MA: Harvard University Press, 1999.

Wayne, Valerie. "The Sexual Politics of Textual Transmission." In *Textual Formations and Reformations*, ed. Laurie E. Maguire and Thomas L. Berger, 179–210. Newark: University of Delaware Press, 1998.

Webster, John. *The Duchess of Malfi*. Ed. Leah S. Marcus. Arden Early Modern Drama. London: A&C Black, 2009.

Wellek, René, and Austin Warren. *Theory of Literature*. New York: Harcourt, Brace, 1949.

Wells, Stanley, and Gary Taylor, et al., eds. *William Shakespeare: The Complete Works*. Oxford: Clarendon, 1986.

Wells, Stanley, and Gary Taylor, with John Jowett and William Montgomery. *William Shakespeare: A Textual Companion*. New York: W. W. Norton, 1997.

Werstine, Paul. "Close Contrivers: Nameless Collaborators in Early Modern London Plays." In *The Elizabethan Theatre* XV, ed. A. L. Magnusson and C. E. McGee, 3–20. Toronto: P. D. Meany, 2002.

———. "Compositor B of the Shakespeare First Folio." *Analytical and Enumerative Bibliography* 2, no. 4 (1978): 241–63.

———. "More Unrecorded States in the Folger Shakespeare Library's Collection of First Folios." *The Library*, 6th ser., 11 (1989): 47–51.

———. "Shakespeare, *More* or Less: A. W. Pollard and Twentieth-Century Shakespeare Editing." *Florilegium* 16 (1999): 125–45.

Werth, Barry. *The Scarlet Professor: Newton Arvin: A Literary Life Shattered by Scandal*. New York: Doubleday/Nan A. Talese, 2001.

Whigham, Frank, and Wayne A. Rebhorn, eds. *The Art of English Poesy by George Puttenham: A Critical Edition*. Ithaca, NY: Cornell University Press, 2007.

Whitaker, John. *Mary Queen of Scots vindicated*. 3 vols. London, 1787.

Whitney, Geffrey. *A Choice Of Emblemes, And Other Devises*. Leiden: in the house of Christopher Plantyn, by Francis Raphelengius, 1586.

Whythorne, Thomas. *The Autobiography of Thomas Whythorne*. Old-spelling ed., ed. James M. Osborn. Oxford: Clarendon, 1961.

Williams, Mary B. "Species: Current Usages." In *Keywords in Evolutionary Biology*, ed. Evelyn Fox Keller and Elisabeth A. Lloyd, 318–23. Cambridge, MA: Harvard University Press, 1992.

Williams, Raymond. *Keywords: A Vocabulary of Culture and Society*. Rev. ed. New York: Oxford University Press, 1983.

———. *Marxism and Literature*. Oxford: Oxford University Press, 1977.

Willinsky, John. *Empire of Words: The Reign of the OED*. Princeton, NJ: Princeton University Press, 1994.

Willoughby, Edwin Eliott. *The Printing of the First Folio of Shakespeare*. Oxford: Oxford University Press for the Bibliographical Society, 1932.

Wilson, Bronwen. *The World in Venice: Print, the City, and Early Modern Identity*. Toronto: University of Toronto Press, 2005.

Wilson, Eric. "London's ABCs: Urban Studies and the Reformation of Vernacular Literacy." Unpublished paper.

Wilson, H. A., ed. *Constitutions and Canons Ecclesiastical 1604*. Oxford: Clarendon, 1923.

Wilson, Thomas. *The Arte of Rhetorique*. London: by George Robinson, 1585. Rpt., ed. G. H. Mahr. Oxford: Clarendon, 1909.

Witmore, Michael, and Jonathan Hope. "Shakespeare by the Numbers: On the Linguistic Texture of the Late Plays." In *Early Modern Tragicomedy*, ed. Subha Mukerji and Raphael Lyne, 133–53. Cambridge, UK: D. S. Brewer, 2007.

Wright, Thomas. *The Passions of the Mind in General*. The Renaissance Imagination, vol. 15. Ed. William Webster Newbold. New York: Garland, 1986.

Ziolkowski, Jan M. "Metaphilology." *Journal of English and Germanic Philology* (2005): 239–72.

———, ed. *On Philology*. University Park: Pennsylvania State University Press, 1990.

Zoppo, Marco. "A putto putting bellows in the anus of another, a third putto on his back and pulling his hair, the scene watched by two men and two boys." Marco Zoppo (or Lord Rosebery) Album. 15th century. Pen and brown ink, with brown wash, on vellum. The British Museum, London. Museum number 1920,0214.1.18.

INDEX

ACKNOWLEDGMENTS

The seed of this book (as we say) was planted years ago at a conference on pre-modern sexuality, as I realized that many of the papers began with a foundation-laying etymology of a sexual term. But the life of books does not simply begin at conception or germination; there were, it turns out, many seeds, a queerer and more plural generation, labor, and dissemination, and this book had the benefit of much conversation and generous assistance—a promiscuous parentage, queerer kinship, and many friends, over many years and venues. I am grateful for all these gifts of Q/cue.

Lynn Wardley gave me a book that launched my attention to the letter Q, and our conversations live and virtual lie at the heart of several other chapters. Much gratitude.

At Northwestern, I am privileged to work with an extraordinary Renaissance studies group. Kasey Evans, Susie Philips, and Will West made this a better book with their insights and their collegiality; Martin Mueller gave me the benefit of his philological erudition. More generous and more intellectually rigorous colleagues than Laurie Shannon and Wendy Wall will not be found; as will be clear, this book benefited from the ambient influence of their thinking on animals and food, respectively. It is a constant pleasure and benefit to work and think alongside Wendy, as I have done now for the greater part of three decades. Remembering still the power of my first real conversation with Laurie at a picnic table in another place, I am grateful now for our scholarly, institutional, and culinary adventures in Chicago. I am grateful for the many and various Qs Laurie and Wendy have each tossed my way.

Current and former colleagues in the English Department and in the Gender and Sexuality Studies Program at Northwestern provided crucial suggestions, provocative queries, and sustaining collegiality; I'm especially grateful to Nicola Beisel, Héctor Carrillo, Nick Davis, Mary Dietz, Brian Edwards, Steven Epstein, Lane Fenrich, Christopher Herbert, E. Patrick Johnson, Lawrence Lipking, Tessie Liu, Barbara Newman, Alexandra Owen, Jan Radway, Carl Smith, Julia Stern, Blakey

Vermeule, and Mary Weismantel. Rebecca Johnson lent philological expertise at a particularly important juncture. Jules Law's rigorous precision—as intellectual, colleague, friend, and chef de cuisine—merits particular mention. Bonnie Honig's brilliant engagement with work far from her own has been transformative.

Many of this book's chapters, in particular its introduction, had the benefit of discussion and critique in seminars, colloquia, and other contexts. I wish that I could enumerate the manifold suggestions I received, beyond debts recorded in the notes and in this regrettably merely alphabetical queue of generous interlocutors: Rebecca Ann Bach, Matt Bell, Thomas L. Berger, Timothy Billings, Catherine Brown, Jim Bulman, Stephen J. Campbell, Christopher Cannon, Chris Castiglia, Roger Chartier, Tom Conley, Bradin Cormack, Stuart Curran, Mario DiGangi, Lars Engle, Carla Freccero, Lisa Freeman, Marjorie Garber, Stephen Greenblatt, Jody Greene, Suzanne Gossett, John Guillory, Heidi Brayman Hackel, David Hall, Byron Hamann, Phillip Brian Harper, Cynthia Herrup, David Hillman, Barbara Hodgdon, Peter Holland, Jean Howard, Shannon Jackson, Heather James, Coppélia Kahn, David Kastan, M. J. Kidnie, Ted Leinwand, Leah Marcus, Gordon McMullan, D. A. Miller, Barbara Mowat, Lucy Munro, Karen Newman, Ricardo Ortiz, Patricia Parker, Gail Paster, Donald Pease, David Porter, Richard Preiss, Mary Beth Rose, Kathryn Schwarz, William Sherman, Susan Staves, Gary Taylor, Dan Traister, Henry Turner, Jonathan Walker, Michael Warner, Paul Werstine, George Walton Williams, and Joseph Wittreich.

I am grateful to my hosts in English departments, humanities centers, gender and sexuality studies programs, Renaissance studies centers, and history of the book seminars at the following institutions for the invitation to present and discuss parts of this book: University of Alabama at Tuscaloosa, Birkbeck College (University of London), Brown, Case Western, University of Chicago, the Chicago Renaissance Seminar, University College Dublin, Columbia University, Cornell, Dartmouth, UC Davis, UCLA, UC Santa Cruz, Denison, Duke, the English Institute, the Folger Library, Harvard, the Huntington Library, University of Illinois at Chicago, Johns Hopkins, King's College London, Loyola, University of Maryland, Miami University, University of Michigan, Middlebury, the Newberry Library, Northwestern, the Ohio Shakespeare Conference, University of Pennsylvania (particularly the Material Texts seminar), Rutgers, the Society for Textual Scholarship, Tufts, the USC–Huntington Library Early Modern Studies Institute, University of Texas at Austin, and Vanderbilt.

At their respective libraries, Edward Gaynor (Albert and Shirley Small Special Collections Library, University of Virginia), Paul Gehl (Newberry), Susan Halpert (Houghton), John Pollack (Kislak Center for Special Collections, Penn), Dennis Sears (University of Illinois), and Georgianna Ziegler (Folger) provided expert assistance, for which I am grateful.

Alongside particular cues, stimulating exchanges with Will Fisher, Carla Mazzio, and Garrett Sullivan helped reframe aspects of this book. Peter Stallybrass's sustaining interest in *Queer Philologies*, as well as his gifts of letters, archival energy, and hospitality, was vital and invaluable. For long-running colloquy and often theatrical hospitality, I thank Ann Rosalind Jones, Meredith McGill, and Andrew Parker. Margreta de Grazia's extraordinary insight as a reader and critic animates many of this book's sentences, perhaps more than she knows; it is impossible to imagine this book without the gifts of her critical support and perception.

I regret that I can't thank in person, for especially formative work and conversation, several scholars who remain with us now in memory and in the brilliance of their published legacies: Alan Bray, Marshall Grossman, Scott McMillin, Jeanne Addison Roberts, and Eve Kosofsky Sedgwick.

In seminars and colloquia at Northwestern and at the Folger Library, Harvard, Michigan, the University of Chicago, and elsewhere, numerous former students—many now colleagues—gave me and aspects of *Queer Philologies* the benefit of their tutelage. Laura Williamson Ambrose, James Bromley, Gwynne Dujardin, Ari Friedlander, Ryan Friedman, Leah Guenther, Hunt Howell, Coleman Hutchison, Peter Jaros, Benjy Kahan, Jeffrey Todd Knight, Jenny Mann, Jessie Mathiason, Dagmar Riedel, Jessica Rosenberg, Marjorie Rubright, Christopher Shirley, and Eric Wilson deserve particular thanks. For the generative provocation of her research and conversation on early modern boy actors, I record a special debt to Emily Drugge Bryan. I am grateful for the adept research assistance at various stages of Andrew Cooper, Gina Di Salvo, David Hacker, Alex Harvey, and Lee Huttner.

In Washington, D.C., a sometime second home to this project, warm hospitality and electric conversations in two households were sustaining—those of Leeds Barroll and Susan Zimmerman, and Jonathan Gil Harris and Madhavi Menon. For me as for so many of us in Shakespeare studies, Leeds's model as a scholar, professional, and wry wit has been a beacon. Well in excess of particular scholarly contributions, the productive pleasure of whispered reading-room conversations with Anston Bosman and Alan Stewart cannot be underestimated. In Chicago and elsewhere, this book was perhaps inadvertently supported through the studiously hilarious erudition of a warm group of friends beyond the academy: Gary Alexander, John Cipriano, Bill Goldstein, Bruce Lederman, Dan Santow, and Blake West.

Several scholars in gender and sexuality studies (among their other specialties) made a particularly deep impression on this book. The scholarly models, conversations, and generosities of Jonathan Goldberg, Stephen Orgel, and Bruce Smith, different as they are, have been enduring, formative, and (high compliment in this book's lexicon) fundacional. I owe particular thanks to Marc Schachter for seminal discussions of queer-philological method, not separable from his particular expertise with translation. Rick Rambuss, consummate host, friend, and interlocutor, has been a longtime companion, ideal reader, and inspiration in this work. I'm grateful, too, for Chuck O'Boyle's brilliant and central role in that conversation and conviviality over many years. Lee Edelman stimulated and spurred this book; David Halperin lubricated and encouraged it; I am grateful to each for many conversations. David Halperin and Margie Ferguson each generously saved me from errors and through their detailed readings of the manuscript added nuance and depth. I am grateful for Ari Friedlander's helpful discussion of a methodological crux in the introduction. With characteristic acuity, intensity, and care, Valerie Traub engaged many of the ideas and chapters in this book from their inception, and her invaluable critique of the complete manuscript at a late stage helped me approach less imperfect imperfection. To attempt adequately to pay tribute to her work, support, and friendship is to practice impossibilities.

I am particularly grateful to several colleagues who generously provided valuable last-moment assistance: Paul Gehl and Bob Williams (Newberry Library), Ann Rosalind Jones, and especially Bronwen Wilson.

At Penn Press, I am beyond grateful to Jerry Singerman for his perceptive engagement with this book from seminar presentation through publication, his patient editorial guidance, and his timely impatience. I am grateful for Christine Dahlin's eagle editing eye and patience with my skaiography. Along with Hannah Blake's assistance with production, Erica Ginsburg's masterful management and careful eye for detail made this book a much better material and digital object. I am grateful to the Press's readers for valuable suggestions and critique.

Queer Philologies was enabled at key points by fellowship and research funding provided by the National Endowment for the Humanities, the Folger Shakespeare Library, Northwestern's Weinberg College of Arts and Sciences and English Department, a Northwestern University Research Grant, and The Graduate School (TGS) at Northwestern. I am grateful for their material support, and to Kate Veraldi in TGS and to Kathy Daniels and Jennifer Britton in Northwestern's English Department for their efficient assistance. Carol Brobeck's warm welcome and facilitation of fellows' lives at the Folger will be much missed.

Earlier versions of portions of this book were previously published; all have been revised and expanded here. I am grateful to the following for permission to reprint material: Columbia University Press (for sections of Chapter 3 earlier published in *A New History of Early English Drama*, ed. John D. Cox and David Scott Kastan), Duke University Press (for versions of Chapters 2 and 9 published in *GLQ* and *Shakesqueer*, ed. Madhavi Menon, respectively), the English Institute (for material in Chapter 1 first published in *Language Machines: Technologies of Literary and Cultural Production*, ed. Jeffrey Masten, Peter Stallybrass, and Nancy J. Vickers), Palgrave (for sections of Chapter 4 in *From Performance to Print in Shakespeare's England*, ed. Peter Holland and Stephen Orgel), and Routledge (for an earlier version of Chapter 6 in *The Body in Parts*, ed. David Hillman and Carla Mazzio).

James and Janice Masten, my lifelong teachers, are the ultimate parents of this book; I am grateful for their unwavering support and all they have given me. Knowing that there are other kinds of families, I am thankful for support we enjoy from the extended Masten-Loutsenhizer and Grossman-Nash clans.

By the time this book is printed and disseminated, I will have been grateful for Jay Grossman's presence in my life for nearly thirty years. He has read and reread, quietly encouraged, queried, heard tell of, and sometimes productively ignored the work of this book. Having endured my preoccupations for some time (and even materially encouraged them with various gifts of Q), he has, with characteristically allusive humor, continued to note that if I could just reach R, it would really be something. To him I dedicate a book that ends with this *our*.

CPSIA information can be obtained
at www.ICGtesting.com
Printed in the USA
FSHW022101290819
61571FS